SHUDDER

CREEPSHOW

FROM SCRIPT TO SCREAM

Foreword by
STEPHEN KING

Afterword by
KIRK HAMMETT

SHUDDER
CREEPSHOW
FROM **SCRIPT** TO **SCREAM**

Executive Producer
GREG NICOTERO

Producer
JULIA HOBGOOD

Writer
DENNIS L. PRINCE

Creative Director & Designer
JOHN J. HILL

Editor
MEREDITH BORDERS

Head of AMC Networks Publishing
MIKE ZAGARI

AMC NETWORKS PUBLISHING

TITAN BOOKS
LONDON

AMC NETWORKS
MATT BLANK – CEO
KIM KELLEHER – President, Commercial Revenue & Partnerships
KIM GRANITO – EVP, Content Room & Integrated Marketing
KEVIN DREYFUSS – SVP, Digital Content & Gaming Studio
CRAIG ENGLER – GM, Shudder
NICK LAZO – VP, Development & Production, Shudder
SEAN REDLITZ – Director, PR & Audience Activation, Shudder
JAMIE GALLAGHER – EVP & General Counsel
MADHU GOEL SOUTHWORTH – SVP, Legal & Business Affairs
ANDREA LABATE – Director, Rights & Clearance and Business Affairs Admin
KORI CLANTON – Counsel
MARNIE BLACK – EVP, Public Relations
OLIVIA DUPUIS – SVP, Public Relations
KATHRYN BRENNER – VP, Public Relations
JESSICA NICOLA – VP, Public Relations
JIM MAIELLA – Executive Vice President, Corporate Communications
DAN McDERMOTT – President, Entertainment and AMC Studios
MIQUEL PENELLA – President, Streaming Services
MIKE ZAGARI – Head of AMC Networks Publishing

CARTEL ENTERTAINMENT
STAN SPRY – CEO
ERIC WOODS – Co-CEO, Cartel Pictures
JEFF HOLLAND – Co-CEO, Cartel Entertainment
LAUREL MURPHY – Coordinator

MONSTER AGENCY PRODUCTIONS
GREG NICOTERO – President
BRIAN WITTEN – Head of TV & Film
JULIA HOBGOOD – Producer

STRIKER ENTERTAINMENT
RUSSELL BINDER – President
MARTINE BERREITTER – Senior Vice President, Operations
MEAGAN RENNER – Vice President, Business Development

TAURUS ENTERTAINMENT COMPANY
ROBERT DUDELSON – Co-Founder, Co-President, COO
JAMES DUDELSON – Co-Founder, Co-President, CEO
JORDAN KIZWANI – EVP of Production

PUBLISHED BY **TITAN BOOKS**
A DIVISION OF TITAN PUBLISHING GROUP LTD
144 SOUTHWARK ST LONDON SE1 0UP

Did you enjoy this book? We love to hear from our readers.
Please e-mail us at: readerfeedback@titanemail.com or
write to Reader Feedback at the above address.

To receive advance information, news, competitions, and exclusive
offers online, please sign up for the Titan newsletter on our website:
TITANBOOKS.COM

Standard edition cover
GARY PULLIN

AMC Networks Publishing exclusive edition cover
SANJULIAN

Contributing artists for this book
MICHAEL BROOM, MATTHEW LINEHAM

Special thanks
SHELLEY VENEMANN, MARCEL FELDMAR, STEVE MARTIN, JUSTIN D'ANGELO, PHIL KARNOFSKY, MICHAEL FLEMING, GRACE TYSON, NICK LANDAU, FRANK GALLAUGHER, SOPHIE JUDGE, PHIL NOBILE, VERONICA OWENS, OCTOPIE ANIMATION STUDIO, ISAAC KRAUSS

SHUDDER'S CREEPSHOW: FROM SCRIPT TO SCREAM Published by Titan Books. Copyright © 2022 Cartel Entertainment, LLC. All rights reserved. Artwork and Supplementary Materials, including images from the Creepshow television series, are © 2019-2022 Cartel Entertainment, LLC. All Rights Reserved. AMC, AMC Networks, AMC Networks Publishing, and the AMC logo are trademarks of AMC Network Entertainment LLC. SHUDDER is a trademark of Digital Store LLC. No part of this publication may be reproduced, stored in a retrieval system, or transmitted, in any form or by any means without the prior written permission of the publisher, nor be otherwise circulated in any form of binding or cover other than that in which it is published and without a similar condition being imposed on the subsequent purchaser. All names, characters, events, and locales in this publication are entirely fictional. Any resemblance to actual persons (living or dead), events, or places, without satirical intent, is coincidental. Printed in China.

A CIP catalogue record for this title is available from the British Library

Standard edition ISBN: 9781803363066
AMC Networks Publishing exclusive edition ISBN: 9781803363349
eBook edition ISBN: 9781803363387
First printing: OCTOBER 2022
10 9 8 7 6 5 4 3 2 1

FOR MORE INFORMATION, GO TO
AMCNP.COM

TABLE OF CONTENTS

FOREWORD by STEPHEN KING 007

INTRODUCTION: IT'LL ROT YOUR BRAIN! 009
Get ready for a blood-curdling journey into the realm of modern horror, one that draws from a deliciously vintage vein...

ONE: LIVING THE SCREAM 019
Meet Greg Nicotero (and his pals). He's got a horrendous history of scaring the daylights out of us. Find out why...

TWO: SHUDDER-ING HEIGHTS 033
Visit the creepy conglomerate responsible for the shriek-filled show that delivers non-stop streaming screaming...

THREE: THE WRITERS' BLOCK 041
Meet the wordsmiths who pen *Creepshow*'s twisted tales. Are they incurably crazed or just weirdly creative? Maybe both...

FOUR: WEIRD WORLDS & DREADFUL DESIGNS 063
Ever seen a nightmarish setting that later gave you bad dreams? Blame these guys...

FIVE: EYE FOR THE UNNATURAL 085
He looks through the camera's lens to focus on your greatest fears. Learn how—and why—he does it...

SIX: CREEPS, CREATURES & ASSORTED ABERRATIONS 101
All the things you wanted to see—plus many you can never un-see—await you here...

SEVEN: THE DIRECTORS' LAIR 145
They don't wear knickers nor woolen berets, but they do have a flair for classic horror. Meet them now...

EIGHT: UNUSUAL AFTER-EFX 161
Post-production polish, illustrated splash pages & transitions, and even musical "stingers" give every episode that pulpy pre-code goodness...

NINE: DEVILED EGGS 189
If you love a good egg hunt, keep your eyes peeled for these hidden gems lurking in each episode...

TEN: COVER GHOULS 199
A gallery of the *Creepshow* comic covers. It's fiendish fine art that will have you shrieking for the next great issue...

ELEVEN: THE *CREEPSHOW* COMPENDIUM 209
[SEASONS 1 - 3]

AFTERWORD by KIRK HAMMETT 235

BIOGRAPHIES / INDEX / ACKNOWLEDGEMENTS 236

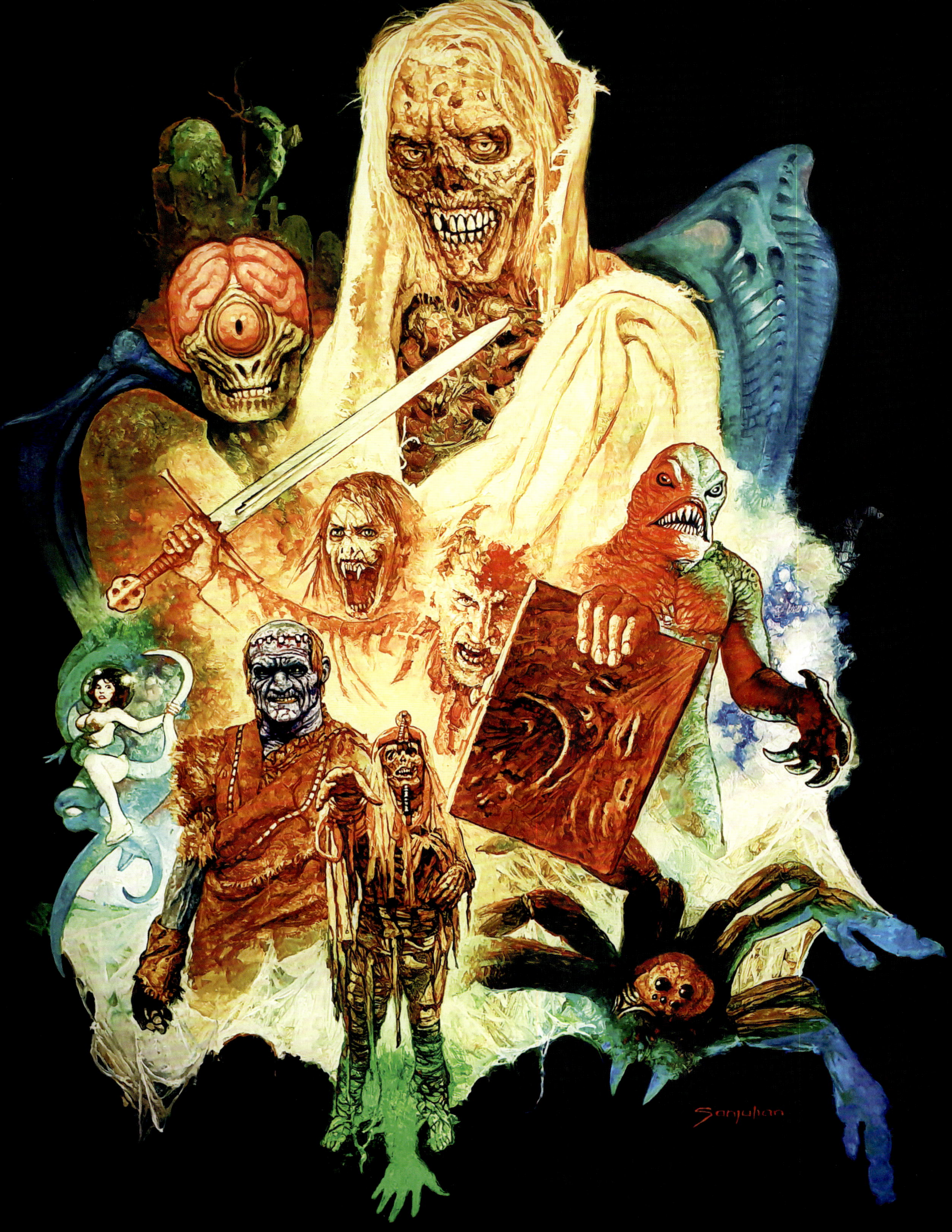
Sanjulian

FOREWORD
by STEPHEN KING

I got my big break in showbiz from George Romero.

In 1979—maybe it was 1980—he asked if I'd play a rube in *Knightriders*, and I said yes. You can look me up on IMDb, where I'm listed as "Hoagie Man" (my wife, in her only screen appearance, gets credited as "Hoagie Man's Wife"). Thus began my career of playing such country-fried assholes as a farmer named Jordy Verrill, a janitor named Johnny B. Goode, and an unnamed trucker with a mouthful of chaw. None of these roles, needless to say, was of Academy Award caliber.

During a break in the filming, George asked me if I'd be interested in working with him again, not as an actor (for which I have little talent) but as a writer (for which I have a little more). As someone who'd never written a screenplay, I was flattered and excited by the possibility of working with such a talented young (he was forty at the time) director. I asked what he had in mind. George shrugged and said, "What do *you* have in mind?"

After several more hoagie-munching takes while I struggled to get my few lines right, I suggested something I called "the good parts." It would be, I said, like comedy blackout sketches...only horrifying rather than funny. Maybe even both, because I've always believed that humor and horror are fraternal twins. Take the old pie-in-the-face gag. It's funny when it's whipped cream, but it's horrible if the whipped cream is filled with flesh-eating parasites that have human faces.

That wasn't the example I used with George that day. What I suggested was this: A nasty old woman dies on her birthday, then comes back from the grave to get her cake. Simple. Right to the point, the point being a good scare.

George said it reminded him of the EC horror comics that had been censored out of existence in the '50s, and wondered if we could possibly adapt my Good Parts idea into an anthology film that used one of those gory old comic books as a framing device. I wasn't immediately wowed. I pointed out that many horror movies had been done that way before—*Asylum* and the extraordinary *Dead of Night* are just two examples—and none of them had been what you'd call box-office smashes.

George slung an arm around my neck and said, "Steve, that's because *we* haven't done it."

I had to laugh. George had a wonderful way of making you feel like you were part of the club: *his* club. I never worked on a project where so many of the crew (all of them, really) were part of the director's fan club.

"All we need is a title that will sell the project. Can't use *The Vault of Horror* or *Tales from the Crypt*, they're copyrighted."

I didn't even have to think about it. "*Creepshow*," I said.

George grinned. "Beautiful. Now write it."

I did, in two weeks. George came back with a suggestion for a wraparound story, featuring "something from the funky ads they had in those books." I thought up a story about a little boy—he ended up being played by my son, Joe Hill—who sticks pins in a voodoo doll to get back at his bad-tempered Dad.

From then on, it was all George Romero. He used the framing device beautifully, and added a riff where each story ended with a freeze frame that morphed into a comic book picture. Each shot in the film looked like a comic book panel, complete with global lighting changes from natural to green or red. Getting those right was a pain in the ass, but he did it.

Audiences responded. The movie grossed $21 million, which would equal more than $60 million in 2022 bucks. The screenplay (along with *Storm of the Century*) remains one of my absolute favorites, and nothing has ever beaten E.G. Marshall's pitch-perfect, almost Shakespearian reading of my lines. ("Although they're [i.e., the bugs] essentially brainless, you have to watch 'em. Because they creep up on you.")

It *wasn't* Shakespeare, but audiences enjoyed the crazed mixture of scares and belly-laughs enough to spawn two sequels and the current TV series, which finally named the host of the fearsome festivities. Calling that guy "The Creep" makes perfect sense; only wish I'd thought of it.

The [Shudder] series has succeeded as other anthology series haven't, possibly in part because of its brilliant colors and in part because of its goofy, gross-out charm. Produced and often written by Greg Nicotero, who understands the genre and loves it, the stories are allowed to go anywhere. In one, a grouchy hermit spills beer on a severed finger which morphs into a weird lizard-thing he calls Bob. In another, a penniless college kid finds a man in a suitcase who produces gold coins when tortured.

All of them hew closely to the horror comics of the '50s, and the production teams of all three films and the TV series—especially the series—have made the most of short money. In fact, the low-budget look seems to be both an emblem of pride and part of the fun. It's also fun for me to think that what George and I brainstormed on the set of *Knightriders* between takes is still alive and well and scaring the crap out of people.

STEPHEN KING
MAINE, 2022

WELCOME TO SHUDDER'S CREEPSHOW! I AM THE CREEP, AND I'LL BE YOUR GHOULISH GUIDE FOR THIS EYE-POPPING EXCURSION INTO THE SHOW THAT DARES TO ASK--IS HORROR BAD FOR YA?
LONG AGO, DURING THE GLORIOUS GHOUL-DEN AGE OF HORROR COMICS, SOME PEOPLE SCREECHED AT WHAT THEY CALLED "THE PERILS OF PULP."
THEY SAID A HORROR COMIC WAS DANGEROUS TO IMPRESSIONABLE YOUNG MINDS. THEY EVEN DARED TO DECREE...
DRACULA
A SPECIAL OFFER!
CREEPSHOW
GET THESE PREVUE EDITIONS!
JOIN TODAY! FILL OUT THE COUPON AND ENCLOSE FIFTY CENTS FOR EACH EDITION OF YOUR CHOICE!
STRANGE, EERIE, TERRIFYING
10¢
CREEPSHOW
TALES OF SUSPENSE AND HORROR!!
MICHAEL BROOM 2021

IT'LL ROT YOUR BRAIN!

It's Wednesday, April 21, 1954. Americans are bedeviled by suspicion and awash with worry. Senator Joseph McCarthy continues his commandeering of the broadcast airwaves, warning us that Communism has infiltrated our institutions, even the U.S. Army. Elsewhere, Vice President Richard Nixon has been issuing grim assessments of a potential Russian nuclear attack; it could happen at any moment. And within Room 110 of the United States Courthouse on Foley Square, Lower Manhattan, another televised inquiry is underway, this one desperate to expose and thwart a new and most insidious affront to our American way of life: *comic books!!*

Chairman Robert C. Hendrickson provides oversight for the *Senate Subcommittee Hearings into Juvenile Delinquency, with special focus on Comic Books*. The attending lawmakers, squeezed almost shoulder to shoulder in the cramped dais, listen intently to expert witness Dr. Fredric Wertham, M.D.—he's a specialist in psychology, brain pathology, and neural development. Seated at the polished cherrywood table positioned opposite the dais, Wertham unleashes his warning of the dire and irreversible effects brought on by comic books.

"[Why] does the normal child spend so much time with this smut and trash? [...] It is my opinion, without any reasonable doubt—and without any reservation—that comic books are an important contributing factor in many cases of juvenile delinquency."[1]

Brows furrow with concern. Chins are rubbed, anxiously.

Wertham picks up a comic book from the stack next to him. Yes, issue #19 of *The Haunt of Fear* will easily demonstrate the deplorable nature of the assault: specifically, a story titled "Foul Play!"[2] He points to a page enlargement displayed for the dais' inspection.

"Mr. Chairman, I can't explain for the reason that I can't say all the obscene things that are in this picture for little boys of 6 and 7. This is a baseball game where they play baseball with a man's head; where the man's intestines are the baselines. All his organs have some part to play. The torso of this man is the chest protector of one of the players. There is nothing left to anybody's morbid imagination."[3]

ABOVE: A smiling child, her faithful dog, and a selection of entertaining comics. What's wrong with this picture? Nothing.

[1] Session transcript (afternoon), Senate Subcommittee Hearings into Juvenile Delinquency, April 21, 1954.
[2] 1953, *The Haunt of Fear* #19. Illustrated by Jack Davis. Written by William M. Gaines and Al Feldstein.
[3] Session transcript (afternoon), Senate Subcommittee Hearings into Juvenile Delinquency, April 21, 1954.

FEAR
HERE ARE TALES THAT WILL USHER YOU INTO
THE HAUNT OF
FEAR
AN ENTERTAINING EC COMIC
NO. 19
JUNE
10¢
FEATURING...
THE OLD WITCH
THE VAULT-KEEPER
THE CRYPT-KEEPER
GHASTLY

OPPOSITE: An efficient executioner does his duty, as seen on the cover of *The Haunt of Fear* #19 (May-June 1953).

LEFT: In Shudder's *Creepshow*, the EC horror style lives on...and on...and on...

Shocking! The senators exchange troubled glances, and, upon additional damning testimony from Dr. Wertham, they unanimously agree with his assertion that these comics are insidiously destructive devices, especially heinous in that they have been disguised as child-friendly "funny books!" Who is responsible for the proliferation of such morally corrosive content?

William M. Gaines, publisher of Entertaining Comics—that's "EC" for short—had printed the "Foul Play!" story the previous year. His company's horror and crime comics are wildly popular with kids of all ages. Besides *The Haunt of Fear*, EC also publishes *The Vault of Horror*, *Tales from the Crypt*, and *Crime SuspenStories*. Now it is Gaines who is seated at the cherry-wood table.

The 32-year-old Gaines has a stout presence, though his ill-fitting suitcoat, shirt, and sagging necktie undermine his credibility. His round-framed eyeglasses upon his round face make him appear bookish and a bit mousey...and vulnerable. Nevertheless, he confidently provides his rebuttal.

"What are we afraid of? Are we afraid of our own children? [...] We think our children are so evil, simple-minded, that it takes a *story* of murder to set them to murder, a story of robbery to set them to robbery [...] Our American children are, for the most part, normal children [...] but those who want to prohibit comic magazines seem to see [children as] dirty, sneaky, perverted monsters who use comics as a blueprint for action."[4]

Gaines goes on to explain the obvious morality within each of the stories he publishes. Comeuppance is central to practically every EC story. Acts of greed, graft, and self-aggrandizing abuse of others routinely trigger the most severe types of judgment and punishment...and, yes, the "Foul Play!" midnight baseball game that incorporates the body parts of opposing player Herbie Satten *was* morally justified. The win-whatever-it-takes pitcher had laced his spiked cleats with lethal poison that killed the opposing team's star player. He murders his opponent...then he pays a compensatory price. It's so plain to see, and Gaines contended that his readers, even kids, *did* see it.

Despite his faithful testimony on that April day, Gaines' petitions fell on deaf ears. The committee members willfully refused to hear the truth, appearing almost desperate to bury it. Did the morals of the EC stories hit too close to home in comparison to the lawmakers' own political ambitions and personal aspirations?

While actual legislation was avoided (the senators feared being accused of censorship in America more than anything they decried within EC's pages), the Comics Code Authority (CCA) was established, instead. By that, comic publishers would "voluntarily" submit their content for inspection and approval, hopeful to earn the CCA Seal. Without approval—that is, without presence of the CCA Seal—distribution and sales of any unapproved comic were cut off at the knees. And when use of the words "horror," "terror," and "crime" in comic book titles was prohibited, Gaines' top-selling books were doomed. EC was finished. The "establishment" had won.

Or had they?

EC's lineup of comics was halted, save for a cleverly reformatted comic-turned-magazine that delivered heavy doses of politically scathing and socially biting humor: *Mad Magazine*. "Magazines," by definition and presence of their larger format, weren't subject to CCA inspection and interference. It proved to be a handy loophole, one that would allow the resurgence of illustrated horror during the 1960s, easily found within new publications like Warren's *Creepy*, *Eerie*, and *Vampirella*.

But the original EC horror style—what became of that? In a way, it flourished. In 1972, UK-based Amicus Productions released their EC-leveraged *Tales from the Crypt*. Lifted directly from the pages of Gaines' most revered book, the film iconized the portmanteau method of anthology storytelling: a collection of self-standing elements tied together by a connecting narrative (The Crypt Keeper has detained five people and reveals to them, one by one, the heinous deeds they're capable of committing... and the judgment that awaits them).

Genre afficionados will point to 1945's *Dead of Night* film as an early example of the portmanteau method, and they will rightly make mention of Amicus' previous anthology outings like *Dr. Terror's House of Horrors* (1965), *Torture Garden* (1967), and *The House that Dripped Blood* (1971). But it was *Tales from the Crypt*, that fourth film in the Amicus line of horror anthologies, that gained producers Max J. Rosenberg and Milton Subotsky their greatest success and highest praise yet. They quickly rushed to release the non-EC *Asylum*, also in 1972, followed by a second EC adaptation, *The Vault of Horror*, in 1973. Horror anthologies on the big screen had become big business, in the UK as well as in the US. EC horror had transcended from the printed page to the big screen.

But...but...comics cause a degeneration of the mind and can only lead to dysfunctional behavior, right?

Time for a bit of our own inquiry.

Many creative talents—artists, writers, filmmakers—have cited EC as a source for their own creative inspiration. Take, for instance, writer/director Joe Dante. He was a New Jersey kid,

[4] Session transcript (afternoon), Senate Subcommittee Hearings into Juvenile Delinquency, April 21, 1954.

OPPOSITE: "They won't stay dead!" 'Nuff said? Original 1-sheet art for George A. Romero's Night of the Living Dead (1968).

born in 1946. His dad, Joseph James Dante, was a pro golfer, but Joe Jr. loved movies—especially horror and science fiction films. Naturally, when young Joe grew up, he wanted to become a cartoonist. He drew his own comic stories and he read comic books—EC comic books.

"Comic books, of course, because that's the way kids learn to read. Comic books always get a bad rap but [they're] a great entrée to getting kids to read."[5]

But that comic terror and horror; surely it leaves psychological scars on kids, right? Well, nowhere near as much as the Cuban Missile Crisis of 1962. *That* was real terror, not at the hands of imaginative writers and illustrators but, rather, at the hands of bickering governments and trigger-ready military forces. Now there's something to terrify America's youth, specifically the 16-year-old Dante and his pals who were preoccupied as they wondered what it would be like when the bomb dropped.

"On that fateful weekend [...] we literally thought there was going to be no school on Monday, and no school ever again—because the world was gonna end."[6]

Thankfully, the world didn't end but, interestingly, Dante didn't go on to become a cartoonist; he transitioned to writing. He was published in *Famous Monsters of Filmland* magazine ("Dante's Inferno") then served as occasional writer and editor for *Castle of Frankenstein* magazine. Ready to jump headlong into filmmaking, he went to work for Roger Corman where he was assigned to cut trailers, edit features, and eventually direct (*Hollywood Boulevard*, *Piranha*). Later came *The Howling*, *Twilight Zone: The Movie*, and, of course, *Gremlins*. His directing credits stacked up from there—*Innerspace*, *The 'Burbs*, *Matinee*, and more. He's well-traveled, well-respected, and well-regarded. Doesn't sound like much of a comic-poisoned delinquent, does he?

Next, say "hello" to John Landis. Born in Chicago in 1950, he relocated to Los Angeles with his family when he was only four months old. As a filmmaker, he insists that he has far too many influences to single out any one type or genre, and he easily recognizes the similarity between horror and comedy. Wait—what?!

"A tenet of comedy—and horror—is anarchy. The Marx Brothers and Laurel & Hardy will create anarchy in a social situation, and it's funny. And in a horror film, [you have] the loss of control, [which] is what anarchy means, and that can be pretty damned scary."[7]

The affable Landis says he loves all genres—westerns, musicals, animation—but he's best known for the laughs he delivers with his comedic gems, including *Animal House*, *The Blues Brothers*, and *Coming to America*. Of course, in the horror genre, he's best known for his horror-comedy, *An American Werewolf in London*. So, he's a success, too. He's had plenty of youthful EC influence, but he goes for the laughs, more often than not. What's so scary about him?

And then there is Mr. Romero.

Six years the elder of Dante and a full ten years senior to kid-Landis, George A. Romero enters this cross-examination analysis, if you will, as our surprise witness, a patriarch among his EC-era peers. He was born and raised in the Bronx, a graduate of Pittsburgh's Carnegie Mellon University in 1960, and an aspiring filmmaker right out of the chute who would take most any project—even Mister Rogers' tonsillectomy. If you've boned up on your Romero history, you'll probably know that lovable Fred Rogers gave the freshman director his first paying gig. "It was the scariest thing I ever filmed," Romero laughingly revealed. "I was scared shitless while I was trying to pull it off!"[8]

Of course, Romero later turned the tables and scared *us* out of our wits with *Night of the Living Dead* in 1968. His film exposed raw nerves (literally) as it eviscerated societal and establishment constructs of the day. During the late 1960s, western culture was overwrought with matters of oppositional conflict by way of war, civil unrest, and clandestine government malfeasance. *Night of the Living Dead*, like the EC stories before it, used horror as a tool—as a mirror—to raise our awareness.

Later came Romero's follow-up, 1978's *Dawn of the Dead*. In it, Romero delivers a terrifying look at rampant consumerism, projecting zombies as shoppers, shoppers as zombies. In a world of mindless consumption, Romero hints at the horrible consequences when gluttonous consumer culture is disrupted... and it sparks a savage turnabout.

Salah Hassanein, whose United Film Distribution Company (UFDC) dared to release *Dawn of the Dead* in its unrated and explicitly violent form, now sought Romero's final chapter in his zombie trilogy. Romero would deliver, but only if Hassanein agreed to fund it as part of a three-picture deal. As Hassanein considered the proposal, Romero busied himself with another project, one with horror author Stephen King.

Romero and King first met when Warner Bros. paired them for a theatrical adaptation of King's second novel, *'Salem's Lot*. But as other directors were also paraded into and out of the project's development, and many hands attempted and failed to convert the author's 400-page vampire story into a competent screenplay, the effort failed (it ultimately found success as a two-part television miniseries directed by Tobe Hooper). No matter, King and Romero were now friends and sought to collaborate.

They set their sights on adapting King's epic post-apocalyptic odyssey, *The Stand*. Both men were eager to bring the big project to the big screen—*their way*. They'd need studio involvement, but they didn't want any creative interference. None. Their stipulation: King, and *only* King, would write the screenplay. He wouldn't trust anyone else with his grand work. Romero, of course, would direct.

Its epic scope would require a suitable budget, more than Romero could fully secure. Their solution: they'd do another smaller-budget film together first, earn half or more of what they'd need for *The Stand*, then visit a backer with one of their pockets already full and a collaborative film success already under their collective belt; they'd just need an advance to fill the other pocket. So, who would finance this first, smaller film? That would be Salah Hassanein of UFDC, under the previously mentioned three-picture deal. Hassanein agreed, and the first picture would be Romero's *Knightriders*.

King conjured an idea: fast-hitting vignettes that quickly usher the viewer to "the best parts," he called them. "I said [to George], 'What if we did a whole bunch of things of varying lengths—some would be almost like comedy blackouts, only scary, little set-pieces, and some longer ones.'"[9]

Romero loved the notion and considered mixing film styles: color, black & white, super widescreen, even 3-D. Eventually, they came down to Earth and settled on an EC comic format,

[5] *Post-Mortem with Mick Garris: Joe Dante*. December 26, 2016. Nice Guy Productions, Inc.

[6] Joe Dante on "Matinee." July 31, 2015, filmSCHOOLarchive.

[7] "*Post-Mortem with Mick Garris: John Landis*." September 22, 2014. Nice Guy Productions, Inc.

[8] May 23, 2016, MentalFloss.com: When Mr. Rogers Gave George Romero His First Paying Gig.

[9] 1982, Fangoria magazine, Issue #20: "On (and off) the Set of *Creepshow*."

THEY WON'T STAY DEAD!
An IMAGE TEN Production
NIGHT OF THE LIVING DEAD
They keep coming back in a bloodthirsty lust for HUMAN FLESH!...
Pits the dead against the living in a struggle for survival!
Starring JUDITH O'DEA · DUANE JONES · MARILYN EASTMAN · KARL HARDMAN · JUDITH RIDLEY · KEITH WAYNE
Produced by Russel W. Streiner and Karl Hardman · Directed by George A. Romero · Screenplay by John A. Russo · A Walter Reade Organization Presentation – Released by Continental

The Masters Of Terror And The Macabre
GEORGE A. ROMERO
Director of "Night of the Living Dead" and "Dawn of the Dead."
STEPHEN KING
Author of "Carrie," "The Shining," "The Stand," "Firestarter," and "Cujo."
CREEPSHOW
The Most Fun You'll Ever Have BEING SCARED!
ADMISSION
·ADULTS
·CHILDREN
ADMIT 1
Starring HAL HOLBROOK · ADRIENNE BARBEAU · FRITZ WEAVER · LESLIE NIELSEN
CARRIE NYE · E.G. MARSHALL and VIVECA LINDFORS as Aunt Bedelia
A LAUREL® PRODUCTION "CREEPSHOW." A GEORGE A. ROMERO FILM
Production Design CLETUS ANDERSON Makeup Special Effects TOM SAVINI Director of Photography MICHAEL GORNICK Associate Producer DAVID E. VOGEL
Executive Producer SALAH M. HASSANEIN Original Screenplay STEPHEN KING Produced by RICHARD P. RUBINSTEIN Directed by GEORGE A. ROMERO
R RESTRICTED UNDER 17 REQUIRES ACCOMPANYING PARENT OR ADULT GUARDIAN
DOLBY STEREO IN SELECTED THEATRES
Read the Plume Paperback
Soundtrack on Varese Sarabande Records
Technicolor®
DISTRIBUTED BY WARNER BROS
A WARNER COMMUNICATIONS COMPANY
©1982 Warner Bros All Rights Reserved

video favorite and go on to be hailed as a cult classic in the decades to come.

Creepshow effectively resurrected the anthology format, inspiring additional offshoots and adaptations. Romero's co-produced Laurel Entertainment television series, *Tales from the Darkside*, arrived in 1983, a show that ran for four well-received seasons—90 episodes in total. It spawned a film treatment in 1990, *Tales from the Darkside: The Movie*, directed by *Creepshow* alumni John Harrison. There was *Creepshow 2* in 1987 and then *Creepshow 3* in 2006. Then, appearing from within the *weird world web* in 2009, we got an experimental internet webisode of *Creepshow RAW*, produced by HDFilms in association with Taurus Entertainment. And...well, by now it's evident that this is a healthy bloodline, still pumping and pulsating, which has led us to...

Shudder's *Creepshow*!

The EC tradition continues, decades after its presumed demise. Apparently, those on that senate subcommittee didn't stop anything; they served as pawns in their own game of deceit, deflection, and deplorable demagoguery—and those who partook in the perverted prosecution are now gone. Dust. Their names have long been forgotten, although we pay our proper respects by digging up some of those names, just the same. And the man they pasted up as their poster boy for persecution, William M. Gaines? Well, sadly, he's gone, too, but his work is iconic. His show of spirit and determination, poured into every story and every issue of his wickedly entertaining comics, continues to inspire new generations of writers and filmmakers.

So, it seems nothing can put a stop to EC influence. Somewhere, even today, a kid is probably hunched over a horror comic, "poisoning" his little mind.

And, exactly, how is that a problem?

OPPOSITE: Step right up for your ticket to terror! Original 1-sheet art for *Creepshow* (1982). Art by Joann Daley.

THIS PAGE, LEFT: Of corpse! It's still the most fun you'll have being scared! Shudder's *Creepshow* early mock comic cover.

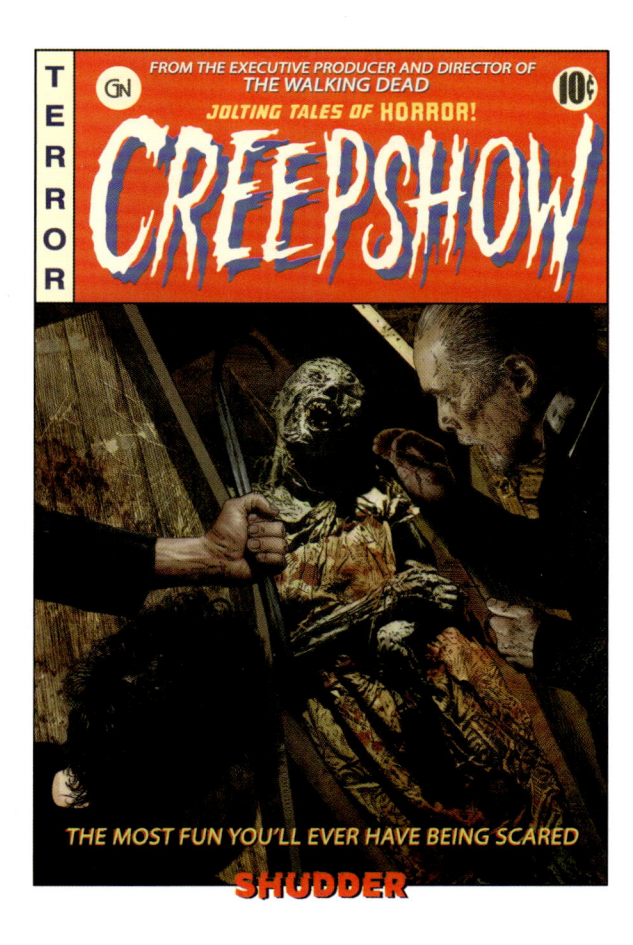

as suggested by Romero, blending horror, gore, gallows humor, all seasoned with a satisfying dose of that ol' comeuppance (audiences *love* to cheer the unmerciful demise of the bad guy... or girl).

"And because we had talked so much about comic books—EC comic books, particularly," Romero explained while introducing the film for Cinemax's 1998 airing, "Steve said, 'Let's do a format like that,' and the next morning he came down to the hotel and said, 'I've got the title—it's called *Creepshow*!'"[10]

As his first-ever screenplay, King delivered "five tales of jolting horror," each springing from the pages of a young boy's comic book, much to the ire of his verbally abusive father. To wit: a vengeful patriarch returns from the grave; a reclusive yokel mishandles a strange meteorite; a collegiate thirst for knowledge unleashes a 200-year-old hunger for flesh; the acts of a jealous husband incite a watery retribution; and a germophobe mogul, consumed by his own power over others, will soon be consumed by what he despises most.

The five stories are faithfully presented in EC comic style, right down to the flipping comic pages and quick glimpses of cons and come-ons promising X-ray vision, massive muscles, and voodoo vengeance. The live-action stories are infused with deeply saturated colors, mood-setting frame masking, and in-camera background bursts—all that keeps you cheerfully confined within its pulp sensibility.

Creepshow had all the earmarks of a hit—a top writer, a renowned director, and plenty of big-name stars. It prompted big studio Warner Bros. to come crawling to Romero and King to secure a big-money distribution deal. They did, and *Creepshow* was a hit. Released nationally on November 12, 1982, the film grossed $5.8 million in its opening weekend, pushing *First Blood* off the No. 1 spot. It would go on to gross over $20 million during its theatrical run. In the following year, it would become a home

SEE, WE ALWAYS SAID HORROR IS *GOOD* FOR YA...BUT YOU ALREADY KNEW THAT. NOW, LET'S MOVE ON AND MEET A KID WHO NEVER LET *BRAIN ROT* KEEP HIM FROM THE CREEPY THINGS HE'S LOVED-- AND I'LL BET YOU'RE GONNA *LOVE* HIM, TOO!

[10] 1998, Cinemax airing of *Creepshow* and *Dawn of the Dead* in a Halloween double-bill.

INTRODUCTION 15

A REAL MOBILE TANK

OVER 6 FEET LONG

LARGE ENOUGH FOR 2 KIDS INSIDE

ONLY $4.98

★ Intercom System ★ Revolving Turret ★ 75mm Cannon
★ Machine Gun ★ Real Periscope ★ Radio Controls
★ Absolutely Not A Cardboard Box ★ A Flag

It's Mobile - Pilot gets INSIDE - Guns Swivel - Turret Turns

Imagine your thrill when you get inside this authentic replica of the mighty ARMY TANK and power forward to adventure! This six foot hunk of equipment is so realistic with it's mighty cannon, swiveling machine gun, simulated treads and other authentic tank features that it's bound to bring squeals of delight from any young warrior. And, when you and a pal get right down into the fully equipped control room and close the cockpit cover–you can bet your using the mobile power to devastate every imaginary enemy in your path!

10 Day Free Trial
Order this sensaional TANK on 10 day free trial and if you are not 100% delighted, then return your purchase for a full refund.

MONEY BACK GUARANTEE!

Rush my TANK at once. If I am not 100% delighted, I may return after 10 day free trial for prompt refund of the full purchase price.

☐ I enclose $4.98 plus 62¢ shipping charge.
☐ Send C.O.D. I will pay postman on delivery plus C.O.D. and shipping charge.

Name _____
Address _____
City _____ State _____ Zip _____

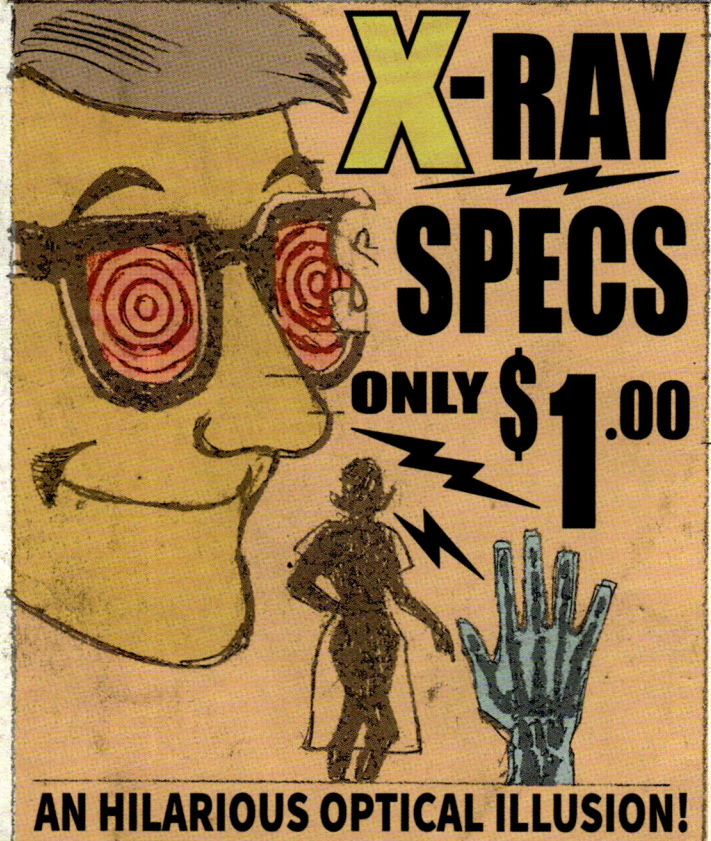

X-RAY SPECS

ONLY $1.00

AN HILARIOUS OPTICAL ILLUSION!
SEE THROUGH CLOTHES! THROUGH SKIN! THROUGH BONES!
THRILL AND EMBARRASS YOUR FRIENDS!

FREE ONE MILLION $ CASH! $

FOOL YOUR FRIENDS!
You'll get a MILLION $$$ worth of laughs with these exact reproductions of old U.S. Gold Banknotes (1840)! They're FREE when you send for our brand new **"FUN CATALOG."**
Send only 35¢ (coin) for shipping

LIVE SEAHORSES $1 EACH

Order a live Seahorse shipped to you from Florida for only $1 each, or send $2 for a Mated Pair. (Include 25c postage, all order.) Get started with this interesting hobby... fascinating project for young and old. Raise them in an ordinary goldfish bowl or jar. Most unusual and intriguing to watch. Hours of fun... see th FATHER Seahorse give birth to live baby Seahorses! Free food and instructions included. Live delivery guaranateed. Special Offer: Order 2 Mated Pairs for $2.98.

MATED SEAHORSE CO.

DARLING LIVE PET MONKEY!

$18.95

This Squirrel Monkey makes an adorable pet and companion. Show it affectiona and enjoy its company. Almost human with its warm eyes, your family will love it. The YOUNG monkeys grow about 12 inches high. Eats same food as you do. Even lolipops! Simple to take care of and train. Live delivery guranateed. Only $18.95 express collect.

Scary, Giant Size
ALIEN - EYE
CREATURE!
Obeys Your Commands!

ONLY $2.00

7 FEET TALL!

HURRY!... Be the FIRST!

This thing from another world acts as though it were alive! Imagine how scared and amazed your friends will be when they see this thriller floating towards them, with its tentacles reachign out. Rises, jumps, darts, in air! Floats up to 50 feet! Satisfaction guranteed.

Send just $2 + 25¢ for postage and handling to:

Zone T_____
_____
STREET _____
CITY _____
STATE _____

SOLD OUT!

CREEPSHOW COMIC ADVERTISEMENTS FOR AMUSEMENT ONLY.

OK, KIDS-- LET'S JUMP INTO THIS JARRING JOURNEY BY MEETING OUR OWN GRUESOME GUARANTOR OF GHOULISH DELIGHTS, GREG NICOTERO.
HE SAYS HIS STRANGE UNDERTAKINGS ARE DESIGNED TO DELIVER EVERYTHING THAT MAKES LIFE WORTH... LEAVING! HEH-HEH
LET'S CRAWL UNDER HIS SKIN, SEE WHAT MAKES HIM TICK, AND DIAGNOSE WHAT'S DRIVING HIS PECULIAR PASSIONS. HE'S NOT WORRIED--HE INSISTS HE'S...
MICHAEL BROOM 2021

LIVING THE SCREAM

The room is dark, save for a spot of light in the far corner. A boy is seated at a small desk—hunched over, obscuring the view of what he's secretly doing. He reaches for the knife.

The edge of the No. 11 X-ACTO blade glints momentarily under the desk lamp, then the boy angles its surgically machined tip downward. It's a delicate procedure. He steadies his hand, and then *scrape-scrape-scrape*.

The bottom half of the "3" is gone. Easy. He picks up the Flair pen, then carefully inks in the bottom half of a "2." Perfect.

He blows lightly at the surface of his doctored learner's permit.

Yessiree—it says I'm 17.

But what's he thinking; he can't buy beer in Pittsburgh at 17— and with a learner's permit?! C'mon, kid.

Who said anything about beer? This is to see *Dawn of the Dead* at the Gateway downtown. It's unrated and no one under 17 can get in—something about shocking scenes.

Well, I'm in!

And he was in. And he would be in...over his head. The year was 1979 and this *Dawn of the Dead* picture that he so anxiously anticipated would be an experience completely unlike anything else. Sure, he had seen *Jaws* here (many times) a few years before, and the shark—yes, it had changed him. He'd studied those lobby cards outside the auditorium, but that didn't compare to seeing the Great White in action, gliding through the ocean and striking at its would-be hunters. Oh, and there was that shocking bit-off leg of the estuary victim. It just sunk downward and laid there on the pond floor, the fleshy end belching out blood. It was unforgettable, unmatched, unbeatable. He imagined that someday he could build a shark like that. Someday.

But there were no lobby cards for *Dawn of the Dead*; only an artsy one-sheet featuring a tattered zombie head ominously rising from a black horizon, and the film's title printed in a sort of pukey-green color. And then there was that warning: "There is no explicit sex in this picture. However...." It was the "however" that intrigued him the most. And that was his only preparation going in.

He took a seat just as the auditorium houselights went down. There were a few previews, then the picture began. Immediately, it's frantic. A television studio is in chaos. A talk show host is yelling at his guest, some doctor or something who says the dead are returning to life and eating the living. "They kill for food."

Yep, expected that.

Suddenly, it switches to a rooftop scene where national guardsmen are blowing away a bunch of gun-wielding thugs holed up in a tenement building.

Wow—so much blood!

ABOVE: Young Joe Aurora (Brock Duncan) puts together his Victim kit, piece by piece, then tears apart his bullying uncle, limb by limb. It's penalty by plastic, from "Model Kid."

ABOVE: The Godfather of horror himself, George A. Romero.

OPPOSITE: Godzilla...plus gore?! What better way to launch *Starlog*'s new sinister sister mag, *Fangoria* #1 (August 1979).

IT'S... IT'S... IT'S...
SATURDAY... SATURDAY... SATURDAY...
NIGHT... NIGHT... NIGHT...
TIME FOR... FOR... FOR...
CHILLER... CHILLER... CHILLER...
THEATER... THEATER... THEATER...

The guardsmen make their way into the building from a rooftop stairway, then they run wildly down the tenement hallways. A door gets kicked in and—BLAM!—some guy's head explodes, blown clean off by a shotgun blast. Blood and brains fly everywhere.

What the fuuu....?

It's only twelve minutes into the film, and now a gray-faced zombie lumbers out of a room and bites a massive chunk out of a woman's neck...and then her forearm. Right there...in plain sight...flesh torn away...gushing all kinds of blood!

At that moment, 16-year-old Greg Nicotero knew he couldn't trust whatever this movie might throw at him next. He settled—no, *pushed*—himself back into his chair, gripping his Twizzlers strip so tightly that its ridges dug into his palm. His jaw went a bit slack. He was uneasy. He was unsure. He was unprepared for this.

And he liked it.

It's not that he was unfamiliar with horror; are you kidding? Greg was weaned on the stuff. Mom and Dad—and Grandpa, too—loved horror and science fiction films, and they shared that love and fascination with Greg and his younger brother. If not carting their boys to local showings of *Dracula: Prince of Darkness* or *Planet of the Apes*, Mom and Dad kept the home 8mm projector perpetually threaded with Castle Films' condensed horror features, eight-minute digests of *Frankenstein Meets the Wolf Man*, *Creature from the Black Lagoon*, or *Dracula*.

When not being fed by whatever was on the family projector, Greg's steady diet of monster fare was served up by Pittsburgh's own Bill Cardille, that is, "Chilly Billy Cardille-y" and *Chiller Theater*.

Greg tuned in to WPXI's Channel 11 faithfully for his weekend dose of horror thrills, and Chilly Billy never disappointed. The smartly coiffed Cardille served up plenty of classic horror and B-grade groaners. During each telecast, he inserted film breaks to perform playful skits, tell bad jokes, and entertain special guests. One such guest was Pittsburgh's own aspiring filmmaker, George A. Romero.

"I knew who George was and I knew about *Night of the Living Dead*," Greg reminisces, "because he literally filmed it about 40 minutes from where I grew up, [plus] my uncle was a local actor and actually had a part in George's *The Crazies*. And my Uncle Sam [Nicotero] wrote a really great retrospective article about George for *Cinefantastique* magazine. But one of the most meaningful experiences for me was when Bill Cardille played *Night of the Living Dead* on television, *uncut*. That was unheard of. This was in 1976 or '77, and I was, like, thirteen. I remember watching it late at night and it just *terrified* me. And George was on during one of the commercial breaks and announced that he was making a sequel."

Romero kept that promise and, a few years later, there sat Greg, disoriented, a bit distraught, and absolutely unsure of what might happen next over *Dawn*'s remaining 114 minutes. It was that feeling of unease and the sense of distrust that Greg would later regard as the most poignant aspect of the film: being instantly put off guard and off balance from the moment the movie began. Everything, and anything, was on the table.

No. Holds. Barred.

"And that's the greatest element of *Dawn of the Dead*," Greg insists, "and I love that. I still love that."

Look, Greg loved the shark—he always would—but *this* was leagues beyond how *Jaws* affected him. This was an entirely new experience, one that would ultimately compel him to step into this blood-soaked corner of horror and learn how the tricks were done.

The premiere issue of *Fangoria* silently crept onto magazine racks that same year, almost unnoticed. The Godzilla cover art made it appear as just another monster magazine, but the full-color, freeze-frame photo of that exploding head just a few pages in screamed otherwise. Here, Greg found some of the answers he was looking for, and it's where he first read about the creator of *Dawn*'s over-the-top carnage, Tom Savini.

A fellow Pittsburgher, Savini was born in 1946 and, at the age of 13, discovered his life's calling to performance and makeup artistry after seeing the Lon Chaney biopic, 1957's *Man of a Thousand Faces*. As he told *Fangoria* magazine in that first issue, the film inspired Savini to create his own makeups and costumes, and later refine his skills in local theater productions. His first film work came in Bob Clark's 1974 pictures *Deathdream* and *Deranged: Confessions of a Necrophile*. But when George

20 CHAPTER ONE

STARLOG presents
GIANT COLOR POSTER
FANGORIA
$1.95
K49129
MONSTERS • ALIENS • BIZARRE CREATURES
#1
PREMIERE ISSUE
25 Years with GODZILLA
"Dawn of the Dead"
Dr. Who Invades the U.S.
Galactica's Lost Aliens
Interview: Christopher Lee
Making of "The Creature from the Black Lagoon"
Preview: New Fright Films
PHOTO PREVIEW
"ALIEN"

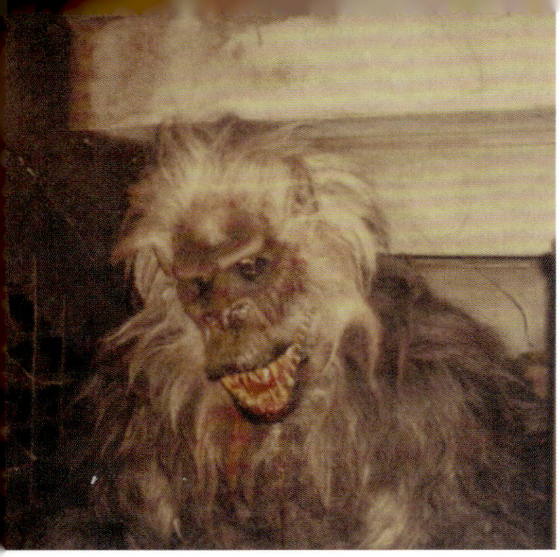

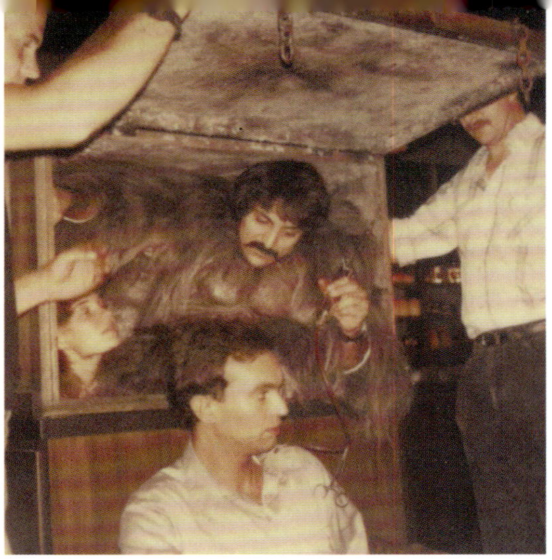

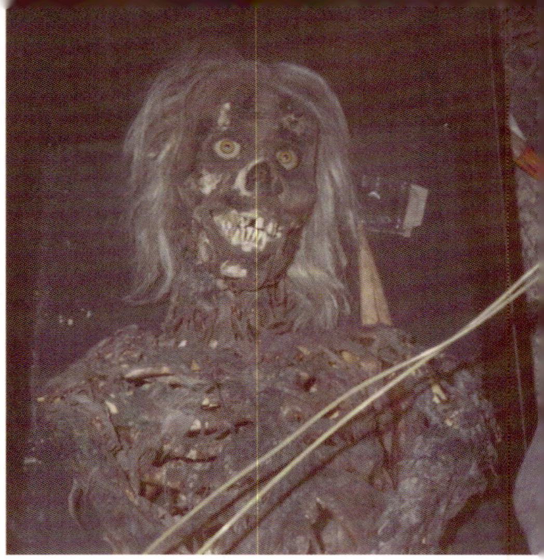

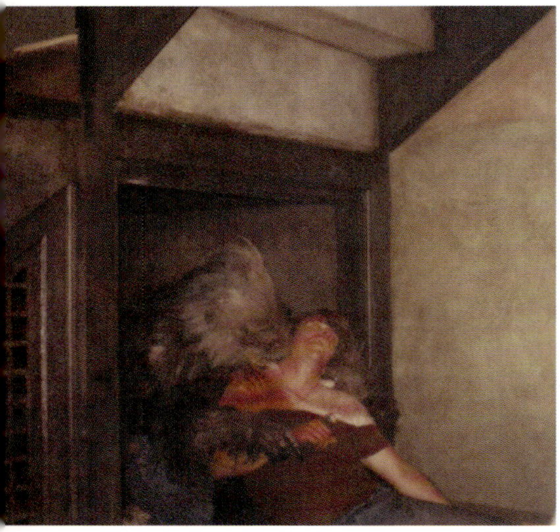

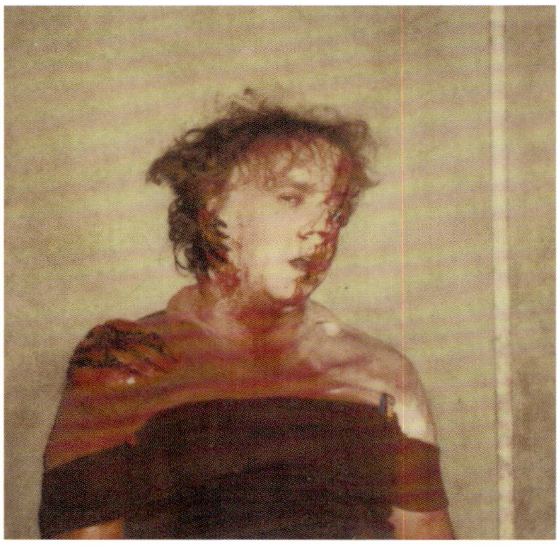

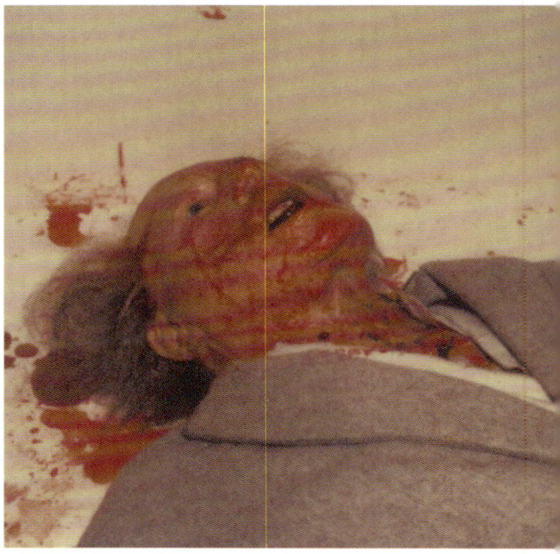

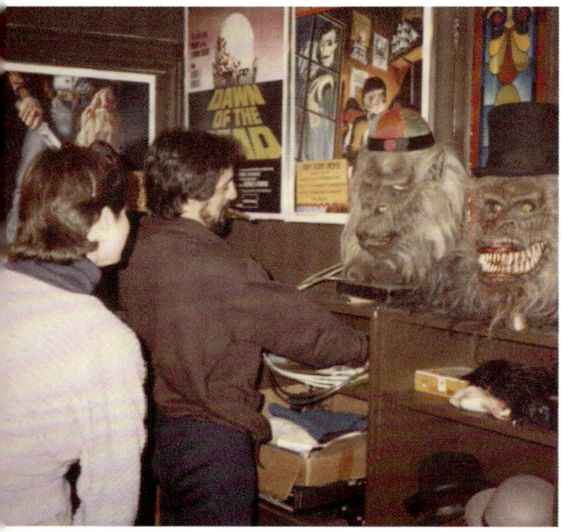
DAWN OF THE

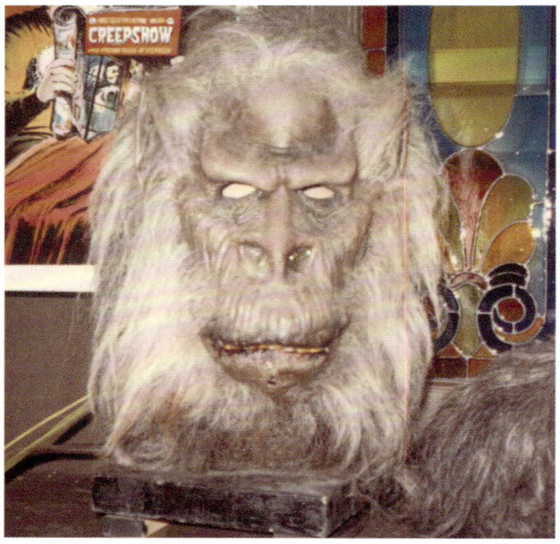
CREEPSHOW

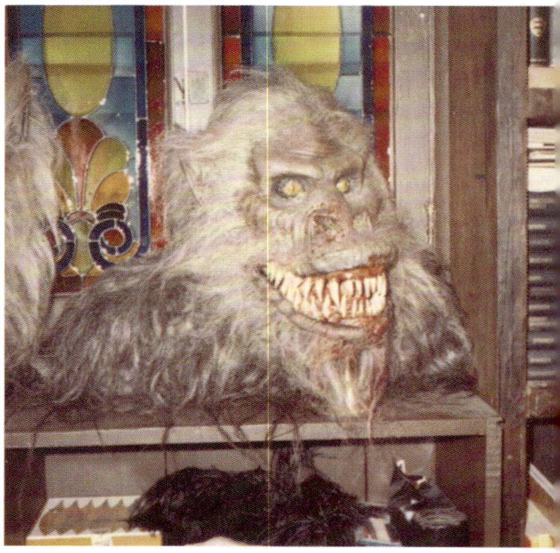

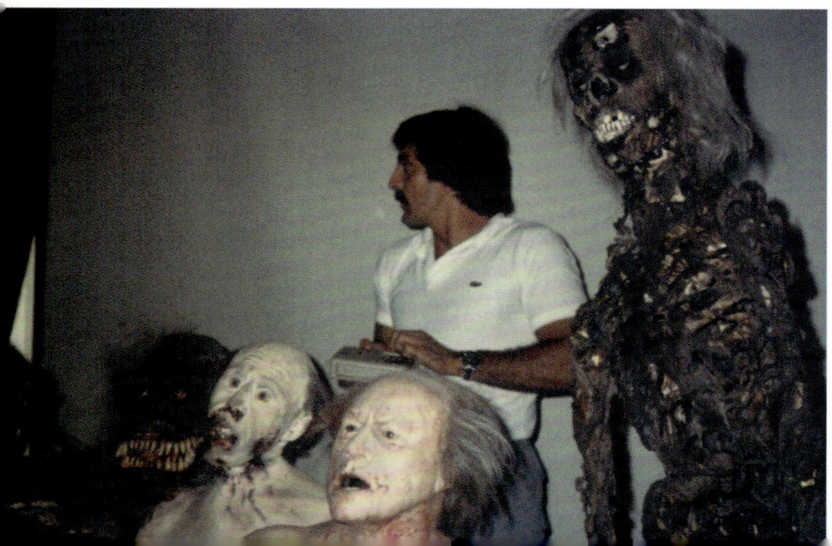

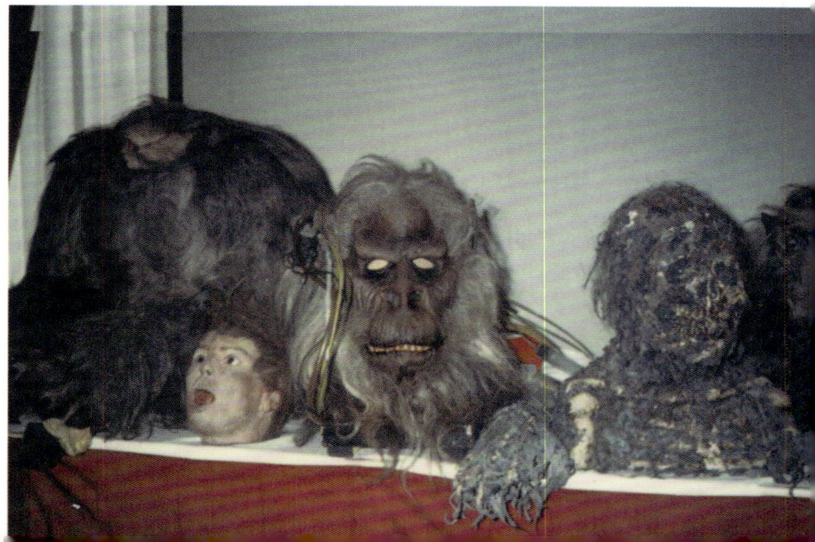

Romero needed a convincing wrist slash for his quasi-vampire tale, *Martin* (1976), Savini showed how it could be done...and blood spurted everywhere! Romero loved it and subsequently hired Savini for *Dawn of the Dead*. With that, plus his inventive gore effects for Sean S. Cunningham's *Friday the 13th* (1980), Savini gained top status in the emerging "splatter film" sub-genre.

"*Dawn of the Dead* and *Friday the 13th*—those two films were like a one-two punch that made Tom Savini a household name," Greg recalls. "Instantaneously, his name became synonymous with the horror genre in the '70s. And then it was *Maniac*, and *The Prowler*, *The Burning*, and *Eyes of a Stranger*, and so on. From 1978 to, like, 1984 or '85, the makeup artists were now on the marquee, right alongside the actors...and Tom was one of the first guys who led that revolution of makeup artists who were able to elevate material based on their effects."

Yes, Savini was a gore *artiste*, and Greg was eager to learn more about the craft—just for fun, anyway. His first brush with a "makeup man's" materials came by way of Pressman's Movie/T.V. Monster Make-Up Kit (with exclusive "Flex Flesh"). Developed in association with makeup master Dick Smith (*The Exorcist*, *The Godfather*, etc.), the kit included a collection of vacu-formed molds and the gelatinous flex flesh mix. Add a little hot water and—*presto!*—you're making latex-like scars, gashes, and so on. It was a step up from Imagineering's Scar Stuff, Face Fur, and Vampire Blood, but it was still rather crude, more for play than practical use. But it was fun and, for Greg, it was a start.

He continued to seek out and absorb every bit of information available about new makeup effects, anything he could find published in the go-to magazines: *Famous Monsters of Filmland*, *Cinefantastique*, *Starlog*, and now *Fangoria*. He studied the work of filmdom's most prominent makeup artists—Jack Pierce, Dick Smith, John Chambers—while closely tracking the emergence of the new breed of effects pioneers—Rick Baker, Rob Bottin, Stan Winston, and Tom Savini.

He scoured the broadcast airwaves for features related to the horror genre, dutifully standing by the REC button of the family's Betamax to capture televised interviews with makeup men and moviemakers. Bit by bit, he assembled his own video reference library. Still, it wasn't enough. He wanted to step deeper into this fascinating world of movies and makeup. He felt almost compelled at times to become a practitioner himself—but how? Well, there would be that chance encounter in Rome...

The Nicotero family was enjoying a vacation in Italy when Greg spied none other than George Romero in a restaurant, seated just across the room. When Romero stood up to leave, Greg rushed over to greet him. Amused by Greg's excitement and energy, Romero invited him to visit his hometown office.

"When you're back in the 'Burgh," Romero cheerily offered, "come drop by. I'm on Fort Pitt Boulevard."

Invitation accepted! As soon as Greg got his driver's license (legit, this time), he drove to Fort Pitt to visit Romero and talk movies. The two became friends and, a couple of years later, Romero was back in Monroeville (the site of the *Dawn* shopping mall) and reached out to Greg to make an amazing offer.

"We're getting ready to prep a new film—it's called *Creepshow*—and I thought you might like a job as a production assistant. Whaddya say?"

"Well...no," came Greg's surprising response. "I'm actually getting ready to go back to college—premed, gonna be a doctor like my dad—so I really can't take the job. Thanks, though."

"Gotcha. No problem, Greg."

"But, y'know...if you wouldn't mind me coming over to visit on the weekends, I'd love to just hang out while you work."

"Yeah, sure, that'll be fine. Come on by."

And so, on Saturdays, Greg would visit while Romero was developing *Creepshow*. And, as fate would have it, this is when Greg would meet and befriend Tom Savini. With Betacam in hand, Greg would document the creation of "Fluffy," the ravenous beast in the crate; this was far beyond anything he could record from a segment on *Evening Magazine*. In time, his intended visits with Romero became lengthy study sessions with Savini, instead.

"Greg—wha...wha...? Where'd ya go? Whaddya doin'?" Romero would ask, befuddled yet amused.

"Oh, yeah. I was over in Tom's lab watching him build stuff." Romero only laughed.

On it went, premed classes through the week, then weekends with Romero and Savini, watching them prep *Creepshow* and talking about all things film. The trio traded movies they had collected on videotape and helped each other fill the gaps in their respective collections. At that moment, Greg realized the significance of this friendship; he was helping this amazing director expand his personal library of most-loved films. Beyond this, Greg was also enlisted by Romero and Savini to lend a helping hand in their actual film work.

"So, Tom and I just got to be friends," Greg recalls, "and he kinda took me under his wing. And when he was doing conventions in Pittsburgh, I would help him pack all his props up. I helped him pack up the Fluffy heads and Raoul [the *Creepshow* spectre] and everything. There was a convention he did in downtown Pittsburgh where he did a whole presentation and had all his stuff from *Creepshow*, and I helped load and unload all of that. And, of course, I took pictures of everything."

Those pictures, incidentally, tell an even bigger story. Greg found himself increasingly drawn into the world of filmmaking, even though he considered himself just a kid from Pittsburgh. The notion of entering the realm of special effects and movies appealed to him, but he was studying to be a doctor, to take over his dad's practice as a kidney specialist someday. Movies and effects—that was just a fun hobby. Besides, he had no ambitions to relocate to the west coast.

"You don't have to live in Hollywood to make movies," both Romero and Savini told him; they had already proved that.

Indeed, Greg's "big break" wouldn't happen anywhere near the lights and excitement of Beautiful Downtown Burbank; quite the contrary. His big leap was a jump into the Wampum Mines, a reclaimed underground limestone quarry located just off of Old Route 18 in Pennsylvania, where Romero would film his third zombie movie.

No glamour. Kinda gloomy. Definitely chilly. In other words, perfect!

OPPOSITE: A crate-full of classic *Creepshow* thrills!

TOP ROW (LEFT TO RIGHT): Fluffy lurks; Savini tests an attack; The Specter "Raoul."

2ND ROW (LTR) - Fluffy bites; Just a flesh wound?; the Mr. Pratt dummy.

3RD ROW (LTR): Savini shows the faces of Fluffy; stoic Fluffy; starved Fluffy.

BOTTOM ROW: Savini showa off his Creepshow handiwork at a Pittsburgh convention.

CHAPTER ONE 23

With the first two movies of that three-picture deal with UFDC—*Knightriders*, *Creepshow*, and "Zombie Movie 3"—in the can, Romero was ready to tie up his Dead Trilogy with *Day of the Dead*.

In this final installment, the zombie apocalypse had descended into a dire state of savage warfare. The original script told of a sort-of despot, Gasparilla, who established a fortress on an island off the coast of Florida. There he was training an army of zombies, fed on human flesh, to battle in mankind's final face-off. Greg jokingly called it *The Ten Commandments* of zombie films. But, no joke, this was the film for which Greg was enlisted, never considering that being hired on could be called a "real job."

"When George and Tom offered me this job, there was no way I was gonna say no this time. I got hired onto *Day of the Dead*, but my intent was to work on the film for six months then go back to school and finish my premed at Westminster. Then I was going to go off and take my medical school entrance exams and I was going to med school. But I just thought that, 'I want to try this once,' because I always loved horror, even though I always looked at it as a hobby. It never really dawned on me that this was an opportunity opening in front of me. I never put two and two together...weirdly enough."

July 23, 1984: Greg shows up for his first day of "work" on *Day of the Dead*. He reports to Tom Savini's home and begins his journey. From July through early September, he'd work under Savini's tutelage and alongside Mike Trcic, David Kindlon, Derek DeVoe, and John Vulich. Come mid-September, Savini's crew would relocate to the Wampum Mines to prep for shooting. On October 1st, George Romero would shout "Action!" But, truly, by the end of that first day in July, Greg admitted to himself that he'd never be going back to school.

Sure hope Mom and Dad take it well.

"It was like, all of a sudden, I was sitting in these meetings with George Romero and we're talking about killing zombies and I'm thinking, '*This is the coolest thing.*' And then they decided to put me in the movie. In the original script, one of the soldiers is killed and his reanimated head comes back to life, and the guys said I should just play that part because they'll have to make a head and so they'll just stick me in as an extra in the background. They cast my head and started making the effects head, and then the realities of the budget sunk in."

Salah Hassanein was elated to know the film was underway... until he saw its budget. He made his position perfectly clear: he could not possibly back an unrated eight-million-dollar movie. Romero, in his typical fashion, would refuse to cut any of the gore effects, thereby eliminating any possibility for an "R" rating. It would have to be an unrated "no one under 17 admitted" affair, like *Dawn* before it. But, no, Hassanein remained firm in his stance, and the budget was slashed from Romero's desired $8 million to just $3 million. The script was also slashed and the grand zombie army confrontation was cut with it. Romero reworked the story, tightened it to center around a handful of medical and military personnel, and made it a more confined (literally) experience.

But they still had an animatronic head of Greg.

BELOW: Greg Nicotero gets a head start in horror. Private Johnson's reanimated head from *Day of the Dead* (1985).

OPPOSITE: "Now, George Romero takes us out of the night, beyond the dawn, and into the darkest day of horror the world has ever known!"

First there was
"NIGHT of the LIVING DEAD"

then
"DAWN of the DEAD"

and now
GEORGE A. ROMERO'S

DAY OF THE DEAD

United Film Distribution Company presents A Laurel Production
George A. Romero's "DAY OF THE DEAD"
Starring Lori Cardille, Terry Alexander, Joe Pilato, Richard Liberty, Production Design Cletus Anderson
Music by John Harrison, Director of Photography Michael Gornick, Makeup Special Effects Tom Savini
Co-Producer David Ball, Executive Producer Salah M. Hassanein, Produced by Richard P. Rubinstein
Written and Directed by George A. Romero © 1985 Laurel-Day Inc.   © 1985 Dead Films, Inc.

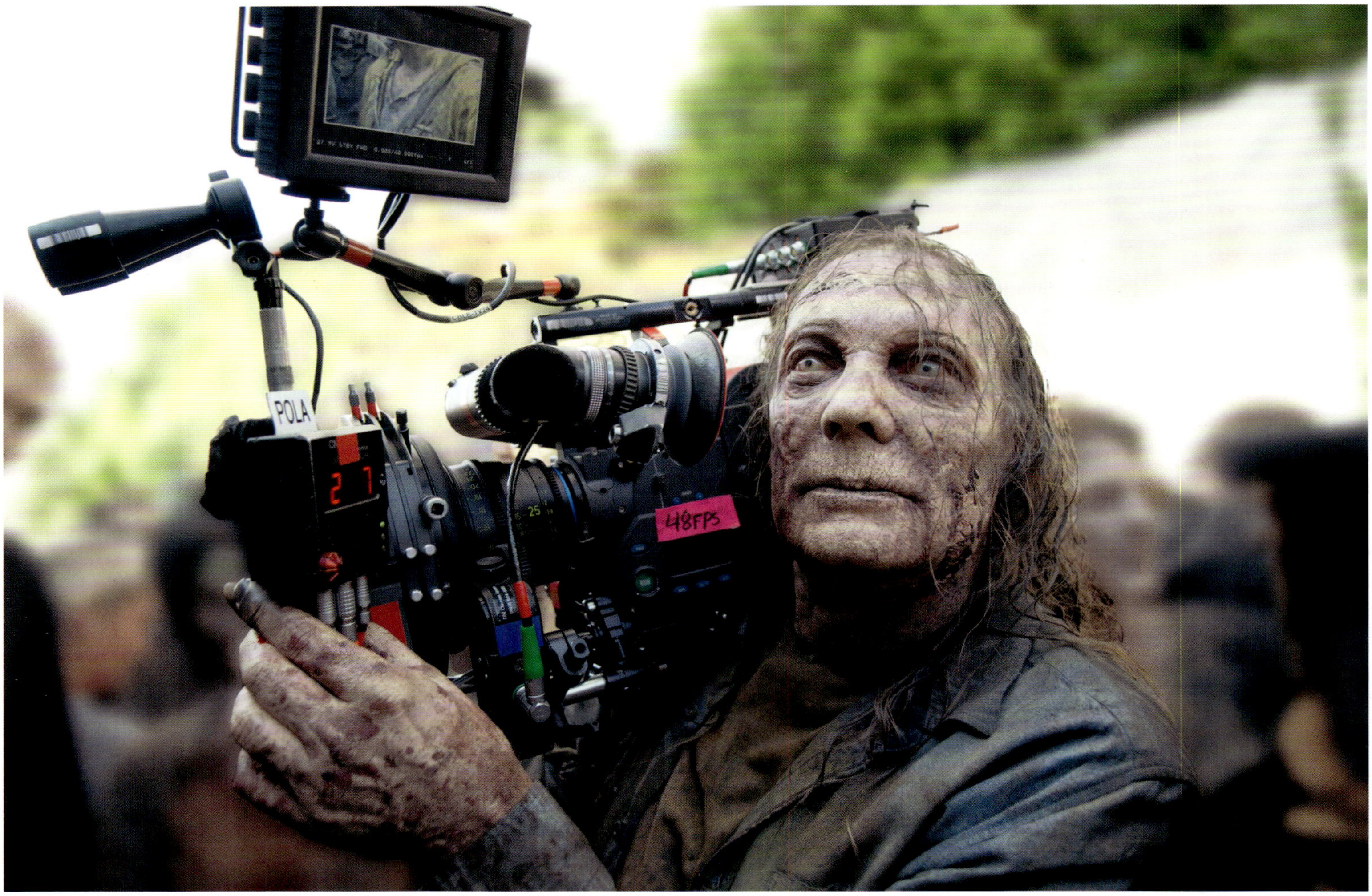
POLA
48FPS

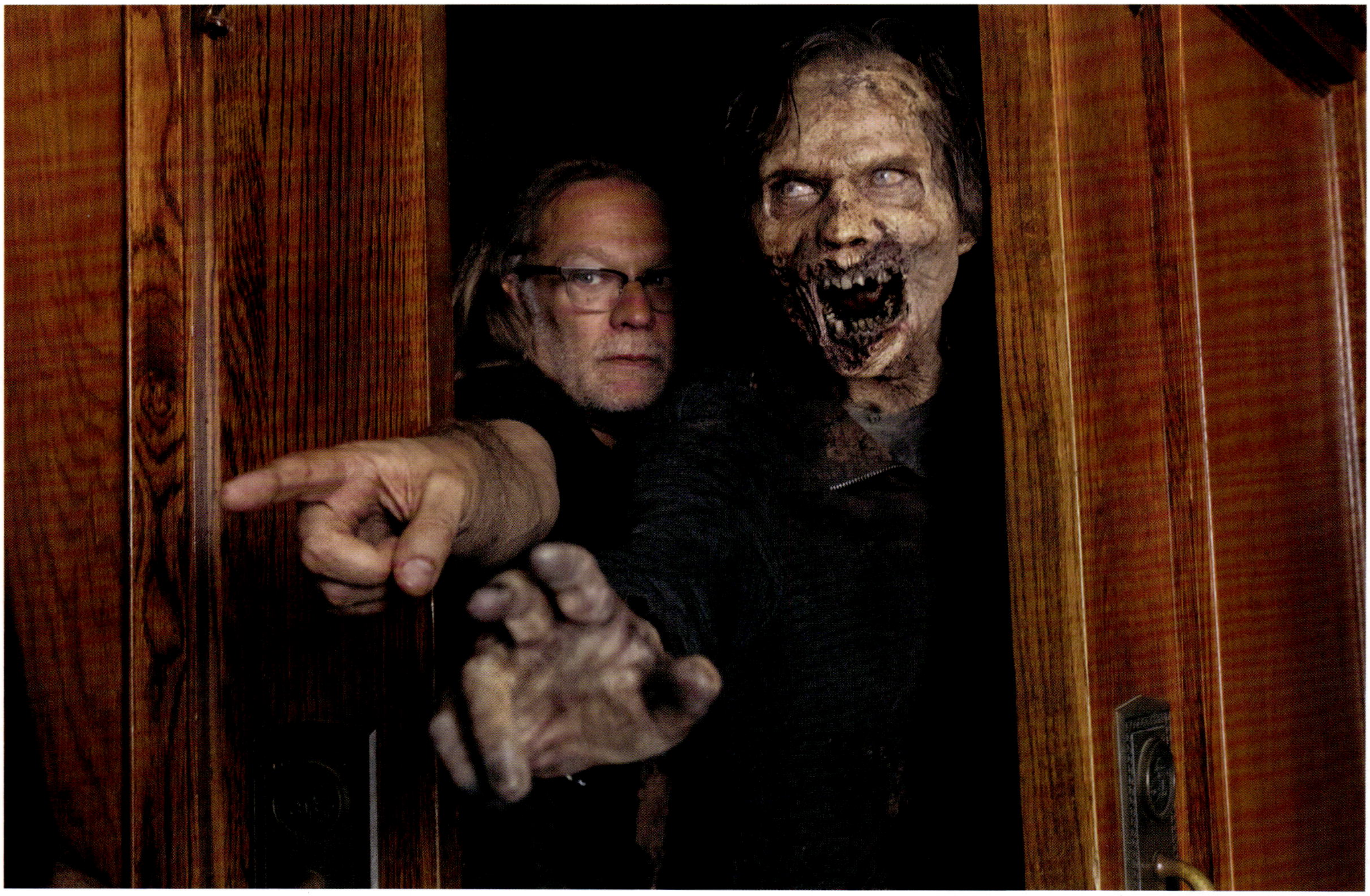

OK, so Greg's a character in the revised script—Private Johnson—and he's given a few lines of dialogue, a handful of faux reefers (unfiltered tobacco doobies that made him dreadfully ill), and a *Playboy* magazine. It was his first acting role, and all because they had a special effects animatronic head of him sitting on the shelf.

Ah, the big breaks of show business.

Upon completion of *Day of the Dead*, Greg lowered the boom on his parents: nope, not gonna be a doctor. They supported his decision and were even amused to learn he'd become a sort of de facto medical advisor during the *Day* shoot.

"Hey, Greg—when we chop off Anthony's arm, do we cauterize it right away; is that how it works?"

"Nah—you have to tie off the main artery first to slow the blood, then you can cauterize."

"Cool. Thanks, Greg!"

And Greg's mom would be especially proud of her son's work. During end-credit crawls of the films he would work on, she'd never hesitate to ask nearby patrons and theater ushers to please wait until her son's name rolled by: "Yes, there he is. OK—thank you for waiting."

After *Day*, he was off to New York where he would serve as a production assistant on Romero's *Tales from the Darkside*, then later it was back to Florida to assist Savini with the Chuck Norris ass-kicker, *Invasion U.S.A.*, then Romero's adaptions of three more Stephen King stories for *Creepshow 2*. After a bit of uncredited work with Stan Winston's team on *Predator*, it was off to work with Sam Raimi on *Evil Dead II*...and then...

And then came KNB EFX Group.

Three freelancers—Robert Kurtzman, Greg Nicotero, and Howard Berger—met up, individually and collectively, on various genre pictures in the late 1980s. Shortly after their joint efforts on *Evil Dead II*, they formed KNB EFX Group to pool their resources and establish a firm footing in the practical effects industry. Early going was a bit tough, sometimes losing money on the jobs they bid for (see *Gross Anatomy*), but they were building a portfolio that would launch them into the upper echelon of effects companies. When they demonstrated their abilities for non-genre effects (*Dances with Wolves*, *City Slickers*), they established their reputation as a go-to practical effects company...even if there aren't any zombies or monsters in the picture.

KNB gains awards galore for their impressive work: an Oscar and BAFTA for *The Chronicles of Narnia: The Lion, the Witch and

OPPOSITE: Gross Encounters of the Decayed Kind? Greg directing on *The Walking Dead*.

BELOW: Greg discusses a scene with Brock Duncan on the set of "Model Kid."

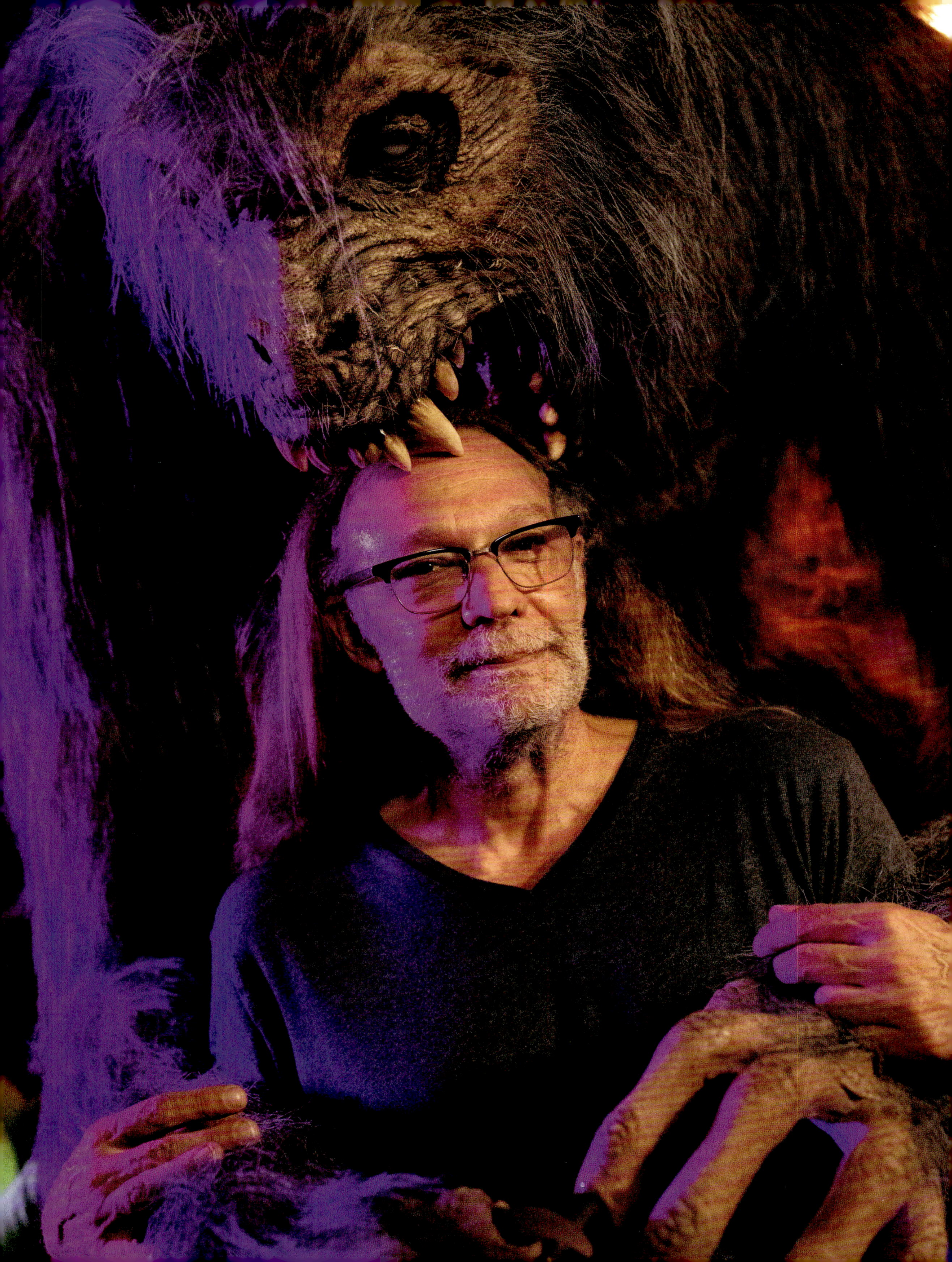

OPPOSITE: Greg and Big Bob on the set of "Shapeshifters Anonymous"

LEFT: Greg explores Celia's innermost thoughts on the set of "Lydia Layne's Better Half"

the Wardrobe, multiple Emmy awards and nominations for TV's Dune, The Pacific, Breaking Bad, and The Walking Dead. Plus, the company amasses a plethora of additional awards including CableACE, Saturn, OFTA, and more. Working from a state-of-the-art facility in Chatsworth, California, their phone never stops ringing.

And although he was up to his neck in work at KNB, Greg had an eye on the director's chair, too. Having taken on second unit directing duties as far back as 1992's Severed Ties, he figured this would be the natural segue that would take him further into his craft. He'd act as second unit director for Wishmaster, Land of the Dead, The Mist, The Vampire Diaries, and, soon, The Walking Dead (and let's not overlook the beloved United Monster Talent Agency, an endearing short film that he wrote, produced, and directed during the spring of 2010). As a director, he proved himself to be a quick study, an apt pupil, a model citizen, and devoted torch-bearer for genre moviemaking.

He advanced to front-line directing on The Walking Dead with Season 3's 2012 episode, "Judge, Jury, Executioner." He'd continue balancing his work across KNB's *very full* roster of film projects while directing even more in the ever-expanding The Walking Dead universe (including webisodes and spin-off series). To say he was "busy" is a vast understatement. Vast. But, amid everything that he and his cohorts were already elbows-deep into, there would come a new opportunity, one Greg simply couldn't reject, refer away, or resist; Shudder's Creepshow would mark Greg's return to his roots, to the bare beginnings of his unexpected journey into effects and film.

To say that the prospect excited him…well, that, too, would be a vast understatement. Creepshow would be his homecoming; he would be going back to his old stomping grounds, and he was returning with every experience, every skill, and every notch on his gunstock that he'd tallied while he'd been away. But he had never gone "away" from what he loved, had he?

He would later joke, perhaps with a slight wince, at the enormity of what he was taking on. Likening it to grabbing a wild bull by the horns, he knew there would be plenty of expectations to live up to, success points to satisfy, and fans to feed. He'd have to hang on, ride the ride, and tame the beast. He couldn't let anyone down.

And he wouldn't.

"It's in my blood. I can't *not* want to scare people. I can't *not* want to make some great shows that are funny and emotional and scary and touching, all at the same time. And it feels really good."

And really, in his heart, that's what makes Greg tick.

> SO, HOW 'BOUT OUR SCREAM-MEISTER, OL' GRUESOME GREG? HE'S JUST THE SORT OF CREEPY KID FIT TO WRANGLE A *GAGGLE OF GHOULS*, RIGHT? NEXT, LET'S SLITHER AHEAD TO EXPLORE THE DREADFUL DESTINATION HE DEEMS HIS FAVORITE *PORT OF CRAWL…*

HORROR SHOCKERS
8mm & SUPER 8 MOVIE FILM!

NOW THESE FABULOUS TERROR THRILLERS CAN BE YOUR VERY OWN! THE SAME BIG FILMS YOU READ ABOUT IN CREEPSHOW CAN COME ALIVE ON YOUR HOME SCREEN. YOU CAN RUN THEM AGAIN AND AGAIN. UNLESS OTHERWISE STATED, FILMS ARE APPROX. 200 FEET IN LENGTH (ABOUT 15 MINUTES OF CHILLS) AND MOST ARE AVAILABLE IN SUPER 8MM AS WELL AS REGULAR 8MM SIZE.

The "Original" CREATURE
The immortal Bela Lugosi shall not die! Now he lives again, undead, flickering across your home movie screen in Tod Browning's masterpiece, DRACULA! This is the film that convinced the world Lugosi was, indeed, the Prince of Darkness! 200' reel. Specify #2226 THE "ORIGINAL" DRACULA $7.99

REVENGE OF THE DEMON
In supernatural technicolor and black and white! Christopher Lee as one of the greatest Frankenstein monsters ever! 200' reel. For the BLACK & WHITE film, specify #2222, REVENGE OF FRANKENSTEIN $9.95. For the TECHNICOLOR film, specify #2223, REVENGE OF FRANKENSTEIN $19.95

CREATURE FROM BLACK HILLS
A SOUND FILM! At last, available to private collectors. Edgar Allen Poe's never-to-be-forgotten classic with James Mason's masterful narration. Ultrasonic sound. 200' reel. When ordering, specify #2231 POE'S TELL-TALE HEART $19.95

THE "ORIGINAL" FRANKENSTEIN
Starring Boris Karloff as the Frankenstein monster. This is a must for all horror film buffs. 200' reel. #2201 THE "ORIGINAL" FRANKENSTEIN $7.99

CROG THE UNBELIEVABLE
Armed with his huge spiked tusks and horrid scales and talons, Varan claws his way up from the world below! 200' reel. #2212 VARAN THE UNBELIEVABLE $7.99

THE DEADLY DINOSAUR
Down from the heavens swoops a gigantic mantis to prey upon all humanity and wreak doomsday destruction upon all in its path! 200' reel. #2204 THE DEADLY MANTIS $7.99

NIGHT OF THE MUMMY
In the steaming depths of the Amazon's Black Lagoon, a gill-man creature from 150 million years ago prowls! 200' reel. #2205 CREATURE FROM BLACK LAGOON $7.99

DOCTOR ROBOT
Conjured up by the devil-worshipping cult of the evil Dr. Kaswell, to wreak its unleashed terror upon mankind! 200' reel. #2206 CURSE OF THE DEMON $9.95

BATTLE OF THE GIANTS
Dinosaur buffs take note! Fantastic film of prehistoric battles between the world's earliest creatures! Real action! Death battles! 200' reel. #2207 BATTLE $7.99

KONG'S KID
Sequel to the film KONG, with special effects again by Willis O'Brien. Truly memorable! 200' reel. #2208 SON OF KONG $7.99

THE HUGE CLAW
Indestructible bird-like beast from the distant past now attacks the world! Clashes with science & the air force! 200' reel. #2209 THE GIANT CLAW $9.95

CREATURES WALK AMONG US
Sequel to THE CREATURE FROM THE BLACK LAGOON. Prehistoric creature is operated upon to be turned into a man. 200' reel. #2210 CREATURE WALKS AMONG, ETC. $7.99

ATTACK OF THE PYGMY
Atomic activity hatches a giant prehistoric bird. The bird is hungry and scours entire horrified nations for sustenance! 200' reel. #2211 RODAN, THE FLYING MONSTER $7.99

THE WEREWOLF
Strange howlings in the church cemetery bring the startled townspeople to the scene of a murder... and the only clues are wolf tracks! 200' reel. #2213 THE WEREWOLF $9.95

A CYCLOPS
Reversing the powers of nature via atomic energy, Dr. Cyclops reduces human beings to the pitiful size of mice... then toys with them! 200' reel. #2219 DR. CYCLOPS $7.99

THE ARACHNID
A mad scientist's experiments with a small spider and it grows monstrously huge and ravages first the lab and then the city and keeps on growing and devouring! 200' reel. #2203 TARANTULA $7.99

I WAS A TEENAGE MANTIS
A mad doctor creates the most fearsome monster ever: a teen-aged Frankenstein, combining boy's body and monster's mind! 200' reel. #2214 TEEN-AGE FRANKENSTEIN $7.99

SON OF FRANKENSTEIN
Bela Lugosi & Basil Rathbone are featured in one of many masterful sequels to the original fright classic! A must! 200' reel. #2215 SON OF FRANKENSTEIN $7.99

CREEPSHOW COMIC ADVERTISEMENTS FOR AMUSEMENT ONLY.

ACTUAL SIZE!
CREEPASAURUS REX
OVER 18 INCHES TALL

MOVING MECHANICAL PREHISTORIC ANIMAL HOBBY KITS
WIND-UP MOTOR INCLUDED — NO BATTERIES NEEDED —

The mighty behemoth roars! And it is answered by a challenging bellow. Two mighty prehistoric beasts charge. There is a clash as the two meet, teeth to teeth, claw to claw. Is this a scene from the latest Harryhausen film? No! It is a battle of moving monsters created from heavy duty, quality plastic and brought to life by your skill. Eight terrific kits! Eight moving marvels! Each comes complete with all the parts and instructions for assembly. A wind-up motor is included. Simply construct the figure, attaching the motor to the arms and legs as outlined. Then wind the key. The motor does the rest. Your miniature monster lurches forward and stalks across the room. The motor emits a lifelike roar. Each is approximately 10" from nose to tail. Own a herd! Each $3.50.

BRONTOSAURUS #2442
IGUANADON #2443
DIMETRODON #2444
TYRANNOSAURUS #2445
STEGOSAURUS #2446
ANKYLOSAURUS #2447
STYRACOSAURUS #2448
TRICERATOPS #2449

CREEPSHOW COMIC ADVERTISEMENTS FOR AMUSEMENT ONLY.

EVER WONDER WHERE EXACTLY WE HARBOR OUR HORDE OF HORRORS?
Y'KNOW, IT ISN'T EASY TO CORRAL SUCH A CAVALCADE OF CONTORTED CREATURES, MARAUDING MONSTERS, AND BUG-EYED BEASTIES... BUT WE DO IT JUST FOR YOU...RIGHT ATOP THIS HORRIBLE HILL.
HOP INTO MY TERROR TRAM AND I'LL TAKE YOU ON A TOUR OF OUR DISPENSARY OF DREAD. IT'S A PERFECTLY PETRIFYING PLACE WE AFFECTIONATELY CALL...
GUIDE
PITTSBURGH MAP
MICHAEL BROOM 2021

SHUDDER-ING HEIGHTS

The origin of Shudder's *Creepshow* is a fantastic story in its own right. It's practically one of those truth-is-stranger-than-fiction affairs, full of coincidence, circumstance, and fortuitous revelations. When you learn about the trail of chance encounters, aided by uncanny timing, you might think this could only have been scripted, but it wasn't. Was it all just accidental, then, or were these unlikely proceedings guided by some ethereal hand of fate? That's a fun and appropriately spooky notion to ponder, so let's explore it. Fittingly, it's the kind of story that begins with the tried-and-true lead-in, "It all started when...."

While attending the 2018 Electronic Entertainment Expo (E3), Russell Binder, founding partner of entertainment licensing and merchandising company, Striker Entertainment, happened upon Jordan Kizwani of the Taurus Entertainment Company. The two men already knew each other, although they hadn't connected in recent years. This was a happy encounter and a moment for professional reacquaintance. The two exchanged the usual pleasantries—*Hi, how ya doing?* and *So, what have you been up to?* These were the customary greetings of this sort of chance encounter, but then...

"We have the rights to *Creepshow*," Kizwani abruptly said.

Binder's eyes widened. Over the past fifteen years, Striker had amassed an impressive list of properties in the horror genre and was always on the lookout for more. For Binder, *Creepshow* had been a long-time favorite. He was intrigued by Kizwani's statement, but cautious; the property had a rather complicated history of ownership.

Taurus Entertainment Company, founded by Stanley, Robert, and James Dudelson, had acquired the United Film Distribution Company (UFDC) catalog of films back in 1991, and that acquisition included *Creepshow*. Despite attempts to reinvigorate the title and further expand the brand, none had taken hold. Binder, though, took hold of Kizwani's unexpected offer for new licensing and development of the property. In short order, Striker and Taurus had struck an agreement. That done, Binder made a call to his friend and industry associate, Stan Spry, co-CEO of Cartel Entertainment.

"Russell has long been a friend of mine," Spry explains, "so when he called me and said he was working with the guys who controlled *Creepshow*, and he asked if I could do anything with it, I said 'Yeah, absolutely!' Russell then brought in Jordan

BELOW: An early announcement that dared viewers to confront their fears. Don't blink. Don't breathe. Don't turn away!

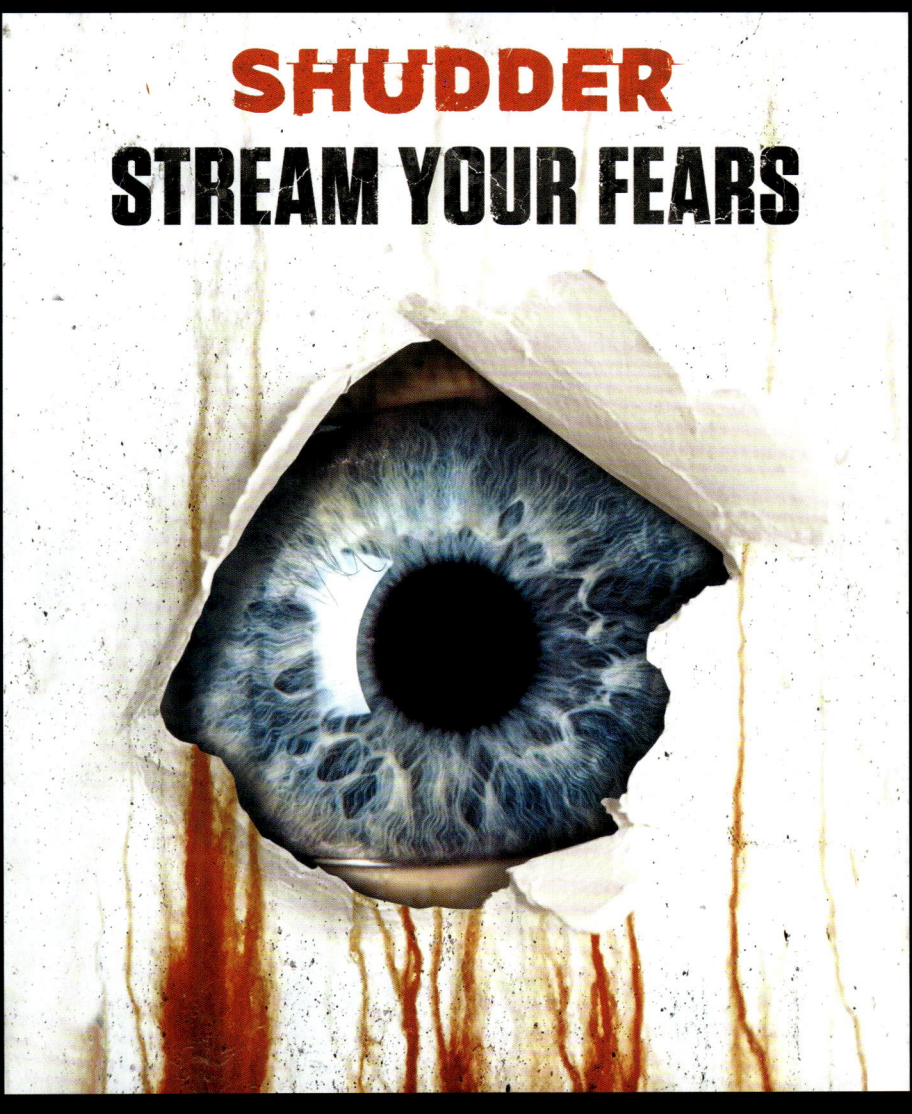

SHUDDER
STREAM YOUR FEARS

ABOVE: Fright at your fingertips—a carefully curated library of the best in horror from around the globe. (Image from Season Three's "A Dead Girl Named Sue")

OPPOSITE: Don't look away now—Shudder has such sights to show you. An early advertisement for Shudder's *Creepshow*.

Kizwani and Robert Dudelson, and I told them that I'd do a chain-of-title search—the rights were quite murky at the time—but if the rights were clear, I'd be one hundred percent in and I'd make an offer that day. And the rights were clear and we made a deal with them and with Russell."

With that done, Spry made a call of his own, this being to Craig Engler, general manager at Shudder. As a new horror streaming service owned by AMC Networks, Shudder—that is, Engler and his team—was on the lookout for original and exclusive material to add to its offerings.

"Look—we've got the rights to *Creepshow*," Spry told Engler, "and we're going to take it out and shop it, but I know you and Shudder are trying to create original content; do you want it?"

"Absolutely we want it," came Engler's reply. "Let's get a deal done. How do we want to structure this?"

Spry had it all worked out: The Cartel would be the production company and the studio backing the show. They'd partner with AMC Networks and Shudder for release. The Cartel would find a showrunner to complete the creative package, then work jointly with AMC/Shudder to get the show off the ground.

For Shudder, *Creepshow* was a no-brainer and, for Engler, there was already a connection to the work of George Romero.

"It's a bit of a weird story," Engler begins. "Before I joined Shudder, I was a writer/producer for *Z Nation*, and through that I had gotten to know Jonathan Maberry, who writes a lot of books about zombies. We became friends and he reached out to me to say he was doing an anthology book with George Romero, set in the world of *Night of the Living Dead* so, technically, it would be canonical to that world. And he asked if I would like to write an introduction or a foreword for that book."

Maberry's book would be titled *Nights of the Living Dead* and would contain a collection of "meanwhile" stories set on the same evening as the farmhouse standoff where Ben, Barbra, and the others fought the reanimated dead.

Of course, Engler was thrilled to contribute to the project, but he asked Maberry if there would be room for a story of his own to add to the collection; that is what appealed to Engler most, especially since this would become canon for Romero's original tale. Maberry enthusiastically accepted Engler's offer and Engler delivered an inventive revenge encounter with zombies and vigilante townspeople in his story, "A Dead Girl Named Sue."

Now, here comes a real-world "meanwhile" twist: before Engler assumed the role of General Manager for Shudder, his business manager had been Stan Spry. When Engler took the lead at Shudder, he told Spry that the channel would be interested in original new material, as well as established properties that could be secured for revisited treatment. Of particular interest to Engler, at that time, was *Creepshow*. Unbeknownst to Engler, Spry was already in negotiations with Taurus to clear a path forward for the property.

Now, here's a second twist: While the rights for *Creepshow* were being cleared and Spry was pitching it to Engler, Greg Nicotero was on a flight out of Australia and, by the fluke of a finger swipe on his tablet reader, he discovered Maberry's *Nights of the Living Dead*. He thought it presented a clever take on the *Night* storyline, especially as a collection of "meanwhile" short stories. Of particular interest to Greg was Engler's story. He was drawn to its premise, so much so that he wanted to produce some sort

34 CHAPTER TWO

CREEPSHOW

GREG NICOTERO

STEPHEN KING

JOE HILL

JOSH MALERMAN

JOE LANSDALE

THE MOST FUN YOU'LL EVER HAVE BEING SCARED!

A **SHUDDER** ORIGINAL SERIES

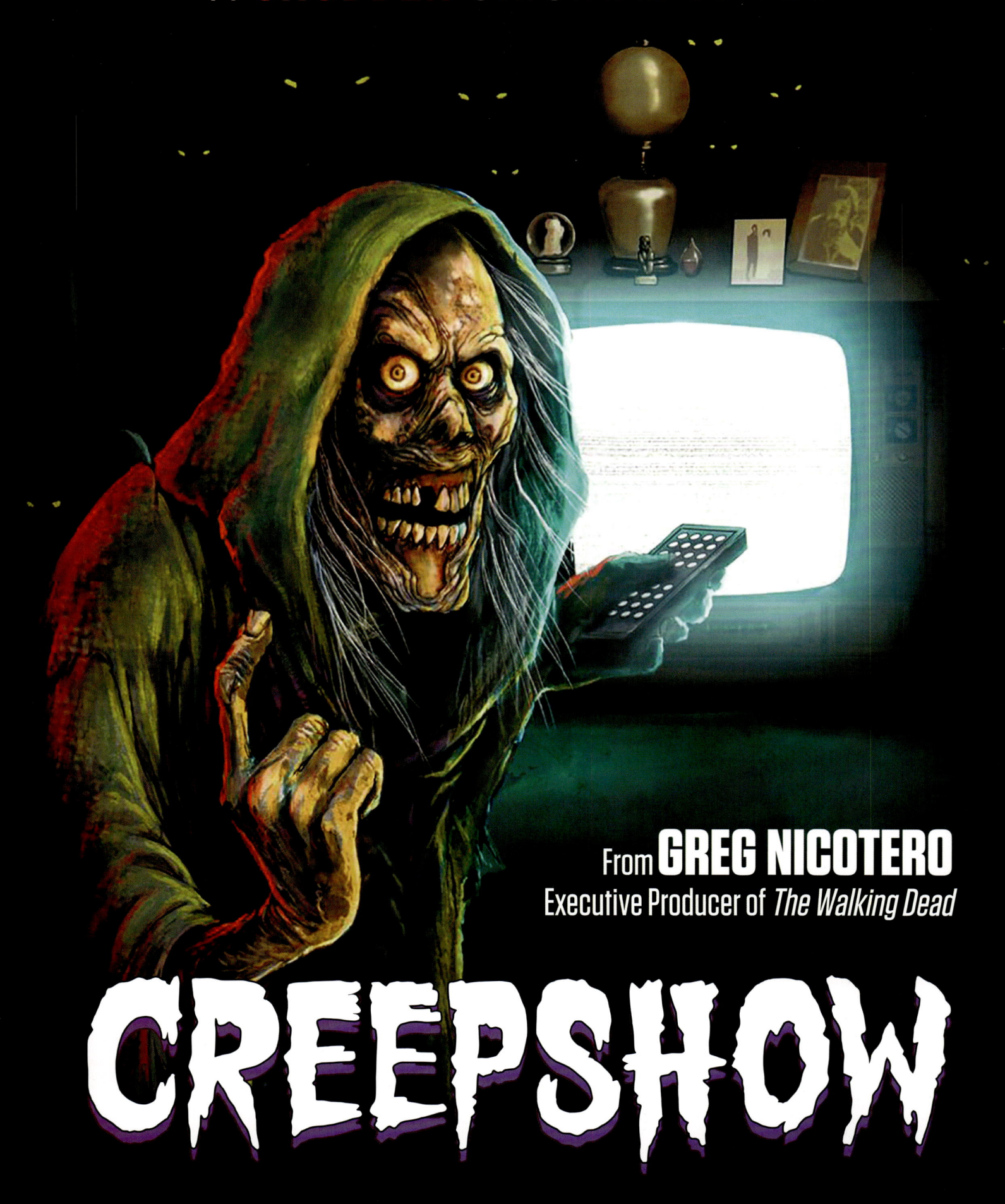

From **GREG NICOTERO**
Executive Producer of *The Walking Dead*

CREEPSHOW

12 TERRIFYING TALES OF TERROR!

STRANGE, EERIE, TERRIFYING CREEPSHOW
TALES OF SUSPENSE AND HORROR!!!

OPPOSITE: The Creep's ready for his small screen debut. An early advertisement for Shudder's *Creepshow*.

LEFT: The bold *Creepshow* episode header promises thrills, chills, and some well-deserved kills!

of short film of it. So, Greg contacted Brian Witten, his partner at Monster Agency Productions, and asked Witten to make an inquiry call to Engler's still-listed business manager, Stan Spry.

"Sure, we can talk about that," Spry told Witten, "but we're also working on *Creepshow* over here. Do you think Greg would have any interest in that?"

Jaw drop.

"You mean 'Creepshow'-*Creepshow*? That *Creepshow*?" Greg asked, slightly astonished, mostly excited, when Whitten relayed the message.

Yes, that *Creepshow*. It was as if the stars had aligned in surreal happenstance (see, we told you). Greg's journey in effects and filmmaking that started with *Creepshow* had now come full circle. Yes, he would become the showrunner and would set off to make this *his* continuing vision of *Creepshow*.

So, was it all that simple? Was everyone on board and in unanimous agreement—just like that? Well, not exactly. The idea of producing a new anthology horror series was greeted with mixed reactions. While Craig Engler believed that *Creepshow* must stay true to its anthology roots, the amazing success of long-form serialized television (think *Breaking Bad* and *The Walking Dead*) had some top brass at AMC Networks hem-hawing at the proposal. They were accustomed to the long-form, season-based approach where, week by week, a slow-boiling narrative would unfold, tension and intrigue would build, and well-placed twists and turns would compel viewers to tune in week after week. That's fine for those shows, but *Creepshow* is an anthology vehicle, through and through; any deviation from that formula would be a betrayal to fans. More importantly, the format would entice viewers, offering them an alternative to the long-term investment required in keeping up with a serialized program. Anthology delivers quick stories that are easily accessible and offer a wide variety of settings and situations—sort of like a comic book (wink-wink). It's a time-tested winner, in film, in fiction, and in illustrated storytelling. It had always worked, and it would continue to work.

And it did.

Shudder's *Creepshow* surprised everyone. Upon its debut, it became the most talked-about show of the streaming service and it revealed that viewers had an active desire for anthology content. Engler and his team of content curators discovered that the short story format was, indeed, quite beloved; it was his initial intention to deliver just a small amount of anthology content on the platform until he learned that his viewers wanted more. They wanted good horror, first and foremost, but they also wanted variety in what they watched, supporting the proposition of "well, if you liked that story, you're gonna *love* this one, too!"

"There's something for everyone," Engler adds, "and [the anthology format] allows us to explore a lot of different stories from a lot of different storytellers...and a lot of different directors. We're able to bring in a lot of guest directors, and it's really fun because they each bring their own energy and spin to it. And so, you just never know what you're going to get—in a good way—with Shudder's *Creepshow*."

Of course, Greg knew exactly what fans would get and what he would give to them. The show was his baby now, and his decades of experience—plus his personal connection to and love for the original material—would make him the perfect caretaker to lead it forward.

> HOW'S THAT FOR A TERROR-FILLED TOUR? DID WE LEAVE ANYONE BEHIND? MAYBE? THAT'S ALL RIGHT--THE TENANTS HERE ARE ALWAYS THIRSTY FOR *FRESH BLOOD*. FOR THOSE OF YOU STILL WITH US, COME ALONG-- THE REAL INSANITY IS ABOUT TO BEGIN...

CHAPTER TWO 37

BUILD YOUR OWN MONSTER

HORRIBLE!

GORY!

FRIGHTENING MONSTER—that YOU can own and CONTROL! Greatest illusion ALL your friends will listen to YOU because YOU control him! WALKS—TALKS—EATS—Order your MONSTER PLANS TODAY!

Only $1.00

No. S-91

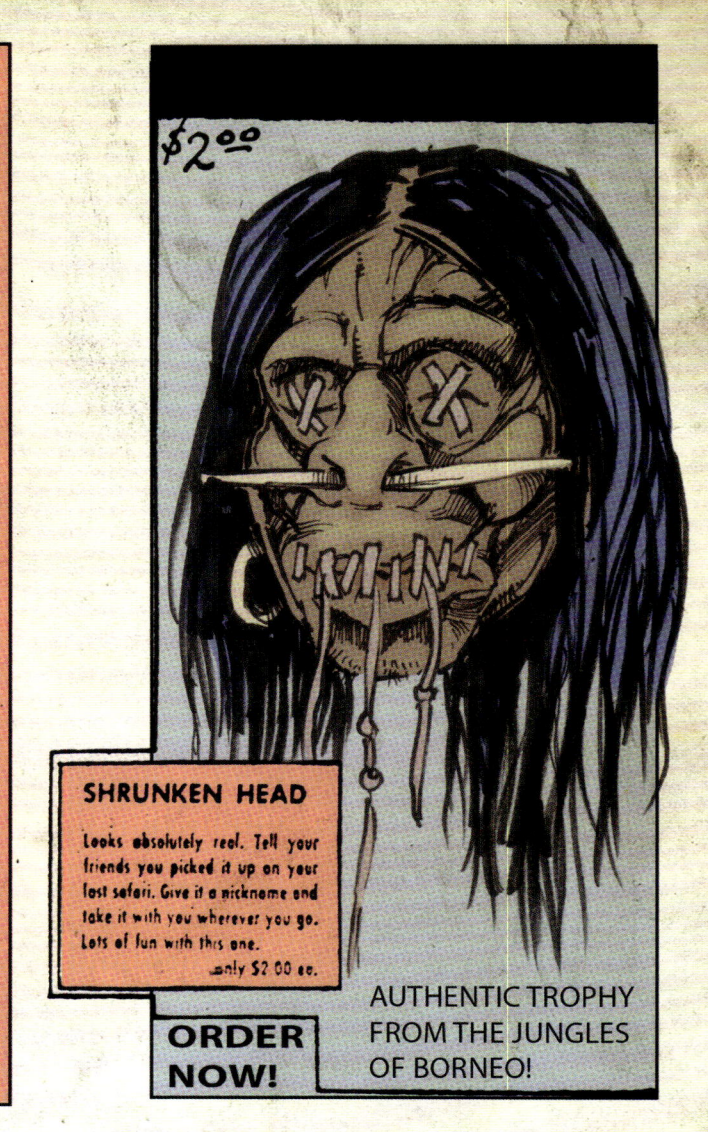

$2.00

SHRUNKEN HEAD

Looks absolutely real. Tell your friends you picked it up on your last safari. Give it a nickname and take it with you wherever you go. Lots of fun with this one.

only $2.00 ea.

ORDER NOW!

AUTHENTIC TROPHY FROM THE JUNGLES OF BORNEO!

THE ZOMBIE MASK

"ACTUAL PHOTO"

This fiendish, evil mask is terrifyingly lifelike in appearance. A hideous greenish color, the Zombie is made of top quality sanitary rubber and can be folded and placed in your pocket. It's lots of fun at parties ...but please...if your friends have bad hearts—don't wear it. With the mask you receive a grotesque Zombie wig of finely spun hair. The combination makes you look like "death takes a holiday."

Price Complete $2.98

FRANKENSTEIN MASK

A partner in crime of the Zombie, this ghoulish mask is a terrifying likeness of the famous monster. Made of sanitary rubber, the Frankenstein mask can be rolled and carried in pocket. Price $2.98

"ACTUAL PHOTO"

Frankenstein Mask, $2.99 _____

SOLD OUT!

ADDRESS _____
CITY _____
STATE _____ ZIP CODE _____

---

38 CHAPTER TWO — CREEPSHOW COMIC ADVERTISEMENTS FOR AMUSEMENT ONLY.

MOVIE MONSTER KITS!

Create your own Classic Horror Characters! Authentic life-like Model Kits made of Styrene plastic! Build yourself with quick dry enamel and watch them GLOW IN THE DARK! Fantastic!

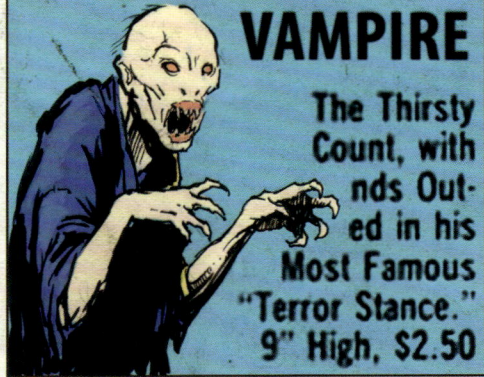

FRANKENSTEIN
YES! The Most Famous of All The Incredible, Fantastic Monsters! 10-1/2" High, $2.50

VAMPIRE
The Thirsty Count, with nds Outed in his Most Famous "Terror Stance." 9" High, $2.50

ZOMBIE
The dead are rising from the grave! Rotten decomposing creature from Beyond! $2.95

ALIEN
Famous Monsters Magazine created this one especially for you! 8-3/8" High. What A Kit! $2.50

MUMMY
You can almost smell the Eerie old Egyptian tombs! 9 inches high $2.50

WEREWOLF
It's a Full Moon — and the Wolfman is out — in all his Gory Splendor, ready for his Next Victim! 8-3/4" High,

DEMON
Summoned from Hell, this monster wants to live on your shelf! 9 inches high $2.95

JACK THE RIPPER
The mysterious killer from the Victorian streets on London was never caught! 8-3/4" High, $2.50

SWAMP BEAST
Horrifying beast that lives in the wet damp areas where most are afraid to go! $2.50

DEMONSAURAUS REX
The Monster from a Million Years Ago! He strikes with the force of a Hurricane! 8-5/8" High, $2.50

THE WITCH
This Evil Lady is shown brewing up some Black Magic! She'll cast a Spell over You! 8-1/4" High, $2.50

SASQUATCH
The legendary hairy creature seen in the Pacfic Northwest attacking hikers and campers! 10 inches high, $2.95

Rush me the following GLOW IN THE DARK MONSTER KITS(S). Enclosed is $ _____ Inclusing 50c postage and Handling for each kit checked.

- ☐ FRANKENSTEIN $2.50
- ☐ VAMPIRE $2.50
- ☐ ZOMBE $2.95
- ☐ ALIEN $2.50
- ☐ MUMMY $2.50
- ☐ WEREWOLF $2.95
- ☐ DEMON $2.95
- ☐ JACK THE RIPPER $2.50
- ☐ SWAMP BEAST $2.50
- ☐ DEMONOSAURUS $2.50
- ☐ WITCH $2.50
- ☐ SASQUATCH $2.95

NAME _____
ADDRESS _____
CITY _____
STATE _____ ZIP CODE _____

CREEPSHOW COMIC ADVERTISEMENTS FOR AMUSEMENT ONLY.

WHAT SORT OF MESSED-UP MINDS CONJURE OUR TWISTED TALES? WELL, WE KEEP THEM ALL HERE, UNDER LOCK AND KEY.
THEIR NOTIONS ARE NOXIOUS BUT THEIR CONCOCTIONS ARE THE SORT OF GORY STORIES YOU SEEM TO CRAVE. SO, WHO ARE THE CRAZY ONES...THEM OR YOU?!
C'MON, LET'S TAKE A STROLL THROUGH THIS PENITENTIARY OF PAIN. IT'S A WAILING WARD WE CALL...
All work and no prey...
All work and no prey...
All work and no prey...
All work and no prey...
All work and no prey...
MICHAEL BROOM 2021

THE WRITERS' BLOCK

When it comes to selecting stories for *Creepshow*, Greg looks for ideas that are fun, entertaining, and that give him a chuckle or two along the way. As he sorts through the multitude of pitches that come his way, he's on the lookout for the ones that have the genuine *Creepshow* vibe—freaky, far-fetched, and full of possibility. And once he finds one...well, that's when the real fun begins.

"Once a *Creepshow* story has been selected by myself and the network," he explains, "and we've made a deal with the writer, I have a brainstorm session—anywhere from forty-five minutes to two-and-a-half hours—where I get on the phone with that writer and we just start riffing ideas...and *that* is probably the most freeing and most rewarding discussion of the entire series. There's no budget involved and no one is telling us what we can and can't do yet; it's just people riffing ideas."

This back-and-forth conversation is open and energetic; it's the first stage of the creative process, and it leaves Greg absolutely electric with excitement. Some initial pitches are little more than one or two paragraphs of a raw concept, so this is where the key details are fleshed out, the characters are refined—who's the good guy, who's the bad guy—and where the creep factor starts to take shape.

"When Josh Malerman and I were going over his story, 'The House of the Head,' there's that point when Evie takes the miniature head out of her dollhouse and throws it, and then she finds it under her bed, full-sized—that was a new idea that came out of one of these calls, the idea that the haunted world of the dollhouse had broken that barrier and entered into the real world. Those are the moments that come out of those brainstorming sessions; they're what make those meetings not only critical but, also, very, very fun."

Greg has written, co-written, and adapted plenty of the stories himself. Some are dark ("Within the Walls of Madness," "Lydia Layne's Better Half," "The Right Snuff"), while others are playfully infused with grim humor ("Skeletons in the Closet," "Shapeshifters Anonymous"), but all come from within his own personal experiences—movies he's loved, stories he's read, and others' work that he's long admired. Each story is infused with something that has spoken to him in a very personal way or has strong connection to the original *Creepshow* world.

Season One, then, gets off to a solid start as Greg immediately drops us into a gooey body horror story with lineage back to the original creative source. "Gray Matter," a short story by Stephen King, was adapted by writers Philip de Blasi and Byron Willinger,

BELOW: A cleverly concocted story takes Greg—and us—to a familiar farmhouse, circa 1968.

CHAPTER **THREE** 41

A harrowing descent into one man's drunken despair, from "Gray Matter."

ABOVE: What will Doc (Giancarlo Esposito, left) and Chief (Tobin Bell) encounter when they come face to face with grief-stricken Richie Grenadine?

RIGHT: Storekeeper Dixie (Adrienne Barbeau) will learn the terrifying truth from Richie's devoted son, Timmy (Christopher Nathan).

and it sets the tone for the new series. It's a dark, dank, and disturbing descent into the decline of a reclusive widower whose dutiful son, Timmy (Christopher Nathan), makes a nightly visit to the corner store to buy his father a case of beer. On this evening, though, Timmy is distraught; he complains to the storekeeper (Adrienne Barbeau), "My daddy's changed; he's sick." It seems that the nightly case of Harrow's Supreme Lager the boy brings home is affecting his father in an odd way—a *really, really odd* way.

Next comes "The House of the Head," a perfectly creepy take on the haunted house sub-genre. Writer Josh Malerman (*Bird Box*) calls it a haunted house *inside* of a house—where six-year-old Evie (Cailey Fleming) is witness to a haunting, not within the home where she and her parents live but, rather, within the dollhouse in her bedroom. Despite her attempts to help the tormented doll family fend off a ghostly presence, the evil stalks each of them, relentlessly, and then it sets its sights on Evie.

"I've always made up little stories, ever since I was young," Malerman shares. "I'd say, 'Oh, this would be a good story to tell or that would be a good story.' As a kid, I was captivated by the first horror film I ever saw; that was *Twilight Zone: The Movie*, and the second horror movie I saw was *Creepshow*." And, for Malerman, it was the variation of the collected stories that inspired his own creativity. He believes that brevity can be a key method to delivering scares.

"Some of the scariest stories that I've ever heard are like just a sentence long. Someone at a party once randomly told me, 'Oh, I once saw my dead aunt peeking at me from behind the furnace.' And then he left. That completely creeped me out, wondering if I'd ever run into one of my dead relatives in the basement. For me, I think the less space there is within a horror story, the less time we have to manage down our tension. I think horror's most natural space is the short story."

LEFT: In "The House of the Head," an uninvited guest has taken residence in a young girl's dollhouse. Can a malicious spirit really haunt a child's play space?

BELOW: Evie (Cailey Fleming) is desperate to save her doll family from the murderous manifestation. Is this really happening, or is it only happening in Evie's head?

ABOVE: When the instinct to "look out behind you" comes a bit too late. Jackson (Andrew Bachelor) was warned that something had followed him. Should've listened. (From "Familiar," the creature played by Brandon Jones.)

OPPOSITE: Kid's play, you say? Well, "Model Kid"'s Joe Aurora (Brock Duncan, pictured top) knows that monsters can be fun...and formidable, as neighborhood bully Billy Niles (Chris Schmidt, Jr., pictured bottom) learns in the clutches of the Frankenstein Monster made flesh (Alex Hill).

What else frightens Malerman? His other *Creepshow* story, "Familiar," offers a clue.

"My mom had an unlabeled cassette tape that she told me never to listen to; it was a recording of a session she had with a psychic. Well, I listened to it and, on it, I heard my mom tell the psychic, 'Everyone in the house has seen a ghost, except Josh.' Years later, when asked what I thought the scariest situation would be, I said it would be visiting a psychic and, during the reading, the psychic silently slips me a note that says, 'Something followed you into this room.'"

And while *Creepshow* is the perfect setting for the things that genuinely spook us, it's also the place to enjoy a fond reverence and tip of the hat for the scary good fun the genre has offered to generations past.

"Honestly, 'Model Kid' was so literally my story growing up with horror," says veteran genre writer/producer John Esposito. "Back in the day, I was lucky enough to have parents who were film fans, and they didn't dissuade me from watching horror. There were the *Creature Features* shows—the horror host shows—and my father was there next to me pointing out to me who Boris Karloff was. Then one day he brings home an issue of *Famous Monsters*, and first I look at all the pictures and then I start to read it and, ultimately, I developed a love for this genre. And the funny thing is that I wrote a line in 'Model Kid' that I overheard being said to my own mom, many times: 'He'll grow out of it.' But, I didn't."

Esposito's "Model Kid" shows loving affection for all the monster kids from decades past. It's the story of millions of other youngsters who felt they were somehow different than the other kids in class and on the playground. They secretly nourished themselves on a steady diet of TV horror shows, monster books and magazines, and Aurora models. Along the way, these youngsters—boys *and* girls, mind you—developed an encyclopedic knowledge of all things horror and sci-fi.

John has been responsible for some true genre gems over the years, writing 1990's *Graveyard Shift* and co-producing 1996's *From Dusk till Dawn*. Throw in his work on *The Walking Dead: Webisodes* and *R.L. Stine's The Haunting Hour* and you've got a talent that knows how to draw on all that horror has given to him over his lifetime. He employs the gamut of his lifelong genre awareness, sprinkling in the sort of esoteric callbacks that are at the heart of the *Creepshow* style. Oh, and stop motion, too!

"'Skeletons in the Closet' was a last-minute thing. Greg called me and said he needed a story, fast; something they could do on one set and could do really quickly. And he always loved the story of the Mount Lebanon cemetery and the Savini/*Dawn of the Dead* skeleton, and we talked about how we could use that idea in a story. And the notion of how we might do a stop-motion

CHAPTER THREE

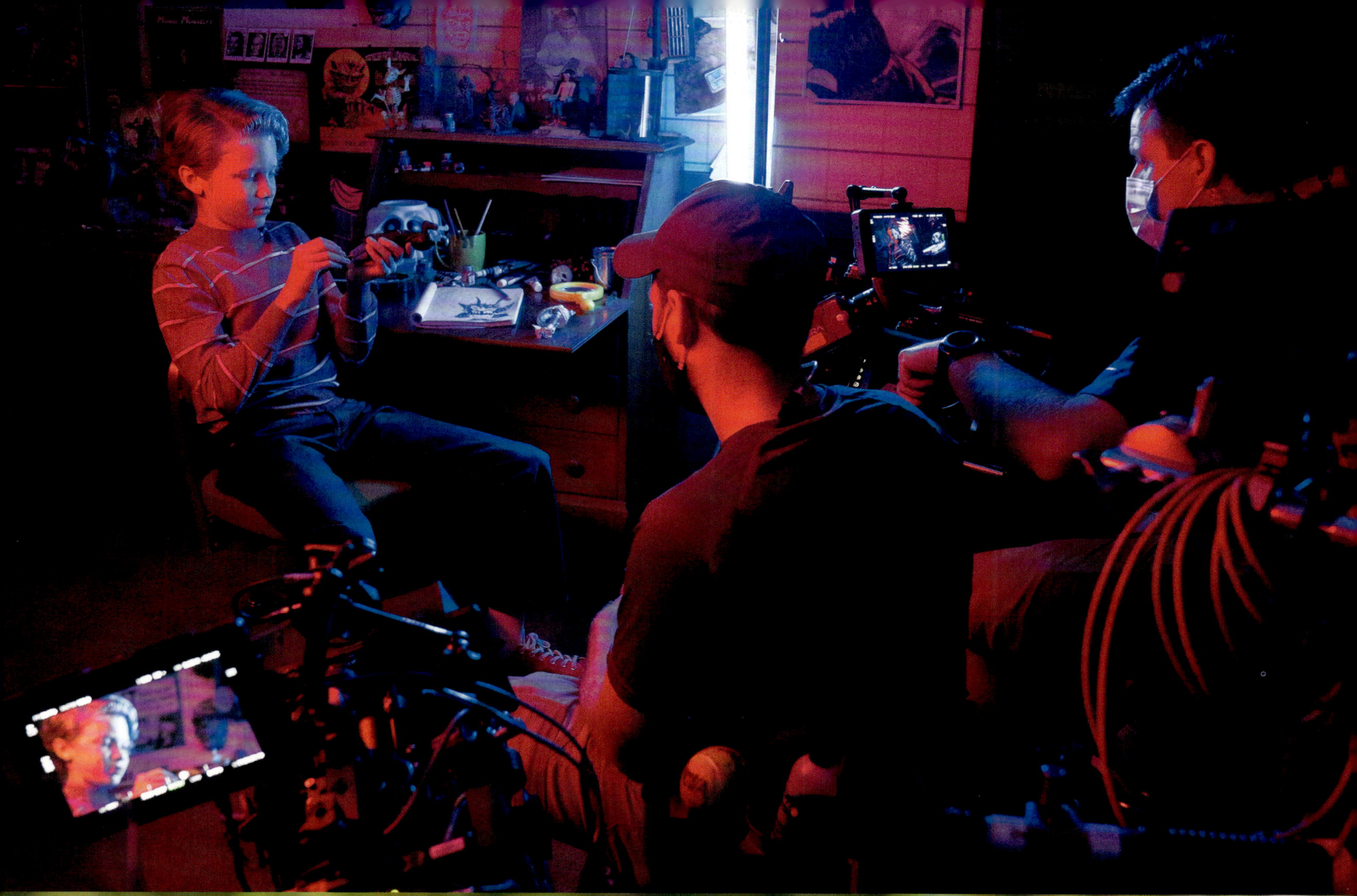

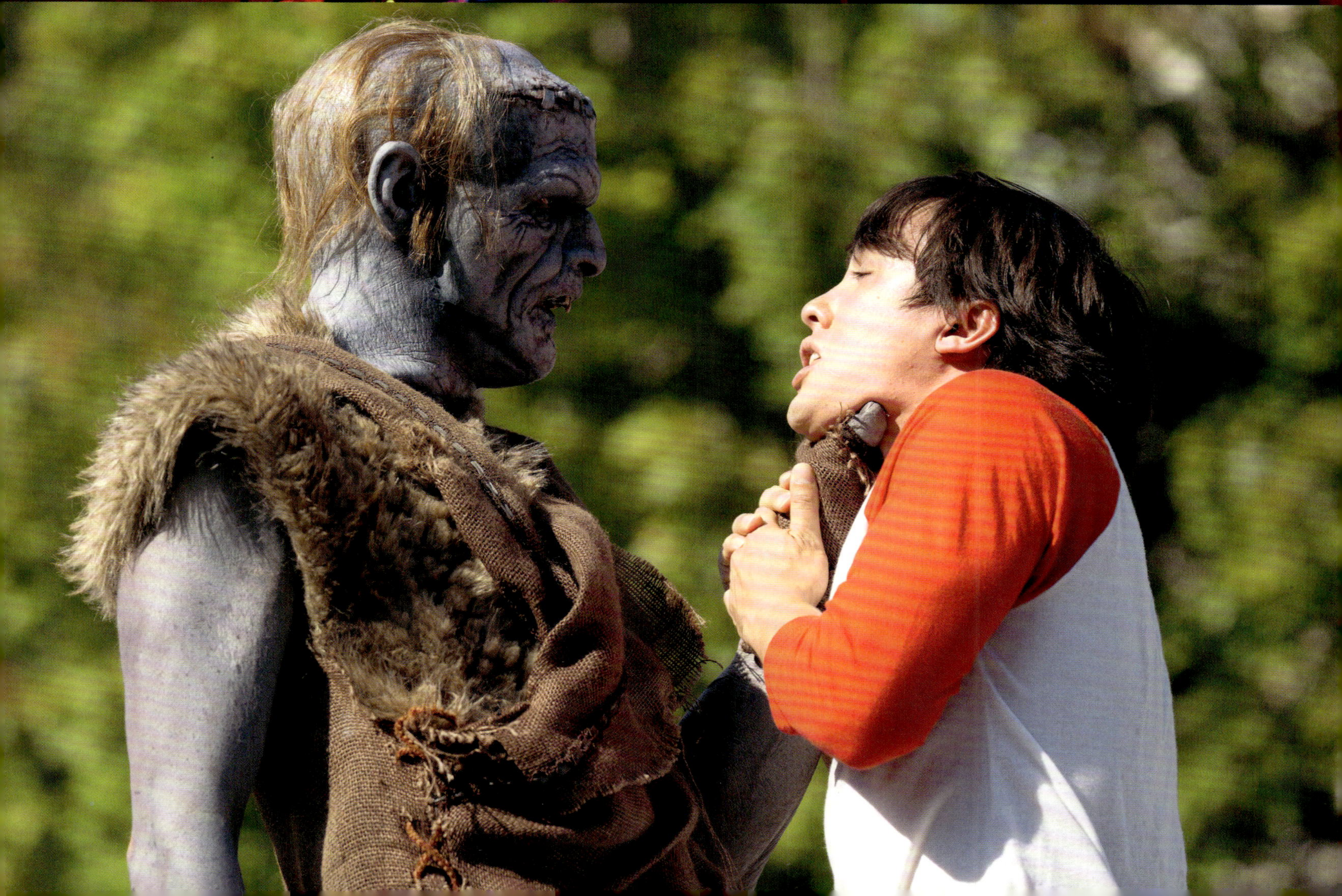

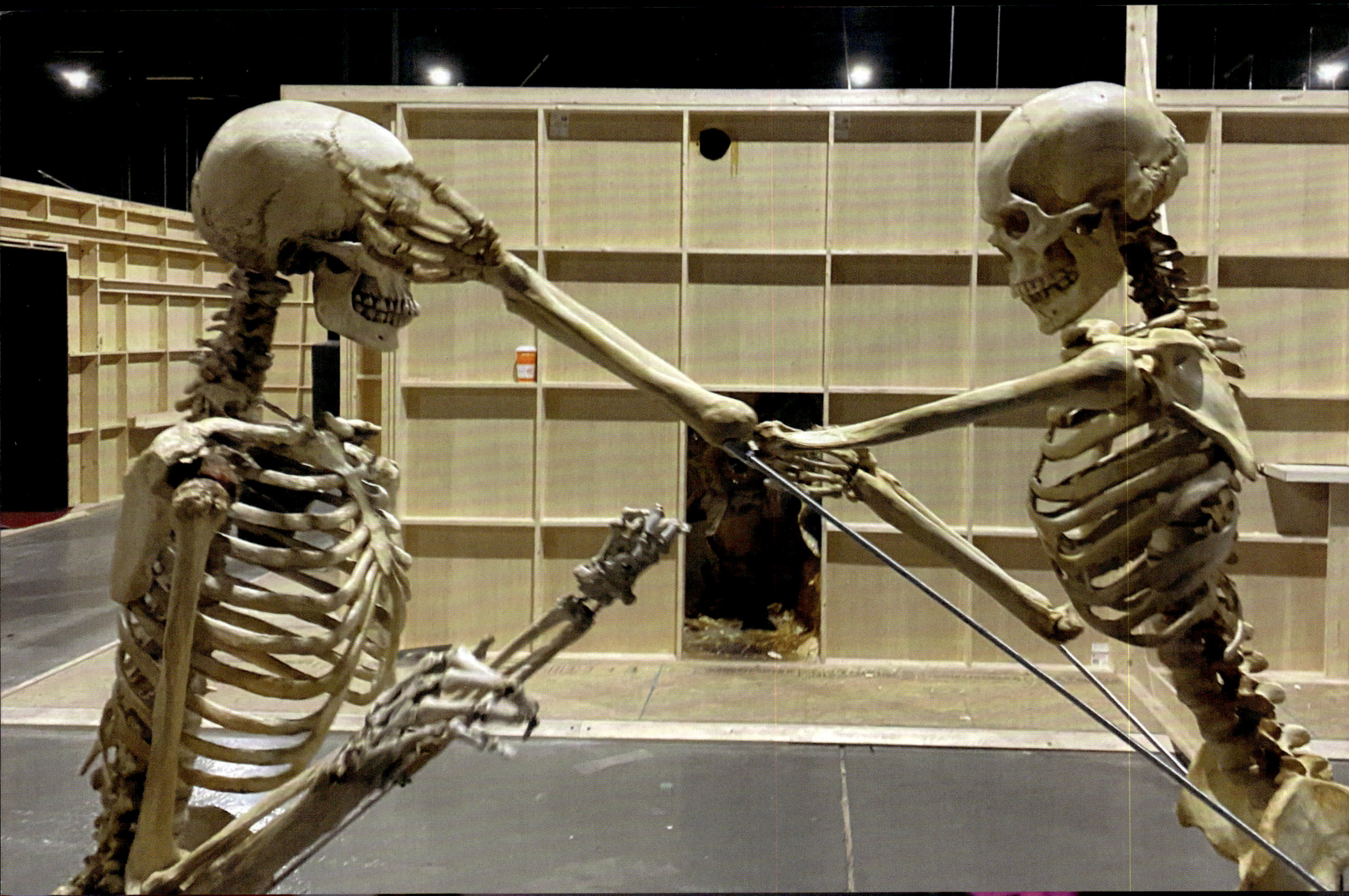

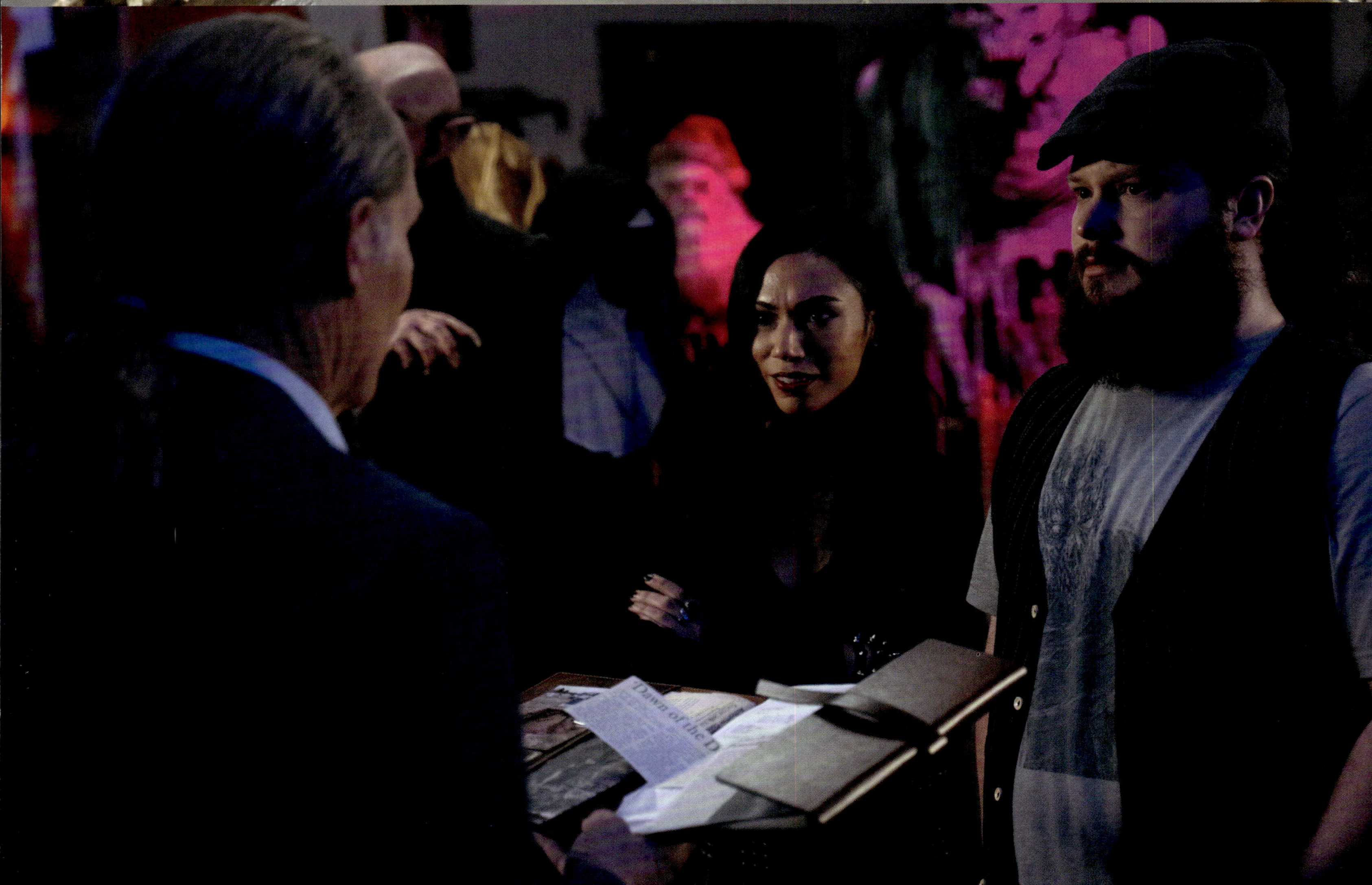
Dawn of the D

skeleton fight at the end came up almost immediately; the real challenge would be convincing the powers that be that the audience would want to see a skeleton fight. We already knew that *we* loved it."

The "Skeletons" script follows a preeminent prop collector and showman, Lampini (Victor Rivera). He's confronted by his rival Bateman (James Remar), a fellow prop connoisseur who covets Lampini's prop museum's recognizable and strikingly realistic "movie" skeletons. Bateman knows the true origins of the skeletons and threatens to expose Lampini's dark secret... unless they can make a deal.

Esposito confesses that it was a ridiculously fast turnaround for a story and, on the evening prior to the start of filming, he and Greg visited the set of Lampini's prop museum, and Esposito's reaction was...terror! The set was still under construction; the paint was still drying and it wasn't yet dressed—and shooting was to start the next day! Greg kept his cool and gave reassurance that all would be just fine. Sure enough, Production Designer Aimee Holmberg and her team—Jason Vigdor, Lucas Godfrey (who has a fun role in the segment), Nick Morgan, and the rest—all pulled off some true magic. Lampini's "Skeletons in the Closet" museum was a horror fan's fantasy!

"All of Greg's love and affection for the material absolutely shines through," Esposito beams. "It operated like a next stage of the 'Model Kid' life story—after models and magazines come movie props. And so many of those props are actually Greg's. In fact, the whole line about the David Warner head from *The Omen* came about because Greg had actually just bought that prop as we were developing the story!"

Reaching further into his bag of horror, Esposito delivered scripts for "Night of the Paw" (a nice twist on the W. W. Jacobs tale), "Within the Walls of Madness" (employing a distinctly Lovecraftian mood), and "Meter Reader" (a sort-of slanted mashup of *The Exorcist* meets *Constantine* meets *28 Days Later*).

"And that's the fun of this series; you never know what you might get in an episode of *Creepshow*. There's something for everyone—Greg makes sure of that."

OPPOSITE TOP: "Why, I oughta!" sez' the slap-happy skeleton to this bony buffoon.

OPPOSITE BOTTOM: Meanwhile, Lampini (Victor Rivera, right) and Danielle (Valerie LeBlanc, center) insist their skeletons didn't come from India. Scheming Bateman (James Remar, left) knows the truth of Lampini's "Skeletons in the Closet."

ABOVE: Anybody up for a game of Hide-and-Schreck?

CHAPTER **THREE** 47

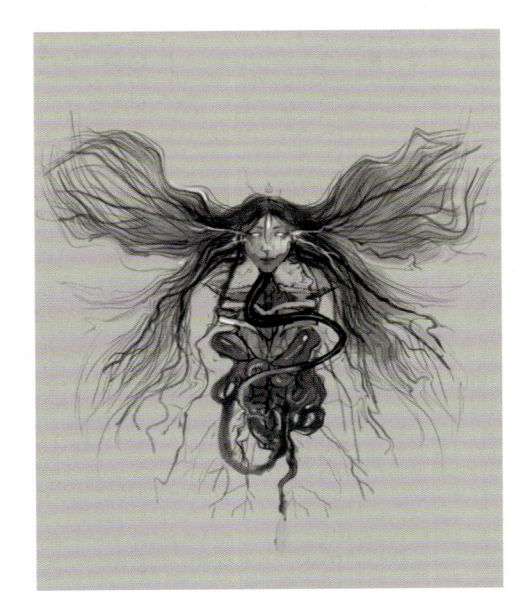

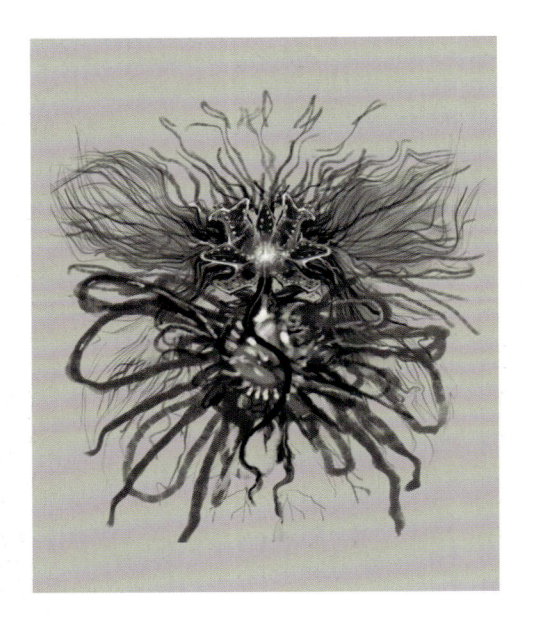

ABOVE: It's not from Lovecraft—it's from Laos! The incredible Krasue is on the loose in "Drug Traffic." Art by Robin Raaphorst.

OPPOSITE: "Going green" takes on a whole 'nother meaning when the Krasue invades your environment. Pictured is Sarah Jon as Mai, prepped by Katie Ballard.

Something for everyone and something from *everywhere*, as we discover in one of the series' most unique thrillers, "Drug Traffic." This is a clever international horror wrapped up in a contemporary conflict at the U.S. border.

"For Season Two, Mattie Do pitched this really interesting, one paragraph idea," Greg explains, "where there's this woman in Mexico and she's trying to get across the border. She's gone to Mexico to get medication that she can't get in the United States, and she gets stopped because the medication is not legal in the U.S., but the medication keeps her daughter from turning into this really weird monster."

"It's called the *Kasu* here in Laos," explains story writer Mattie Do (*Dearest Sister*), "but in Thailand it's known as the *Krasue*—and that's the reference that is used in the story. And it's great that we can introduce it to viewers, a new creature from a different country. I love working in this genre because people are always open to something new, and Greg is definitely into that."

"Right," interjects Christopher Larsen, husband and creative collaborator to Do. "Originally, we were going to have the monster in our story be a werewolf, but it was Greg who urged us to give him something new and different."

"And it was this one little paragraph Mattie pitched to me," Greg adds, "and I absolutely fell in love with their idea and was fortunate to collaborate with her and Chris because it turned out to be one of the favorite things I worked on in a long time."

According to Southeast Asian folklore, the Krasue is a spirit that manifests itself as a young woman, consisting of a floating head with trailing organs and other viscera—heart, lungs, intestines—in search of blood and flesh.

"When Greg told us he was looking for something more outside the box and that we should tap into the Asian culture and the heritage here...well, we've got some fucked up monsters here!"

Larsen adds that, upon the actual airing of the episode, he noticed enthusiastic chatter arising on social media as individuals from around the world began weighing in on the Krasue's origins and its differing manifestations from country to country—Thailand, Indonesia, Vietnam, Japan, and more.

"And as I was watching this online chatter," Larsen recalls, "I realized that we tapped into something multi-cultural. We gave it a specific Thai-Lao presentation, but this monster connected with a population area of almost two billion people! There was an excitement shared by almost a third of the world that seemed to be saying, 'I tuned into *Creepshow* and there was *my* monster.'"

Veering from Asia and over to Europe—Germany, specifically—we're presented with a traditional monster encounter—a

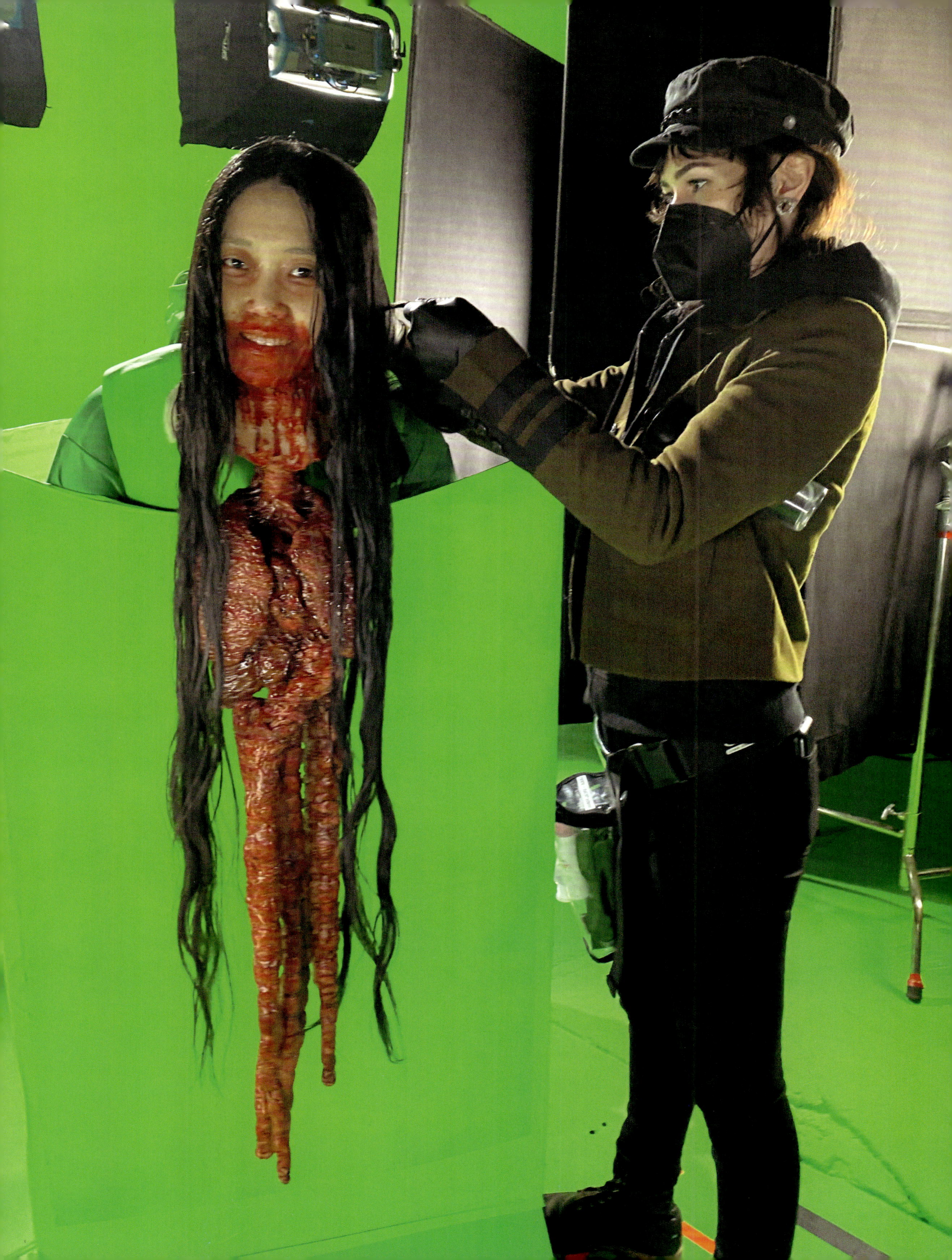

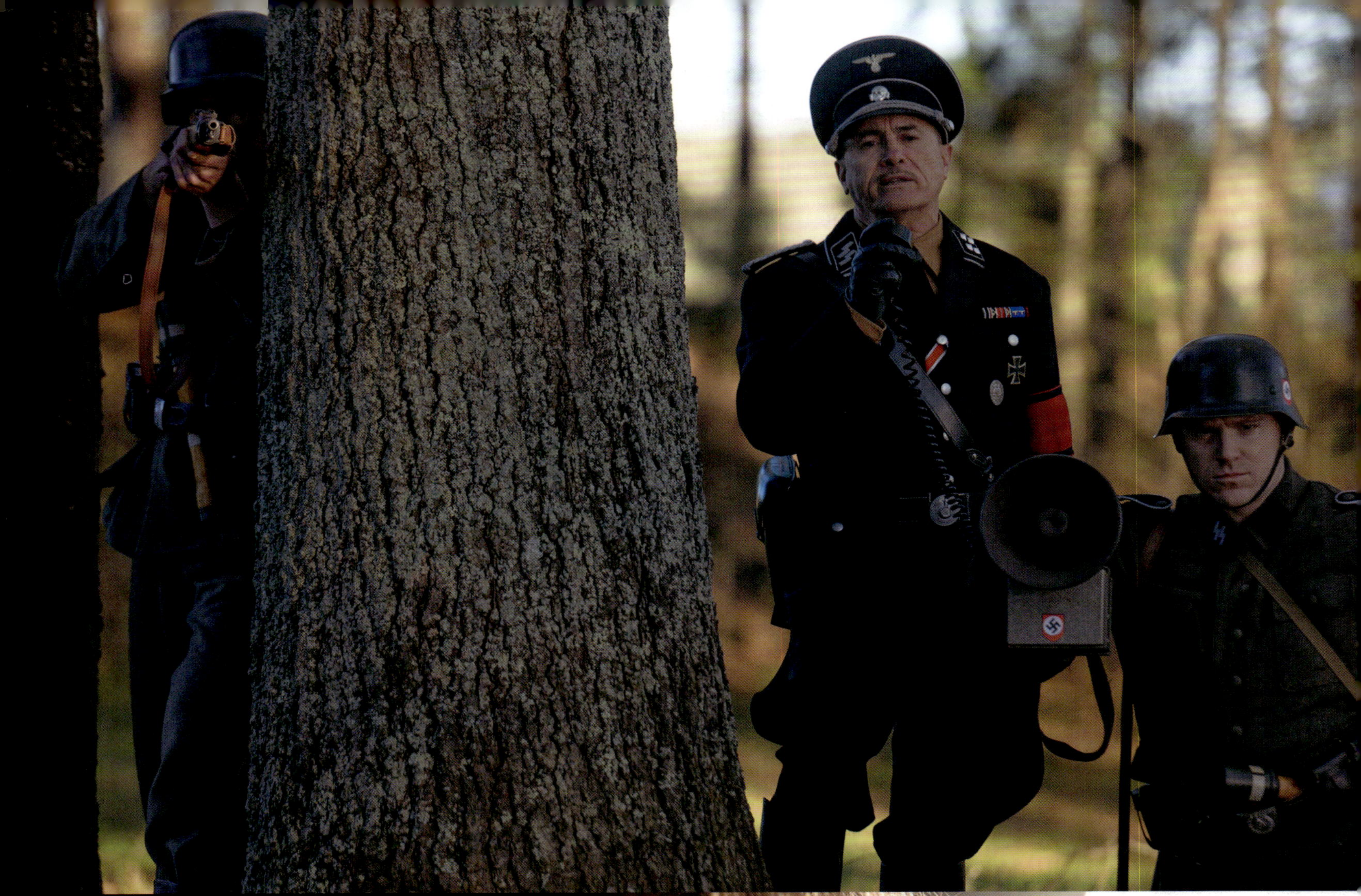

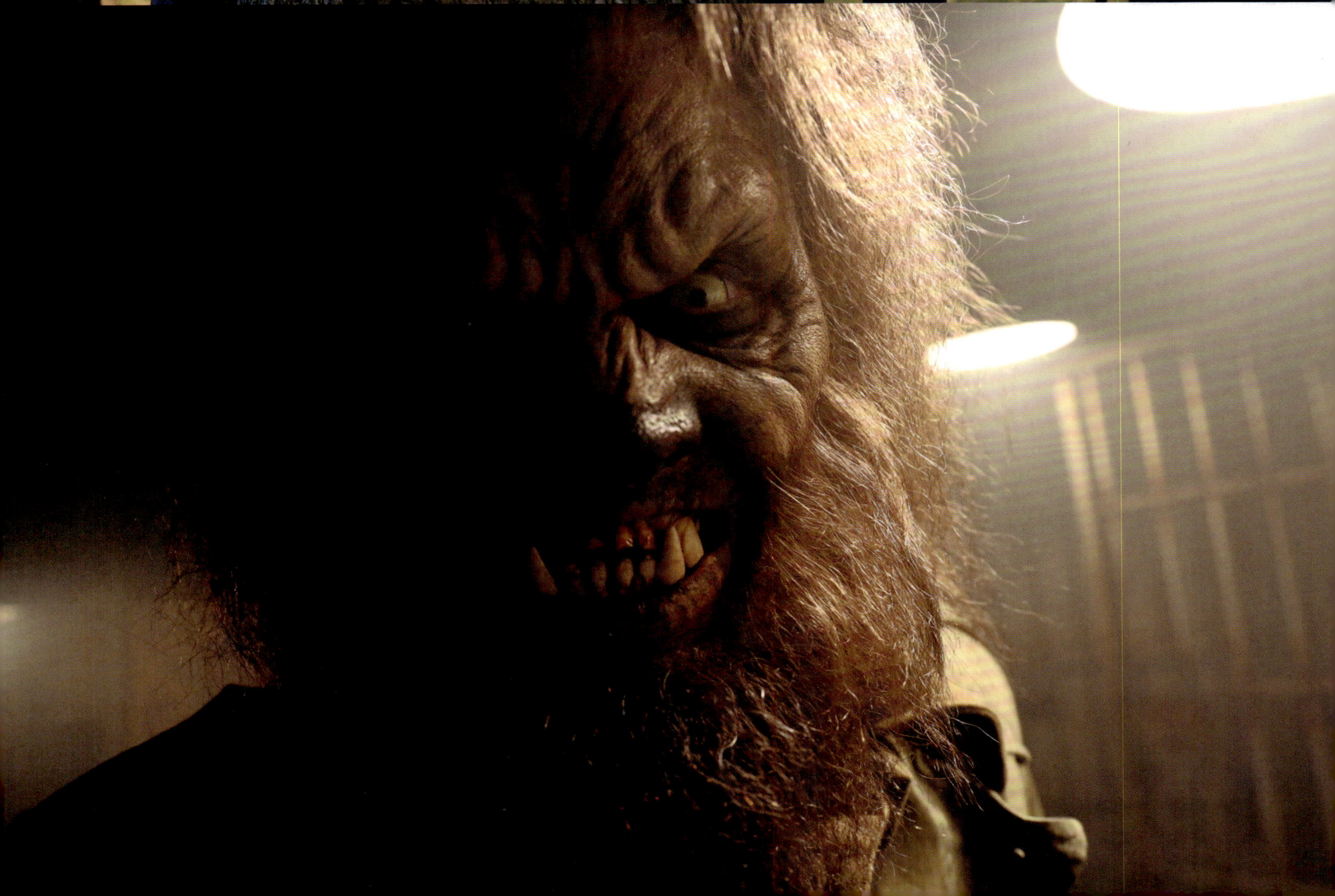

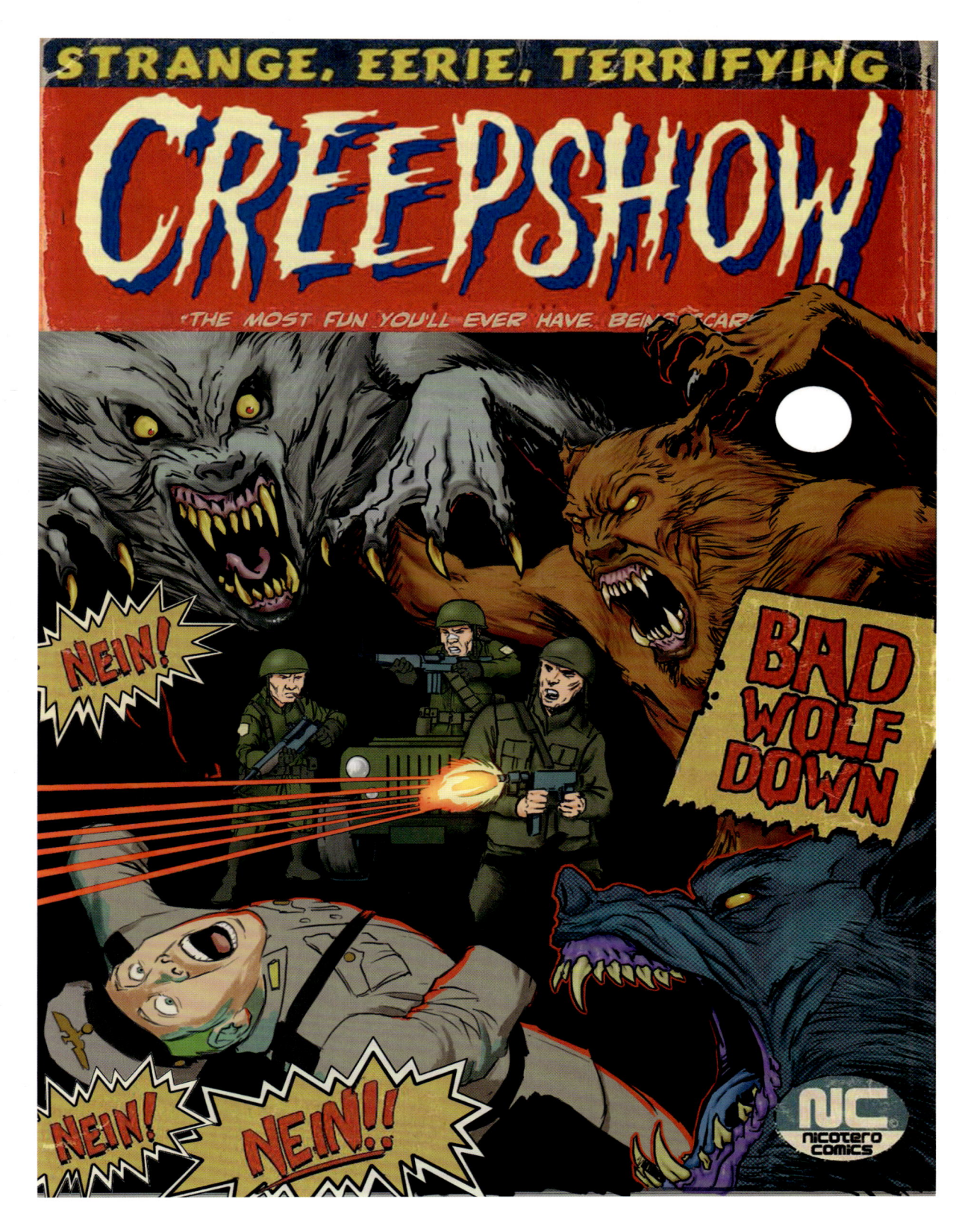

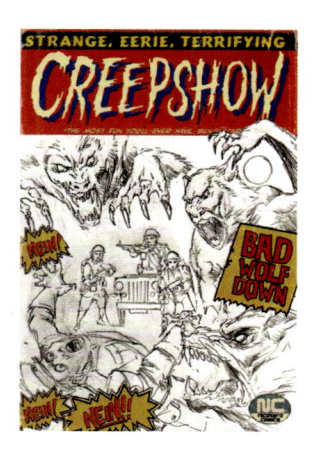

OPPOSITE TOP: When writer/director Rob Schrab is on the job, things can get mighty hairy, and Commandant Reinhard (Jeffrey Combs) is about to learn that you can't keep a "Bad Wolf Down" (flanked by Daniel Stone [left] and Ryan Dempsey [right]).

OPPOSITE BOTTOM: Captain Talby (portrayed here by stuntman Andy Rusk) would go to any lengths—come Hell or high water—to overpower the German aggressors.

LEFT and ABOVE: Conceptual art by Rob Schrab sets the mood for some howling good fun!

werewolf—although there's not much that is traditional about this lycanthrope's manner of manifestation. Writer Rob Schrab (Monster House) leads us onto a WWII battlefield where a small group of American soldiers take desperate measures to defend themselves against an isolated Nazi siege.

"For a little background, I had written a script about killer octopi that lived in the sewers, and in the script, I had some characters talking about the Creepshow movie, citing lines and just bonding over it. Well, my friend, Derek Mears, sent the script to Greg, then Greg later invited me out to KNB to look around...and in his office was the original crate from Creepshow. It was the best day of my life, and Greg and I just nerded out talking about the movie and all sorts of stuff. So, when I learned about the Creepshow series, I reached out to him to see if I could contribute a story."

Schrab caught Greg's attention with two of his pitches, "Bad Wolf Down" and "Public Television of the Dead." Schrab was elated and immediately wanted to know what kind of budget would be available for what he might write. "Don't worry about that," Greg advised, "just write a good script and we'll figure it out."

Schrab concocted an esoteric approach to his writing which, by his estimation, would help him deliver a truly authentically styled story. He referred to a copy of Stephen King's original Creepshow movie script, then painstakingly transcribed it, verbatim, to get a feel for the mechanics of how King structured his work. Schrab says the approach helped him develop the toolset, the style, and the rhythm to write a proper Creepshow story.

PUT BATTLE-SCARRED STRUCTURE IN BACKGROUND (POST EFFECT)

LIKE THE BEACH HOUSE IN 'SOMETHING TO TIDE YOU OVER.'

DEAD FOREST -- ON LOCATION (DAY)

ACTOR WEARS WOLFMAN GLOVE -- HE CONTROLS HOW TALBY'S HAND GOES INTO HIS MOUTH.
(FOR SAFETY & HOPEFULLY MORE BRUTAL PERFORMANCE)

RIPS JAW OFF!

TOSS!

USES LOWER JAW AS HORSESHOE

THE END!

52 CHAPTER **THREE**

CHAPTER THR

PREVIOUS SPREAD: Conceptual storyboard art by Rob Schrab for "Bad Wolf Down."

ABOVE: When antiques attack. The Necronomicon swallows the soul of show host Goodman Tapert (Peter Leake) in "Public Television of the Dead."

OPPOSITE TOP: Have a heart—she's just a kid. Lola Pierce (Maddie Nichols) has her brother understandably upset as she takes "Sibling Rivalry" to a whole new level.

OPPOSITE BOTTOM: Blake's frantic flight of terrified tweets reveals big trouble under the big top, from "Twittering from the Circus of the Dead."

"This was originally a story set during the Gulf War rather than World War II—'Bad Wolf Down' was a play on *Black Hawk Down*—but we didn't want it to be misconstrued as anything political, so we decide to make it a story of werewolves versus Nazis, and it turned out to be great."

For his second story, "Public Television of the Dead," Schrab again used his unusual preparation method.

"This time, I was transcribing script pages from *Evil Dead II* because I wanted to experience what it might have been like for Sam Raimi and Scott Spiegel to write that—and it was so *fun* for me to do that. And so I sent my script off to Greg and later got a call back. He said, 'You're a genius—and *I'm* directing this one.'"

Clearly, there's a story behind the story of every *Creepshow* excursion. The writers' own circumstances are oftentimes as interesting as the actual stories they write.

"I had been one of the lead walkers on *The Walking Dead*," says actor/writer Melanie Dale. "One day, Greg and I happened to be chatting and, since he'd found out I was a writer, he asked me if I wanted to pitch an idea for *Creepshow*. I pitched a story but it wasn't really right for *Creepshow*, but then he spent time with me to explain how to properly twist an ending and how to structure it all, and I realized that I was getting a master class from a master of horror."

A quick learner, Dale delivered a cleverly concocted story, "Sibling Rivalry," where a brother (Andrew Brodeur) is stalking his sister (Maddie Nichols), readying to—what?—kill her?! He's convinced she's a bloodsucking monster while she snarkily rebuffs his ridiculous theory and unfounded aversion to her, up until the point where she invites him over to her side.

Vampires, Dale proclaims, are her most loved monsters within the genre. She devoured Bram Stoker's *Dracula* at an early age and still calls it her favorite book of all time. And this love of vampires led to her second *Creepshow* assignment, a teleplay adaptation of horror author Joe Hill's short story, "Twittering from the Circus of the Dead." While not a vampire story, the task nonetheless appealed to Dale, given that Hill is a favorite author of hers, the man responsible for penning new vampire lore in *NOS4A2*.

Of course, Joe Hill had a few things to say about the adaptation of his story and its treatment within *A Creepshow Animated Special*. "This is actually one of my favorite adaptations. I thought it was really scary and really heartfelt, and it looked great. And the actress, Joey King—ha-ha, I get the joke," he adds about the actress who shares his family name, "did the narration, and she was terrific. And I really thought it was a faithful adaptation of the source material. As a writer, when someone adheres to the source material, you can't help but be flattered; it's like, '*Oh, they're using all my words!*'"

Inasmuch as Joe is pleased to see how Dale stayed within his original story elements, he knows that sometimes that is not the best route in adapting a written work for the screen. "I don't think that adaptation has to be slavishly faithful to the original source material," he clarifies. "What's important is that it comes alive for the filmmaker. If you're taking a novel or a short story, and the filmmaker finds something in that material that excites them to explore...the audiences respond to that; they *feel* the difference between something that was phoned in and something where [...] it all comes alive for [the filmmaker and the actors]."

54 CHAPTER THREE

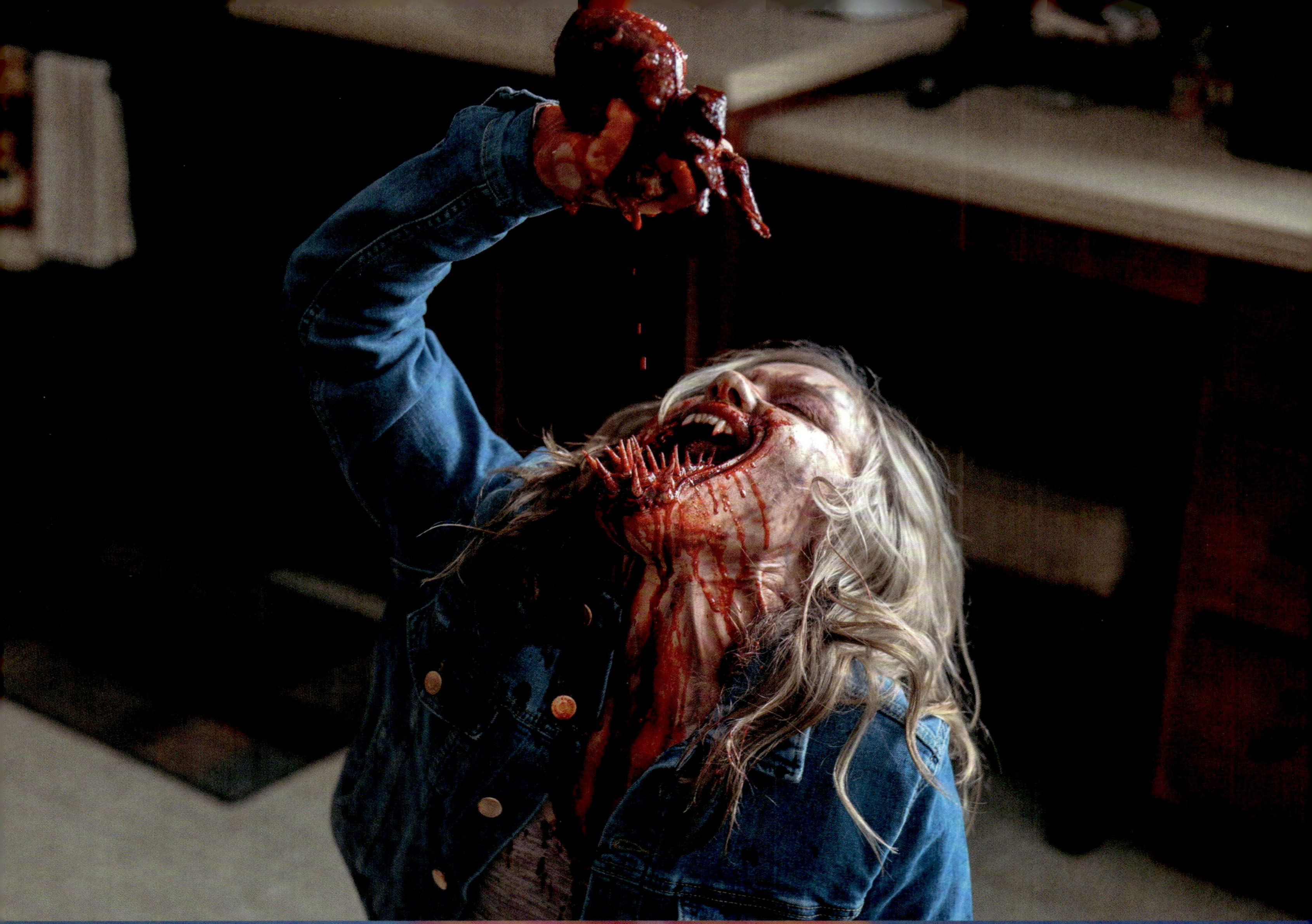

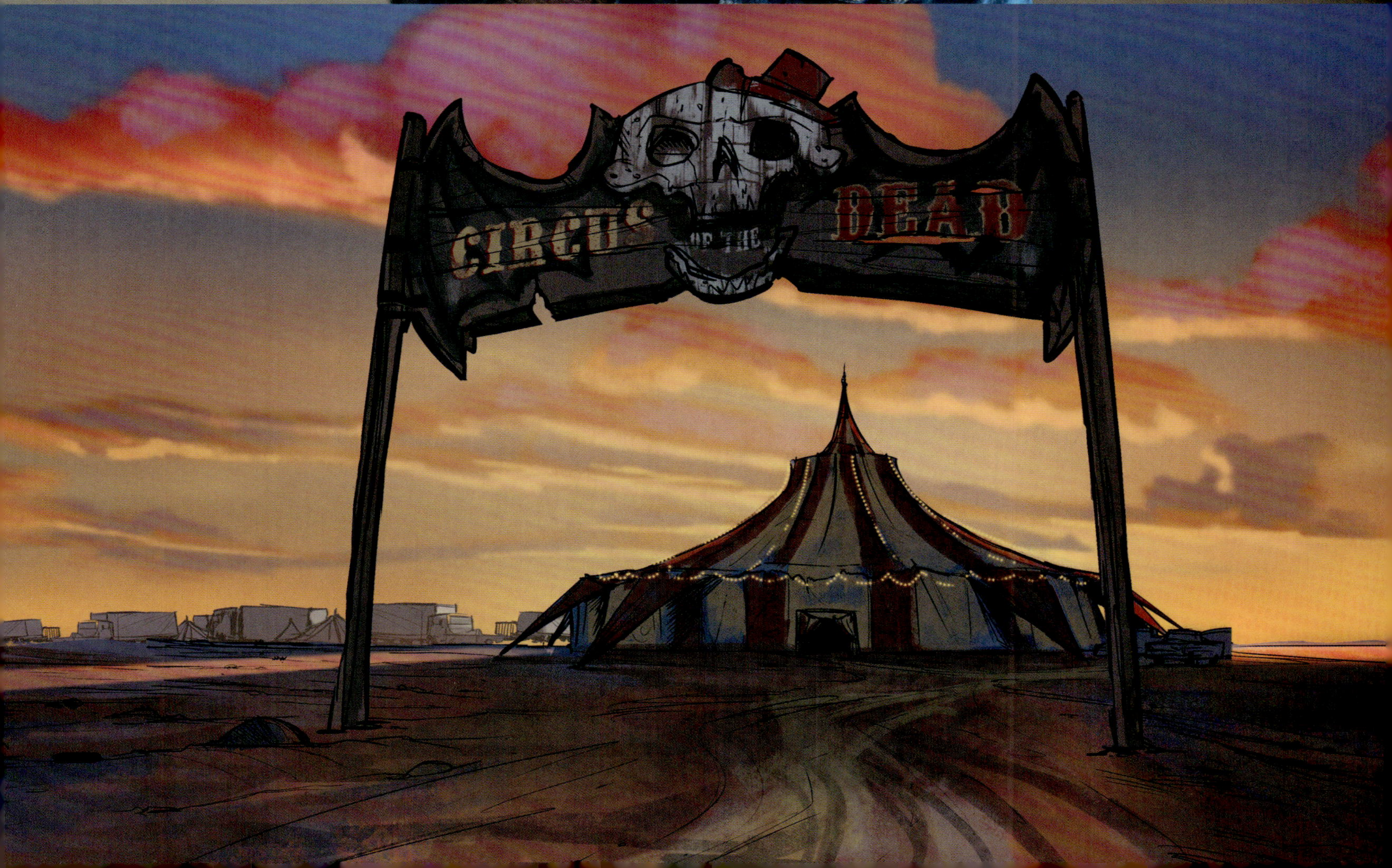

CIRCUS
OF THE
DEAD

ABOVE: There are things more terrifiying than the dead returning to life. Police Chief Evan Foster (Cristian Gonzalez) stares evil straight in the eye, that is child killer Cliven Ridgeway (Josh Mikel) from "A Dead Girl Named Sue."

RIGHT: Pop-star fanaticisim can lead to eye-popping encounters… and beyond, as Trenice (Olivia Hawthorne) and Carlos (Nico Gomez) discover in "Queen Bee."

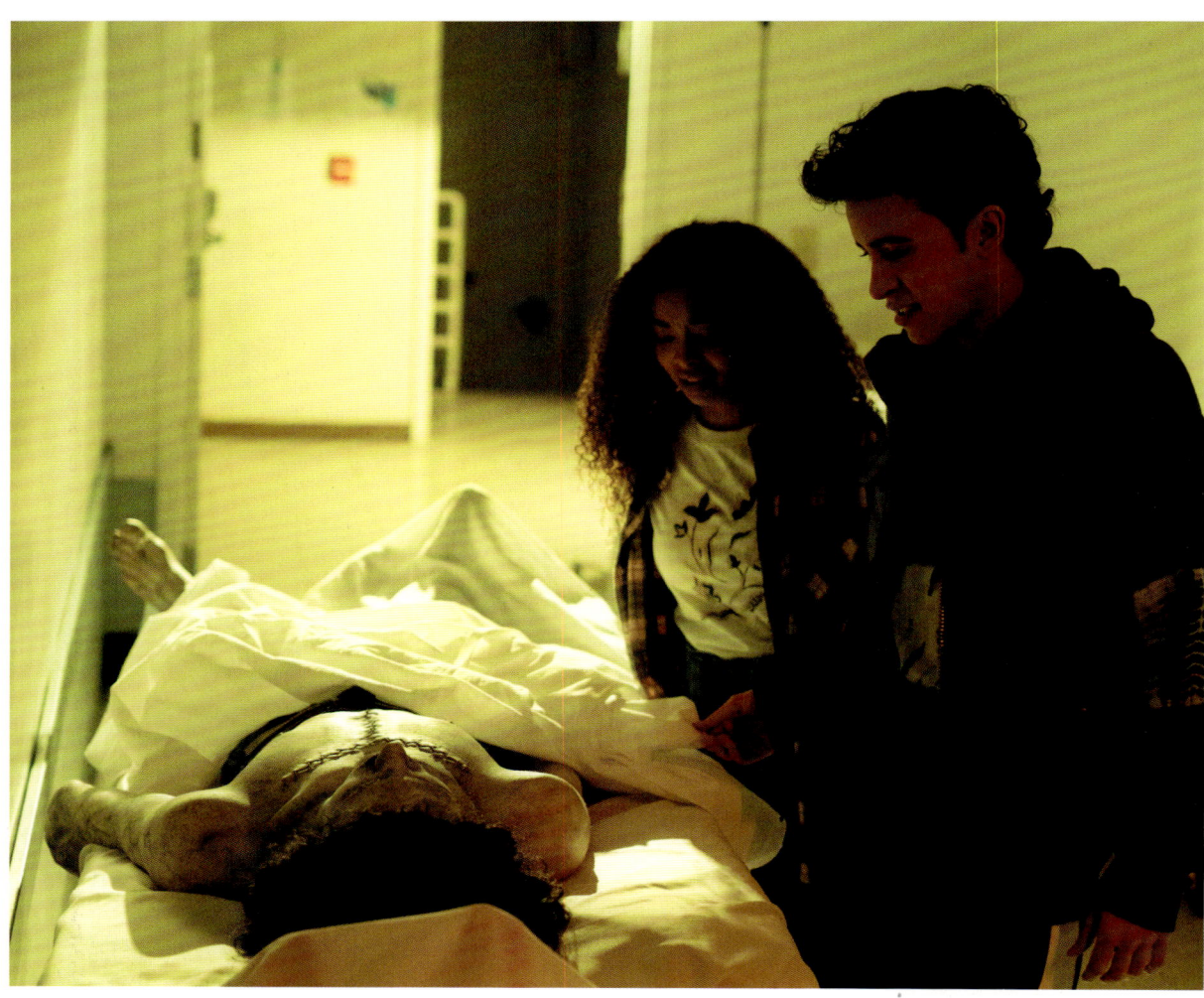

But what about that first story that brought life to this expanded *Creepshow* universe? You remember: Craig Engler's "A Dead Girl Named Sue." Interestingly, it wasn't Engler who wrote the teleplay, and it wasn't adapted by a horror veteran. Meet Heather Anne Campbell, accomplished performer and writer...of comedy! From *Whose Line Is It Anyway?* to *Key and Peele* to *The Midnight Show*, Campbell really needs no introduction...except maybe to horror? Well, no, not exactly.

"Brian Witten reached out to me to say that he and Greg had seen one of the *Twilight Zone* [2019] episodes I had written, and they wanted me to write for *Creepshow*. And I was honored and flattered because I'm a huge fan of the genre. I come from a background of comedy, but one thing I really want to do is to write horror genre stuff, maybe more than anything in the world. Look—the last thing I want to do at the end of a day is to watch the sort of work I've been doing. So, I watch sci-fi or horror or film noir.

"And I realized that horror and comedy are sort of on the same set of tracks, although separated. Laughter is the response we have to anything that surprises but doesn't frighten us, and horror is an artificial terror. I think the reason people laugh in a movie after being frightened is that they remember, 'Oh, yeah, I'm not really in danger'; and that's kinda funny."

While adapting Engler's story, Campbell decided there would be no overt comedy, nor any attempts at laughs.

"My adaptation was pretty light; this was such a remarkable short story that I didn't want to rewrite the dialogue because it already had such a sound. I restructured it a bit at the beginning to establish the stakes and to give the main character a journey—his initial refusal of the call to adventure, then he'd acquiesce, giving him an arc—but, as much as I could, I wanted to put *everything* from the short story into this. It's like, if you're a fan of the short story and then you go into the episode...I didn't want anyone to be disappointed.

"And, truthfully, I think John [Harrison] did an incredible job directing this, and everyone did a fantastic job with this—the acting, the set design, the cinematography, and lighting—everything's incredible and it gives the episode all that atmosphere and energy. I was so proud of the episode, so proud of what they did, and I was almost on the verge of tears. It's the kind of writing I've dreamed about doing, then getting to watch it; I couldn't believe that it was something I got to be a part of."

Continuing with that thread of story-meets-production, some *Creepshow* writers approach their work a bit differently, anticipating the actual production and tailoring their stories to best support the *facility* for that interpretation. That's how collaborators Erik Sandoval and Michael Rousselet approached "Queen Bee" and "Dead and Breakfast."

"Erik and I come from a production background," begins Rousselet, "so we're both very aware of the 'ask' we're throwing at the production folks. We've been in the trenches of filmmaking together from way back when, since college."

"It helps us when writing," adds Sandoval, "because when we think we can do some scene, we stop to think, 'That would need a [production] company move on the day of the shoot; is this *really* necessary?' And that was the great thing about our work with Greg here because anytime we've gotten notes from him, they've been about character or story or pacing, but there were

BELOW: Pam Spinster (Ali Larter) looks to social media to resurrect interest in the Spinster Haunted House. Careful—online trendings can cause untimely endings, in "Dead and Breakfast."

never really production considerations because he indicated that it seemed like we'd already thought of that. We try to never really create scenes that are too large."

"Exactly," Rousselet agrees, "and when we initially pitch ideas, that's the sandbox we're asking about—can we play in this sandbox or can we play in this sandbox [of ideas]? And for the ones they pick, we say, 'All right, this is the world we're building,' and we try to keep it focused, fun, and scary."

"And when we were between drafts of the script and making changes," Sandoval adds, "one of the things we were battling with in 'Queen Bee' was explaining the root [of] what she is—is she a space alien on some mission from Mars or something? Greg reminded us that some of the scariest and spookiest stuff has no explanation. When we leave those little things unexplained, we leave some mystery...and that's fun."

"Yeah, we give you just enough information to make you uncomfortable," concludes Rousselet.

Both "Queen Bee" and "Dead and Breakfast" nestle their horror within the modern-day mentalities of tech-enabled toxic fandom and subversive social media, respectively. "Queen Bee" lands a stinging reproach of overt youth fandom, that which recklessly disregards a protocol of celebrity privacy in blind zeal to post facts and photos from a hospital delivery room. "Dead and Breakfast" shows what might happen to those who'd risk a ghostly encounter in exchange for self-promotion on a social platform. Both stories demonstrate *Creepshow*'s ability to nimbly incorporate topics and trends of the current day just as easily as it traverses time to drop us into any era it chooses. But in Dana Gould's wickedly clever "Night of the Living Late Show," the onscreen horror takes the next step; it bends time, performs a media mash-up, and goes full-on meta. It literally infiltrates the 1972 British creature feature, *Horror Express*.

"Now, my original idea was to have all of this set inside of *Night of the Living Dead*," Gould says, "but I didn't want to do a whole episode of just that film because it wouldn't give me anywhere to go for the end of the story. So, Greg and I were looking at other film titles that we could use in the episode. Well, Greg is a big fan of *Horror Express* so I took another look at that, and what I liked about it is that it's what we call a 'bottle show'; it's all in one location, by and large, and as I watched it, I found scenes where I could insert the character of Simon *into* the film. It really worked out perfectly."

Simon (Justin Long) is a tech wizard and film nerd who has developed a virtual reality home theater system—the

BELOW: Simon (Justin Long) has made it possible to actually enter his favorite movies, assuring his young bride Renee (D'Arcy Carden) that they can write their own ticket with his amazing invention.

LEFT: Renee is aghast at Simon's true intention for the machine as he indulges in virtual ride after ride on the *Horror Express*. (From "Night of the Living Late Show.")

"Immersopod"—that allows him to virtually enter his favorite movie, *Horror Express*. It's an expensive prototype funded by the family riches of his wife, Renee (D'Arcy Carden). Soon, Renee develops suspicions over Simon's infatuation with the movie; it might even be an addiction...or worse. Is it really possible that he's pursuing a VR tryst *inside* the movie?

"You know, you can't *not* put yourself into what you're writing," Gould ventures, "and, as a writer, I rarely set out to do that. But as I was writing this—well, it started out as my homage to the comedy *Dead Men Don't Wear Plaid*—but as this episode went along and [Simon] starts hiding what he's doing, and the couple is growing apart, I realized that I was actually writing about my own divorce."

The catharsis of this story was not only occurring for the characters on the screen but for Gould, as well. "There was a point when I wondered why this was coming out so easily," he laughs, "and then I realized."

And, as all writers we've met here have confirmed, when it comes to writing within the *Creepshow* realm, it always comes back to George Romero.

"By moving the story to *Horror Express*, it allowed us to then go to *Night of the Living Dead* at the end. I felt that, when people see where [Simon] then turns up, and they see the farmhouse and the field, it would deliver such a thrill. It gave us the twist we needed and it also gave Greg a chance to play, recreating that farmhouse set and literally working within that film."

And, finally, there came the twist. It was Renee's revenge. It was the deceptive Simon's well-deserved comeuppance. And it was a shock. It was visceral. It was deliciously visceral.

"Yeah, *that's* a real EC moment," Gould exclaims.

Yes, it was...and it's what *Creepshow* is all about. It starts with unusual and outlandish stories...and then things *really* get crazy.

"And that's kind of what you're looking for in a *Creepshow* story—or in EC Comics," Joe Hill concludes. "You're looking for that stinger, that ooompf! From the time we're children and into adulthood, we long for fairness and justice; we long for karma to be a thing. And the world is constantly slapping with examples of *un*-fairness, of people *getting away with it*. The child inside of us that wants the world to be fair always feels like shouting in outrage—and stories like *Creepshow* are that shout of outrage. For time immemorial, as children, we've been told the world is not fair...but in fiction, we can often get the justice we're denied in real life; we can see the wicked get punished, we can see simple heroism rewarded and kindness rewarded. And our need for that is so intense that we will take it in fiction if we can't get it in life."

Fair enough. On we go....

> WHAT DID YOU THINK ABOUT OUR WRITERS' RANTS? SHOCKING? MIND-BENDING? HORRIBLE BUT HARMLESS? WELL, LET ME SHOW YOU THE *LINGERING EFFECTS* THEY'VE HAD ON OUR OTHER INMATES...*ERR*...INTERNS HERE AT *SHUDDER'S CREEPSHOW*...

CHAPTER THREE 59

HORROR MONSTER MASKS!

DELUXE FULL-OVER THE HEAD MASKS

| VAMPIRE | SEA MONSTER | SASQUATCH | WITCH |

DELUXE FULL-OVER THE HEAD MASKS

| VAMPIRE MUMMY | VOODOO ZOMBIE | LADY FRANKENSTEIN | WEREGORILLA |

| SCARECROW | CREEP | GENIE | HEAD |

RUSH ME the following RUBBER MONSTER MASKS: Enclosed is $ _____
INCLUDING 50¢ POSTAGE AND HANDLING FOR EACH MASK CHECKED

- ☐ #2501 VAMPIRE
- ☐ #2505 SEA MONSTER
- ☐ #2513 SASQUATCH
- ☐ #2514 WITCH
- ☐ #2518 VAMPIRE MUMMY
- ☐ #2508 VOODOO ZOMBIE
- ☐ #2507 LAD[Y FRANKENSTEIN]
- ☐ #2503 WER[EGORILLA]
- ☐ #2506 SCAR[ECROW]
- ☐ #2509 CREE[P]
- ☐ #2516 GENI[E]
- ☐ #2517 HEAD

CITY _____
STATE _____

SOLD OUT!

CHAPTER THREE — CREEPSHOW COMIC ADVERTISEMENTS FOR AMUSEMENT ONLY.

CREEPSHOW FAN CLUB

You can't possibly be a CREEPSHOW Reader without being a CREEPSHOW FAN CLUB Member! Look what you get! n 8x10 FULL COLOR PORTRAIT of the CREEP, suitable for framing.
The OFFICIAL CLUB PIN IN FULL COLOR & sturdily constructed. The Wallet-Size OFFICIAL MEMBERSHIP CARD with your own individual Member number. You won't believe how super creepy this fan club kit is until you see it for yourself! The cost for a lifetime membership to this ghoulish fan club is ONLY $2.00

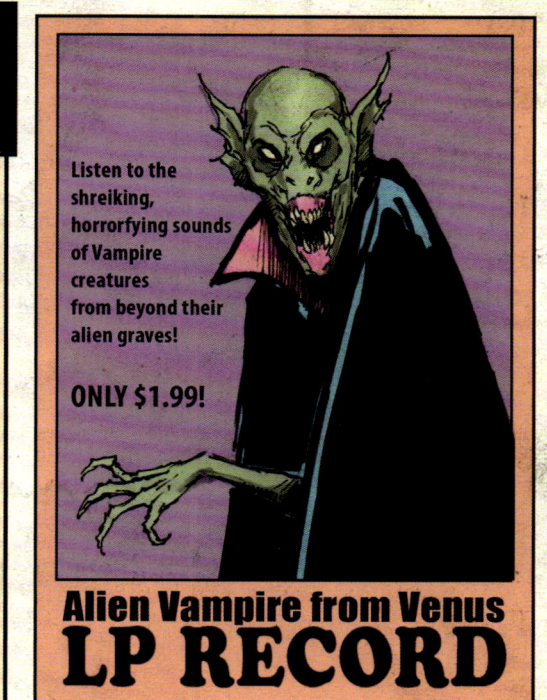

Member Number - 537673

Listen to the shreiking, horrorfying sounds of Vampire creatures from beyond their alien graves!

ONLY $1.99!

Alien Vampire from Venus LP RECORD

GIANT LIVING DEAD GORILLA
GLOW-IN-THE-DARK POSTER

Own a 24x36 glow in the dark horror poster of the gruesome simian creature that lives after death! Printed on high-quality heavy paper in durable bright, long-lasting color! Scare your friends and family with this original art from the famous movie 'Living Dead Gorilla from Hell'!
#234550/$4.95

FRANKENSTEIN VS FRANKENZILLA

A mad scientist on a tropical island experiments with cadavers and dinosaur DNA. He brings to life two of the most terrifying monsters of all time, who immediately go to battle with one another! A film not to be missed! $7.99

THE SLIME

An alien creature lands in a small Iowa town, overtaking local residents and eating as much livestock as it can eat! How long before it destroys the town and takes over the entire world??!
THE SLIME! $5.99

CREEPSHOW FAN CLUB ☐   FRANKENSTEIN VS FRANKENZILLA ☐
ALIEN VAMPIRE LP ☐   THE SLIME ☐
LIVING DEAD GORILLA ☐

NAME_____
ADDRESS_____
CITY_____
STATE_____ ZIP CODE_____

I enclose _____. Please send me the subscription checked above.

In Canada & outside U.S.A., add $4.00 to all rates

CREEPSHOW COMIC ADVERTISEMENTS FOR AMUSEMENT ONLY.

PLEASE EXCUSE OUR DUST--BONE DUST, THAT IS! HEH-HEH
OUR HANDY HOBGOBLINS ARE BUSY CUTTING, CHOPPING, AND SLICING THROUGH EVERYTHING THEY NEED TO GIVE EVERY CREEPSHOW SET THAT "JUST DIED-IN" LOOK.
THESE FETID FABRICATORS HAVE A NASTY KNACK FOR RENDERING DARK REALMS AND LOATHSOME LOCALES, THE KIND THAT ARE SURE TO PRICKLE YOUR SKIN WITH GRODY GOOSEFLESH, A WRETCHED REACTION YOU'LL ATTRIBUTE TO THESE...
BUCKET OF BLOOD
MICHAEL BROOM 2022

Weird Worlds & Dreadful Designs

With the stories chosen, the plot and character details largely hammered out between Greg Nicotero and the writers, and the shooting scripts (usually) in hand, the *Creepshow* team is called into action. Each story gets another review, individually and collectively, in another spirited collaboration session. During this round, it's time to ensure suitability of each story—they'll now become "segments"—for production; that is, not only must each story thematically fit within the *Creepshow* universe but, also, they must fit within the production's allowances.

Time. Budget. Location.

Mostly time.

Their home base is Atlanta, GA, or the "Hollywood of the South," as the Georgians say. For Seasons One and Two, the team worked in a production office located on the west side of Atlanta. The facility served them well enough to get the show established, even though the team was cramped within the two conjoined stages while Greg bristled at the incessant construction noise on the other side of his office wall. Near the end of Season Two shooting, as the company transitioned directly into Season Three production, the crew relocated to a larger production park. Their challenge in this was to maintain a build and shoot schedule while coinhabiting both studios concurrently.

Challenge. Yeah, there's a lot of that going on here.

Don't fret for the team, though; they love the crunch. They work in what can rightly be called an "organic" process; it's all done in rapid progression (*really* rapid), and, since no two segments are ever the same, they're perpetually starting from scratch with each set (or sets) for each segment. This is their method. This is their challenge. Every time. Every segment. Every three and a half days.

None of this scares Production Designer Aimee Holmberg. Take a look at her long portfolio of work and you'll see that she's had experience in practically every capacity of production design—as designer, art director, set decorator, and set builder.

LEFT: As Lampini says in the Season 3 episode "Skeletons in the Closet": "Unlike stars themselves, props never die."

"I love building anything that's not based in reality," she says, "anything where you do not have a foundation based in the real world, and we have to reimagine each world from scratch. I guess I'm a bit of a masochist for that, but so are the people who keep coming back to work with me." Laughing, she adds, "They know what to expect, so it's their fault at this point. Some people don't make it, but the ones that do seem to enjoy this sort of sleepless thrill."

At the start of each season, she and Greg share what she calls "a somber moment." The two of them look over the proverbial cliff, high above the creative valley they're about to jump into, and consider the impossibility of what they'll attempt. They assess the enormity of the situation, they ponder it for just a bit longer, and then they agree to jump in for a helluva ride.

But *Creepshow*, she says, takes on a life of its own. "It's amazing how each segment becomes its own entity and has its own energy. And when what we've done actually becomes its own character, that's when we know we've succeeded with the set...but we never really know where we're going until we get there."

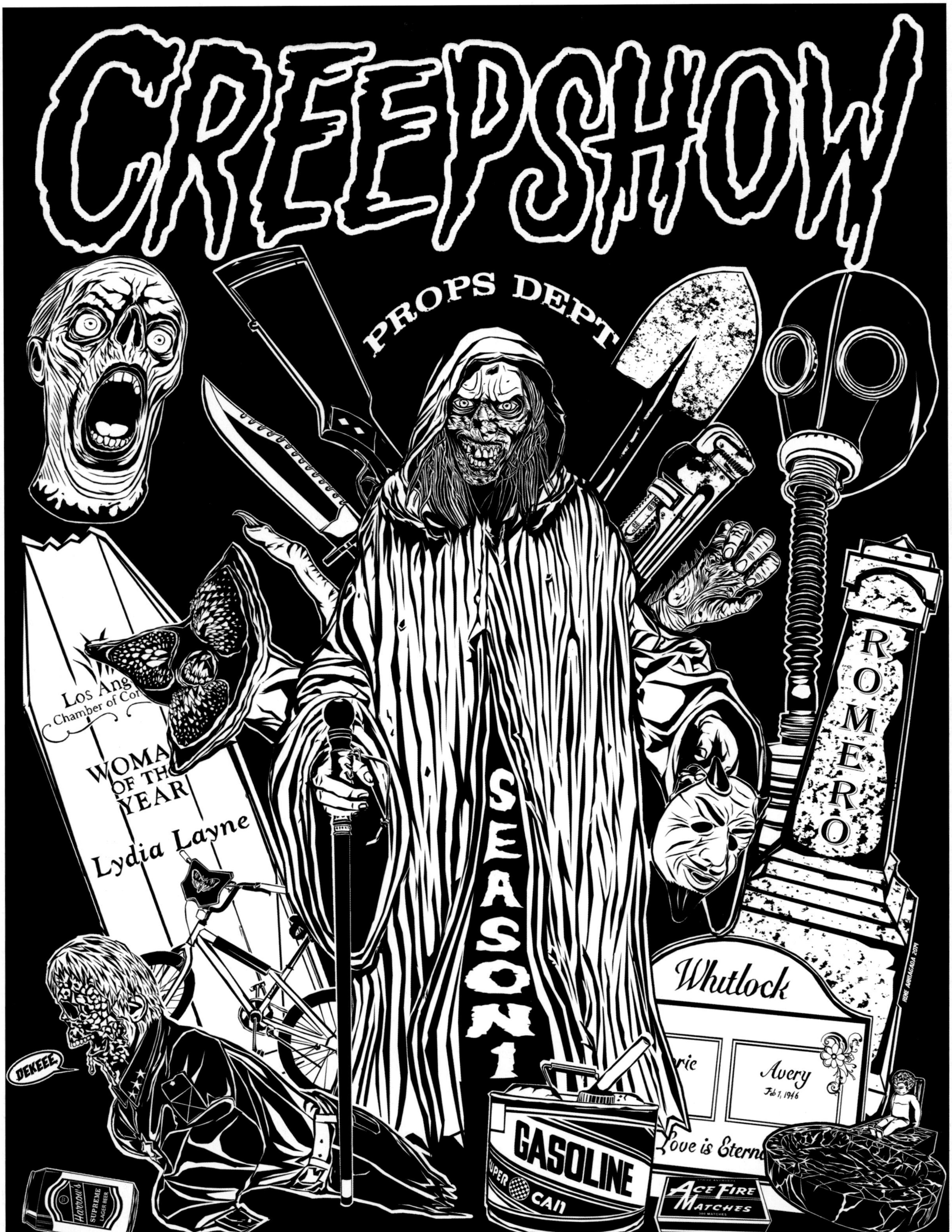

CREEPSHOW
PROPS DEPT
Los Ang
Chamber of Co
WOMA
OF TH
YEAR
Lydia Layne
SEASON 1
ROMERO
Whitlock
Avery
Feb 1, 1946
Love is Etern
DEKEEE
SUPREME
LAGER BEER
GASOLINE
SUPER CAN
ACE FIRE MATCHES

"This is how productions run in the real world," Greg chimes in. "There's rarely, if *ever*, that perfect situation where there's lots of time to consider and review and revise the production. They're all under constraints and limits, but that's when the teams get to their most creative moments."

With a tight schedule and ever-changing set needs, there's little, if any, time for design iterations, set models, or pre-build samples, but the team has gained Greg's trust for delivering whatever's needed, whenever it's needed, even if it's out of the usual scope of duties for any member of this art team.

A running joke within the team, as Aimee shares, is that many designs begin with a napkin drawing. She says they're not much to look at, but they're enough to motivate her team to begin sharing ideas and developing their approach. Series Art Director Jason Vigdor kids her for the approach, but then adds that the team is able to take one of those napkin sketches and actualize a set design and build from it.

"And, for the first two seasons, I was pulling double-duty between art direction and graphic design," Jason shares, "but that leveled off with Season Three; that was when I needed to make twenty gallons of fake slime for the 'Queen Bee' segment. We needed it to be drenched over all the cells of the honeycomb and have it ooze over…and it was really cool, but it was a process I really had to figure out and explore. UltraSlime wasn't gonna do it because we needed it to stay in place. So, working with new materials, and being able to play and explore a little bit…I think that's kind of unique to this kind of show."

He goes on to call this the DIY spirit of the show. "It's kind of the 'Romero Way'—just a bunch of people figuring this stuff out. There is no playbook for how to achieve these things because some of these things haven't been done before."

Does he consider this an exercise in stress or exhilaration… or both?

"Yes, yes, and yes. I do think that iteration is the best way to get something 'right,' but in this business it's really easy to think something to death, and kind of squeeze the life out of it; having meetings and talking about it and scouts and pre-planning and pre-production and pre-visualizing…and I'm like, 'Fuck it—just do it!' And that's when there's something we can capture—something real or cool or different—that wasn't necessarily intended."

Jason says his work on the show is a "condition of circumstance," made possible by his years-long working relationships with the design team. "A lot of these people are who I've been working with in Atlanta. I've done a ton of shows with [Set Decorator] Nick [Morgan], I've done a bunch of shows with [Prop Master] Lucas [Godfrey], Cameron Boling, our UPM [Unit Production Manager], and then Aimee Holmberg—she and I kind of came up the ranks together. I art directed her second feature, and we kind of just stuck together after that."

Aimee calls this an "art family," each member bringing their own unique strengths, developed over years of practical practice in set design, construction, decoration, and more. And, since

OPPOSITE: Prop Master Lucas Godfrey and his team have their claws full juggling everything from headstones to, well, heads.

ABOVE: The birthing room, so to speak, from "Queen Bee."

"The grubs in the 'Queen Bee' segment…I used them for when we built the bee hive. We did fake larvae inside the cells behind the transparency films, and the grubs the KNB team created were so realistic, and heavy…about the size of a loaf of bread. They were so amazing."

—Jason Vigdor, Art Director

CHAPTER FOUR 65

they've worked together for so long, they can usually anticipate what each other might want or need—or *say*—next.

"Yeah, we have a bit of a running joke about that, too. I might be thinking about something I want on set, a hero object or a ringer or something, and I'll ask Nick to keep his eyes out for it, and then he'll put it on my desk almost immediately, knowing that I'd be asking for it, saying, 'I already have it.' Although, other times, I forget to tell Jason about something that I need and he'll say, 'I haven't quite been around you long enough to read your mind yet; you'll actually have to say those things out loud.'"

As amusing as this sounds, the team insists that, without that sixth sense among them, they wouldn't be able to operate at the speed the production requires, nor deliver the sort of uniquely character-infused sets they stand up in front of the camera.

The key responsibility of the art department is the telling of each story *visually*, in ways that can't be easily told through exposition or by the actors. "Even before an actor appears," Jason says, "we need to be conveying a lot of information, and I think the best way to learn about characters is by showing their personal space. That's one of our favorite things, being able to see somebody's bedroom or their house."

In "The Finger," we meet Clark Wilson (DJ Qualls), the victim-turned-victor-turned-victim-again (it's complicated), and upon first sight of his darkened, claustrophobic, and severely cluttered home, we learn that this guy is a hoarder. "Not only a hoarder," Jason clarifies, "but also what *kind* of hoarder, by the kinds of things he keeps. Those spaces are always the most fun for us."

At the opposite end of the spectrum is "The Last Tsuburaya." Self-aggrandizing billionaire art collector, Wade Cruise (Brandon Quinn), has connived his way into ownership of a rare and unusual painting. In a shocking act, he destroys the rare piece after laying eyes on it; *he* will be the only person to have had privilege to see it. Of course, in classic *Creepshow* style, he'll see so much more.

RIGHT: Eclectic takes on a whole new meaning in Clark Wilson's world. The set of "The Finger," impeccably cluttered by the Creepshow team of Nick Morgan (Set Decorator), Blake Myers (Set Dec Buyer), Lucas Godfrey (Prop Master), and Rene Arriagada (Asst. Prop Master).

OPPOSITE: The egotistic opulence of narcissistic art collector Wade Cruise is on garish display. Another effective set design that reveals much about a lead character. From "The Last Tsuburaya."

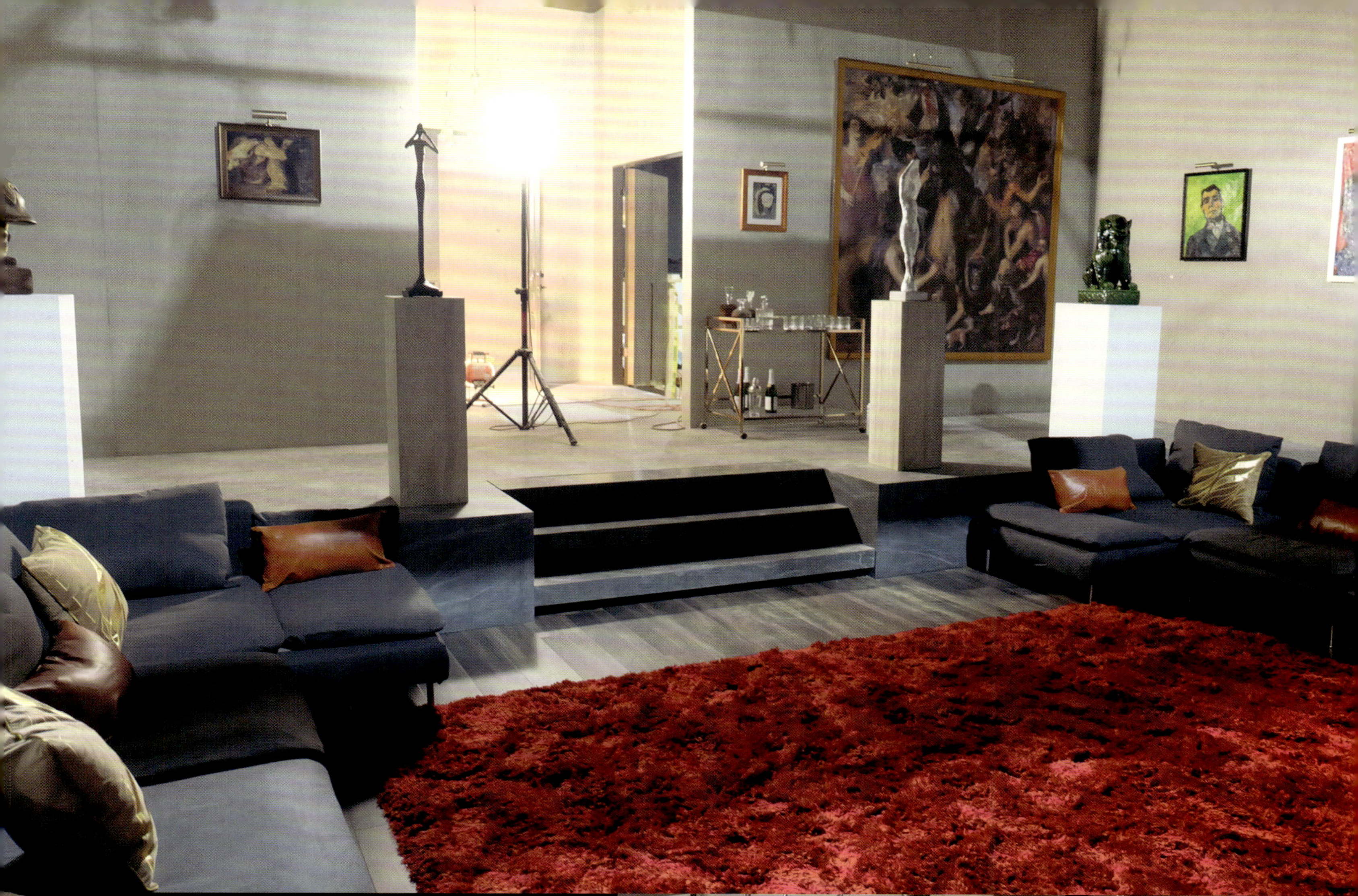

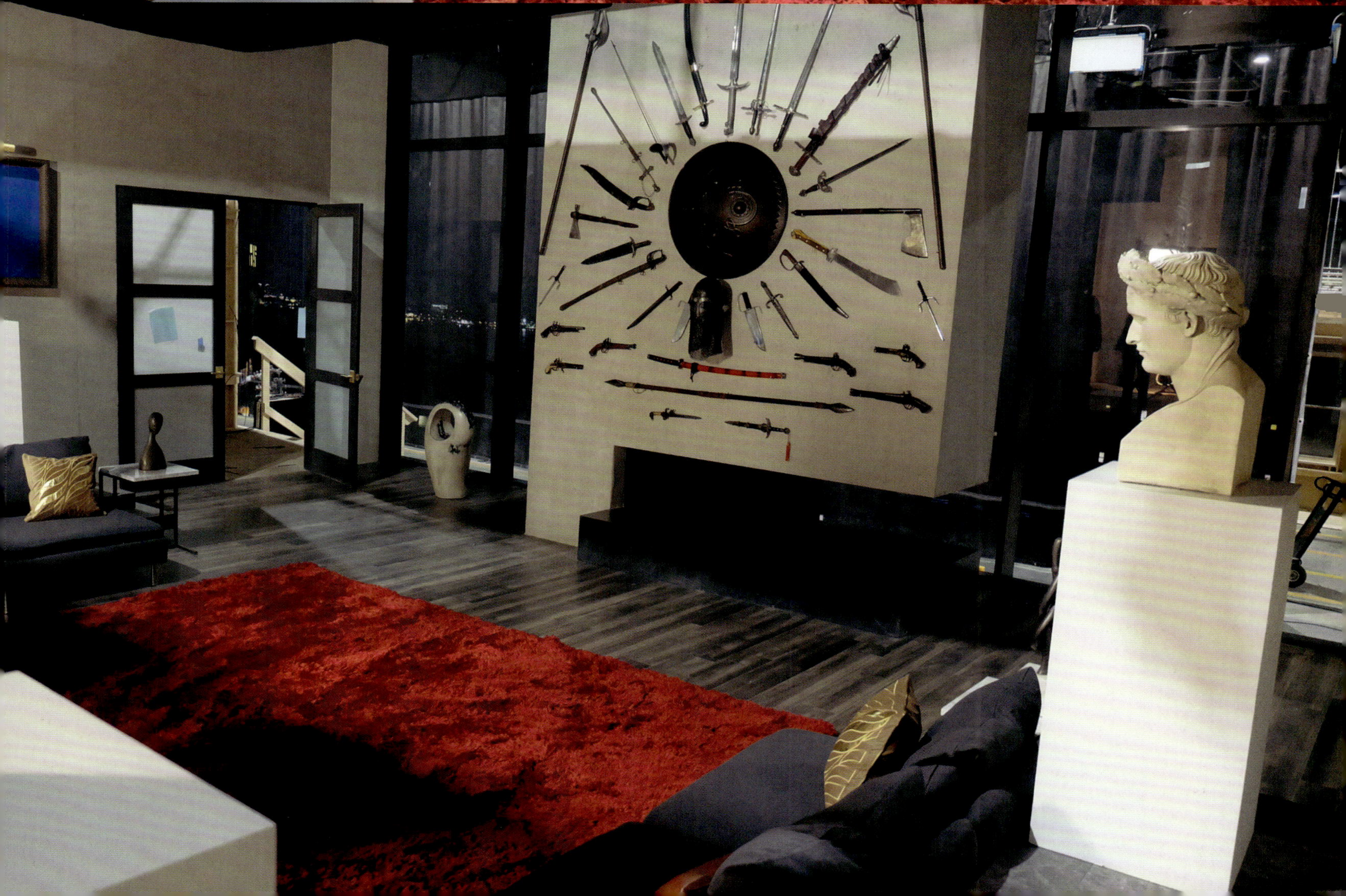

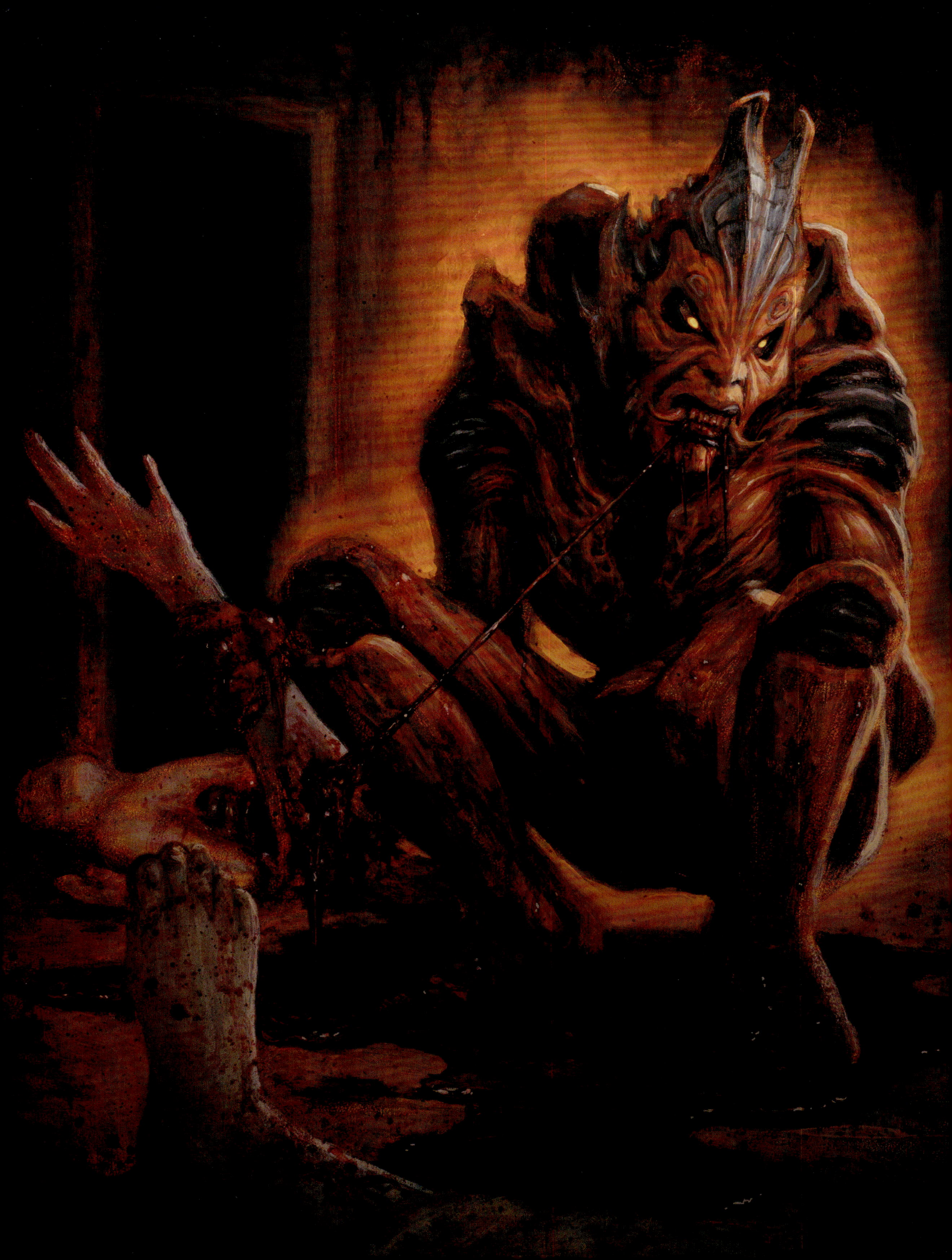

OPPOSITE: The Last Tsuburaya, from the segment of the same name. Original painting by Chet Zar.

LEFT and BELOW: A strangely familiar cabin in the deep woods, as seen in "Public Television of the Dead." Original painting by Bethany Arriagada.

CHAPTER **FOUR** 69

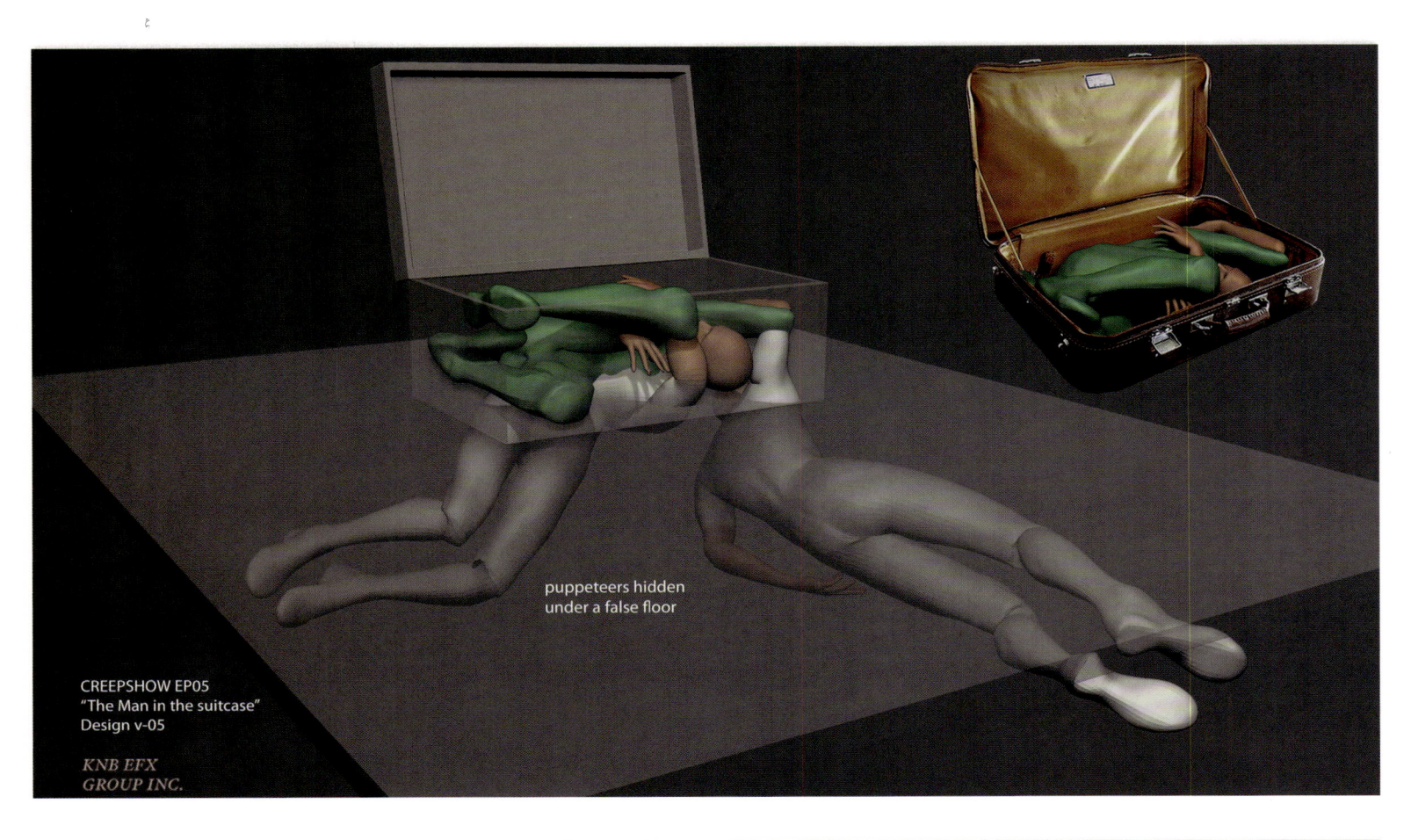

puppeteers hidden
under a false floor

CREEPSHOW EP05
"The Man in the suitcase"
Design v-05

KNB EFX
GROUP INC.

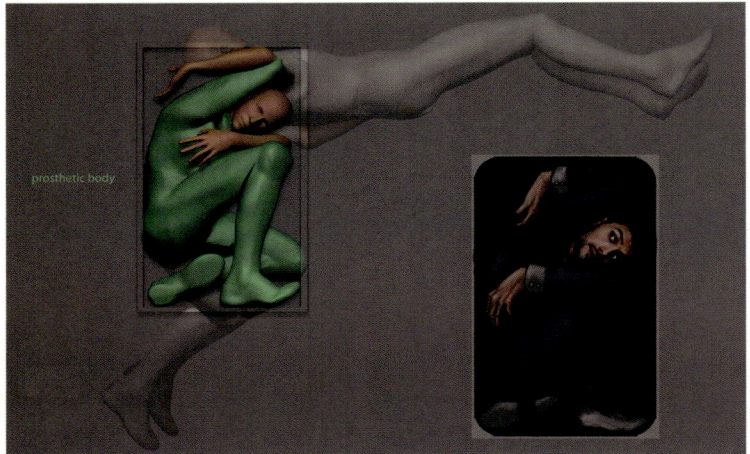

prosthetic body

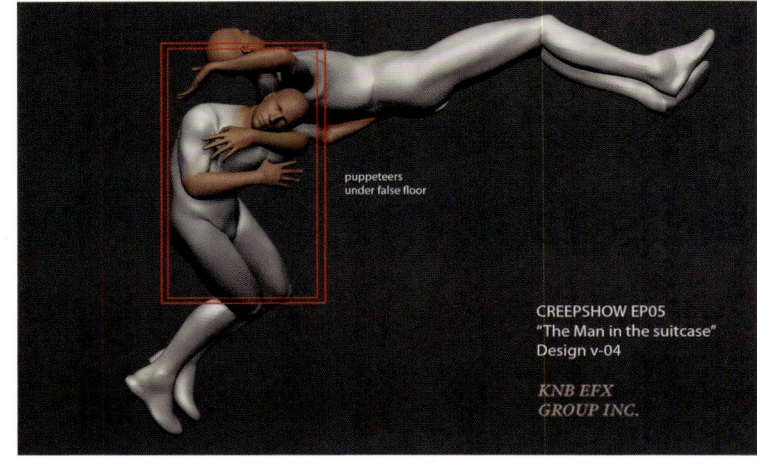

puppeteers
under false floor

CREEPSHOW EP05
"The Man in the suitcase"
Design v-04

KNB EFX
GROUP INC.

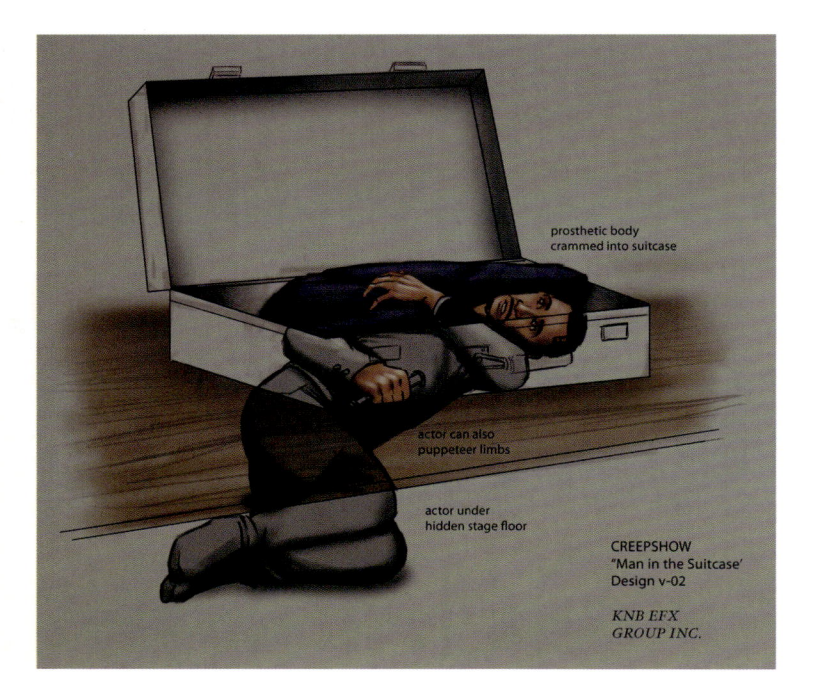

prosthetic body
crammed into suitcase

actor can also
puppeteer limbs

actor under
hidden stage floor

CREEPSHOW
'Man in the Suitcase'
Design v-02

KNB EFX
GROUP INC.

CHAPTER FOUR

"We did a big penthouse. There's a big, sparse space in there with a cold and isolating feeling, and there's very little personal touch. It feels more like a museum [or showplace] than a place where somebody lives."

The expansive penthouse imparts the vacuous nature of Cruise; big and boastful, perfectly appointed, yet morally hollow; again, the set reveals the character. But aside from that character value, there are also the practical elements that are built in, too. The wide open and sparsely decorated set not only telegraphs the grand ego of Cruise, but also accommodates a major fight scene; the story required the extra space for the clash. Of course, the extra space considerations aren't only for the things we see on screen but, as important, for the things we *don't* see.

"On the show, there's so much puppeteering and practical effects, all of which needs to be considered and built *into* the designs, so a lot of these sets end up being built onto decks, three or four feet off the ground, so we can access from underneath."

"The Man in the Suitcase" required stunt coordinator Andy Rusk to position himself below the deck, allowing him to reach up and around actor Ravi Naidu; this enabled arm movement for the impossibly folded over and contorted "Man" in the suitcase. Effects execution—creature placement, puppeteering, and so forth—requires these set elements: platforms, recessed sub-floors, and special wall and ceiling design and construction. These effects' requirements are one of the team's earliest considerations and, once accounted for, the team establishes the setting and character aspects around the false floors and off-camera cubby holes.

So, how is the set characterization achieved? Here's how Set Decorator Nick Morgan explains it: "The writer tells the story through their words. The actor tells the story through facial expressions and tone and movement and the lines they say, and I tell the story by the history of the set that they're in." In this regard, Nick is an artist and the *Creepshow* sets are his canvas. "I don't do what I call 'catalog' or 'magazine' style sets. Just like any artist, I have my own style. I love *real* sets. I don't want people to walk on and say, 'Oh, this is a nice set.' I want people to say, 'Holy shit! This is my childhood living room,' right down to the coffee stains on the table and the boots over in the corner. This is my time to get artistically involved with the story, to tell a story with what's around the room and, a lot of the time, what has *already happened* in the room."

Of course, Nick doesn't work alone in this level of storytelling; his accomplices are prop masters Lucas Godfrey and Rene Arriagada, plus buyer Blake Myers. As a cohesive team, these are the professional hoarders who study the characters in each script, and then breathe additional life into them through the dressing and decoration around them.

"We go back and we look at all the horror films that have memorable props," Lucas begins, "and then we want to create something that's a little bit different; something that stands out as its own thing. And so those are the props we make ourselves, because we don't want these to look like any random store-bought thing or something we ordered from Amazon. We want to make things that only exist in the *Creepshow* world."

From the gnarled cane and beating heart in "The Companion" to Santa's jingle bell mace in "Shapeshifters Anonymous," Lucas and Rene deliver anything odd and unusual to keep viewers locked into the *Creepshow* mood. But then there was "Skeletons in the Closet," where they went beyond the confines of meta sensibility in a genre free-for-all.

OPPOSITE: So how exactly do you get a man in a suitcase? Production designer Aimee Holmberg and KNB team member Joe Giles make it look simple...sort of.

BELOW: See, they're all just regular guys. LTR: Shawn Upthegrove, Lucas Godfrey, Gino Crognale, Dead Uncle, Tom Savini, Jake Garber, Greg Nicotero, Rene Arriagada.

⑧ Axe, Grey wig, dress (wardrobe)
Glasscase mannequin

⑨ Morgan's suitcase/bags

⑩ Wall mount lamp triggers, floor swing open.
Pam pulles a cord, Wall mounted Axe swings
and pierces a chair (Work around set)

⑪ Comic panel?

⑫ laptop, bags, blogger Camera

⑬ Computer Screen, You have 3 new Cancellation
(Small laptop) (Stickers on Back Skull)

⑭ Cable router cables get pulled off, router?
Wire up a modem with Led's

⑮ Table setting for 3?
heavy satchel (Big fake meat with knife)
like Bag, UV lites flashlight, metal detector, Infared
empty hollow goggles, Inflatable Camera Array of tools

~~⑯~~ Ultra wide band radar scanners
Bug Eyed — metal detector infrared Camera
flipping lenses — High tech forensic goggles UV flashlight

⑯ UV light, goggles glowing Stain.
Crowbar, glass bottles in a

Pipe Screams 203-1

Watch or Wrist

Intro
Scene 1

- Beer Stein
- Harrow Beer top
- Cell phone
- Penlight + flashlight

Scene 2

- Cellphone plumber

plastic ✓

- Flashlight Slumlord

focused sharpied Name

- Penlight plumber

Aged white Bucket
Pouch for 5 gallon Bucket

- Victoria flashy Jewelry
- Linus plumber toolbelt + bucket of tools
- map gas torch
- Cat w/ dead mouse

PVC w/ Elbow
11 gal weapons
Weather Gold watch

- Sweat towels or rags bandana
- Linus Watch — maybe a Crate "fluffy"

All of his tools have his Name Sharpied on them

- Cracked laundry Basket to stand on
- tool belt / wrench
- a bit of mouth slime
- Splatter of blood, poofs of Cat hair, Severed Cat 2
- tool Bucket   Set dec 2
- Cockroach MUFX

Scene 3
Again

- foot squish roach
- tool Bucket
- Rag or towel

Cat Collar Pink Squish Fluffy

- Grand father and 2 Kids
- Janet Name tag
- tool Belt + Bucket — Wrench holster
- Wrench as Sword

Victoria Smith
50's Slumlord

Linus Carrothers
40's Plumber

Barbara Crompton
Smoothie Bottle

Janet
Main Apartment

Grandfather
Cane
2 grandsons
Baseball Stack of
Basketball Comics in
Big Comicbook plastic
Back   Bag
Old lady Miss
Brown Ingersoll
Bostonian

Hamid
Frazzled young
Books
or Computer
Phone Bag
Mr. Wass

Mrs Chen
Lyla

PREVIOUS SPREAD: Rene Arriagada's "recipe" for properly dressing a set, *Creepshow* style.

RIGHT: Not just an egg hunt—this is practically a hen house of horror! (From "Skeletons in the Closet.")

BELOW: When a run-of-the-mill cart won't do, Rene Arriagada unleashes his Custom *Creepshow* Cart.

Lucas recounts, "The three of us—me, Rene, and Nick—we were just going mad on that one, finding all those things for that set. A lot of them were actually Greg's; the Michael Myers mask, the Freddy glove, the *Phantasm* ball. Plus, I had to make stunt versions of that ball, one for throwing and the one that gets stuck in my head."

Lucas pauses to smile for a moment, then laughs.

"I remember us sitting in the content meeting for that segment, and Greg just said something like, 'Oh, hey, I think you should play this role,' but all I'm thinking about is how I'm going to find all this shit for the episode, because this is like the biggest thing we've done. So, I just said, 'Well, I don't know....' Then I got out of the meeting and thought, 'What the fuck was I saying? Yes, I'll do this!'"

This is the fun they have, and it fuels them in what they do. But, for as good of a time as they're having, there's still the responsibility to the production in what they bring to each episode.

"It's always a bit weird when the work is coming down the pipeline," says Rene Arriagada, "because they're accepting some scripts and they're rejecting some scripts, so we can't really get too far ahead of ourselves or we'll blow a budget on something that may never happen. So, we're shakin' the dice a lot."

As he implies, the design team gets an early look at scripts under consideration but not yet locked for production. Even so, the prop team needs this early review so they can send their feelers out for particular items. Nick phones his prop vendors to check their inventory while also scouring the Atlanta area (and beyond) for estate sales and the like to see what he can find; they're all on the lookout for anything that can dress a set. "I bought a cow milker recently," Rene recalls, "because I liked how the little attachment pieces looked—y'know, the parts that suck onto the cow udders; they were just these cool-looking machined pieces. We ended up using those on the anti-gravity console in 'The Right Snuff.'"

74   CHAPTER FOUR

ABOVE: The bare beginnings of "Night of the Living Late Show"'s Imersopod.

Additionally, Rene and Lucas will consider what they might need to fabricate specifically, and they often rely on their own stuff. As they review the scripts, they first highlight the sorts of props that they might already own; that saves them a lot of time.

"Yeah, we each dig into our own personal collections of things—anything, really—that we might own and that we could use for a segment, or we'll call people we know or people we worked with on other shows, remembering what those folks might have had that we could use. And then we'll load those things onto our cart and wheel it over when we open set each day."

Cart? What cart?

"I built this huge *Creepshow* prop cart," Rene beams, "it has a side table and a Frankenstein head on the front, and skull lights; it's massive. For the first season, we had this Rubbermaid cart, and it was efficient and all that, but we had so many props and we needed to use so many carts—even shopping carts—to get everything on set, so I decided I'd build a cart. Lucas laughed at the idea, until he saw it. He just said, 'What the fuck did you just do here?' 'Is it awesome?' I asked him, and he said, 'It's amazing!' So, yeah, done. We're using it forever."

One key piece that wouldn't fit onto the prop cart was the Immersopod for "Night of the Living Late Show," although Lucas slyly refers to it as the tanning bed. "We were putting that together just the day before [shooting]. We had to get it off to Paint and Construction to get the base built for it, then all the little cameras inside it were slapped together at the last minute. The VR helmet was fully fabricated by Rene. And Jason designed the honeycomb interior. It wasn't until we had [the electric department] plug in the lights…then we thought, 'Fuck, that doesn't look bad.'"

They start from scratch so often to deliver sets and props for each segment that they really don't have much in the way of "off the shelf" elements to draw from; almost everything they design, build, and dress starts from square one. Of course, Aimee and Jason are mindful of the effort from the team, and they look for every opportunity to lighten the load wherever they can.

CHAPTER FOUR 75

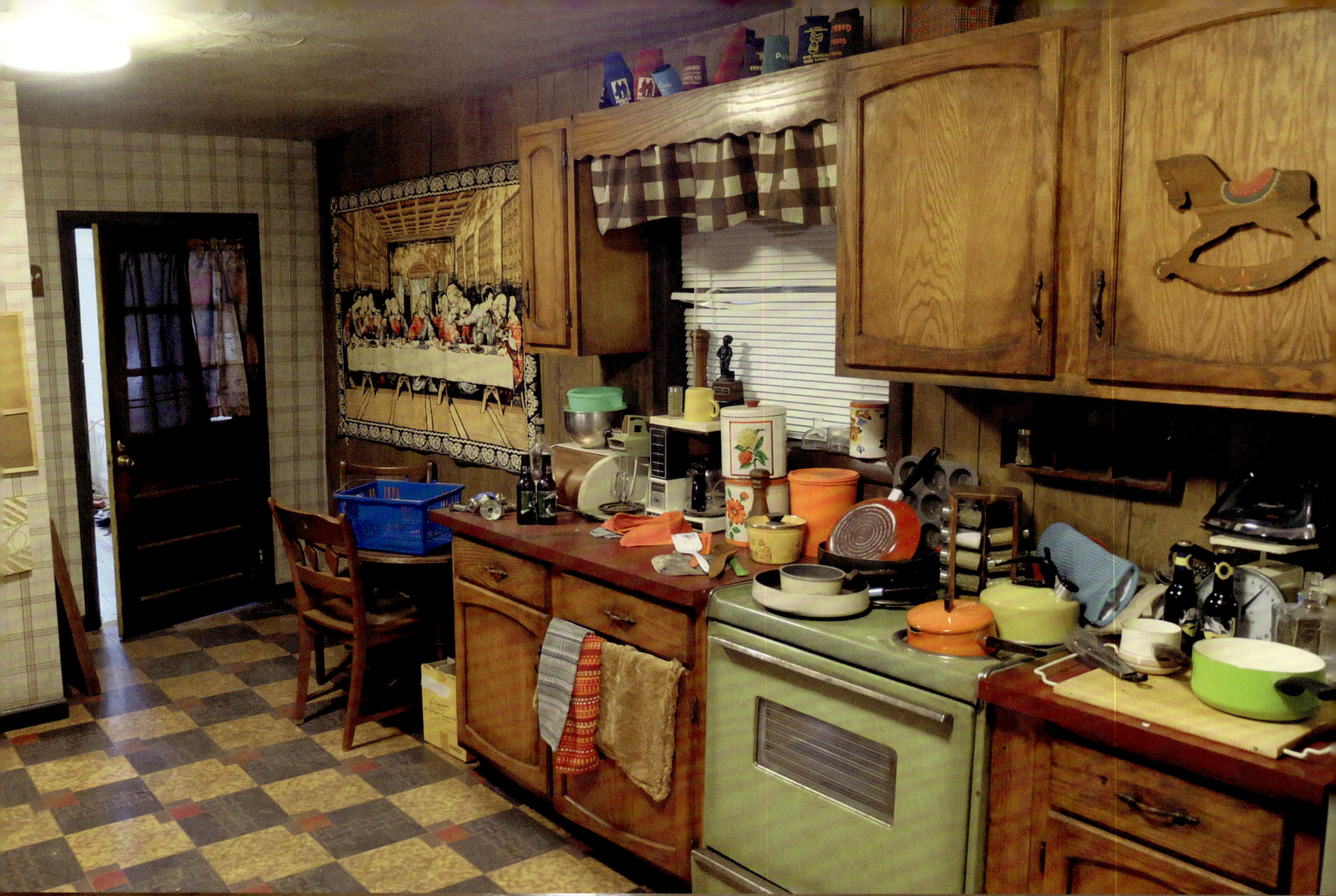

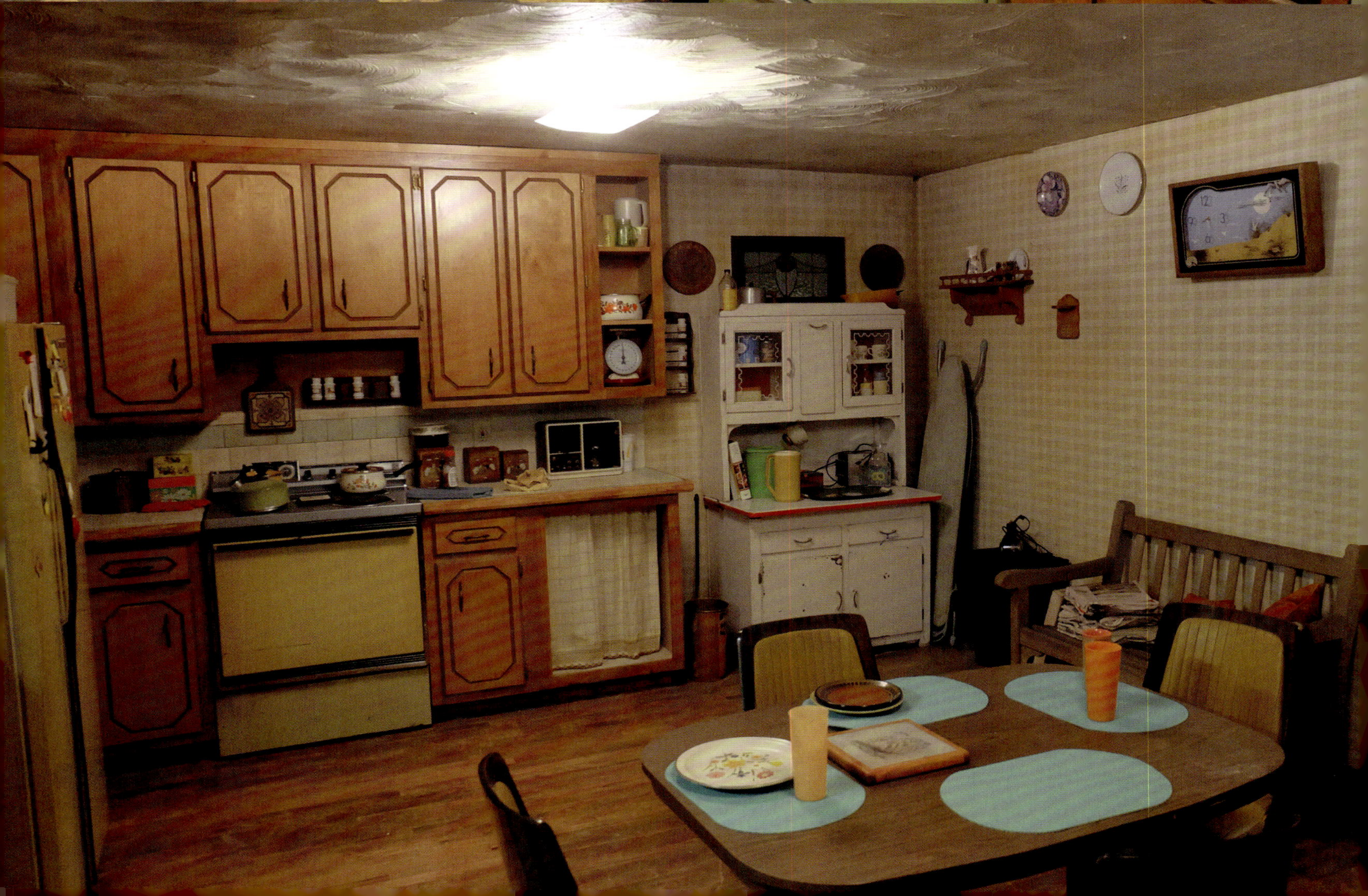

"One aspect of our [production] model—and it's a little unusual—is that we build what we call 'swing sets.' So, at the very beginning [of the season] when I have the scope of the stories, even if they're not one hundred percent locked, I try to figure out how many sets I can fit into five iterations that change. So, we usually build five swing sets, and we figure out how to change them modularly, and use their pieces to cover eighty percent of what you'll see in a season. Each season, there's probably five sets that use the same skeleton."

"That's one of the things that we did—by necessity on this show," Jason reveals, "but it's the only way we could possibly have gotten through it—we always identified sets that we were able to flip between episodes...and those have taken different shapes across the different seasons. That's where we would change the configuration, remove walls, swap walls, slap on a different coat of paint."

Look closely at some of the episodes and you'll be surprised to learn just how the team redressed these modular sets. The house in "The Finger" offers an extreme example of the team's inventive efficiency—they called that set "Megatron." It comprised three sets that were all built together on one deck for easy reconfiguration; they used that set three or four times during Season One.

Of course, there are a couple of wrenches thrown into the works. First, although the design and construction crew work to streamline and modularize some of the set pieces, that only carries them to the end of a season. "We don't actually get to keep anything between seasons," Aimee says. "We don't have a facility to store them and we're always in a different place. If we had those sorts of facilities, we'd probably let our prop makers sleep a little more and maybe the paint wouldn't still be wet when the actors get on the set."

Wet paint was only one of the problems that Scenic Lead Brooke Beall had to contend with. She joined the team in Season Two and bonded immediately. She wasn't fluent in horror, though, when she joined up; her background was theater. No matter. The *Creepshow* experience changed her, probably forever.

"I now love working in horror. It's so fun. It's so dramatic. And there's usually grime, and dirt, and blood. It's very creative, and Aimee gives my crew a lot of freedom. She basically gives us reference photos, then she turns us loose...and so we're working with raw wood and making it look like a nasty, oozing beehive, and on that one we used so much glue, and so much trans-tint, and other stuff, then Jason came in with his amazing goo. So much goo."

While she echoes the challenges of the tight time schedules and the need to flip sets—repaint and redress—in fast fashion, one of her biggest challenges was blood. She couldn't seem to get the walls to stop bleeding.

"The [production] has a special kind of blood, and we tried all sorts of chemicals to clean it up, and then we decided we'd just paint over it after we laid down a coat of primer. This was the 'Drug Traffic' interrogation room, and there had been a lot of blood everywhere, but we needed to flip the set and paint it white...but the blood just kept bleeding through our paint. We tried different things to clean it up, then we later discovered that it comes off really easily with just water—the only thing that we *didn't* try."

OPPOSITE: Looking for a kitchen remodel? This team can do it. Can you spot these classic kitchens in the *Creepshow* segments?

BELOW: The buckets of blood used on the set of "Drug Traffic" proved to be incredibly challenging for the crew to deal with.

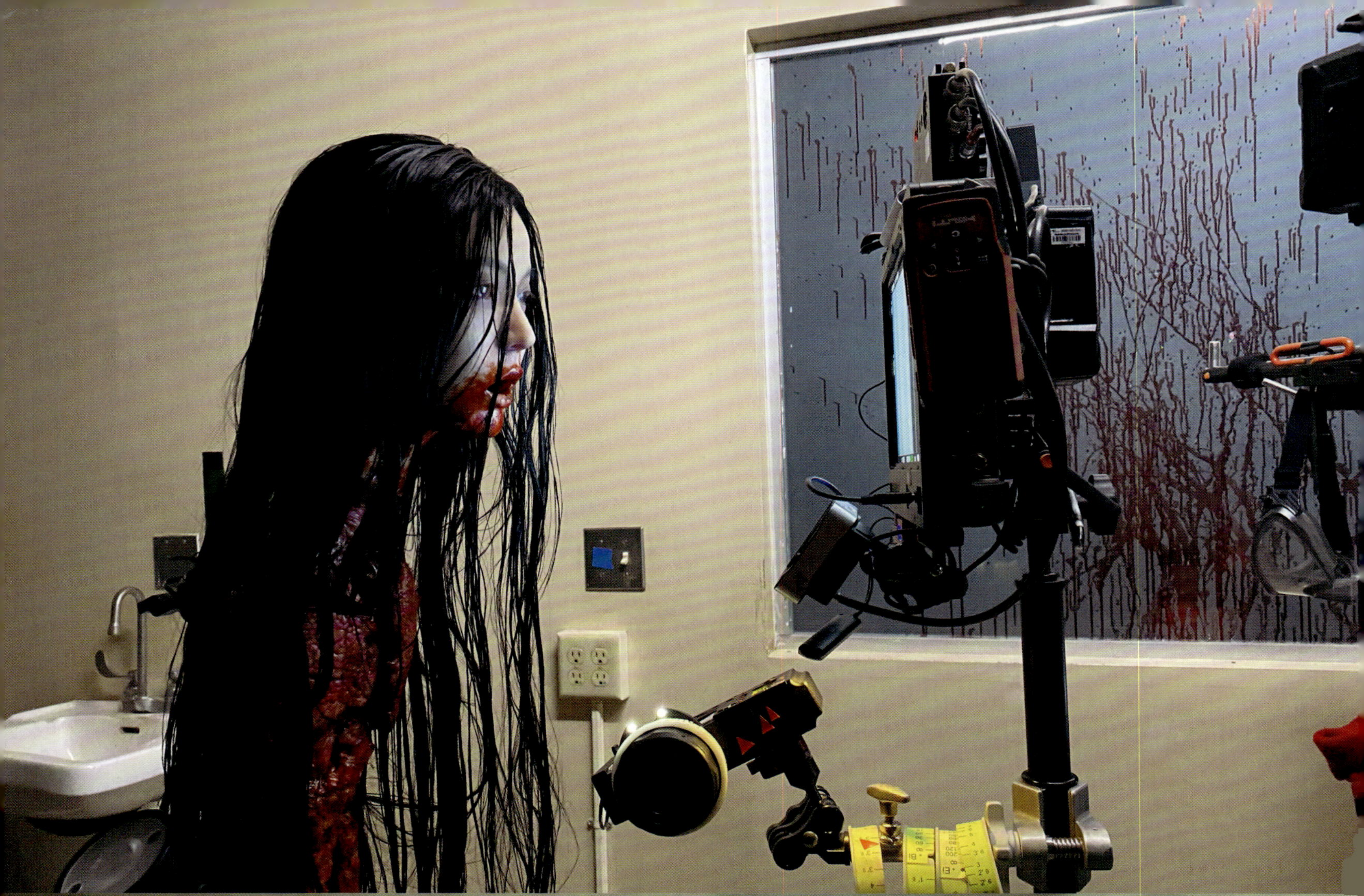

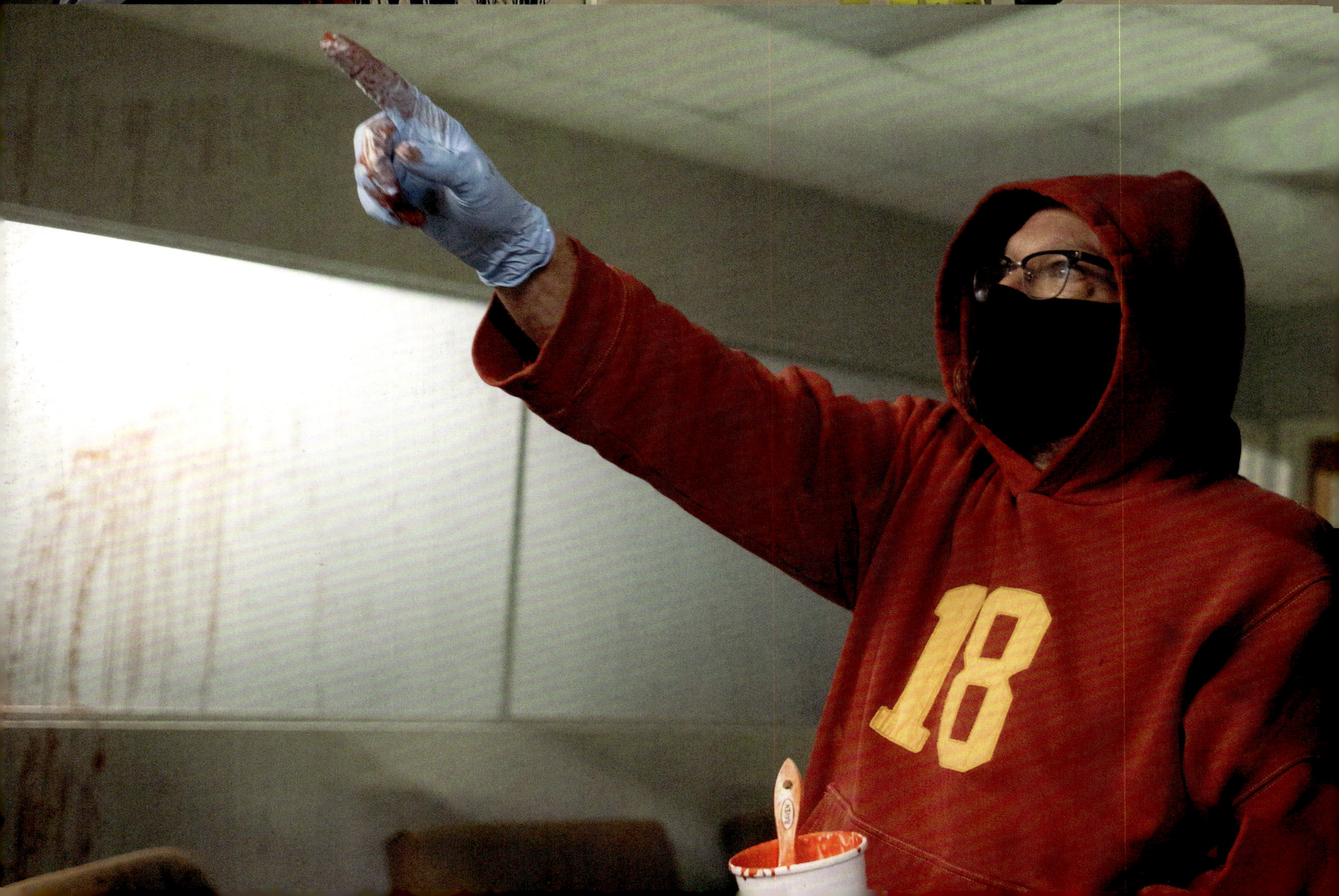
18

Aside from wet paint and bleeding walls, some sets are still under construction when the company arrives to shoot. Case in point: the spaceship in "The Right Snuff" wasn't quite complete by the time the company showed up for the day; the cockpit windshield was still being fitted, this as a finishing part of an overnight build.

And that spaceship—Aimee calls it her favorite set so far. "I was very proud of that one. I've been asking for ten years for somebody to write me a spaceship, and I finally got to build one, even though we only had a few weeks to do it, along with everything else we were doing...but I finally got to build a spaceship."

Jason calls the spaceship the "bear" set of Season Two, alluding to the fact that some sets prove to be particularly challenging to design and build. "It had the dome on top of it, and the CNC panels...and the amount of *math* that had to go in to creating the central room and the hallways. It was like a full-time job, figuring that [set] out, but while that was being built, there were still other sets that had to be built and delivered, too. And *that's* the real challenge of a show like *Creepshow*."

And Brooke? She just calls it "crazy orange."

"Aimee chose this bright orange color, then some reds, and a creamy white. It wasn't the sort of spaceship I would have

OPPOSITE: The incredible Krasue leaves a wake of carnage in its path (although Greg sees a spot that could use an extra splash).

BELOW: Blood, blood, blood! Scenic Lead Brooke Beall says the "Drug Traffic" set was the most difficult to clean and redress.

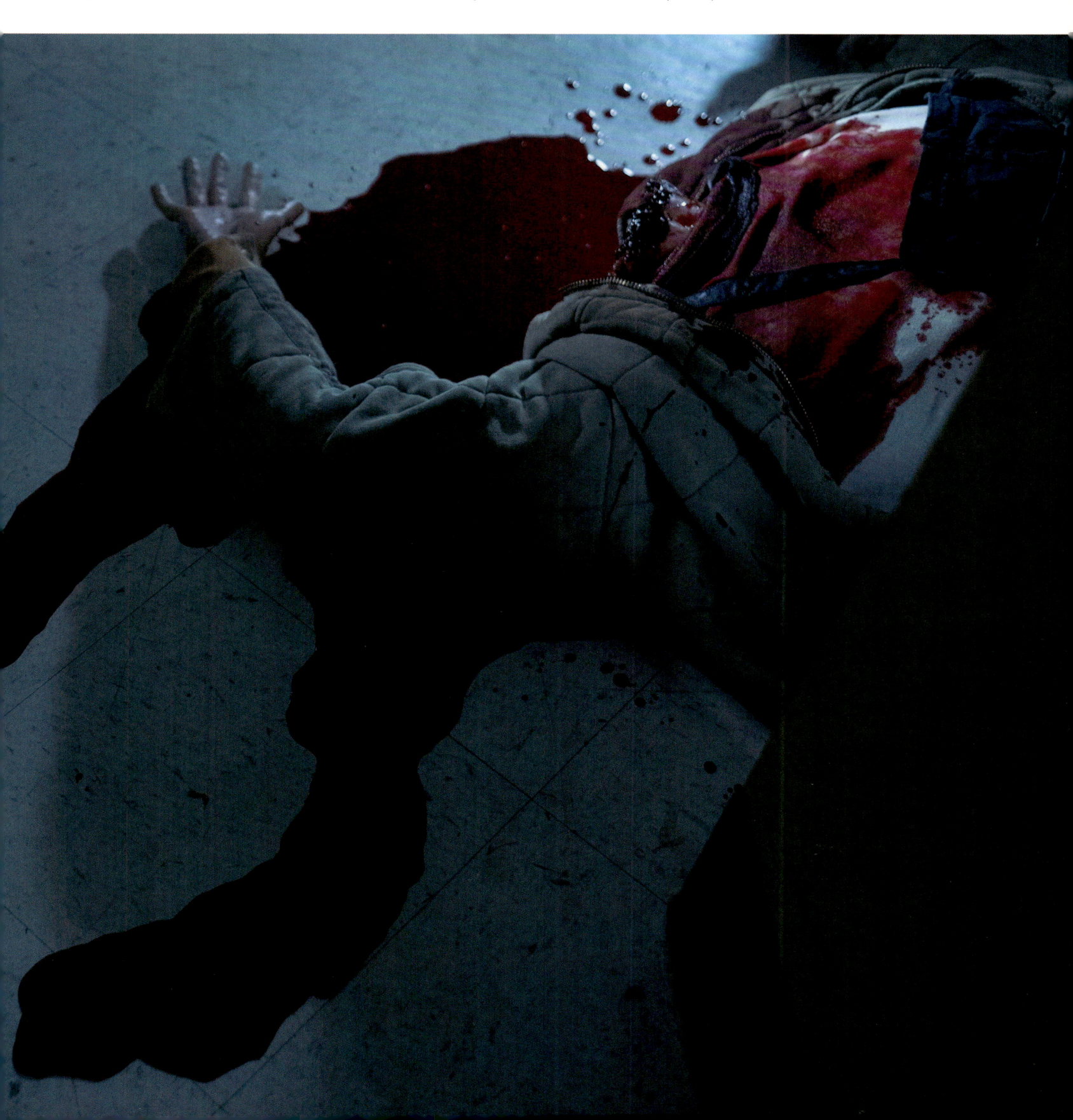

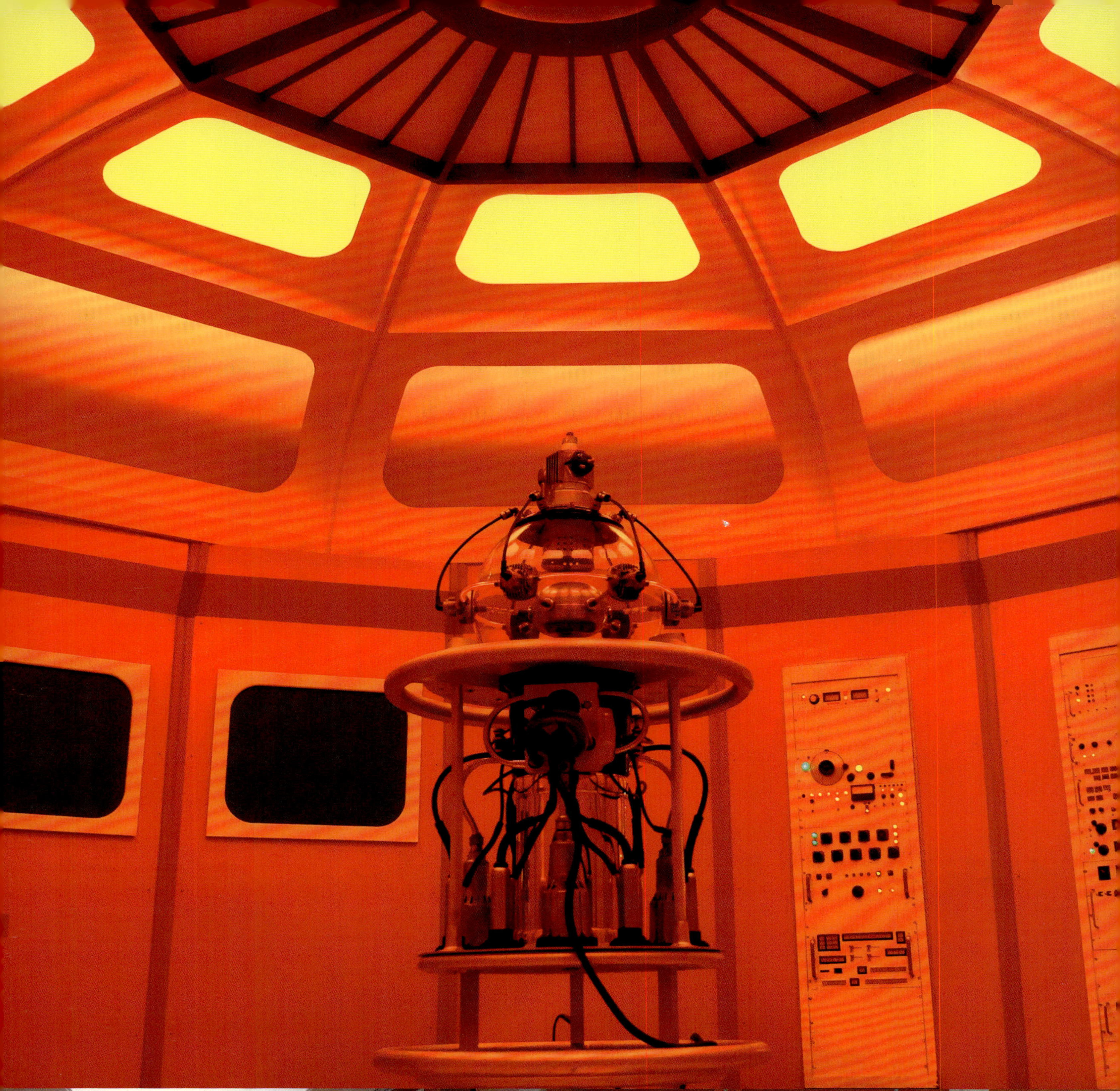

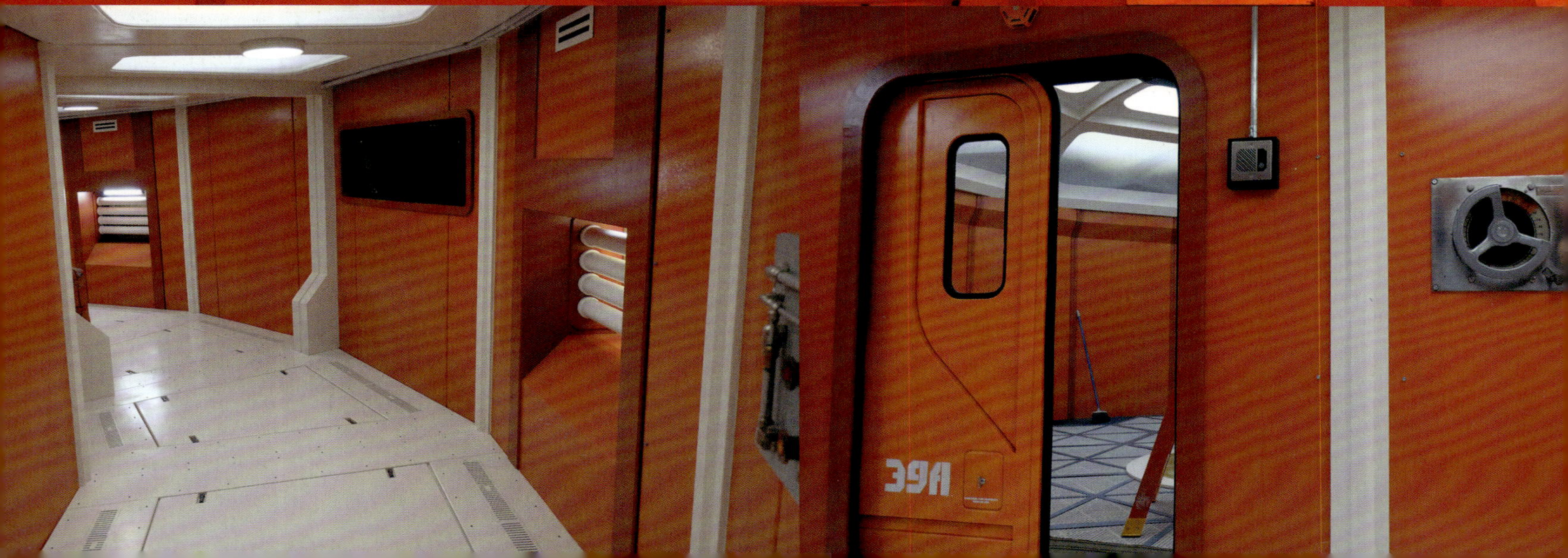

OPPOSITE: Aimee Holmberg gets her wish. The incredible Oculus spaceship set from "The Right Snuff." (Note the cow milker attachments hanging from the central gravity module, courtesy of the udderly inventive Rene Arriagada.)

LEFT: It's amazing what this Production Design team can achieve within a three-day shoot. They can take you to any world...or out of this world!

thought of, but we had so much fun with those colors. It was such a great set."

And all of this only scratches the surface of what this team does to deliver *Creepshow*. They thrive on the material, they live for the variety, and they greet the non-stop hustle with a crazy sort of glee. Their work is indispensable to each segment's eerie moods and lasting impact. Over the course of three seasons—thirty-six segments—they've led us deep into defiled graves and up to lavish penthouses; they've taken us across time to revisit different decades in our favorite genre; they've transported us *into* movies and far out into space. Wherever the story leads, that's where we'll go, thanks to these folks.

"This is such an amazing crew of people," Nick says, "and they all have a true love for horror—and that goes for every department on the show. This is the stuff we grew up on, the stuff we read about in *Fangoria*, and now we get to be a part of it."

> IN THE MOOD FOR A *REVOLTING RENOVATION?* JUST GIVE THESE *REPUGNANT REMODELERS* A CALL! BUT FIRST, LET'S MEET THE TORTURED SOUL WHO CAPTURES THIS ALL IN THE CAMERA'S EYE. HIS ASSIGNMENT HAS LEFT HIM DELIGHTFULLY *DERANGED...*

CHAPTER FOUR 81

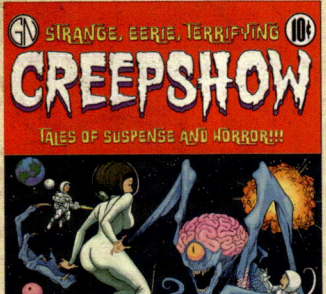

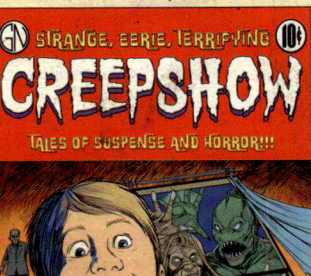

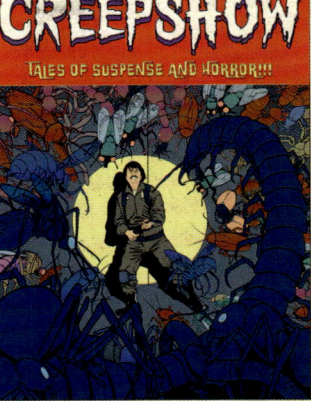

NOW YOU CAN BUY RARE CREEPSHOW BACK ISSUES!

ISSUE #04 ISSUE #05 ISSUE #06

SEND IN YOUR ORDER TODAY!

NAME_____
ADDRESS_____
CITY_____
STATE_____ ZIP_____

CREEPSHOW COMIC ADVERTISEMENTS FOR AMUSEMENT ONLY.

OFFICIAL CREEPSHOW CREEP CLUB

This card certifies that the holder is an official member of CREEPSHOW's CREEP CLUB and entitled to all benefits that it entails.

Member Number 0173

Name _____

CREEPSHOW CRYPT CLUB

JUST WHAT YOU LITTLE CREEPS HAVE BEEN WAITING FOR!!

OOZE YOUR ORBS AROUND THIS PAGE.... IT CAN ALL BE YOURS! AN 8X10 FULL COLOR PAINTING OF THE CREEP AND HIS PALS FROM CREEPSHOW, SUITABLE FOR FRAMING, THE **OFFICIAL CREEP CLUB PIN** (SHOWN BELOW), AND A POCKET-SIZED **MEMBERSHIP CARD** THAT IS AVAILABLE ONLY TO OUR CREEP CLUB MEMBERS. ORDER TODAY!

SOLD OUT!

SEND IN THIS COUPON!

CITY _____ STATE ____ ZIP _____

CREEPSHOW COMIC ADVERTISEMENTS FOR AMUSEMENT ONLY.

READY TO TAKE A LOOK THROUGH THE LURID LENS OF OUR RESIDENT DIRECTOR OF PHOTOGRAPHY, ROB DRAPER? HE'S THE LOCAL SHUDDER-BUG, THE SINISTER CINEMATOGRAPHER WHO GIVES CREEPSHOW ITS UNMISTAKABLY UNCANNY STYLE.
HE BRINGS A TWISTED VIEW TO THE GOINGS-ON HERE. YOU'LL AGREE THAT HE'S GOT A REAL...
MICHAEL BROOM 2021

EYE FOR THE UNNATURAL

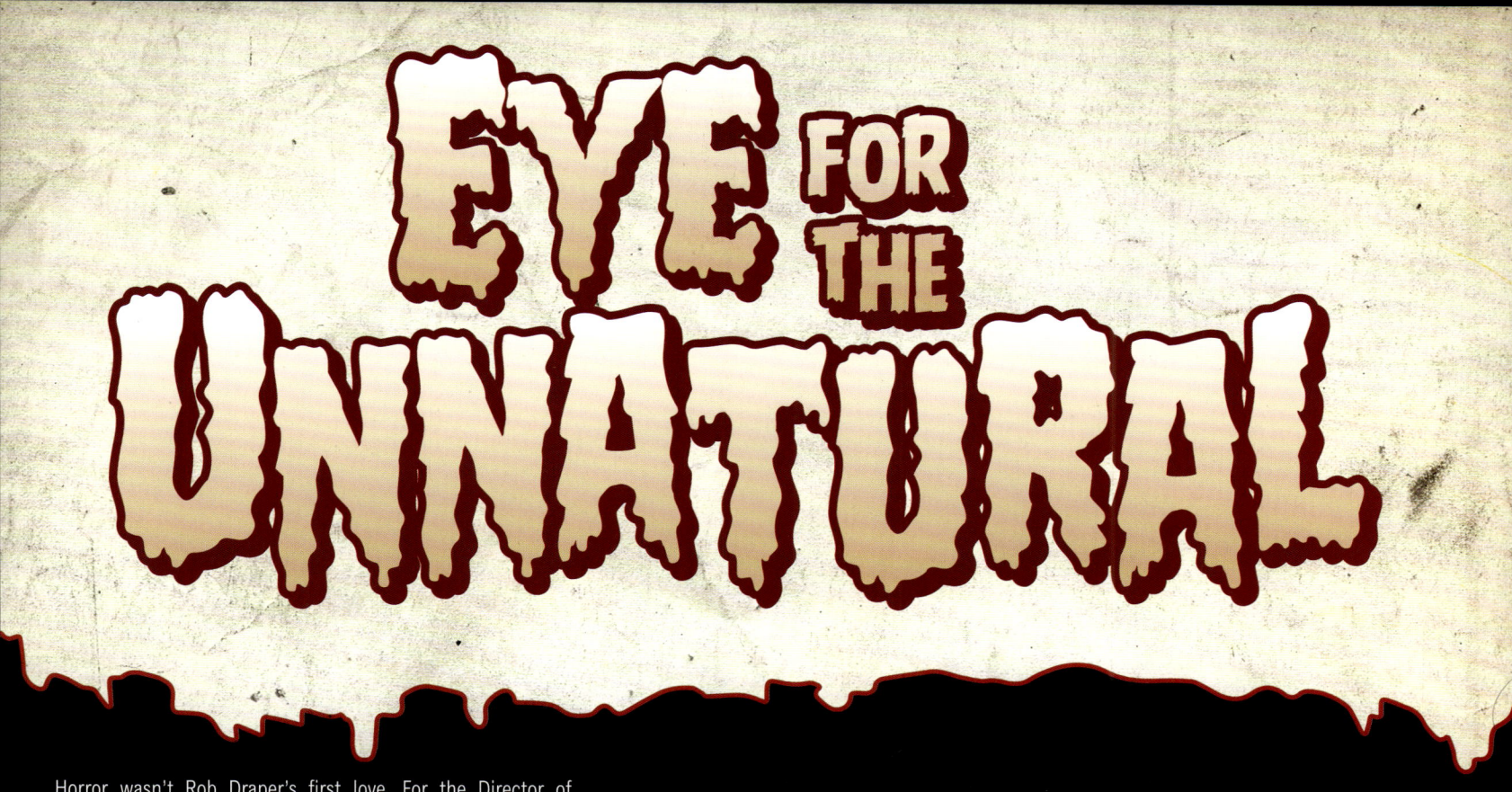

Horror wasn't Rob Draper's first love. For the Director of Photography on Shudder's *Creepshow*—the series' veritable "eye" into the unnatural realms—cinematography, as a profession, wasn't even his original aspiration. He wanted to be a dentist.

Born in Australia, Rob originally studied dentistry at Sydney University, but that was a short-lived endeavor. He switched over to medicine instead, and got a job as a medical technologist working in a pathology lab in Wagga Wagga, Australia. Medicine seemed to suit him more than molars and bicuspids...that is, until he laid his hands on a Bolex 16mm camera.

Despite his initial intention to simply film his wife riding horses, a camera shopkeeper lured him away from the Super-8 and over to the Bolex. *That* was his second love at first sight, and the camera's manual explained all he needed to know about scene structure: start with a wide shot, then a medium shot, close-up, close-up, medium-shot, then back to a wide-shot. He reckoned this would be enough "film language" for him to land a job at a local TV station. And he did.

So much for the medical career.

The camera suited him and, after success in Australian TV and migration from film stock to video, *he* migrated to America in 1980. He developed a maverick approach to his work, always looking for assignments that would stretch his creativity, his on-the-spot resourcefulness, and his natural inclination to take risks.

"I have a philosophy that I learned from Frank Stanley from ASC [American Society of Cinematographers]; he told me 'If you don't take a risk every time you push the button, you're just mediocre.'"

With Shudder's *Creepshow*, Rob pushes that button, pushes the limits, and pushes himself to achieve his best results within the limitations he's given—all with a laugh and a smile. After more than forty years in the business, he brings his own style to each episode and a collaborative ethic that perfectly suits the need and gets the job done.

"I do an enormous amount of prep, even given I'm doing the shooting and I'm not given prep time. I'm prepping while I'm shooting. I have a pretty good idea how I want to see the piece. And then I'll talk to the director to get his or her ideas. And then I'll talk to [Production Designer] Aimee [Holmberg] to see what she has planned. And then I sort of put it all in the mixer and blend 'em all up, and we come up with a visual style."

Of course, *Creepshow* demands its own style—EC comics' influence, remember?—and Rob is dutiful in his adherence to it. He utilizes the usual accent lighting of stark reds and blues as seen in the original film, but he says he doesn't want to copy that work outright. He strives to bring elements of his own style

ABOVE: Rob Draper shows off the latest in camera technology—the Norelco PC-60. Just kidding! It's really a throwback nod to George A. Romero's *Dawn of the Dead* and featured in the *Creepshow* segment, "Public Television of the Dead."

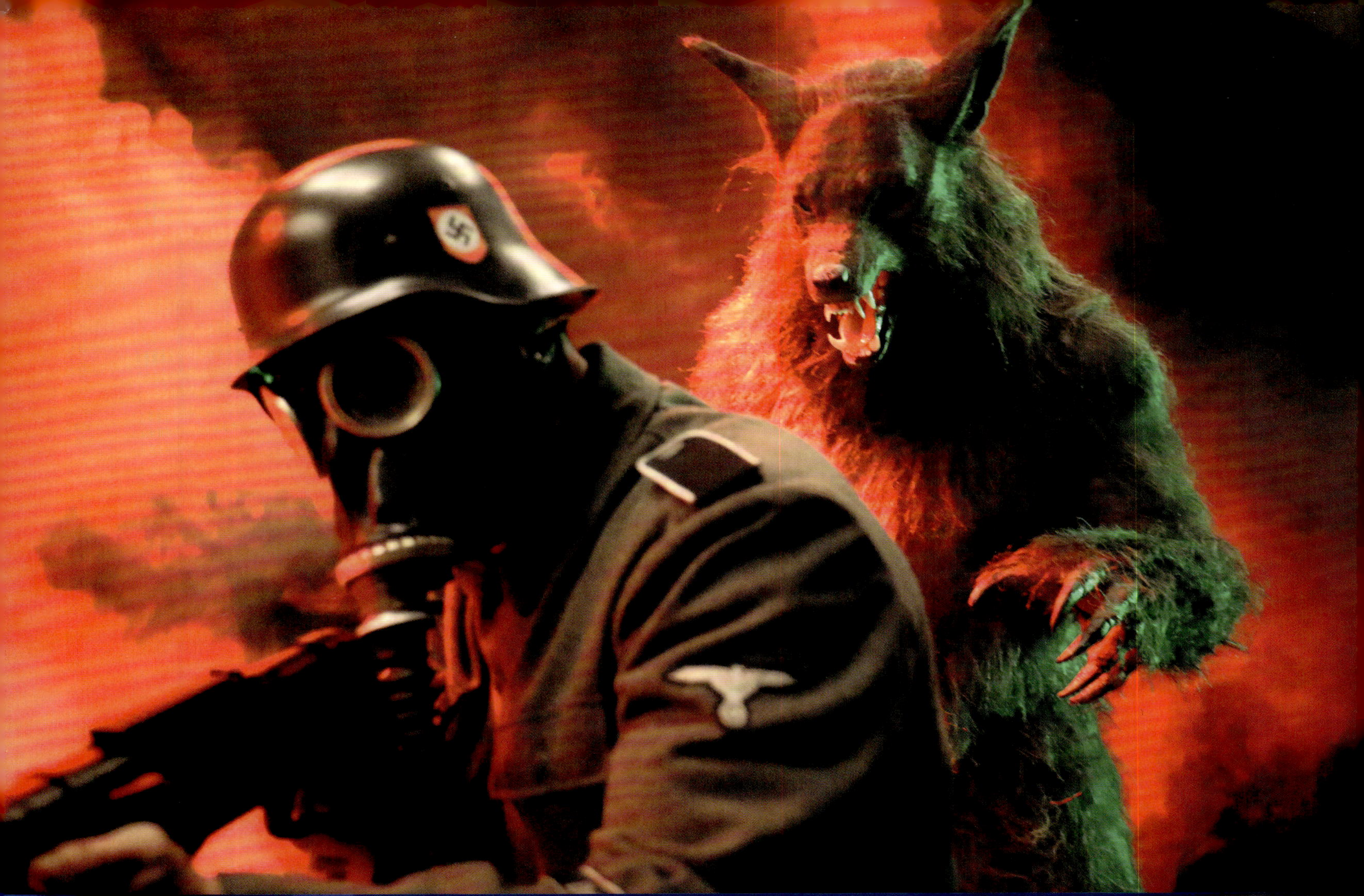

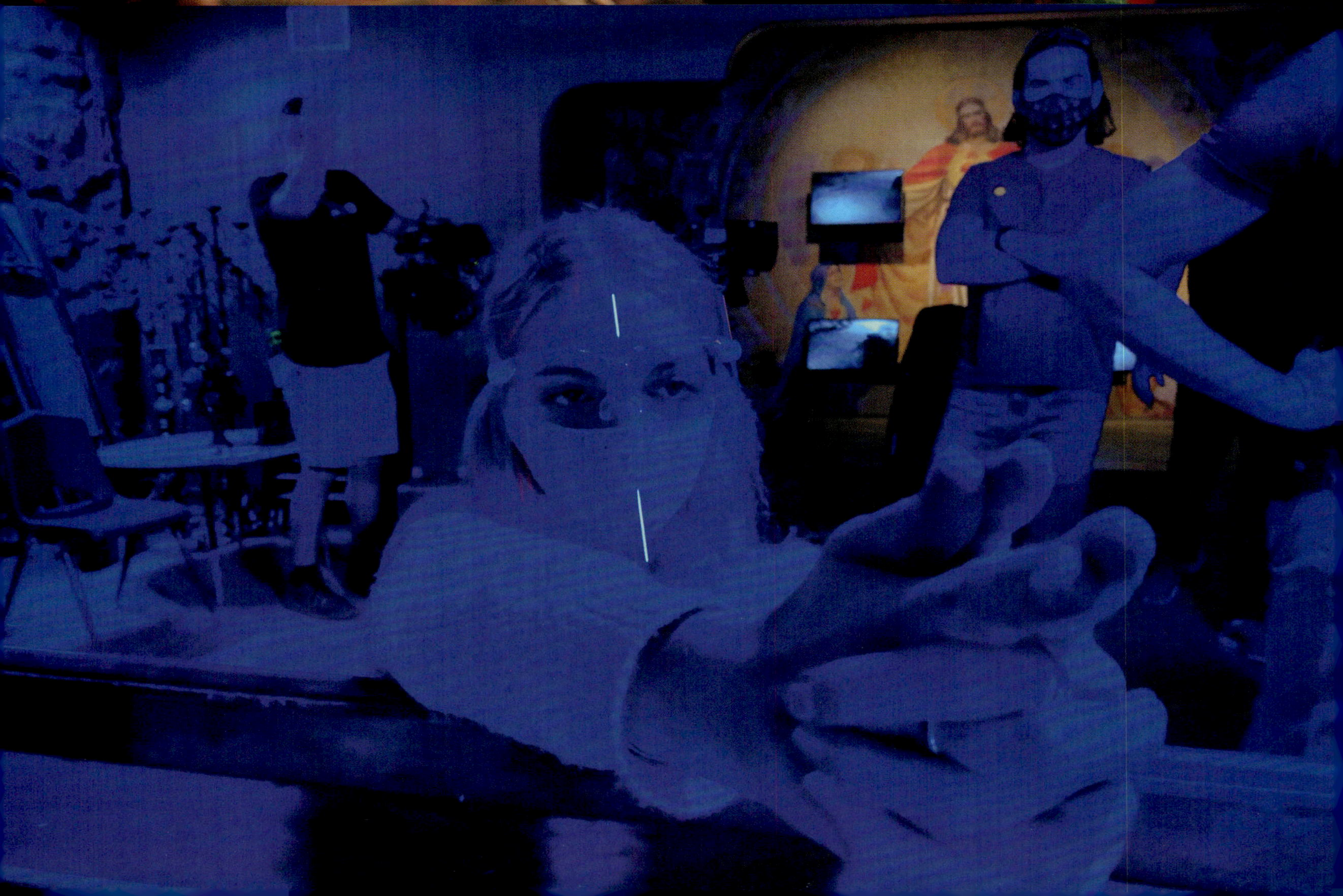

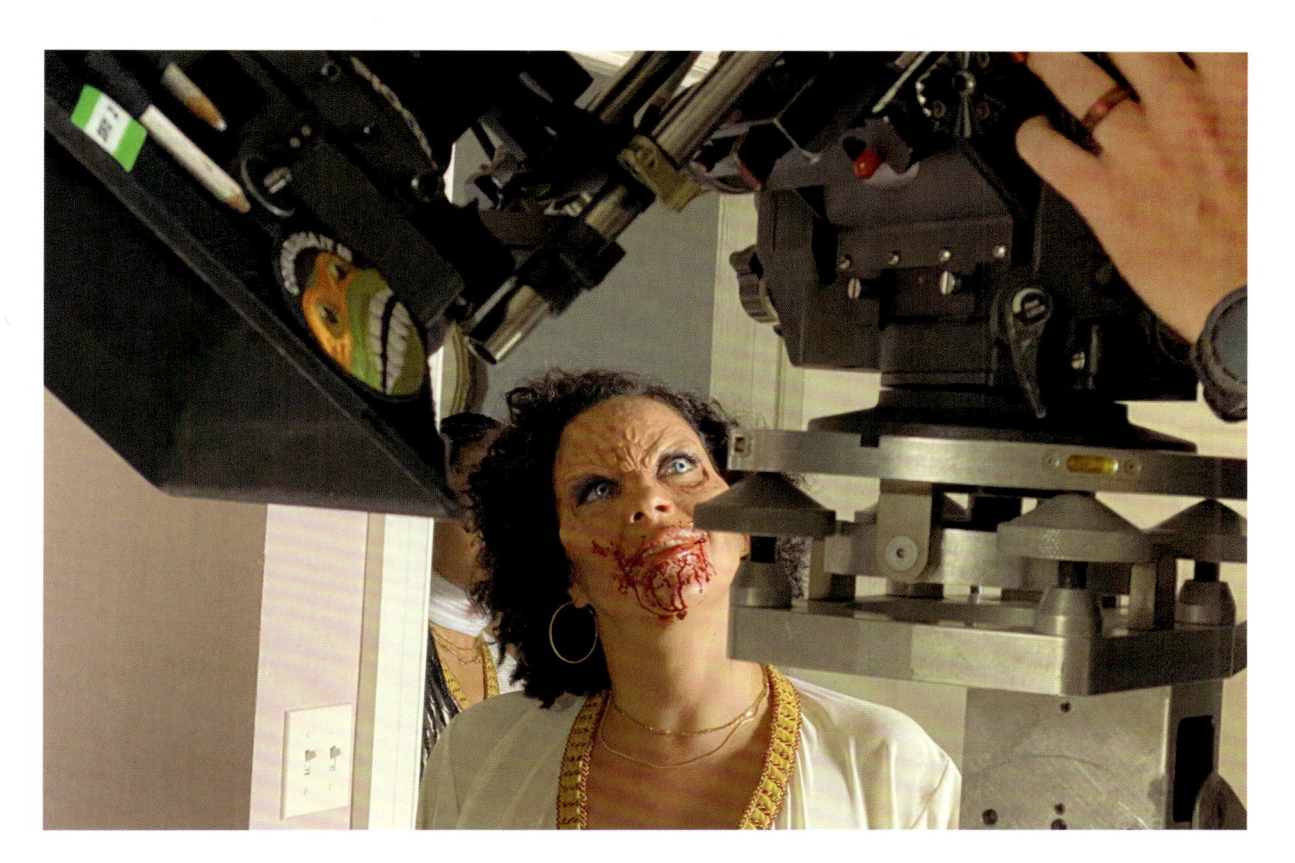

OPPOSITE: Let Rob Draper and crew color your world. From "Bad Wolf Down" (top, werewolf played by Carey Jones) and "Shapeshifters Anonymous" (bottom, pictured foreground are Maddie Rose Chandler and Kevin Marshall).

LEFT: Whether heightening a moment of terror or adding a claustrophic creepiness to a haunted setting, Rob has an eye for the perfect angles to amplify the on-screen fright. From "Stranger Sings" (pictured is Suehyla El-Attar Young).

BELOW: Rob Draper shows off his acting skills between takes on the set of the "Model Kid" segment.

to the show, to bring a bit of a contemporary visual method, all while keeping within Greg Nicotero's vision for the series.

"I spend a lot of time talking to Greg and about what he wanted to see. One of the things we talked a lot about was focal lengths of lenses. With [the art within most] comic books, we get a lot of forced perspective, and we get that by using really wide-angle lenses—and I love using those and getting in close because it engages the audience more. So, that was a big part of the style, using those wide-angle lenses and getting close so we were right on top of the actors a lot of the time. Then, we Dutch the angle on the lens so we get that stretch on the edges of the frame. That's a real 'comic book' feel."

Aside from his continuous collaborations with Greg, the directors, and designers, Rob regularly refers to his own archive of material—artwork, photographs, samples of his own work—to develop his approach for each *Creepshow* segment. He'll review film clips and movies suggested by the directors, taking it all in to put together a suitable visual recipe. Once he has an idea of how he'll approach a segment, he'll bring his vision to the director to explain what he'd like to do, and why.

"As the DP on the series, I can be the guy who's got all the control in terms of how the show looks, but I try to open it up to the directors as much as possible so they feel like they're making a movie. I try to get as much information from them as possible

CHAPTER FIVE   87

ABOVE: The graphic backlighting with contrasting key light is the *Creepshow* style, through and through. From "The Last Tsuburaya." Pictured in foreground are Jeffrey F. January (left) and Rob Draper (right). Nate Andrade played the monster.

and then meld it all together so I can develop and produce a visual style within the budget and time constraints of the show."

And when considering the schedule of shooting a half-hour of material every three-and-a-half days (that ominous seven-day-per-episode shooting schedule), he laughingly says, "We're cookin'. We're making pizzas, mate!" And what's his secret ingredient when cookin' on the *Creepshow* sets? Preparation.

He does an admirable amount of preparation in his work. He never shows up on any shooting day not knowing what he'll do. On the contrary, he has every day planned out before he steps foot onto any set. Armed with his exhaustive script notes, he already knows what lenses he'll use, what exposure settings he'll use, how he'll light the scenes—it's all laid out ahead of a day's work (and, remember, he often does this prep while simultaneously shooting). He makes good use of the Scriptation app, an indispensable tool in his arsenal today.

"I'd make an enormous number of notes on the script pages, then when new pages came out, I had to transfer it all over. The advantage of [Scriptation] is I can put all of my notes into digital form, and then transfer them every time there's new pages or a new script comes out; they just transfer straight over. So, I can have all my photographs and artwork, video clips and anything I want—all my notes and storyboards that I do or blocking diagrams and all that stuff—can just transfer from one version of the script to another."

He adds, with a laugh, "And nine times out of ten, a lot of that changes, but I always go in with a basic plan. For every shot, I note my f-stop, my focal lengths, and all that. And I'll have all

CHAPTER FIVE

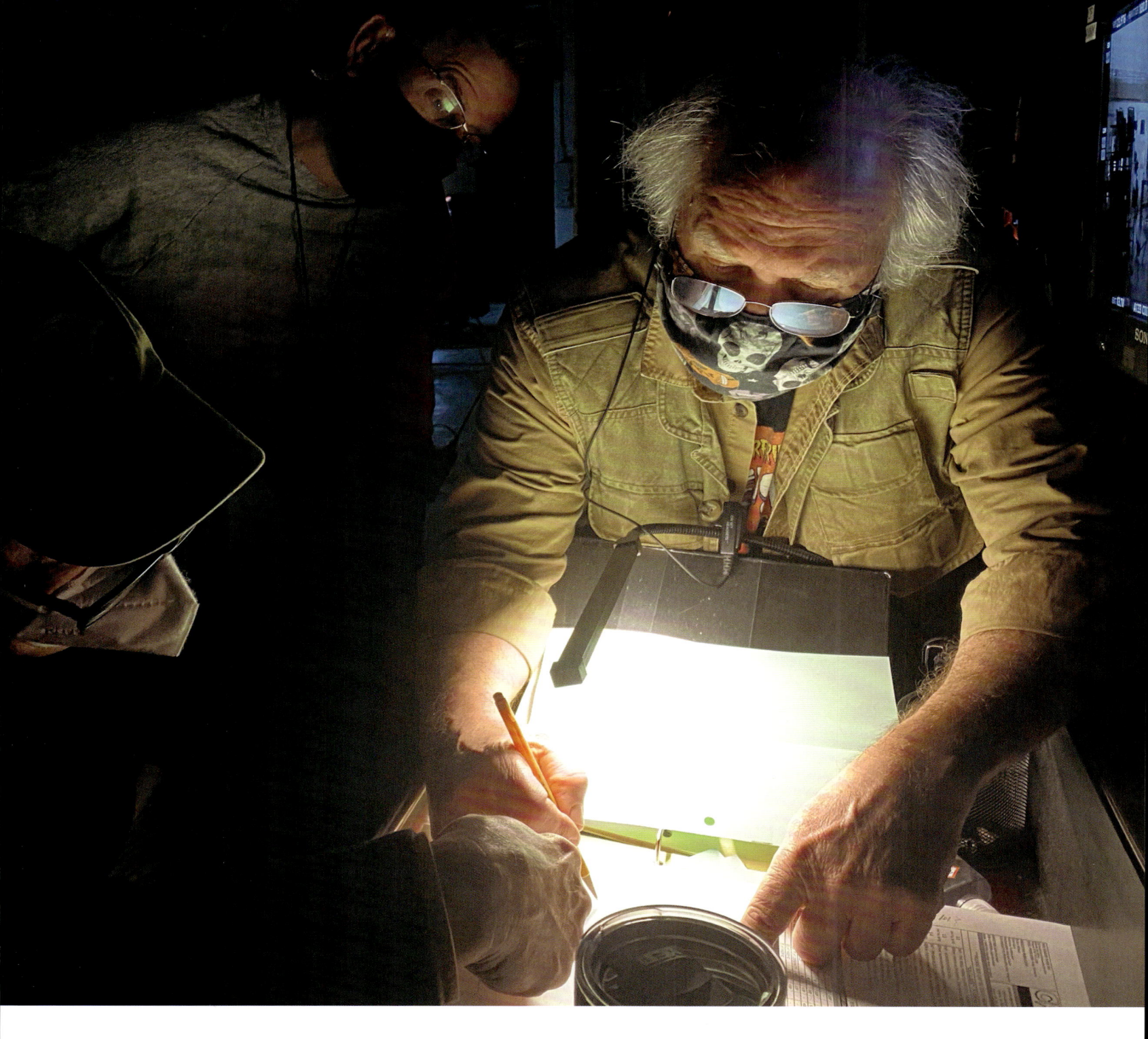

my notes of what I want to do, then I have all the notes of what I actually do. If I have to come back to it later on, or Second Unit has to pick up something, I can give them exactly what they need. But, with that basic planning, it's real easy to make the adjustments that we need to make."

Adjustments? Simple camera settings? A few tweaks to the lighting? Sometimes, but not always. In the Season Three segment "Mums," the driving sequence shot inside the car at the segment's close was originally planned for shooting on the actual road at the location. Upon arrival at the site, Rob was told he couldn't shoot on the road: a thunderstorm had moved into the skies above, not only complicating shooting but obscuring the planned exterior daylight. The sequence would have to be done using green screen, only there wasn't time to return to the studio to complete the shoot there. Rob's answer:

let's use the location lunch tent, push the car into the tent, put the green screen behind it, and shoot it there. And so, they did. To achieve the natural daylight within the tent, Rob bounced lights off the white tent's covering and—*Presto!*—daylight.

"The reason I was able to pull all of that off is because I knew exactly how I wanted it to look; it really didn't matter where we shot it. It was just a matter of setting up the green screen wherever we shot. Later, I shot a background plate myself, dropped it in, and it was fine. But that *all* comes from prep. In my experience, if you don't prep—if you think you can just show up and wing it, especially on a show like this—you're dead."

But he says he likes the stress. For him, there's a refreshing quality in having to shift gears so rapidly. He admits he feels the stress of the budget and the stress of making the schedule.

ABOVE: Although he never steps on set without a shooting plan, Rob's always prepared to collaborate with his team to make on-the-spot adjustments. Pictured on left are director John Harrison (foreground) and David "Muddy" Waters (background).

RIGHT: This impressive cockpit of the Oculus (from "The Right Snuff") was completed just as the film crew arrived on set. "Hey—we're cookin'!" Rob cheerily remarks.

BELOW: Here's a trick: Rob has the lighting he needs installed first, then the set is built around that. Who'da thunk it possible? From "Within the Walls of Madness." Pictured is Drew Matthews.

OPPOSITE TOP: Nope—it's not Orange Crush, it's the Oculus, from "The Right Snuff."

OPPOSITE BOTTOM: The same set in different dimensions? Maybe. The redressed Oculus becomes the airlock in "Within the Walls of Madness." Betcha' didn't even notice.

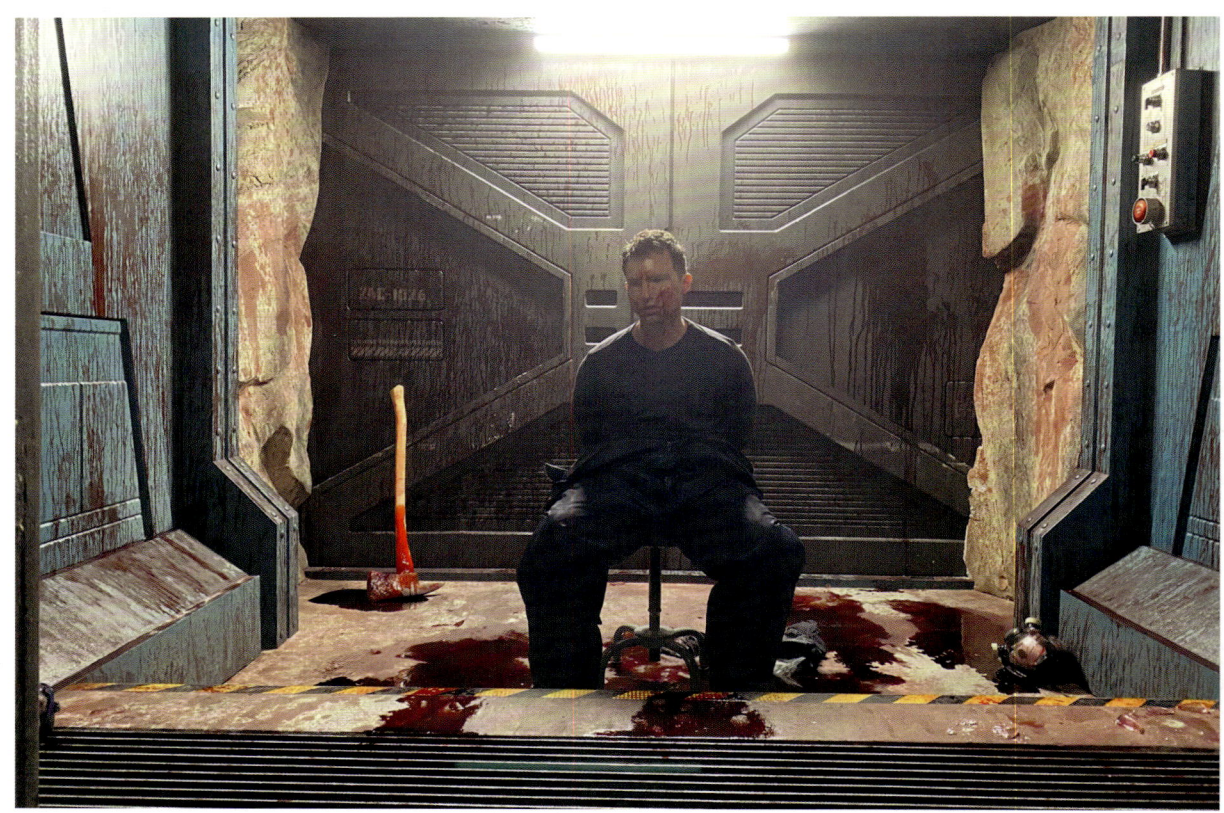

Plus, there's the stress that comes with the fact that many sets are re-skinned and repainted. "I have to make sure—and Aimee and I talked a lot about this each time we went from one set to another—that the audience didn't twig on to the fact that we're shooting on the same set in three stories."

To that last point, he cites the quick re-use of the spaceship sets from "The Right Snuff," repurposed for "Within the Walls of Madness." The cockpit of the spaceship was reworked to become the airlock for "Within the Walls of Madness," while the spaceship's control room was transformed into the central control room of the latter segment.

"The crazy thing with 'Within the Walls of Madness' was that I had to come up with the lighting before the team actually built the set. I needed to light the control room somehow, and I needed to light it from overhead. Once they built the set, there would be no way I could put lights overhead, so we put the lights in and they built the set around them. There was no second-guessing that one! I told the director, 'Look, this is the way I'm gonna light it...and I'm *pretty sure* it's gonna work.' And once they built the set around it, there was no going back."

In other cases, pre-planning takes a back seat to efficiency and simplicity. The dank claustrophobia of the "Gray Matter"

90 CHAPTER FIVE

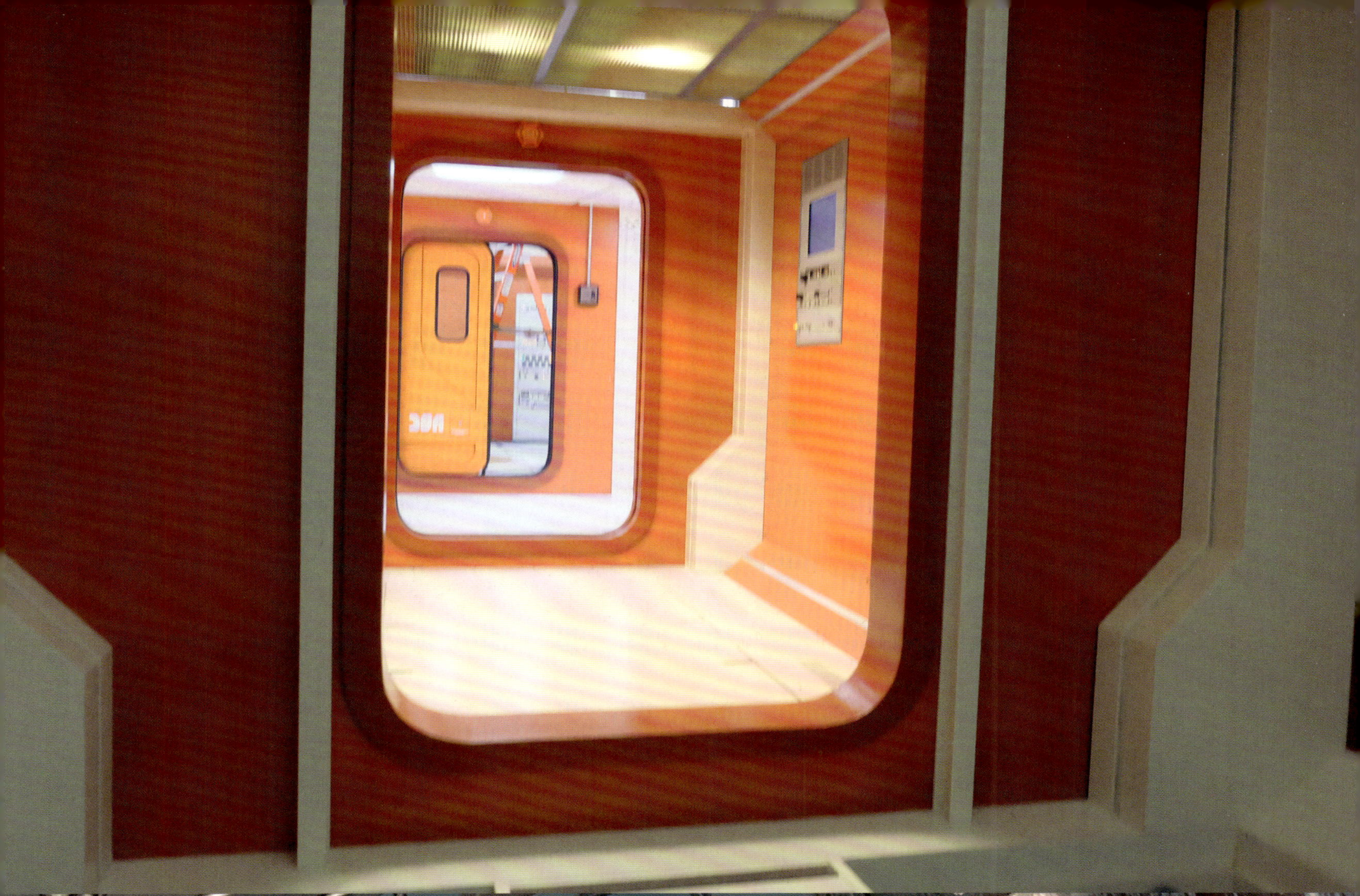

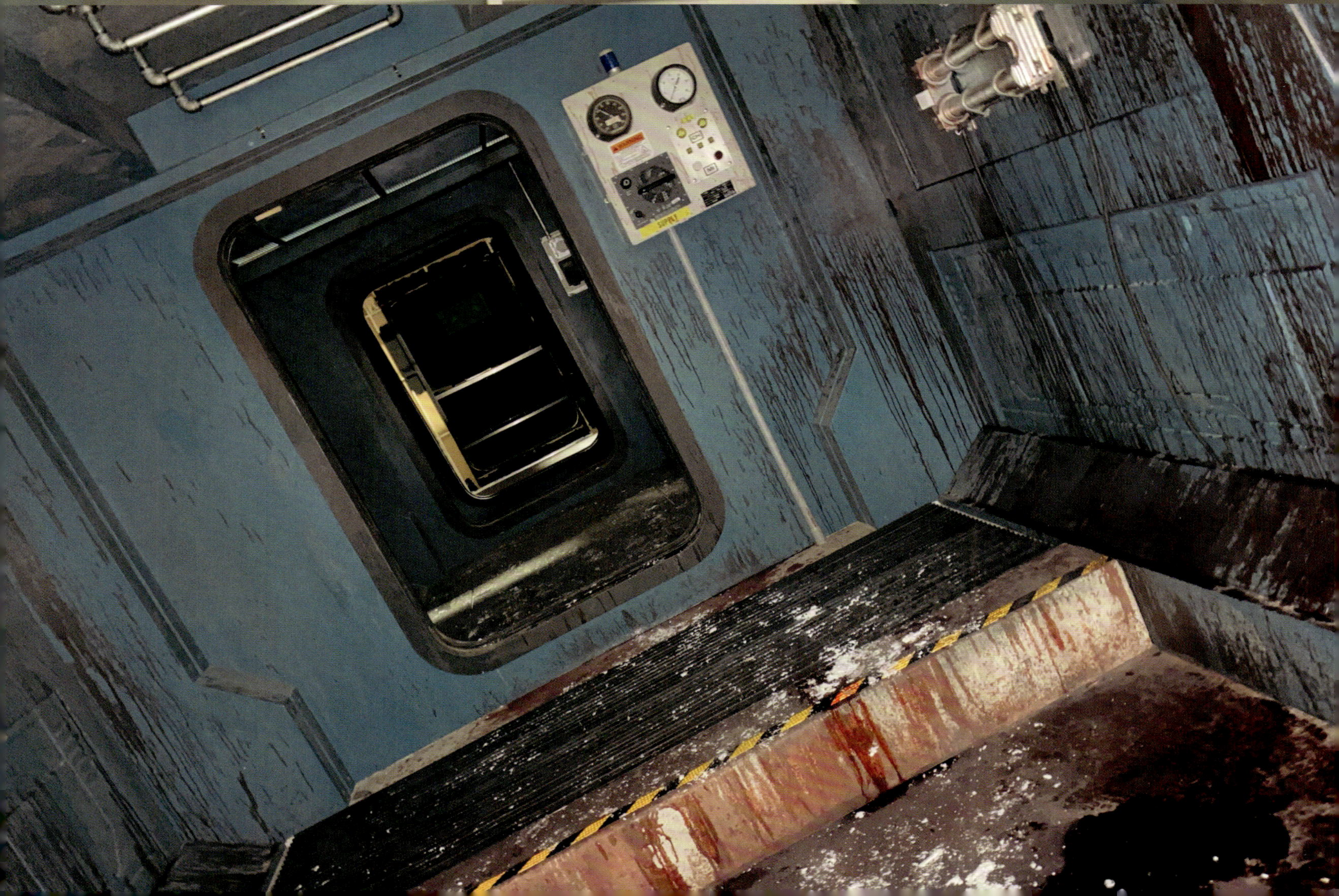

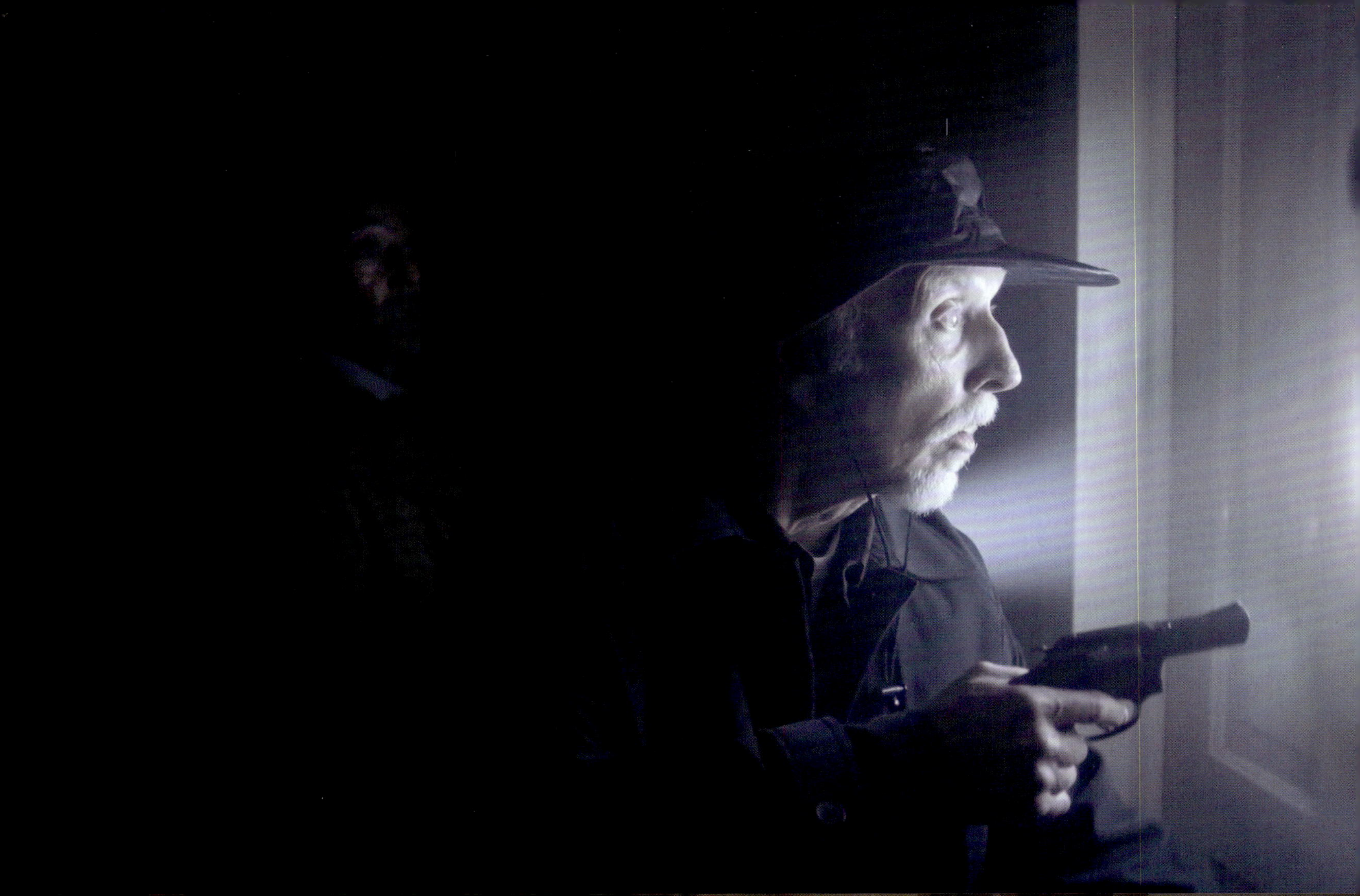

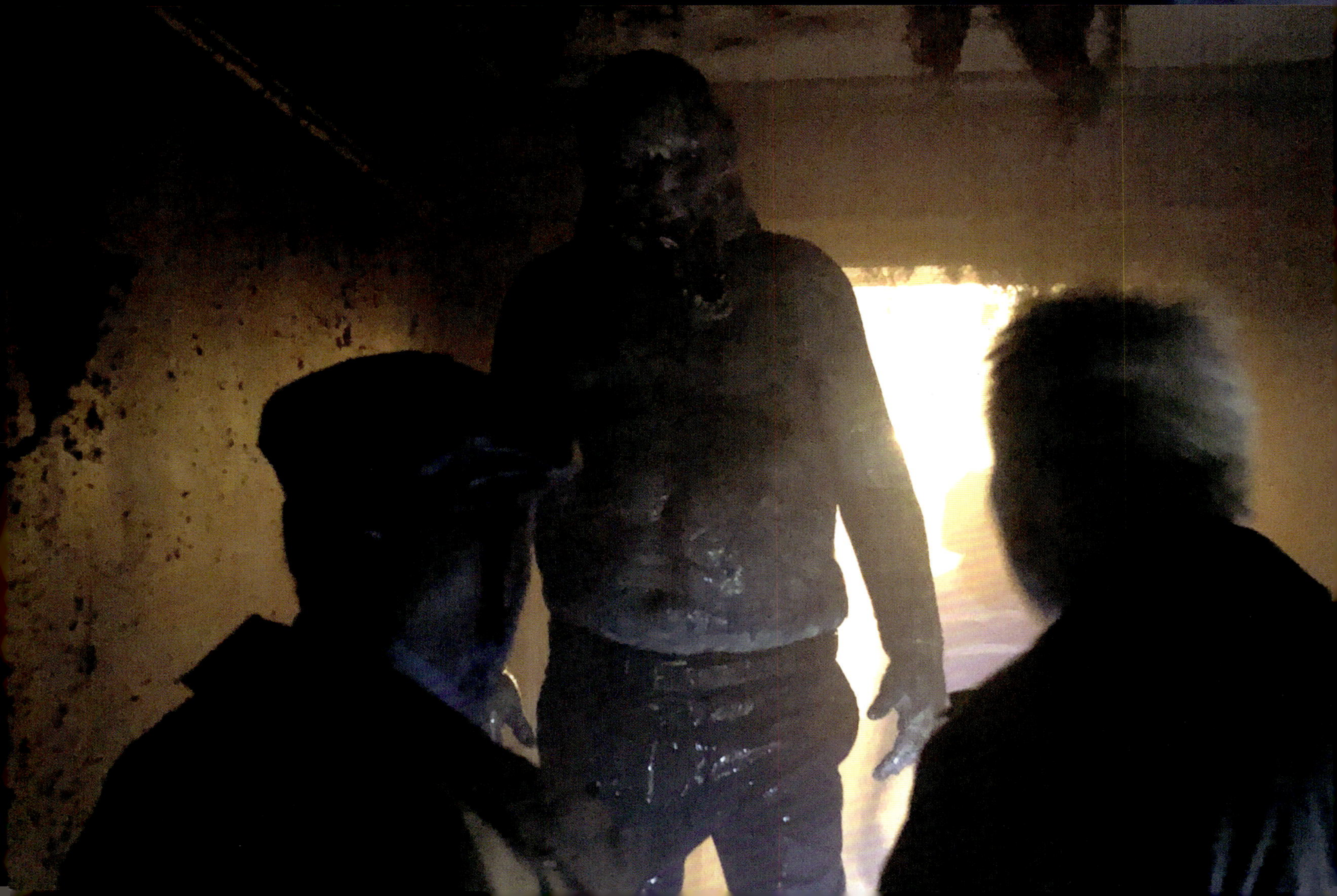

segment was achieved by a suitably dark lighting scheme with tension spiked through the use of the unsteady and uncertain beams from hand-held flashlights. As actors Tobin Bell and Giancarlo Esposito tenuously climb the stairs to discover what's happened to Timmy's dad, only the flashlights provide a narrow view of their surroundings. But was this a lighting choice of Rob's own intention to gain maximum anxiety?

"A lot of the time, I'm just looking for the fastest way to shoot something! And so I was thinking, 'What's the fastest way we can shoot this thing? Flashlights!' But I also told Greg I wanted to shoot the entire scene with only flashlights and no other lighting; that would give him the freedom to move the camera anywhere he wanted. And I didn't want to have lights hidden all over the place and I did want to use smoke because it was supposed to be steamy and sweaty and awful in there. If I had lights hidden all over the place, we would have seen beams coming down from them. But in order to see [the actors], I had little white cards taped up to the walls all around the set. So, they had to come along and hit those little cards with their flashlights; that's how we got enough light bouncing back to see them. And Giancarlo Esposito came to me after we had done a few takes of them coming in the door and going up the stairs, and he said, 'At what point am I gonna be able to do some acting with my mouth instead of with my hand?'"

Rob affirms that it's a fun set and an energized crew and cast, every episode, every segment, every day. He goes on to say that the enthusiasm of the film company comes through in the production and even translates to the actors, who are also energized by the on-set vibe. "I've always believed that, and we have fun on this show. It's never agony going to work. It's always *[motioning with two thumbs up]*, 'Hey! What monsters do we have today and how many blood cannons are we gonna shoot across the set today, and what gore and guts are we gonna see?'"

Like his cohorts, Rob sees this production as all good fun, and maintains that, if everyone is enjoying themselves, then the end product will reflect that organically. And it does.

"When I first started [in this work], I didn't want to do horror films. Well...I *did* want to do the big horror films like *The Exorcist* and *The Shining*, that sort of stuff. But I didn't want to do [typical] horror films, and then my first film was *[laughing] Halloween 5*. I did that after doing *Tales from the Darkside* on TV, then *Tales from the Darkside: The Movie*, and *Tales from the Crypt*, and I was just thinking 'What the hell?!' But the thing that was good about it all is that I was doing different stuff all the time, and it's not like shooting a regular series where you come in and you're doing the same kitchen, living room, dining room, bedroom—day after day after day. [On *Creepshow*], every

OPPOSITE: Of Must and Men? The hideous hotbox that was once Richie Grenadine's apartment, from "Gray Matter." Pictured top is Giancarlo Esposito (left) and Tobin Bell (right). Pictured bottom is Andy Rusk as the unrecognizable Richie, confronting Doc and Chief.

BELOW: Brooke Beall reveals the "Gray Matter" concerns over Richie Grenadine's apartment: "People were saying, 'This looks like it's molding... and I don't really want to go in there.'" Pictured is Giancarlo Esposito as "Doc."

BELOW: Rob Draper encounters a siren's supper, from "Stranger Sings."

OPPOSITE: Setting the graveyard scene from "Night of the Paw."

day it's a different set with a different group of actors, a different story with different monsters. For me, it's a real challenge—and I enjoy it!"

Yes, he's come to love the horror, and the monsters, and the opportunities it all offers to use as much of a practical approach in his work as possible. He considers himself fortunate to have been able to work with Greg Nicotero and Tom Savini early in his career. After all, bringing creatures to life is the name of the game on Shudder's *Creepshow*.

"We were all basically at the beginnings of our careers [when we first started working together], but the thing that was great is they had a really good handle on what made prosthetics and creatures work...and I was able to learn from those guys to modify my lighting styles to really make the creatures come to life."

Like Greg and the KNB EFX team, Rob prefers in-camera practical work. In his camera and lighting setups, he often employs classic theatrical techniques, ones that he especially enjoyed when shooting "Night of the Paw." He achieves an effective time-and-space transition through a clever, if not crude, stylized method that he laughingly refers to as his take on German Expressionism. Mostly shot on a location serving as the Whitlock home, actor Bruce Davison explains the fate of his reanimated wife. In one flashback moment, the audience sees a reaction closeup of the actor that is actually filmed in a studio set with him seated on a dolly chair that is physically moved across the frame (across the camera's view). The key light on his face intensifies while the lit scene behind him fades to black; that is, the flashback is ending. A well-placed cut puts Davison back on location in the Whitlock house, returning to present time as he continues his exposition. Not only does this method achieve a compelling visual transition (tight closeup with fading flashback background), but it also allows for complex storytelling in a time- and cost-effective manner.

"On a show where we only have three-and-a-half days to shoot it, just working out all that stuff can be a nightmare. Also, when

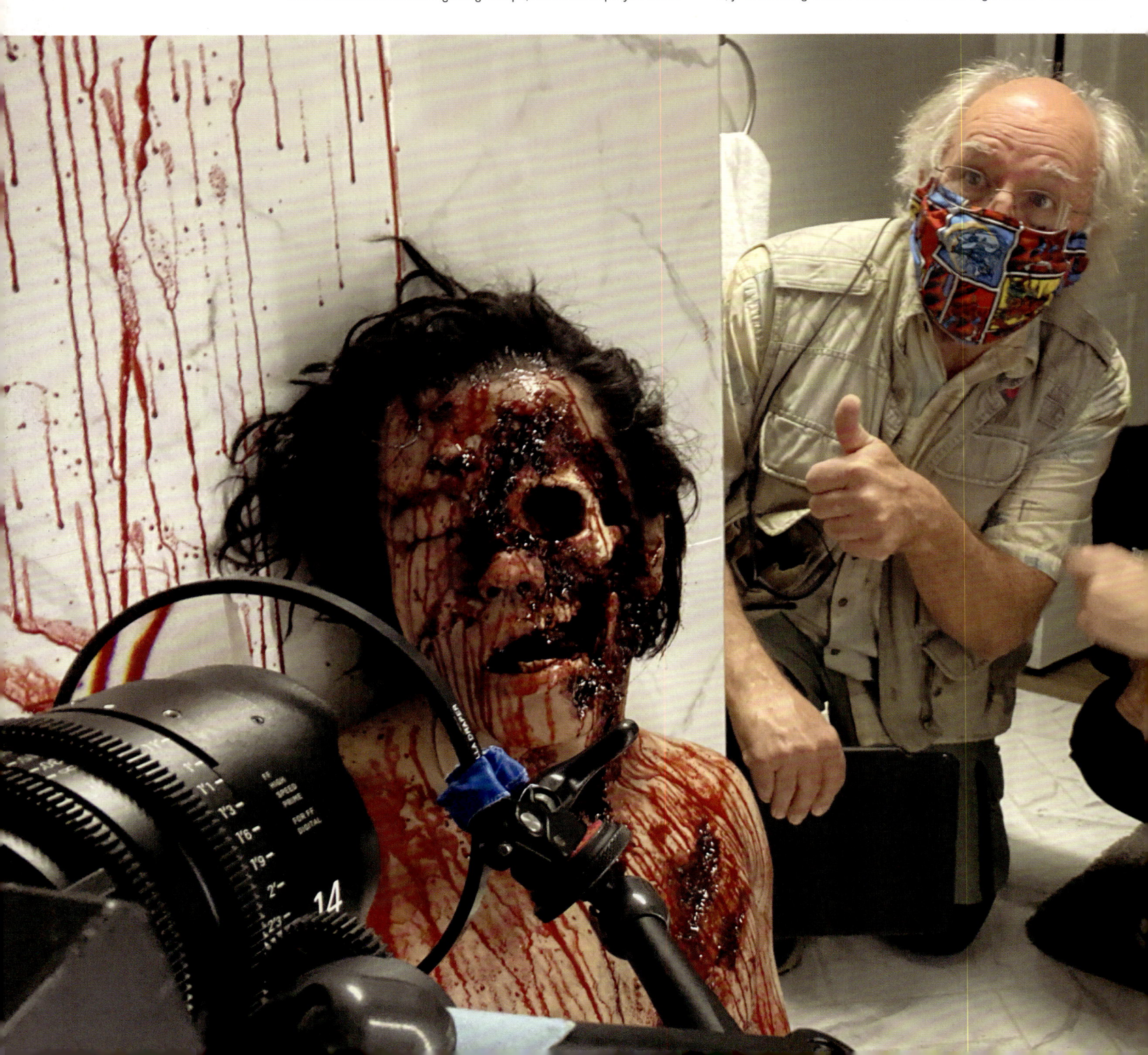

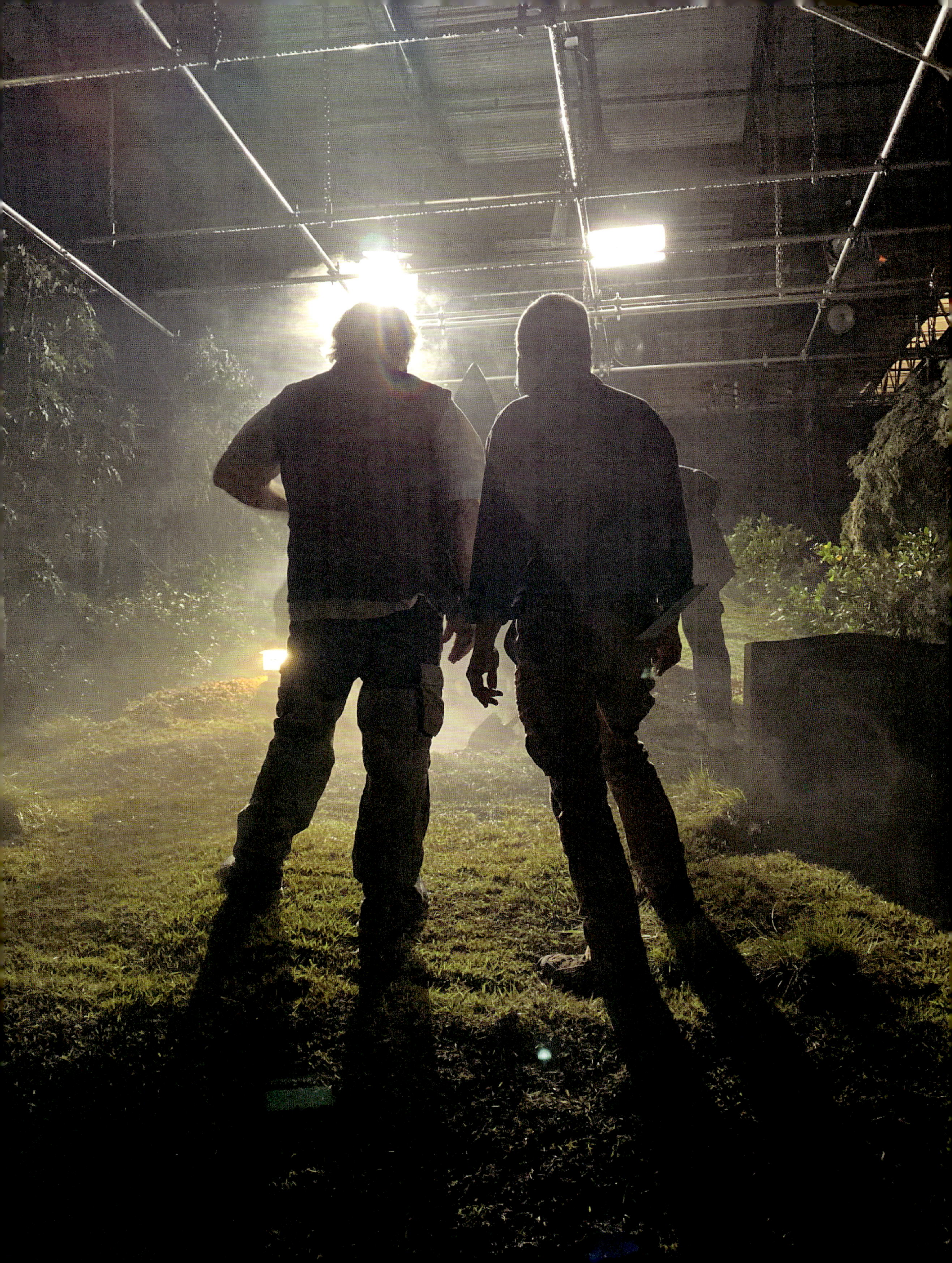

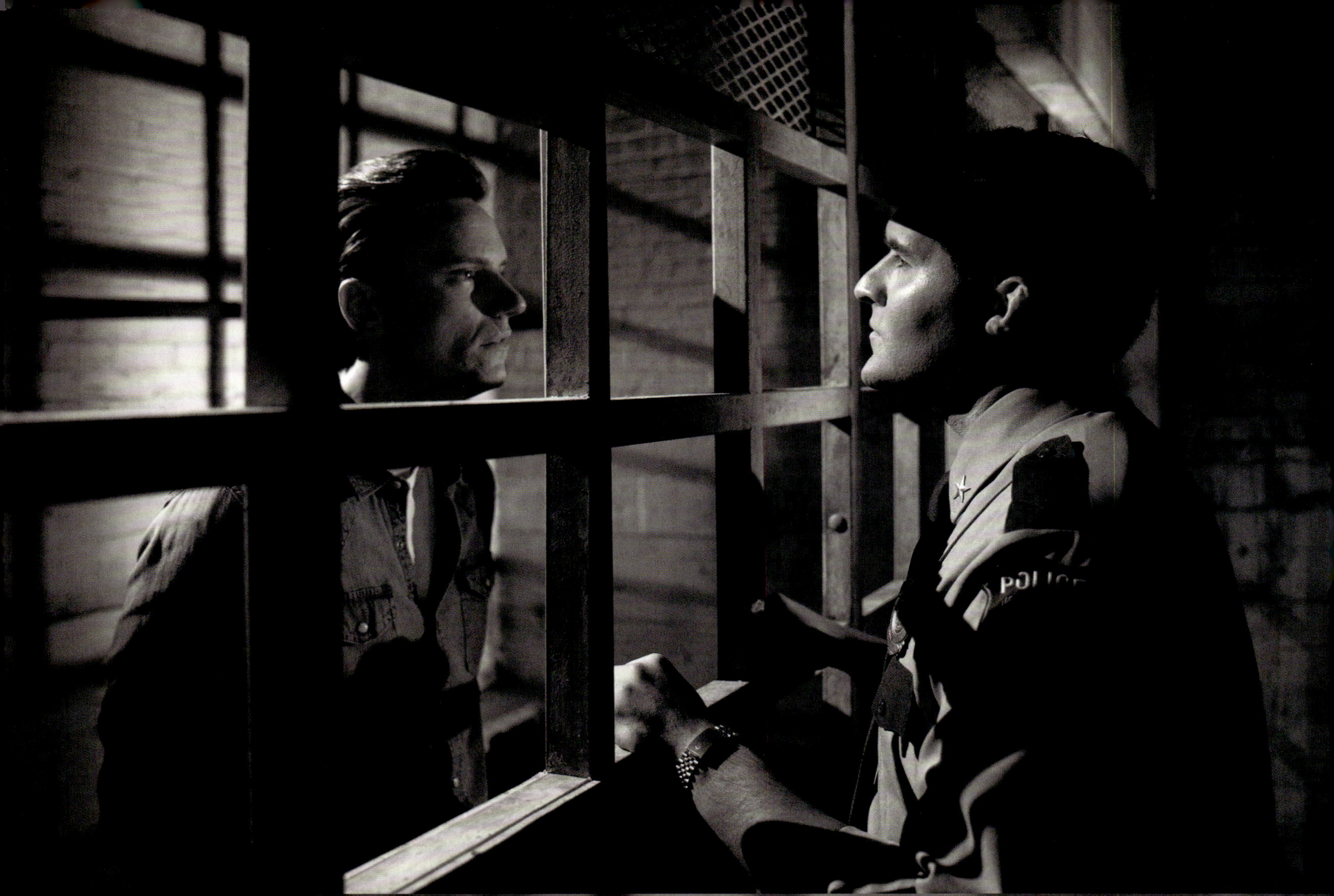

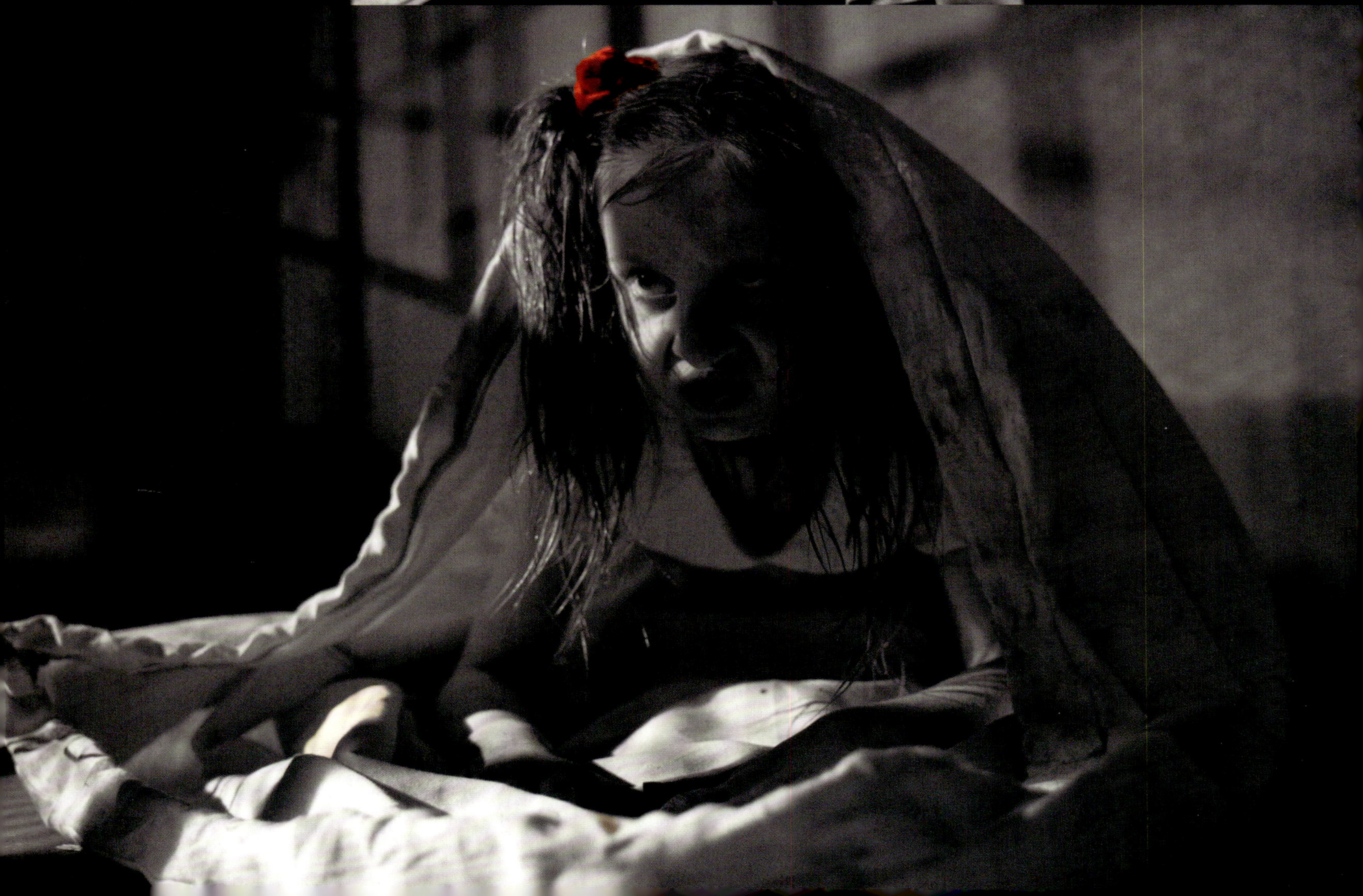

doing the lighting transitions, I had to basically do two lighting setups for each shot; whenever there was a transition, I had to have the lighting for the scene and the lighting for the transition so we could cross-fade."

Again, these are challenges that he gladly takes on, episode after episode. But ask Rob what he's loved most so far—and what he loves most in film—and he'll answer, "Noir!"

He considers himself a "film noir freak" (his words). He loves the starkness of it all: the hard light, hard edges, key light, no fill light, hard backlight. With Shudder's *Creepshow*, he found a kindred spirit in director John Harrison.

"We actually worked together for the first time on an episode of *Tales from the Darkside* ["Everybody Needs a Little Love"]. And he called me and asked, 'So, do you like film noir?' 'Do *I* like film noir?!' And I rattled off my favorite titles, and it was great. They didn't let us do black-and-white for that *Darkside* episode, but when 'A Dead Girl Named Sue' came up, John asked if we could do it in black-and-white, and they said yes. We were so excited. I bumped up the contrast so it looked more like black-and-white film stock, and I lit it with hard light, and gave it real classic noir style, throwing shadows up the wall. And even when we did the Poor Man's Process [rear projection], we shot that purposefully to give that that [unsteady] Poor Man's Process look."

And for the reveal of Dead Sue, the corpse girl's chilling crawl across the floor was achieved through slight under-cranking while filming, then it was turned over to post-production for skip framing. The result was a quirky, jerky, and unsettling movement for the climactic moment. "It really worked well," he says. "I thought it looked fantastic."

As much fun as Rob is having on the *Creepshow* series, he shares his disappointment with much of what he sees in film today, something he's actively addressing with his own online cinematography instruction.

"Cinematography today really pisses me off," he laments. "Everything's starting to look the same because everyone's imitating everyone else. I want to explain to people where you start and how you come up with your own visual style, because I think that's what's missing now. People aren't injecting themselves into their work; they're just copying what other people do and then it all just starts to look the same."

With *Creepshow*, he's already gotten more than thirty opportunities to explore visual style, to apply and extend his own visual sensibilities, and to try new and inventive ways to terrify us.

It's bloody fantastic, isn't it?!

OPPOSITE: A nightmare in noir from "A Dead Girl Named Sue." Pictured top, jailed kid-killer Cliven Ridgeway (Josh Mikel, left) attempts to indimidate Police Chief Evan Foster (Cristian Gonzalez) while, pictured bottom, Dead Sue (Chloe Williamson) readies to take a bite out of crime...and Cliven, too!

ABOVE: Rob Draper explains to Cristian Gonzalez how the noir approach will heighten the dread of the night—"About this high," he says.

HAVE YOU EVER KNOWN ANYONE WHO HAS SUCH FUN MAKING YOUR NIGHTMARES *REEK* WITH SUCH WRETCHED REALISM? WELL, MR. DRAPER HAS SURELY SET THE MALEVOLENT *MOOD*, SO NEXT COME THE FOLKS WHO TURN THE CREEPS AND CREATURES LOOSE! *LOOK OUT!!*

CHAPTER FIVE 97

JOIN NOW! America's only CREEP FAN CLUB

$1.99

GIANT

LIFE SIZE

VENUS VAMPIRE

OVER 6 FEET TALL!

SOLD OUT!

ADDRESS _____

CITY _____

STATE _____

it's all included when you join the **CREEP FAN CLUB**

CREEPSHOW COMIC ADVERTISEMENTS FOR AMUSEMENT ONLY.

GLOWS in the DARK

LUCKY SKULL RING

MADE OF GENUINE ETERNIUM

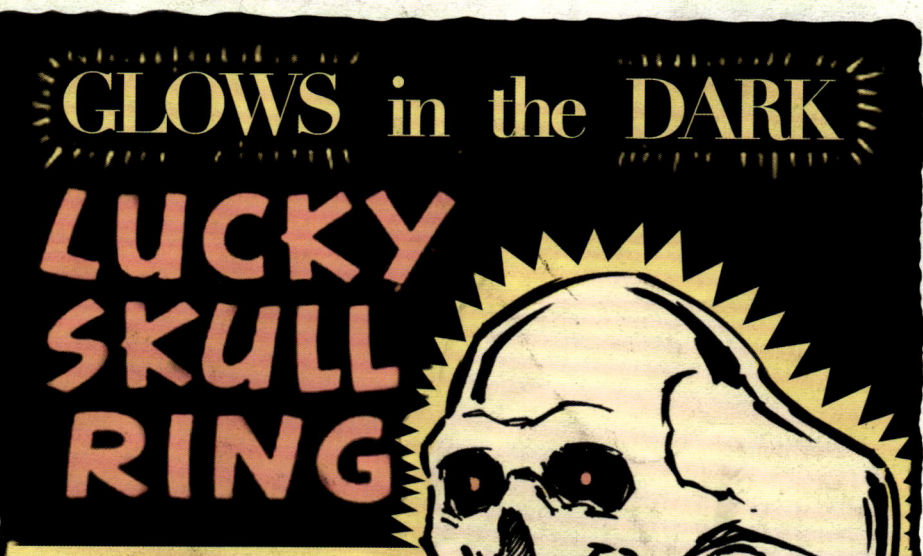

AMAZING
BY DAY an impressive, handsome, mystic skull with flashing ruby-red eyes — massive design — a heavy-duty ring for he-men.
BY NIGHT — glows with mysterious blue fire — a haunting novelty that will make you the envy of your friends
DAY OR NIGHT — packs a wallop

Eternium, "THE ETERNAL METAL," that is actually harder than steel, brilliant as silver, luxurious as platinum, never becomes dull, can't tarnish, can't wear away. SOLID Eternium, not plated. IT LOOKS EXPENSIVE:

sizes (small, med, large or ex. large)

ONLY $2.98 plus tax

BABY ALLIGATORS

PRICE $1.50

How would you like to own a real live baby alligator? Shipped directly to your door by mail, carefully packed - safe arrival guaranteed.

CREEPSHOW MONSTER HATS!

OWN PART OF A BIG LEAGUE UNIFORM
Only $2.98 Postpaid

Cap custom tailored professional Major League Cap. All-wool shaver-proof with genuine leather cushion-edged sweatband. Navy, Royal, Red, Maroon, and Navy-Red, Royal-Red Combinations.
BE SURE TO SPECIFY HEAD SIZE

HAUNTED HOUSE MYSTERY BANK

ONLY $5.95

SHUDDER WHILE YOU SAVE

If you like the chills and thrills of the undead this bank is for you, and it makes saving those coins real fun. Just place a penny, nickle, dime or (if you're independently wealthy) a quarter... on the step of the house. With a groan and rattle the door squeakily opens. The house shudders and quakes. The Horror Head sneaks out of the doorway and snatches the coin back in. The door slams shut and all is quiet again. What? Want to try it again? Go ahead. It's money in the bank!

MONEY BACK GUARANTEE

STURDY CONSTRUCTION
Sturdily constructed of metal and fibreboard for years of saving with fun. It's a perfect gift, too. Comes complete---nothing else to buy. Price only $5.95 plus 35¢ postage and handling.

7 INCHES HIGH
7 INCHES WIDE
9 INCHES DEEP

Satisfaction Absolutely Guaranteed or your money back. $1 each plus 25¢ for postage and handling Rush the Haunted House Mystery Bank to the address below. If I am not delighted with my purchase in every way I may return it within 10 days for a full purchase price refund.
☐ I enclose $5.95 plus 35¢ for postage and handling in full payment.
☐ Send C.O.D. I enclose $1.00 good will deposit and will pay balance plus C.O.D. and postage charges on arrival.

NAME ....
ADDRESS .... ZIP ....

CREEPSHOW COMIC ADVERTISEMENTS FOR AMUSEMENT ONLY.

HERE IN OUR HOME OF THE HORRID, WE HAVE A SPECIAL PLACE WHERE WE TEND TO ALL THE THINGS THAT *LIVE* AND *DIE*--AND SOMETIMES *LIVE AGAIN*--HERE AT *CREEPSHOW.*
OUR LOATHSOME LAB ISN'T FOR THE SQUEAMISH NOR FAINT OF HEART. HERE'S WHERE WE CONJURE ALL THE *GHOULS, GREMLINS,* AND GAG-WORTHY *GROTESQUERIES* THAT MAKE UP OUR COLLECTION OF...
MICHAEL BROOM 2021

Creeps, Creatures & Assorted Aberrations

"I *love* creature effects and makeup effects," Greg Nicotero beams, his eyes gleaming as he smiles wide, "and I still get excited about reading a script and reading about this cool monster. And I'm trying to imagine in my head what it looks like, and how we're gonna build it."

It's no accident, then, that Shudder's *Creepshow* is just the sort of playground where Greg and his KNB EFX gang can play, slay, or decay just about anything they can get their happy hands on. As with anything else in this production, the schedule would become the prime mover, but in the earliest pre-phase of the show, before the green light had officially been lit, the team had time to let their imaginations run wild. To be witness to their enthusiastic exchange of ideas and recollections—from start to finish of creature concept, design, development, and everything in between—is like enjoying an exuberant round of fond *remember-whens* and friendly one-upmanships with your best friends.

ABOVE: Confronting his fears, Greg grapples with a giant tarantula in the KNB shop.

LEFT: Harlan the bug hunter (Josh McDermitt) suddenly has that pesky creepy-crawly feeling. (From "Pesticide.")

CHAPTER SIX 101

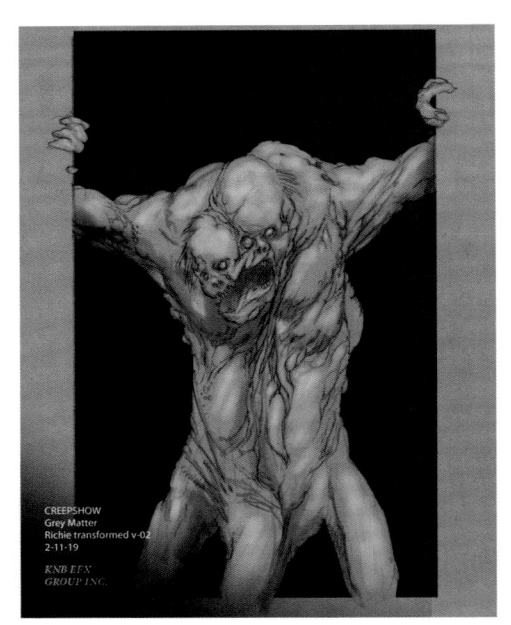

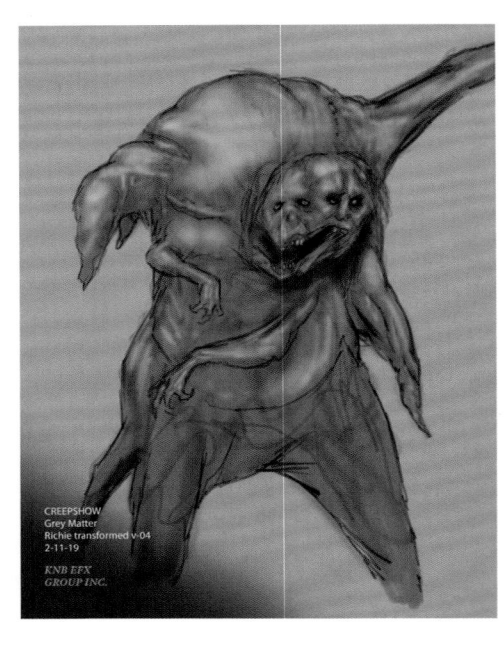

ABOVE: Conceptual art by John Wheaton (top row) and Michael Broom (bottom row) as they imagine the mind-bending metamorphosis of Richie Grenadine. (From "Gray Matter.")

"It started with a barrage of scripts as we were preparing for Season One," begins KNB Shop Supervisor, Carey Jones. He's a real pro, been at it almost two decades, and when he's not creating the creatures, he's often performing as them (in Shudder's *Creepshow*, he appears as the Djinn in "The Man in the Suitcase," the Scarecrow in "The Companion," and the Gill Man in "Model Kid"). "We read all the scripts—the design team here [at KNB] with artists Mike Broom and John Wheaton—and we got together here in the office and just talked about ideas, creatures, and different things like that. And Greg would throw in his ideas...and then we'd all go away. We'd come back later with all of these sketches and designs that we'd put up on the screen in Greg's office, and we'd just sift through them, and we'd critique them: 'Oh, that one's cool,' or 'Maybe take the head from this one and put it on the body of that one.' 'Now, put some spikes on it.' And we had these meetings every week where we'd sit down and go through these ideas, and this is actually the most fun part of this whole process."

For a period of months before *Creepshow* was officially a show, this creature design team considered different approaches for the different monsters lurking within the stack of scripts that Greg had on his desk. And, as previously revealed, while some scripts were fully fleshed out, others weren't scripts at all; sometimes they were as little as a few sentences. And creature details? Well, that was all quite vague, pretty much across the board.

"But that's the best way to design," Cary says, leaning forward. "We weren't locked into what we get a lot of the time: specifics like, 'It has to be this tall' or 'this wide' or 'this color' or whatever. We're able to take the handcuffs off and just go for it. And when there are no limitations on the designs or any constraints about how to execute them, that's the way to get your mind free as to what you can create, and that's why we were able to come up with so much cool stuff."

Concept artist John Wheaton nods his head in agreement, noting that most often, the details of a creature are left unspecified, perhaps by design. "Greg usually has a general idea of what he wants," John says. "He might say he has this piece of art another artist did that inspired him, and other times he might make reference to other films as a source of reference for our designs, but we always try to push the limit and do something that hasn't been seen before—and that's what Greg really likes—something that's really wild and out there."

Michael Broom, the other concept artist who shares an office with John Wheaton, offers insight into his approach during these creative pow-wows: "I usually like to make little thumbnail

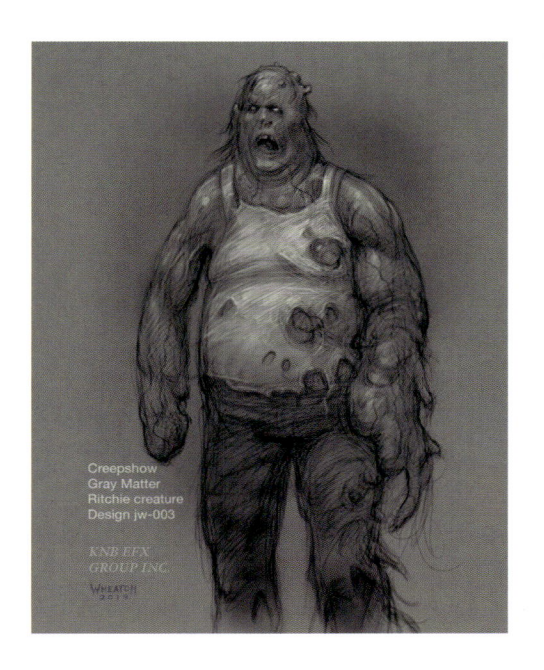

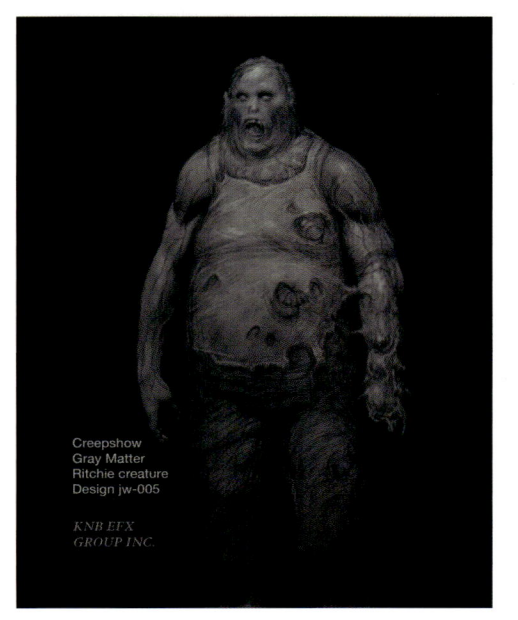

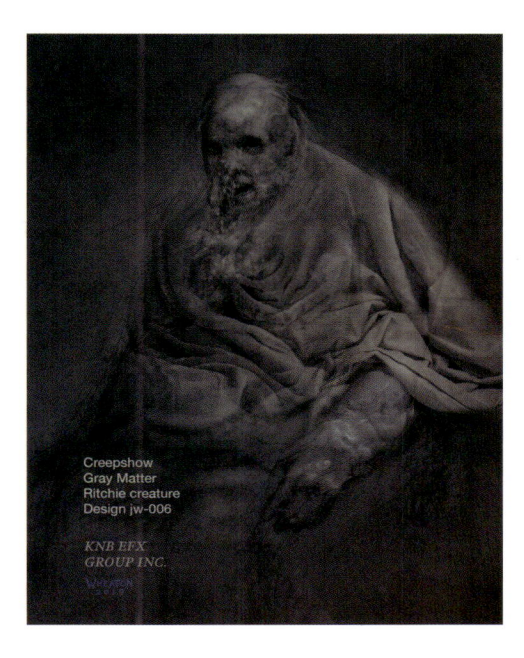

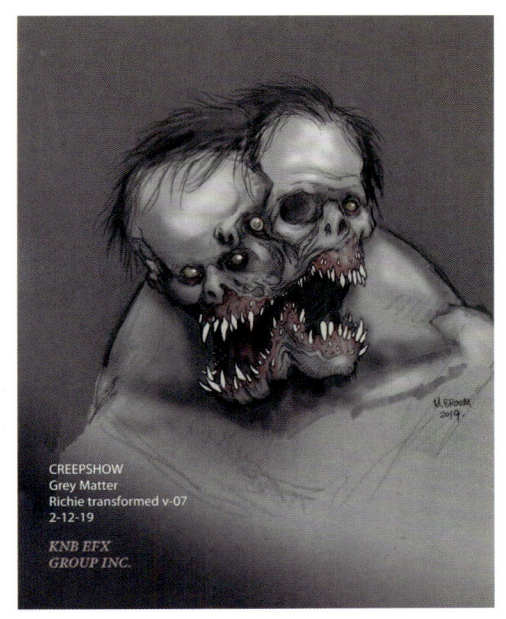

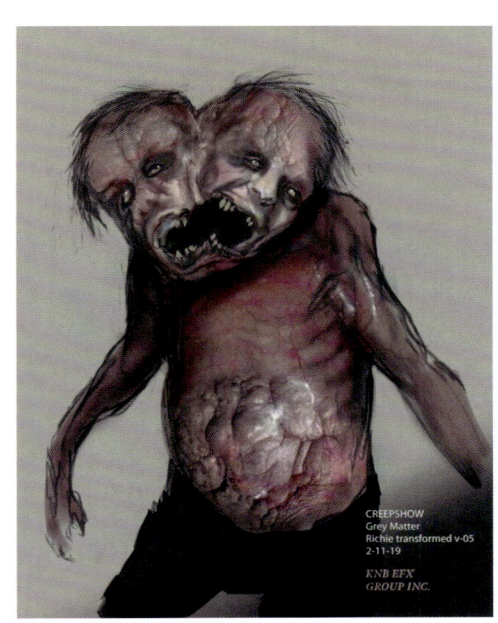

ABOVE: More "Gray Matter" concept art by John Wheaton (top row) and Michael Broom (middle row), plus the Ritchie-monster made flesh in the KNB shop (bottom row).

CHAPTER SIX 103

v-06

v-02

v-03

v-07

v-08

v-04

v-05

CREEPSHOW S2
Alien head options
Design 06

KNB EFX
GROUP INC.

CREEPSHOW S2
Alien head options
Design 02

KNB EFX
GROUP INC.

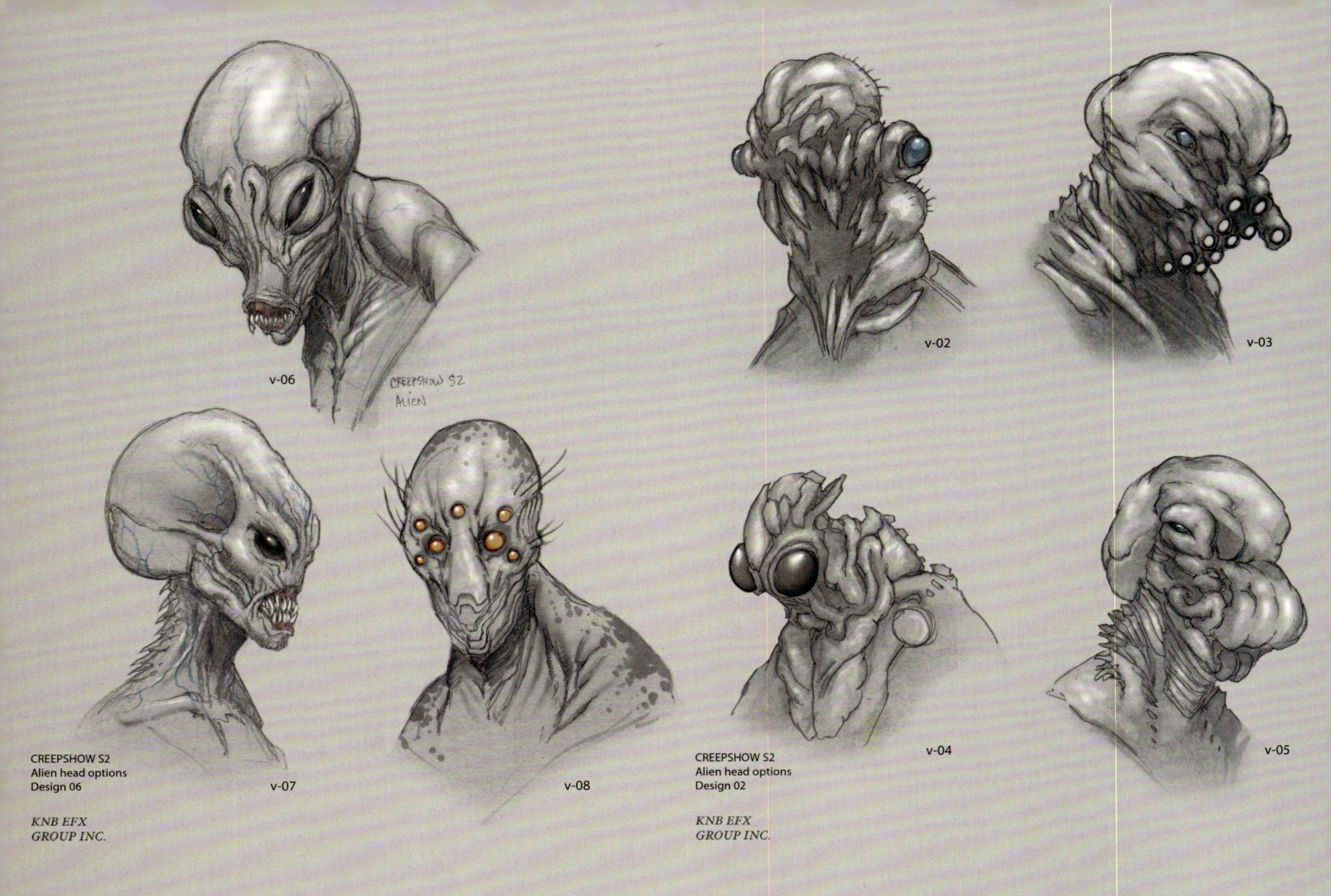

CREEPSHOW S2
Alien options
Design 012

KNB EFX
GROUP INC.

CREEPSHOW S2
Alien options
Design 011

KNB EFX
GROUP INC.

sketches and notes, working with the initial impressions I'm getting from Greg or Carey while they tell me what they're thinking. For me, I think so visually that I try to make those thumbnails as we talk. In some cases, those thumbnails turn out to be pretty dead on to the final design; I just have to rigor it out [to completion]."

OK. He admits that he's not always there with the final, *final* take. "The alien from 'The Right Snuff,'" he recalls, "was one where we used the head I had designed, going back to the first thumbnail I did, but sculptor Dave Grasso sculpted a different maquette body for it. I had done a sort of humanoid body but he had come up with a really cool sort of alien body, so we went with the big-brained, cyclopean head I designed, then added it to the body that Dave Grasso did."

That's the purpose of thumbnails—to put a stake in the ground, to establish that starting point, then allow the creative process to do its thing. It was the same for the demon in "Familiar." Writer Josh Malerman hadn't specified any details of the "demon" that apparently followed Jackson to the psychic's table. Greg simply assured him, "Don't worry. We'll take care of it."

"And that's what made it cool for us," Carey says. "Greg just threw out some obscure references for what he liked, demon-wise. And we told the guys not to worry about how we were going to do it;

OPPOSITE: Evolution of an alien being from "The Right Snuff." Art by Michael Broom.

BELOW: A monstrous mash-up that pairs Michael Broom's alien head design with a new body design conceived by Dave Grasso (top row), then the alien's head takes shape in the KNB shop (bottom row).

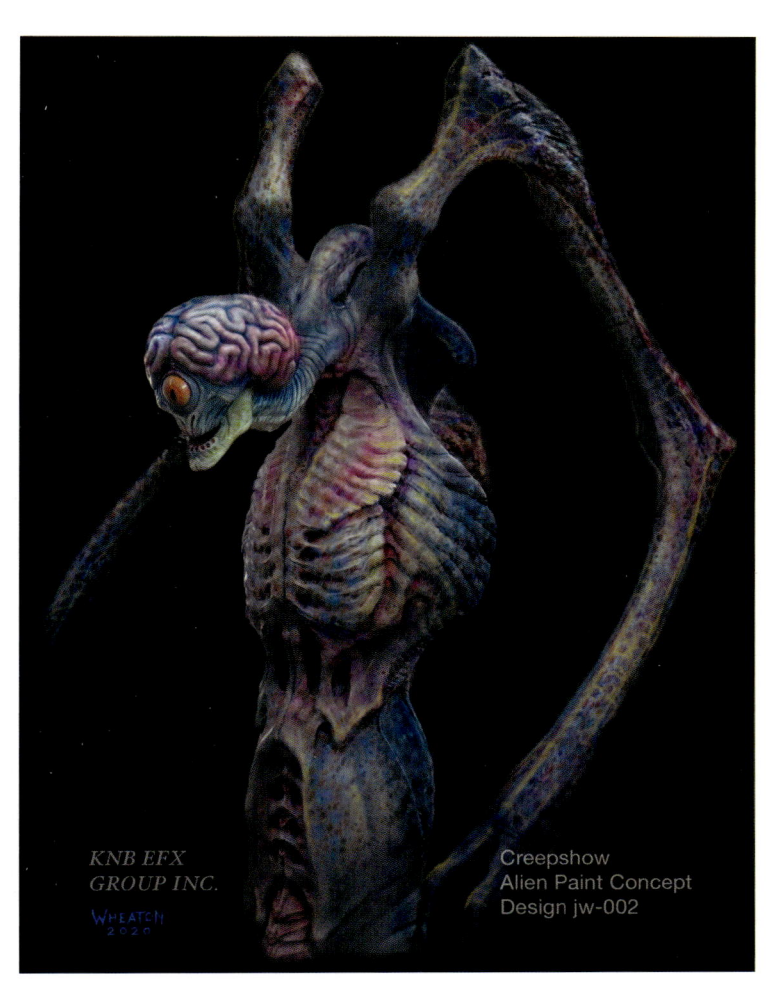

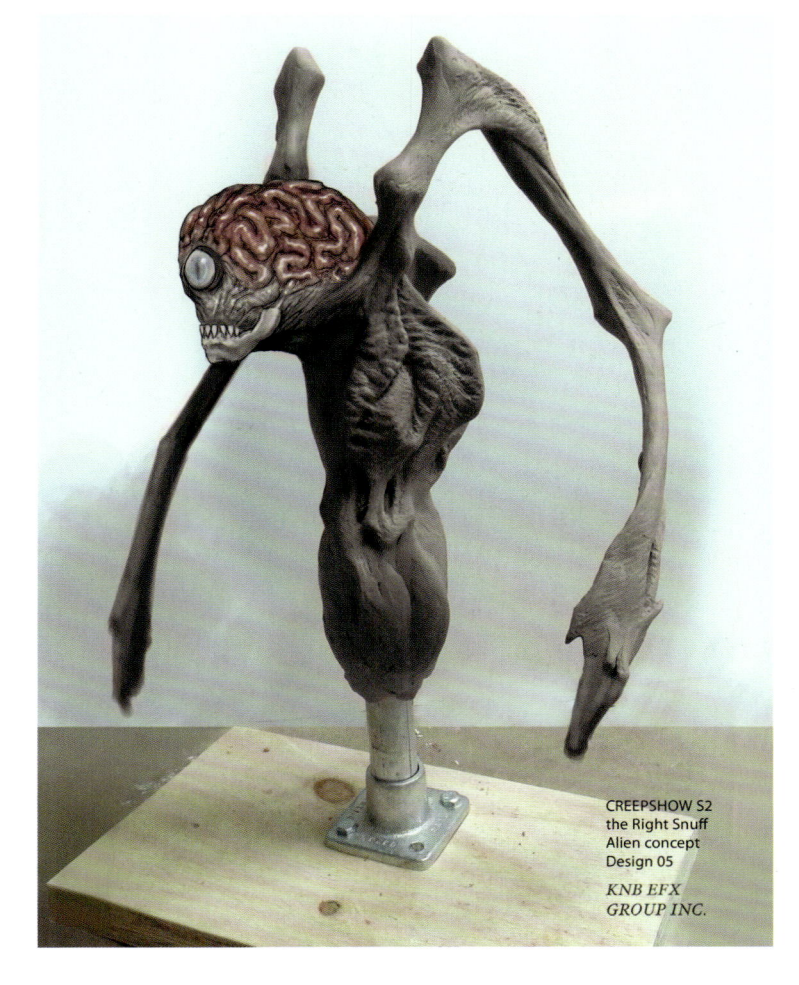

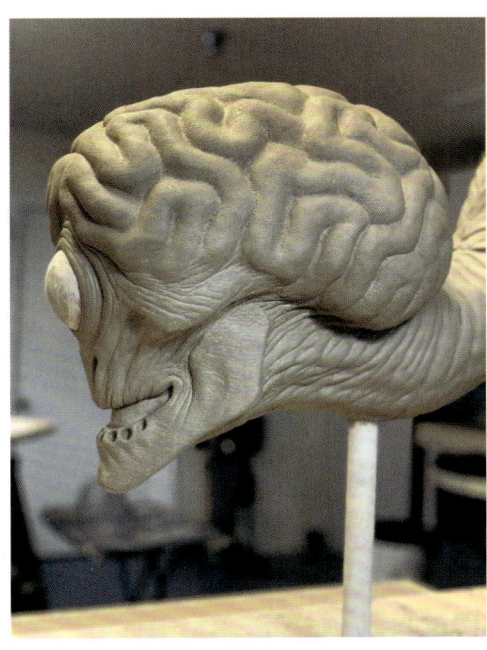

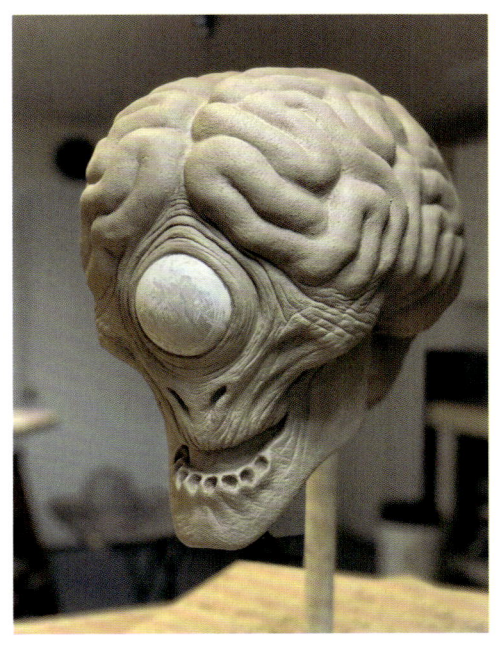

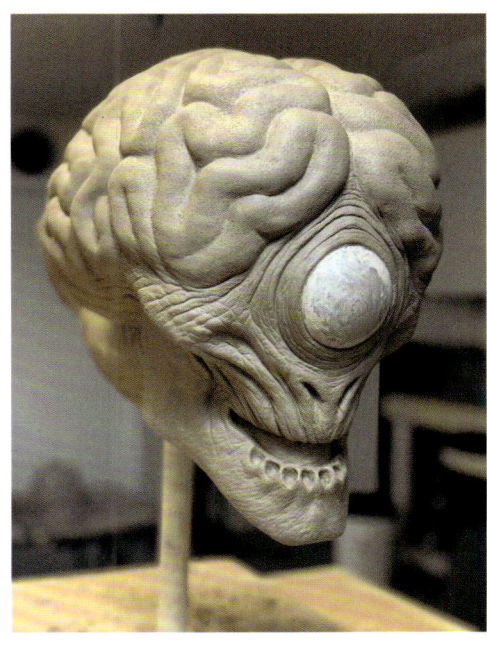

CHAPTER SIX 105

Creepshow S2
Demon
Design jw-007

KNB EFX
GROUP INC.

WHEATON
2020

TOP: John Wheaton's design provides foundation for the "Familiar" demon.

we never wanted them locked in to anything when they were designing it. We kept tweaking and tweaking and tweaking it in design, then we had Jaremy Aiello sculpt it—and, again, even in the sculpture, it gets tweaked. Seeing it on a head-form, then I start thinking, 'OK, this is how we can physically make it work,' and that's when other tweaks happen."

When Carey and team take a refined idea back to Greg for his blessing, he might ask for more adjustments or, with schedule in mind, might say, "Yeah, that's close enough. We'll figure out the rest later."

"Design-wise, it never has to be fully, *fully* developed," Carey continues, "because I know in the process from 'that design' to the 'finished thing,' there's gonna be changes that make it slightly different. We take the design process up to a point, knowing that once we get it farther along, it *is* going to change—and we're OK with that because we know that's the nature of what we're doing. And, a lot of times, the schedule gets us to the point where I have to pull it out of design. We sometimes only have, like, a week to turn this stuff around, so I have to ask if we've got it to where we know the idea's right, and the rest we'll finish in sculpture or 3D design or however we decide to build it."

106   CHAPTER SIX

That "build," then, clearly implies that practical effects are the preferred method for *Creepshow* creatures over digital execution, right? Carey considers for a moment, his eyes searching a bit, clarifying and qualifying his answer in his head before making any proclamation of "yea" or "nay."

"Not...necessarily," he ventures. "Well...yes and no. Yes, it's preferred—in my opinion—as a performer and for other performers. And even for shooting, as directors and DPs, just to have something physically there that they can look at and light...and actors can react to. But, at the same time, there's some times when Vis-EFX makes sense...or a combination of the two makes best sense."

He's right, of course. These days, actors are routinely forced to interact with the colored end of a long stick. Elsewhere, cameramen glide around a person in a black body suit who's being attacked by a horde of ping pong balls. Scary stuff. But, for *Creepshow*, there's an elegant marrying of both: honest-to-goodness ghouls on set, with conscientiously conceived after-effects to give final flavor to the frights...all while keeping the segments on time and within budget.

The "Familiar" demon evolves into the sculpting phase (opposite, bottom), then...look out for the fully realized creature in flesh, blood, and latex (above)!

CHAPTER SIX 107

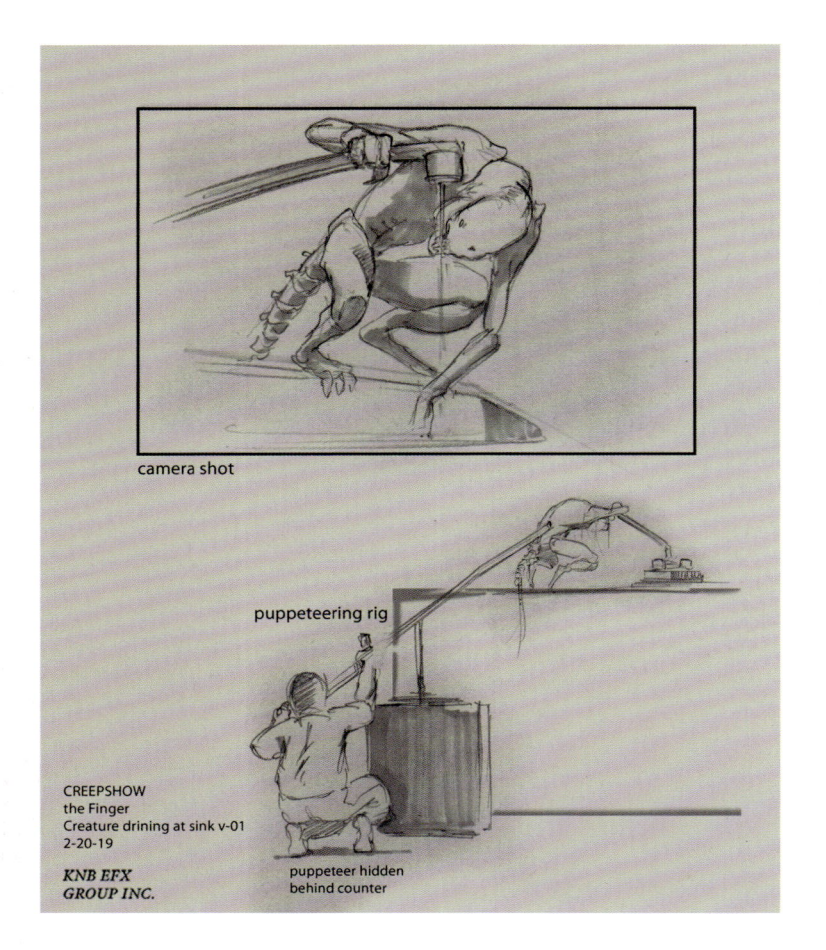

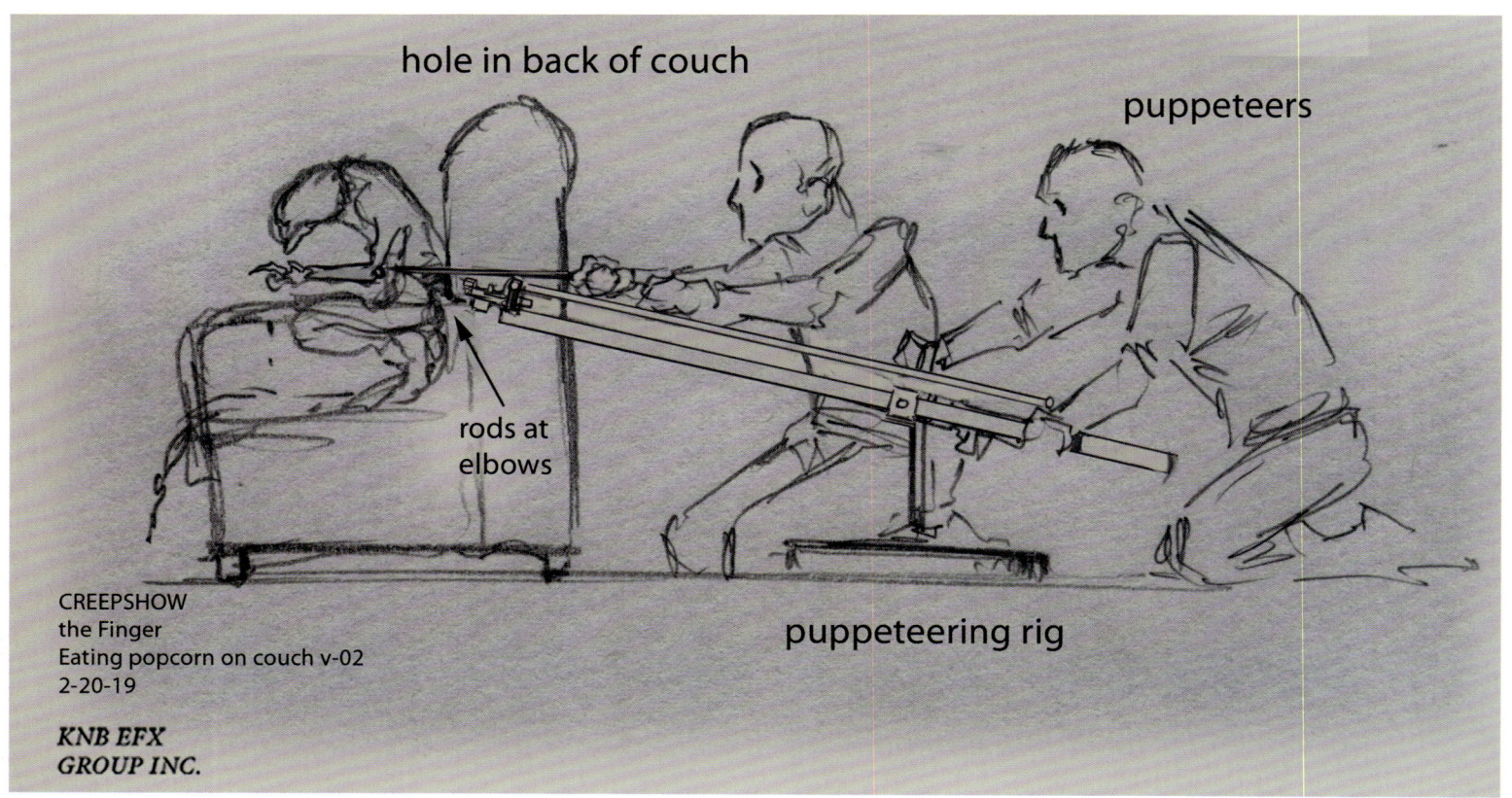

camera shot

puppeteering rig

CREEPSHOW
the Finger
Creature drining at sink v-01
2-20-19

KNB EFX GROUP INC.

puppeteer hidden behind counter

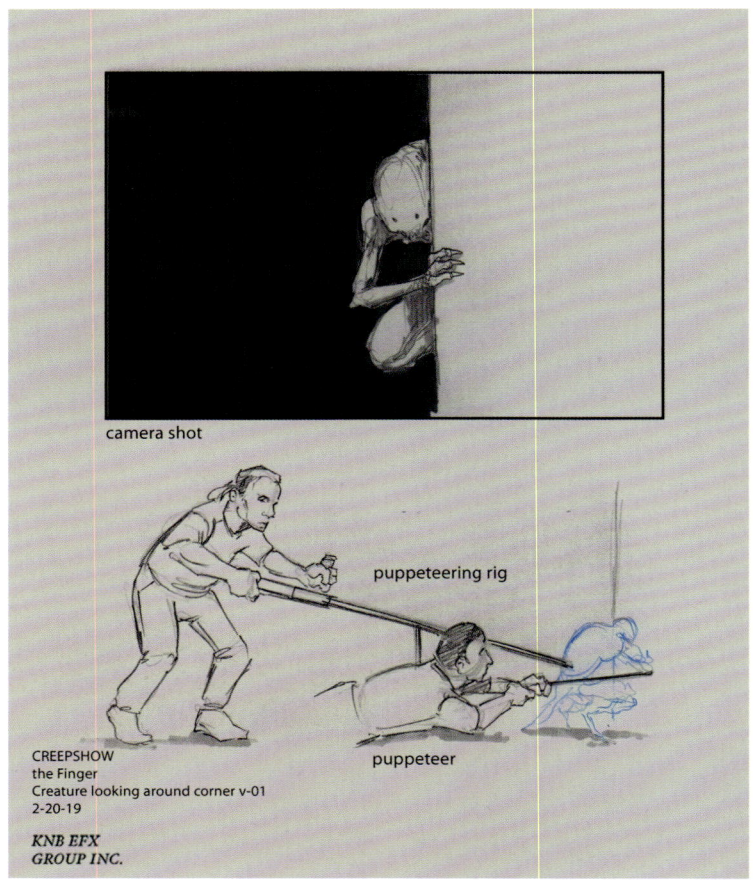

camera shot

puppeteering rig

puppeteer

CREEPSHOW
the Finger
Creature looking around corner v-01
2-20-19

KNB EFX GROUP INC.

hole in back of couch

puppeteers

rods at elbows

puppeteering rig

CREEPSHOW
the Finger
Eating popcorn on couch v-02
2-20-19

KNB EFX GROUP INC.

ABOVE: Designs for puppeteering Bob, the faithful finger-ling to Clark Wilson. (From "The Finger.")

OPPOSITE: The completed Bob, showing off his range of moods and motions.

"Yeah, we did a lot of rod puppets and rod removal, and puppeteer removal, because that made more sense than creating a full digital character. And it looked real because the thing was there—physically there—and it was in the space and everybody was looking at the right thing, and the lighting was right. For [Vis-EFX] to only have to digitally remove the rods and the puppeteers...that was cost effective."

Carey and his team established practical solutions for their practical effects, often employing some truly inventive methods that fooled even the most effects-savvy viewers. Consider Bob of "The Finger," Clark Wilson's home-grown hit pet that likely could be mistaken as H.R. Giger's idea of a housecat. So, when some online wiseguy decried the segment's lousy CGI rendering of Bob, well, the truth was that Clark's lap-sized pal was done entirely as a rod puppet and...wait for it...a stop-motion marionette (for Bob's wide-shot scurrying). So there.

CHAPTER SIX

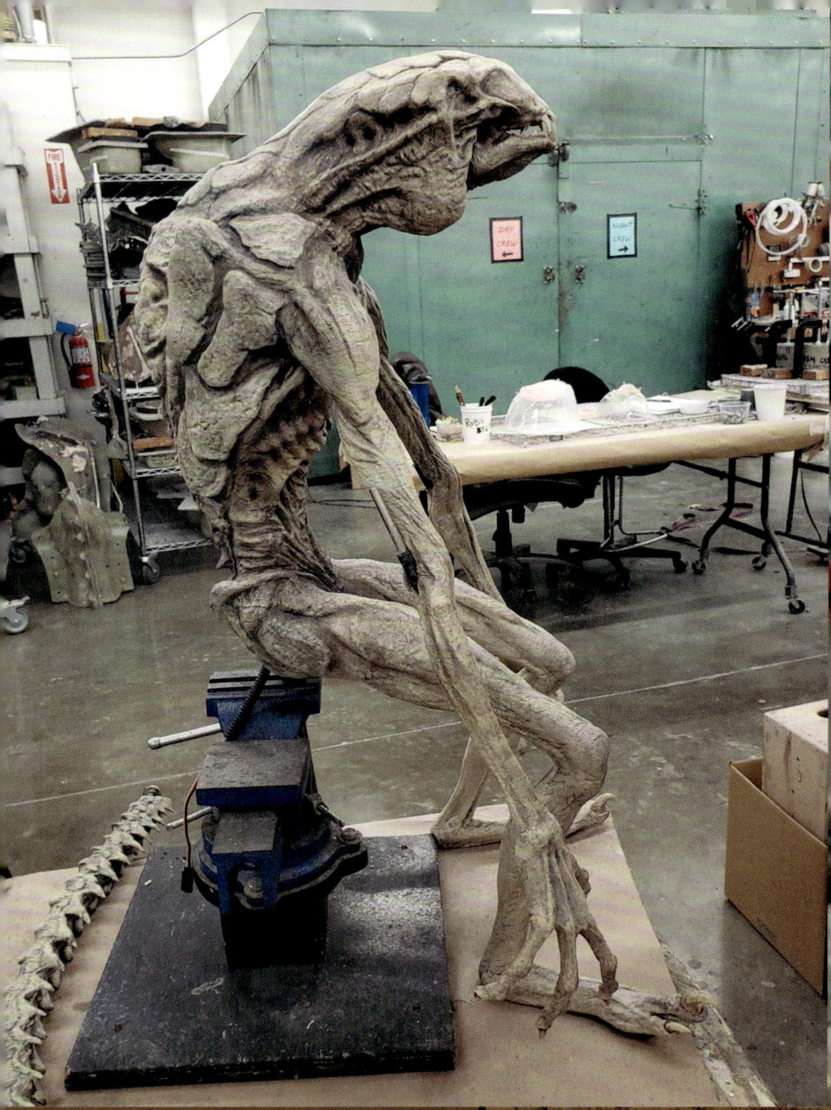
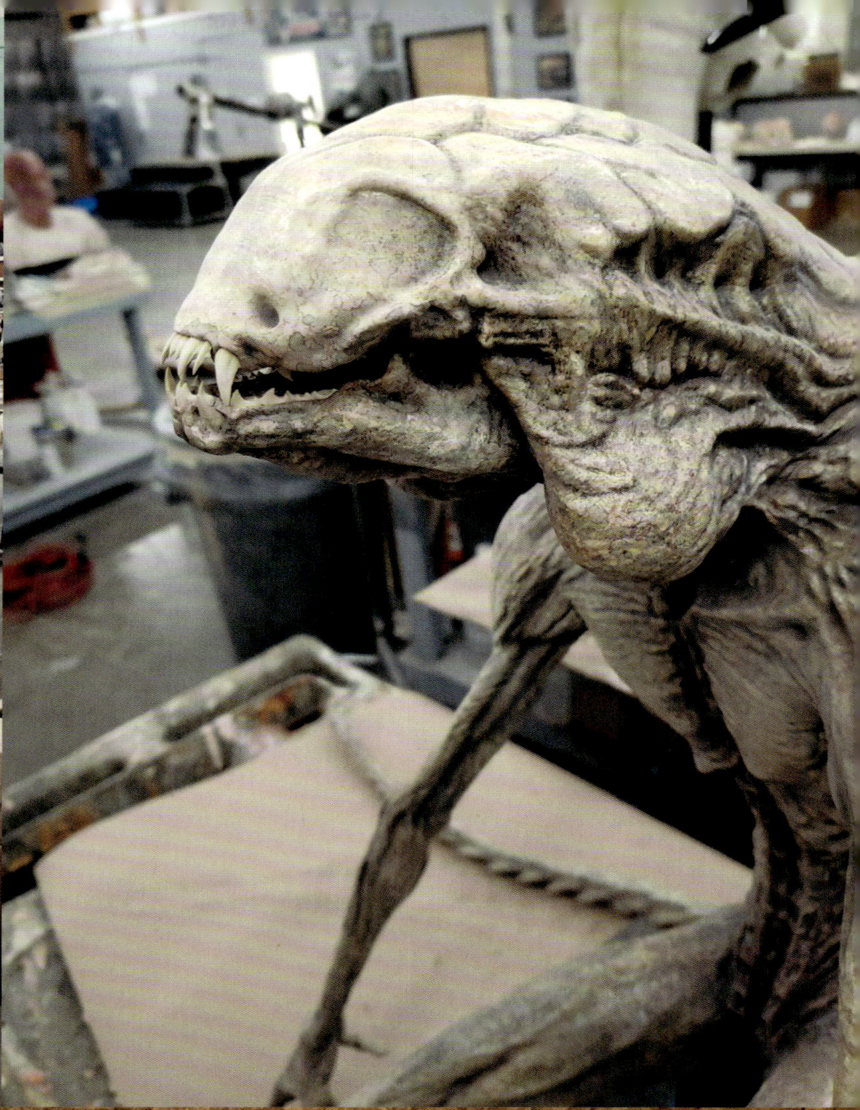
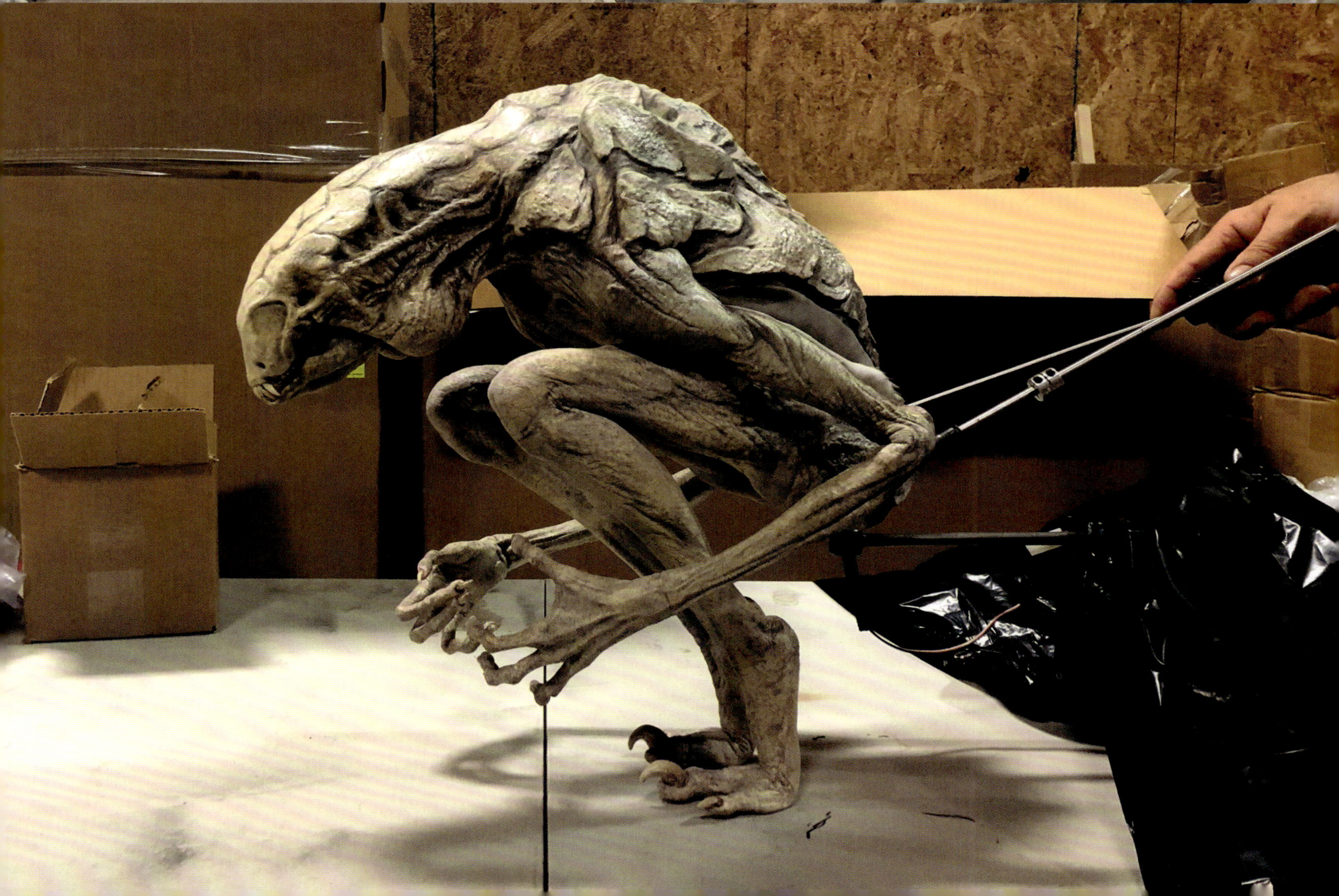

CREEPSHOW S2
Queen Bee
Design 01

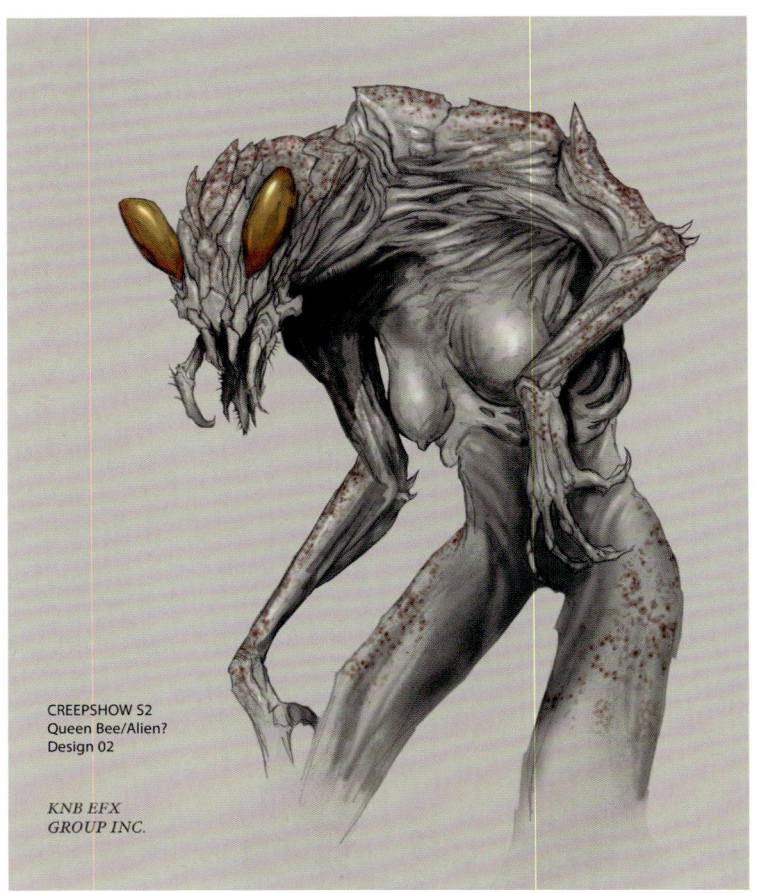

KNB EFX
GROUP INC.

CREEPSHOW S2
Queen Bee/Alien?
Design 02

KNB EFX
GROUP INC.

ABOVE: What's a "Queen Bee" look like when she's in her full glory? From Michael Broom's mind, the options are practically limitless.

OPPOSITE: Michael Broom's design hones in on the horrific honey-beast (top and middle rows) while John Wheaton provides a color design (bottom left), and the KNB team sculpt her in intended third-scale realization (bottom right).

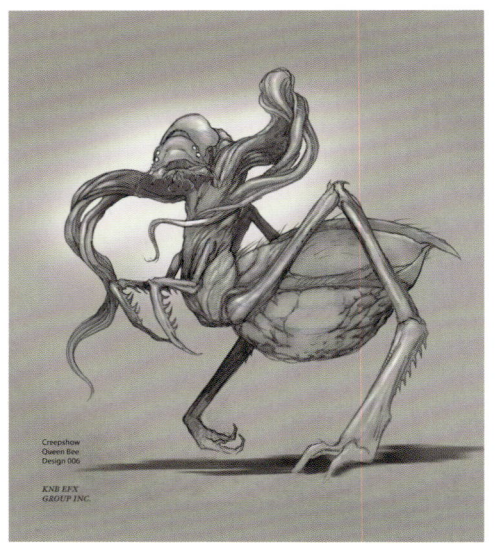

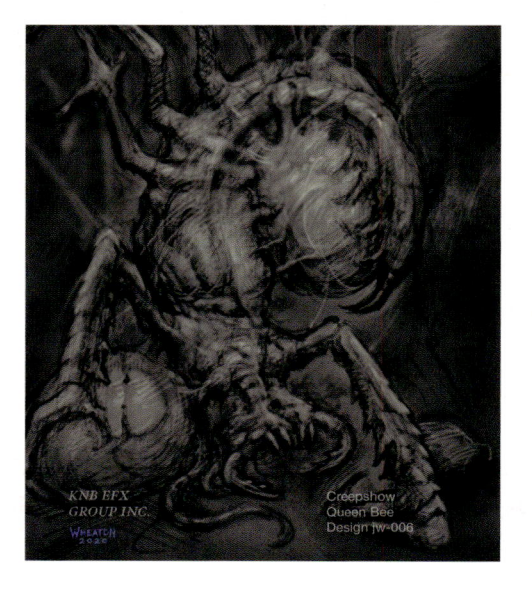

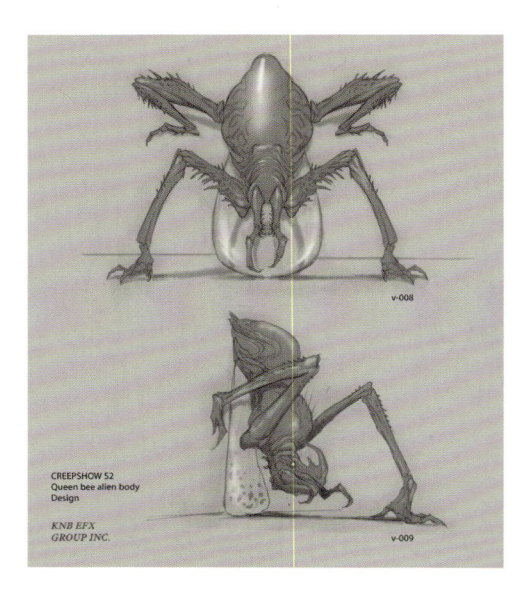

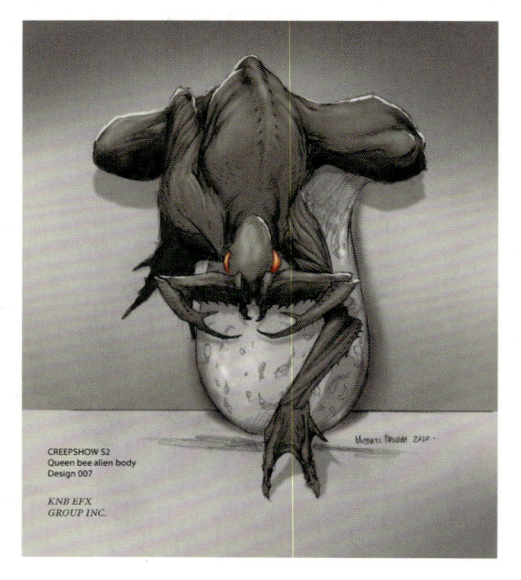

110   CHAPTER SIX

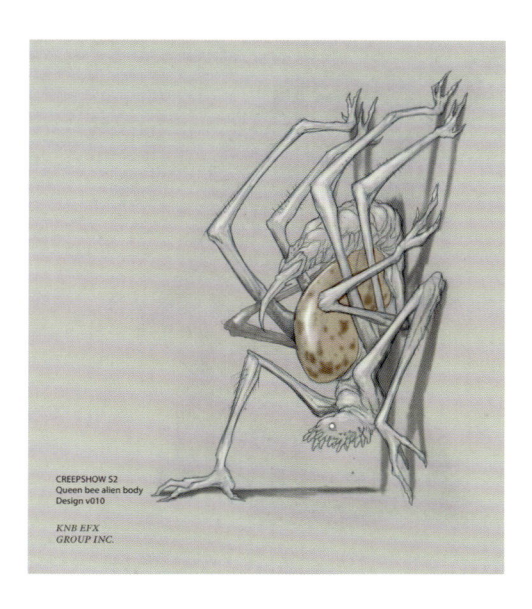

CREEPSHOW S2
Queen bee alien body
Design v010
KNB EFX
GROUP INC.

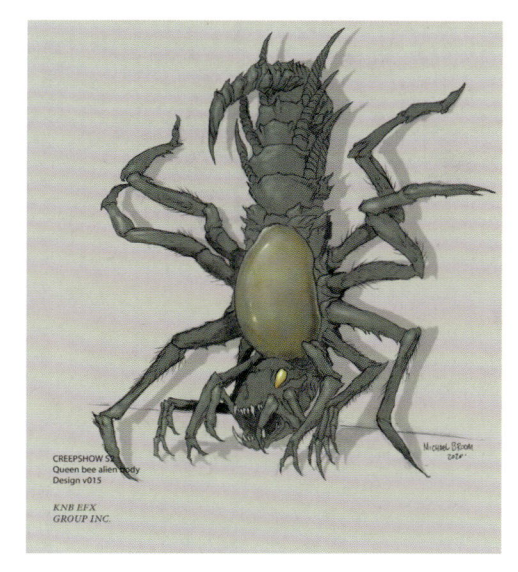

CREEPSHOW S2
Queen bee alien body
Design v015
KNB EFX
GROUP INC.

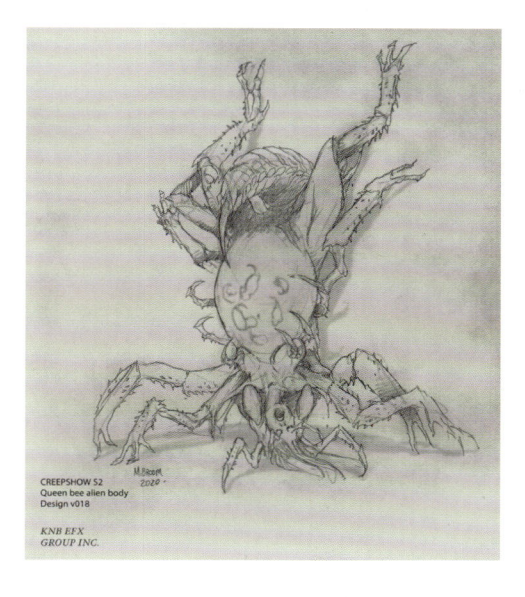

CREEPSHOW S2
Queen bee alien body
Design v018
KNB EFX
GROUP INC.

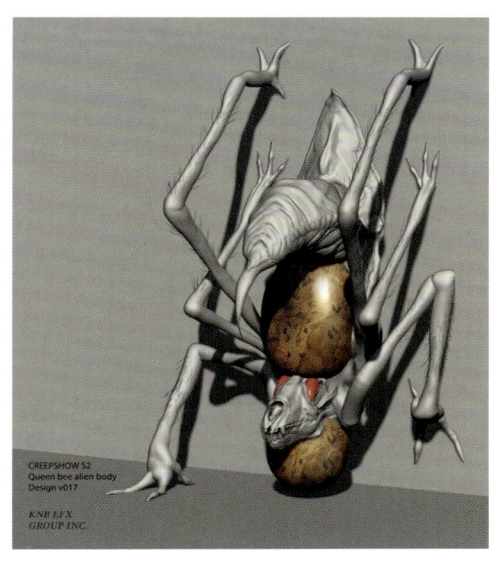

CREEPSHOW S2
Queen bee alien body
Design v017
KNB EFX
GROUP INC.

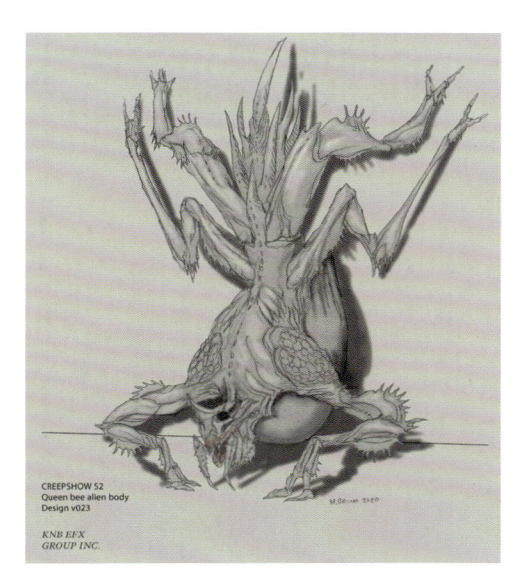

CREEPSHOW S2
Queen bee alien body
Design v023
KNB EFX
GROUP INC.

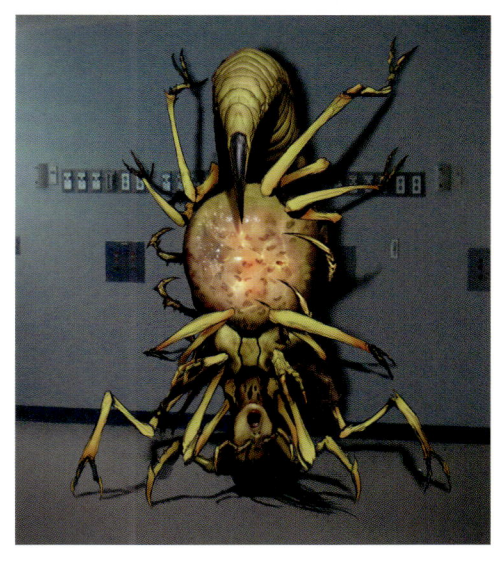

KNB EFX
GROUP INC.

Creepshow
Queen Bee Paint
Design jw-003

CHAPTER SIX 111

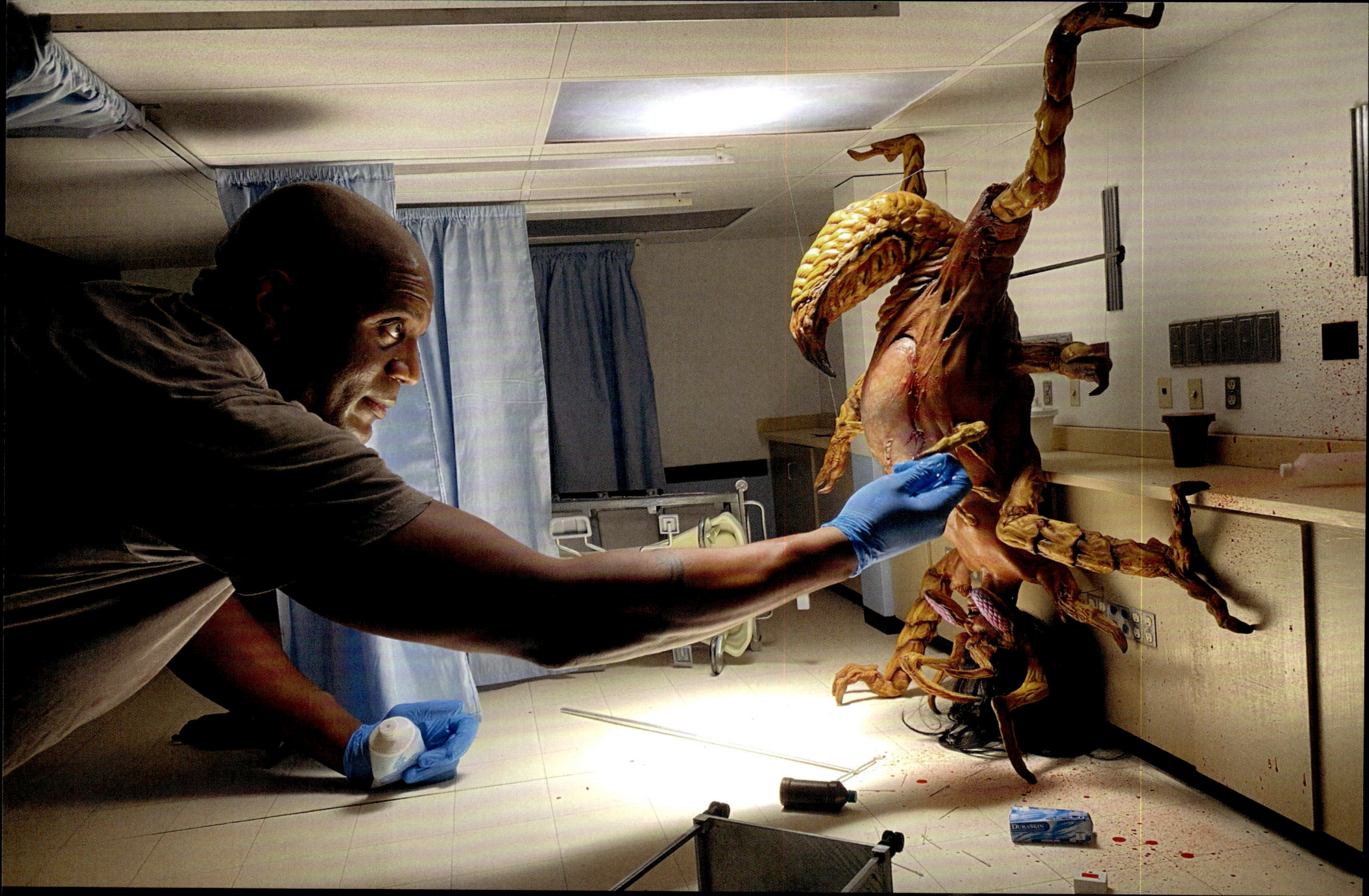
DURASKIN

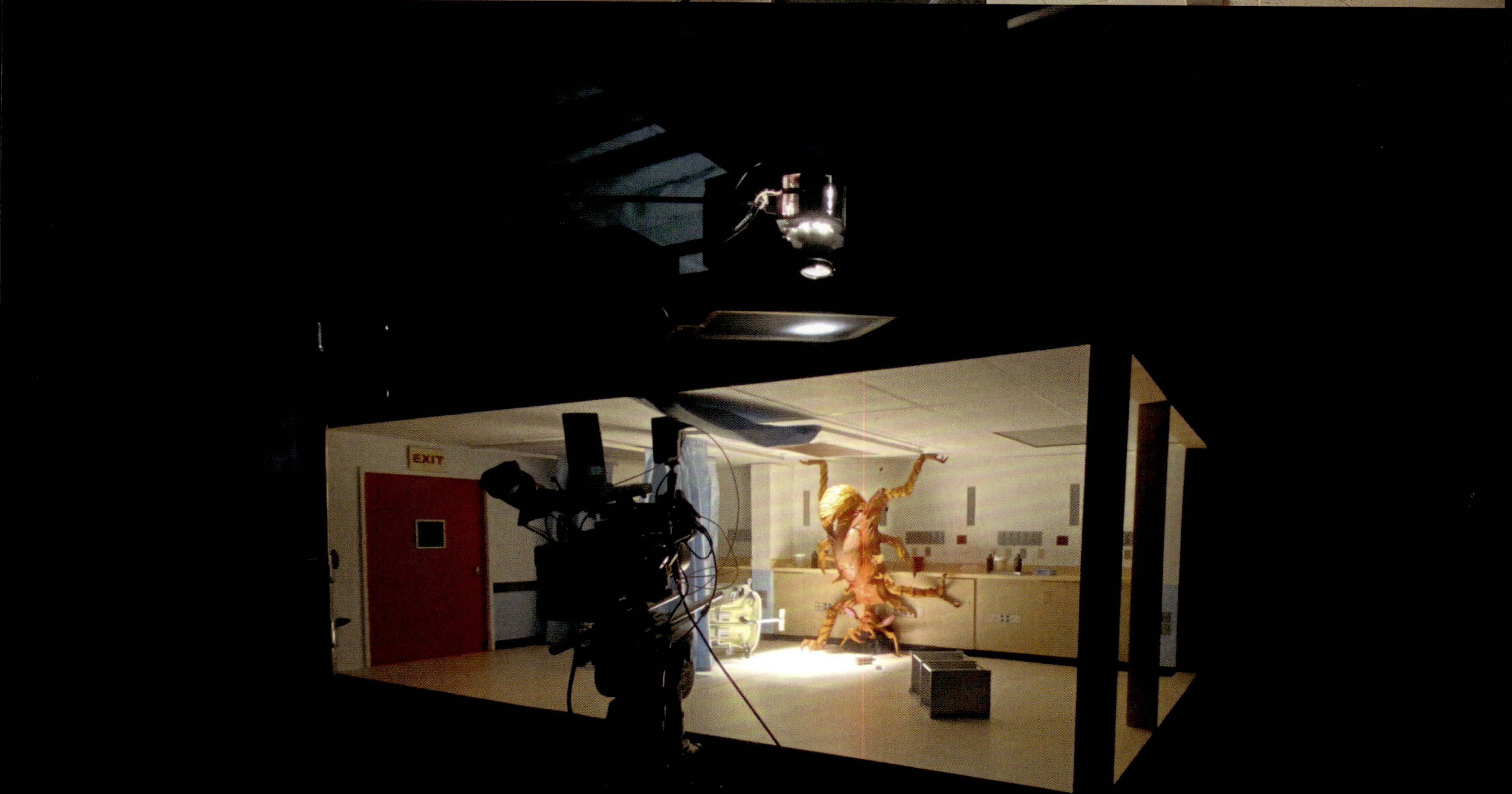
EXIT

Think you got it all figured out? Well, jump over to Season Three's "Queen Bee" and you'll be amazed when you learn that the transformation of the lovely pop idol Regina (Kaelynn Gobert-Harris) into an insectoid superstar was done through a combination of full-sized practical elements and a third-scale miniature.

"That whole transformation was shot as a miniature," Greg explains. "We shot it at KNB a couple of weeks after [principal photography] had wrapped. We designed this cool creature, and she was sort of upside-down, and I loved that the legs were up on the ceiling and the head was upside-down...and that was all a rod puppet."

Adding to that clever third-scale miniature approach, including the intricate Queen Bee armature fashioned by Dave Wogh, there was the perfectly rendered miniature hospital room set, also built by Wogh. The furniture and other pieces in that set were created from digital image scans, rendered by Dave Grasso, and 3D-printed to use as detailed set pieces—all the way down to miniature boxes of rubber gloves and cups and all else you see. Digital, made practical. Why not?

Practically speaking, there does come that physical handoff of the effects elements from the KNB shop to the effects crew in Atlanta, often overseen by Philadelphia-born Gino Crognale. As a veteran special effects artist and performer, he's battle tested in all realms of effects makeup and puppetry—from *The Faculty* to *The Final Destination* to *The Walking Dead*—and he has plenty of boots-on-the-ground stories to tell about how he and his compatriots pull off every *Creepshow* mission assigned to them.

"Like Carey said, we go from script to concept, and we'll kick around conceptual ideas, and that's when Broom and 'Wheaty' [John Wheaton] do some designs, some quick modeling on the computer. Then, KNB has to look at the schedule to see how much time we have to build this and what they can give to me. When that stuff is shipped in [to Atlanta], whatever prosthetics they are, whatever type of puppet—whatever it is, I get it in the state that those guys left it. Sometimes stuff isn't finished or painted; it's as much as they could do in the time they had, so *my* job is the execution of the makeups; whatever shows up, I have to look at it and pre-paint it and make it look like what it's supposed to look like, as best as I can. I'm in the field, guns loaded, and we have to shoot tomorrow morning."

Don't feel too badly for Gino. Like everyone else in the company, he loves this stuff. There's a thrill in his scramble. Given he's been at this for over three decades and has enjoyed a working relationship with Greg for just as long, when the crunch-time moments arise, he's ready and able to respond...with whatever it takes!

OPPOSITE: Carey Jones makes some final touches to the "Queen Bee" (top), and the incredibly detailed third-scale hospital set, built by Dave Wogh.

BELOW: Dave Wogh animates the movements of the raging Queen Bee.

CHAPTER SIX 113

Creepshow
Werewolf V4-A
KNB EFX
Group Inc.

Creepshow
Werewolf V4-B
KNB EFX
Group Inc.

Creepshow
Werewolf V4-D
KNB EFX
Group Inc.

Creepshow
Werewolf V4-C
KNB EFX
Group Inc.

Creepshow
Werewolf V3
KNB EFX
Group Inc.

Creepshow
Werewolf V2-A
KNB EFX
Group Inc.

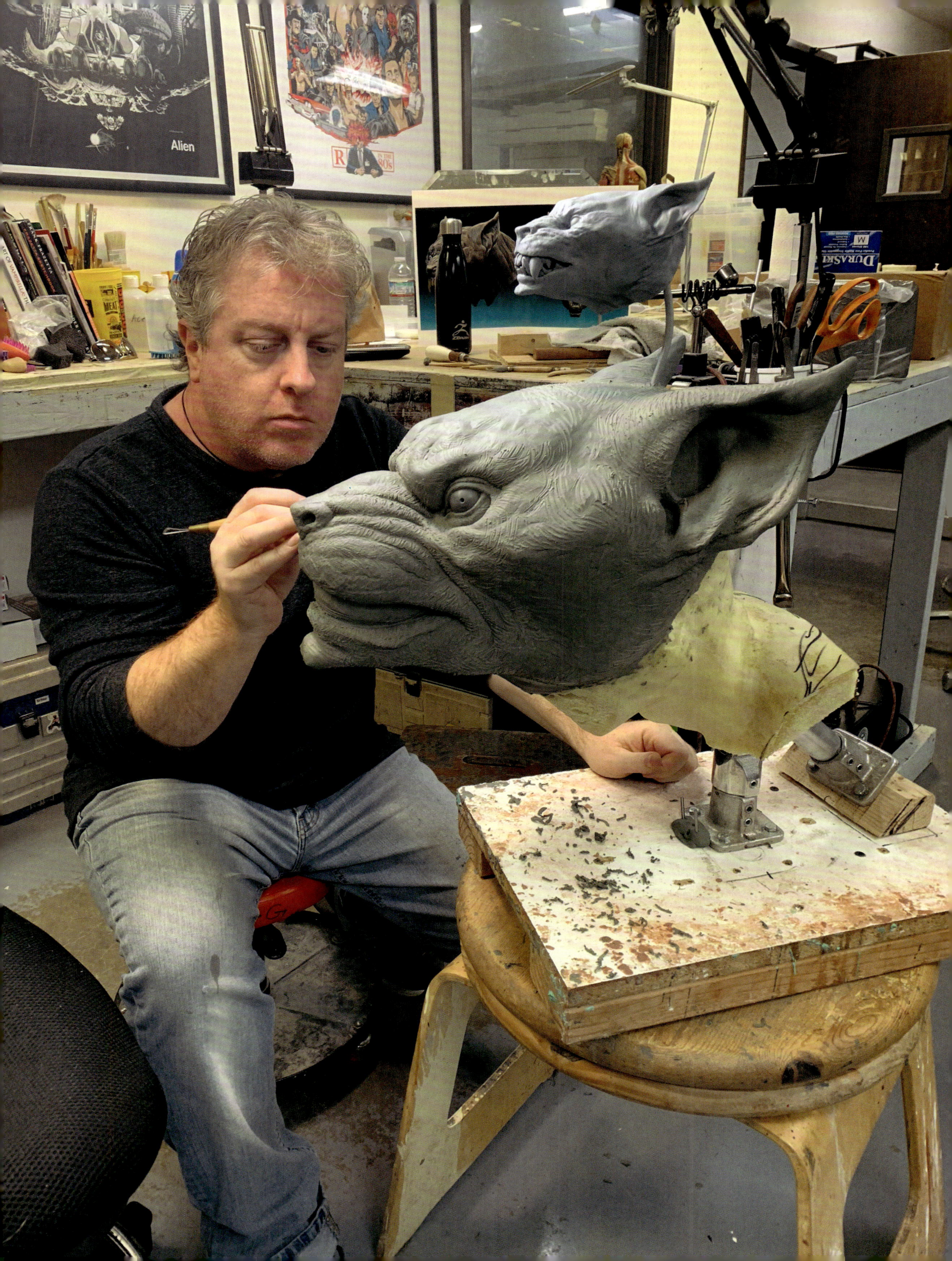
Alien

PREVIOUS SPREAD, LEFT: Where-wolf? Everywhere! Concept art for "Bad Wolf Down" by John Wheaton.

PREVIOUS SPREAD, RIGHT: Dave Grasso sculpts a howlingly-horrific wolf head at KNB.

RIGHT: Michael Broom's werewolf design that would become the Captain Talby wolf (portrayed by Andy Rusk) in "Bad Wolf Down."

OPPOSITE: Howling-good homages to werewolf features we've known and loved—can you guess them? (Pictured top are Jeffrey Combs, attacked by Carey Jones; bottom left is Jonathan Thomas.)

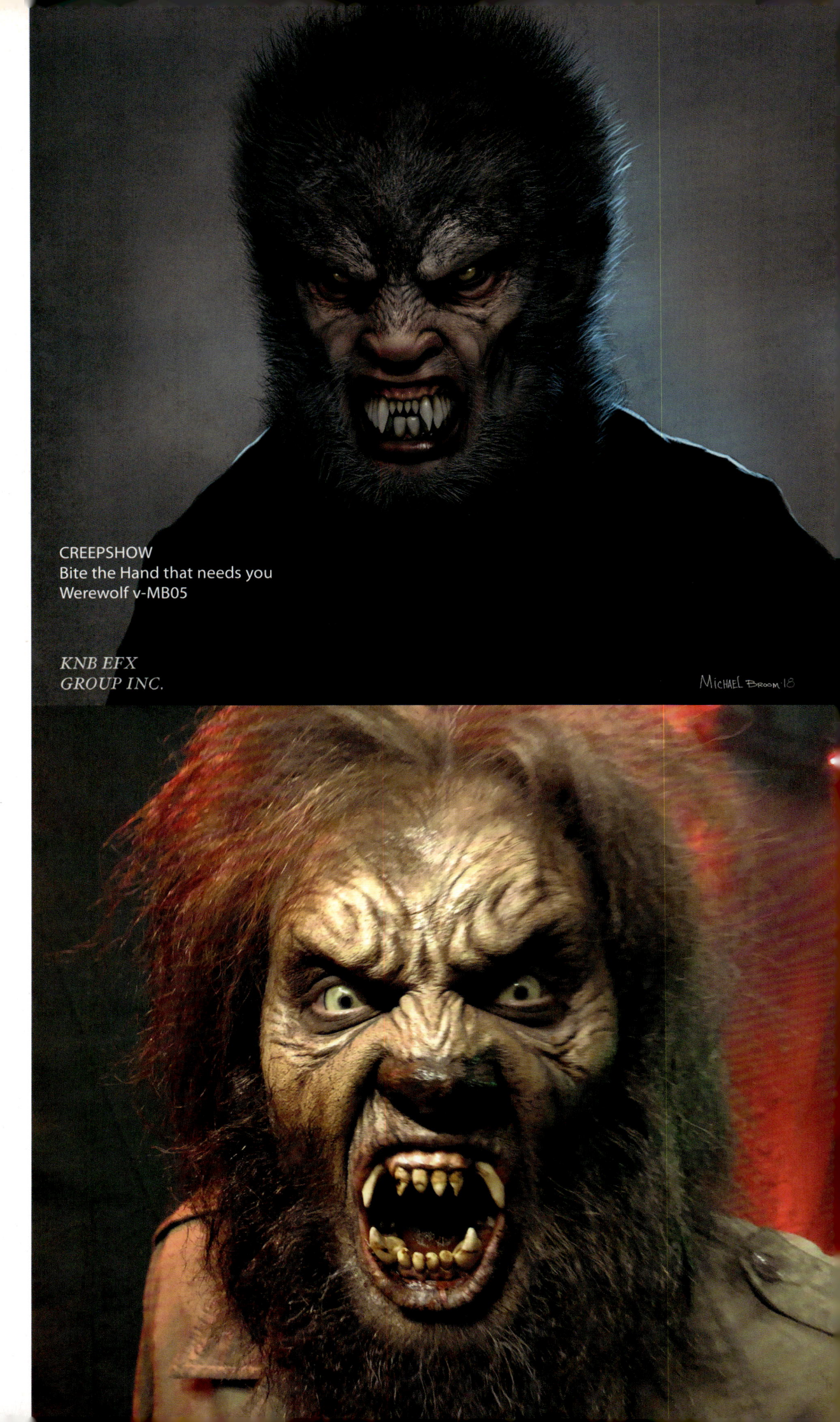

CREEPSHOW
Bite the Hand that needs you
Werewolf v-MB05

KNB EFX
GROUP INC.

116 CHAPTER SIX

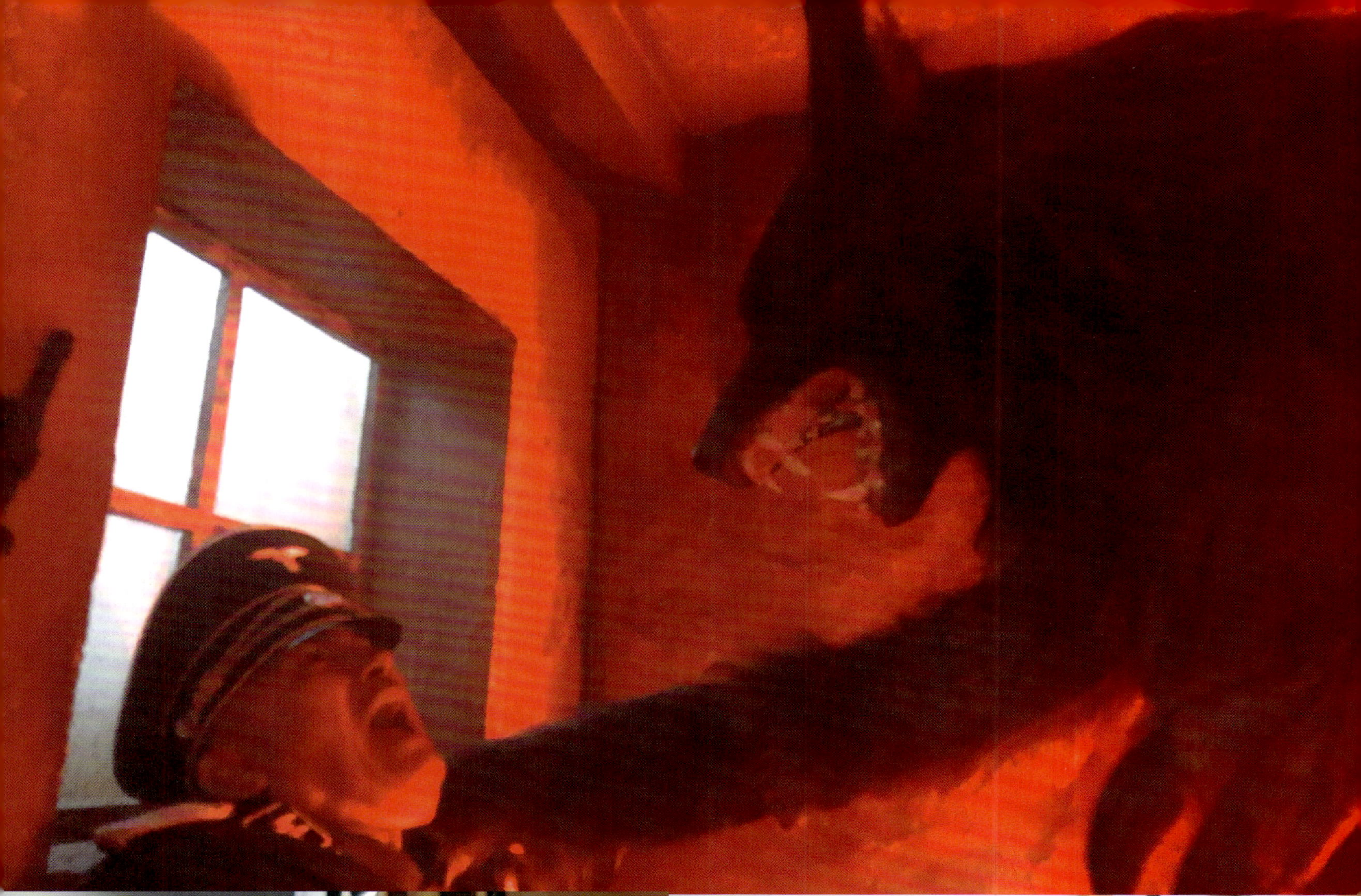

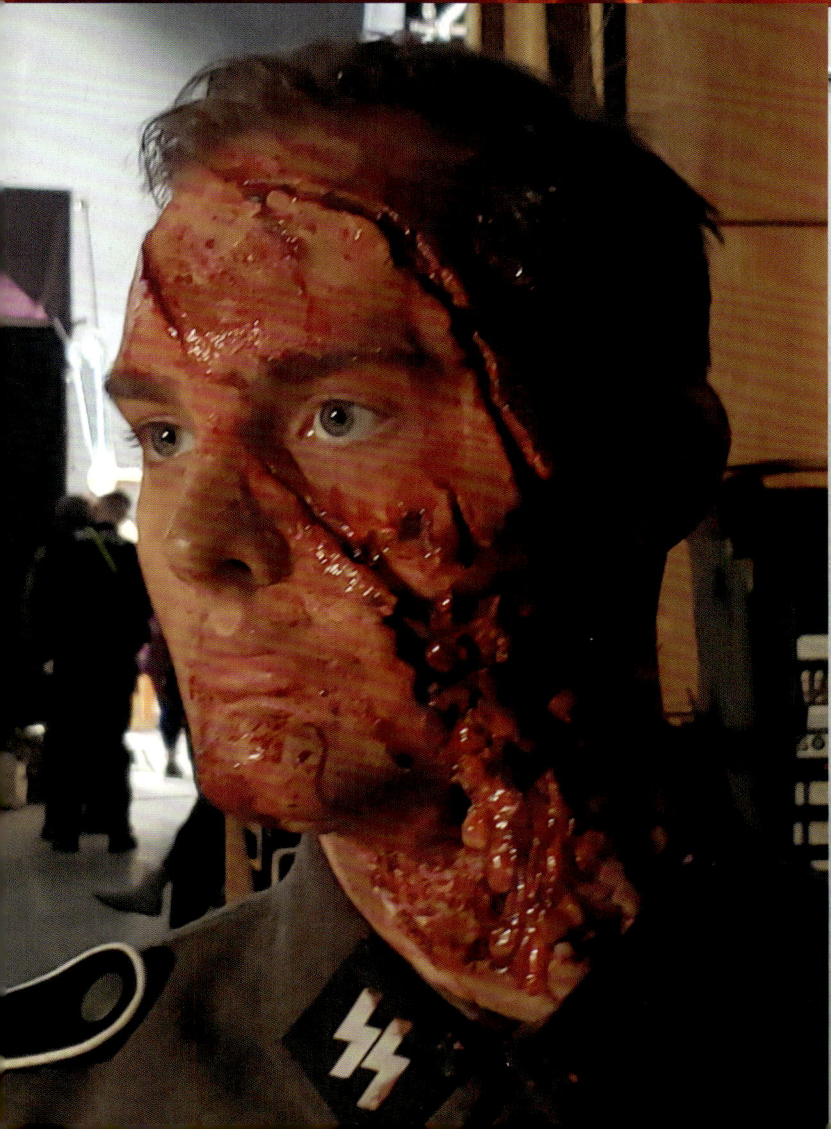

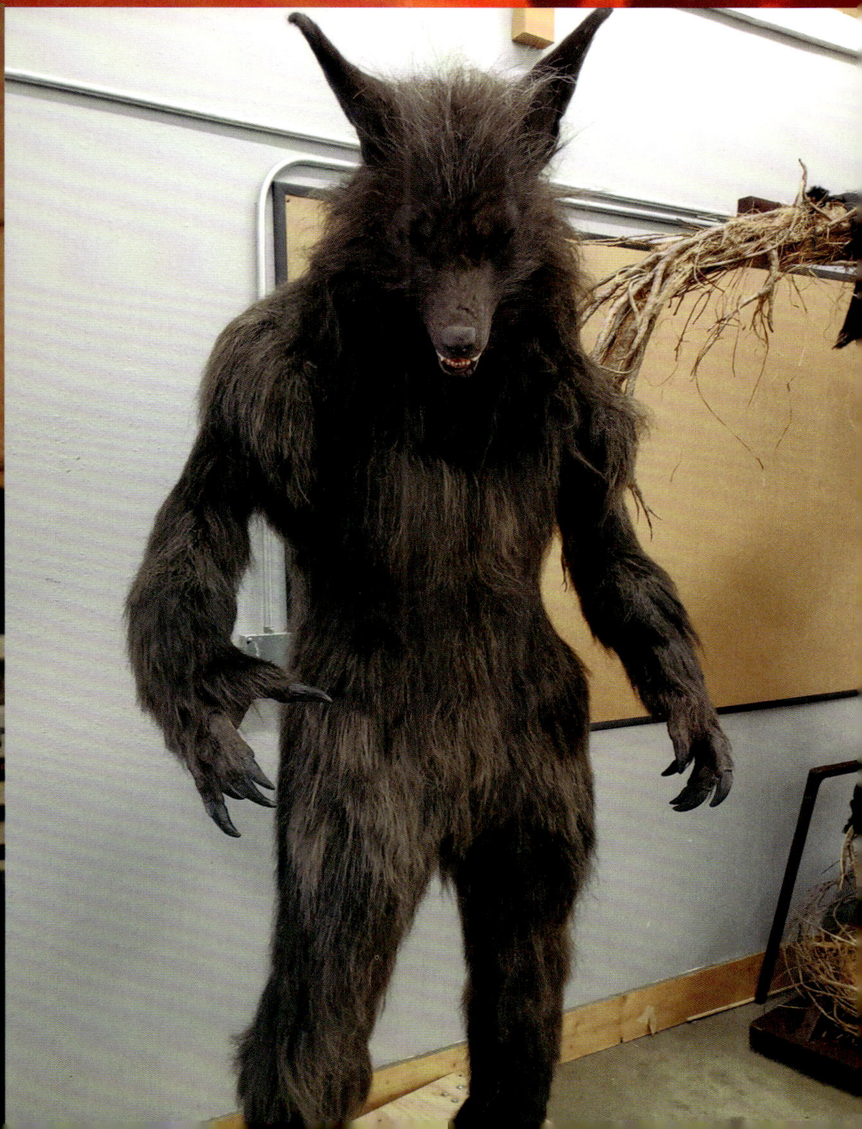

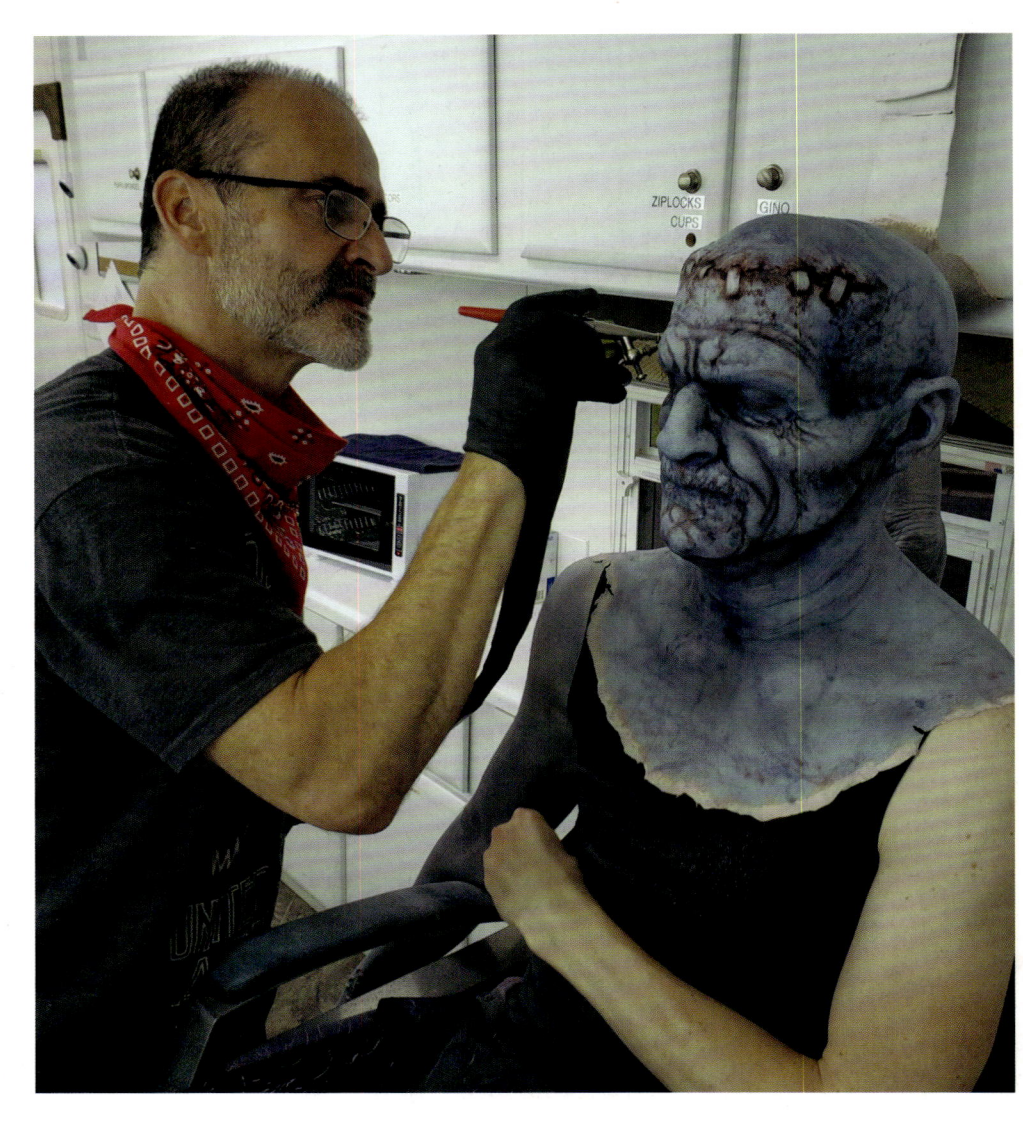

ABOVE: Michael Broom channels some classic Jack Davis while Gino Crognale (right) brings the monster (Alex Hill) to life, from "Model Kid."

OPPOSITE: Even the reanimated dead could use a bit of Gino Crognale's demented dental work.

"In the 'Model Kid' segment, where there's the Frankenstein monster in the street, that makeup was supposed to be a Frankenstein based on the Jack Davis poster. KNB sent me these prosthetics that *weren't* Frankenstein; they actually looked like a caveman-type makeup from another project, maybe. So, I built up a Frankenstein-like forehead out of other prosthetics, you know, just some layers to give it that big bulge and stuff. And for the suture that goes across the forehead, I literally took a plastic bottle of water and cut out little plastic sutures, spray-painted them silver, and then just aged them with paint, and glued them right over the forehead wound. It was crazy, but it worked!"

Then, Gino's eyes glimmer and he laughs. "Oh—and I needed teeth for the Frankenstein actor, but there wasn't time to sculpt and fit teeth for him, so I used the leftover hero teeth from the Were-Boar of 'Shapeshifters Anonymous.' I grabbed those, smashed out the tusks, and re-sculpted the teeth in this fast-hardening material, and I had to sculpt this one buck tooth for the Frankenstein. So, he's wearing that wild boar-man's teeth, re-sculpted, with the fangs missing."

There's definitely a MacGyver-style ingenuity at work here, but don't interpret that as lack of planning; *Creepshow* is a carefully planned and prepared endeavor (as much as it can be—as much as any production could ever be). As Gino explains it, there are literally page-turn reviews of each script, much like actors' table readings, to detail what's needed in effects, stunts, straight makeup, and everything else in order to be ready when the cameras roll. "And because the pace is furious, there's always things that need to be prepared throughout the whole series. It *is* a lot like a military operation—we have Headquarters who pushes down into the ranks the execution of the plan. I'm like Infantry, I'm the guy in the field who's literally in the fight, trying to make this work. 'Jonesey' [Carey Jones] and those guys are more like Headquarters; they're telling us what to do. And Greg fine tunes it; he's the Lieutenant who's telling us, like, 'I need five guys over there, then some others over there,' and he really tightens it up for us to get it done."

Despite the conscientious planning, Gino still has to navigate a minefield of challenges, surprises, and aggravating delays; just-in-time delivery often...*isn't*. "Sometimes things can be held at FedEx in Atlanta. I'll get calls like, 'Uhh, we don't know what this is...this is a giant Devil suit...who gets this?' And, so, we've had late nights where stuff doesn't arrive until like 6pm, and we have to pull it out of the box and take a look at it, and maybe it needs paint or it got damaged and needs to be repaired—and this thing shoots in the morning!"

He goes on to explain the myriad challenges that come with the production—again, it's not unlike any other production where, as Greg has previously said, nothing ever goes perfectly and there's never as much time as you'd wish to get the shot. So, appliances get to Gino but they don't exactly fit the actors; there usually isn't enough time to do actual life masks or body casts. Gino has to jury-rig what are generic prosthetic pieces to fit properly and to work as intended "on the day" (of the shoot), often fitting them to actors that may have been cast for their roles only days before filming begins.

"Like on 'Stranger Sings,' we had two possible prosthetics for [Kadianne Whyte], and the one I chose for her worked well, and

118 CHAPTER SIX

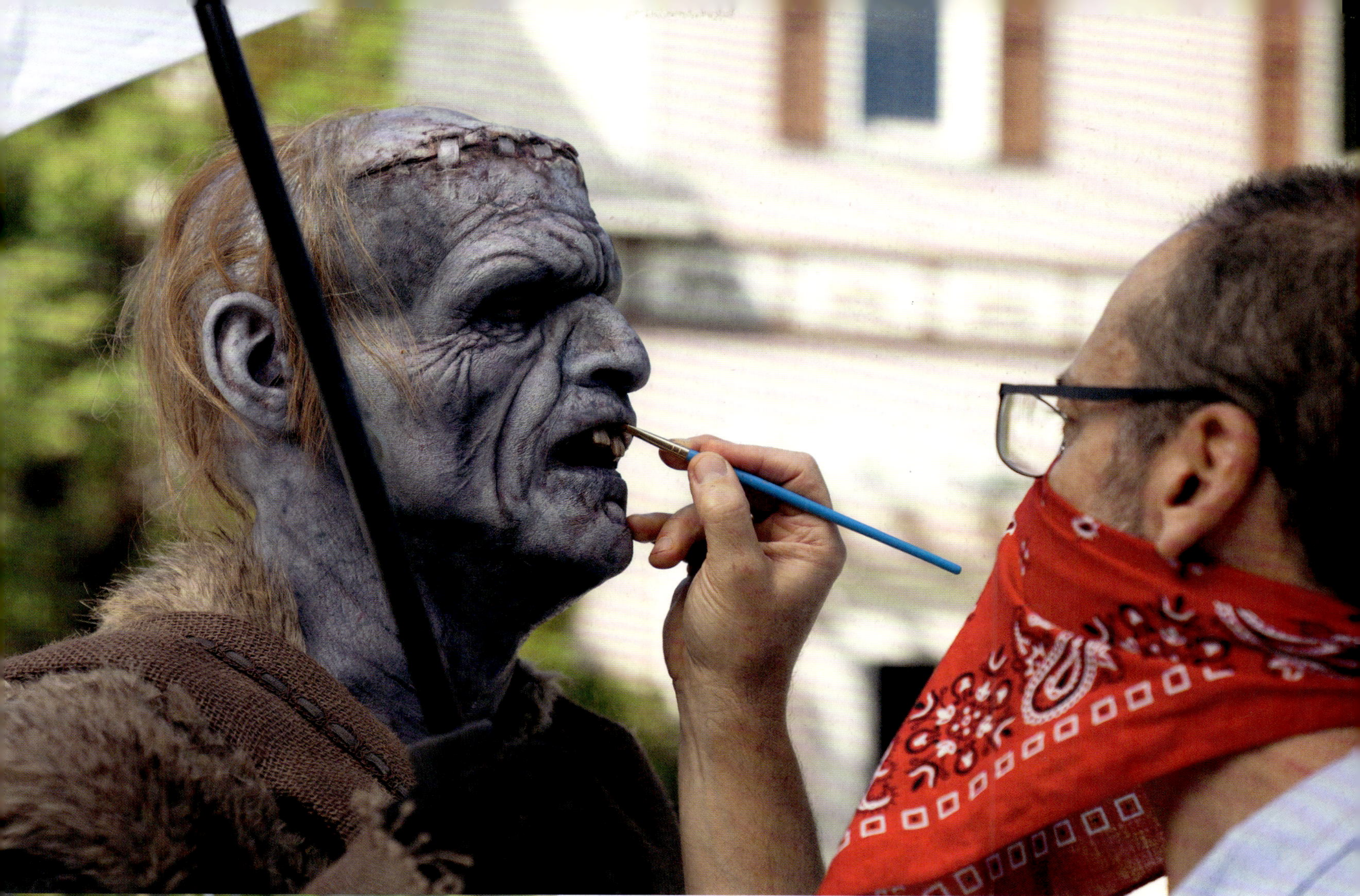

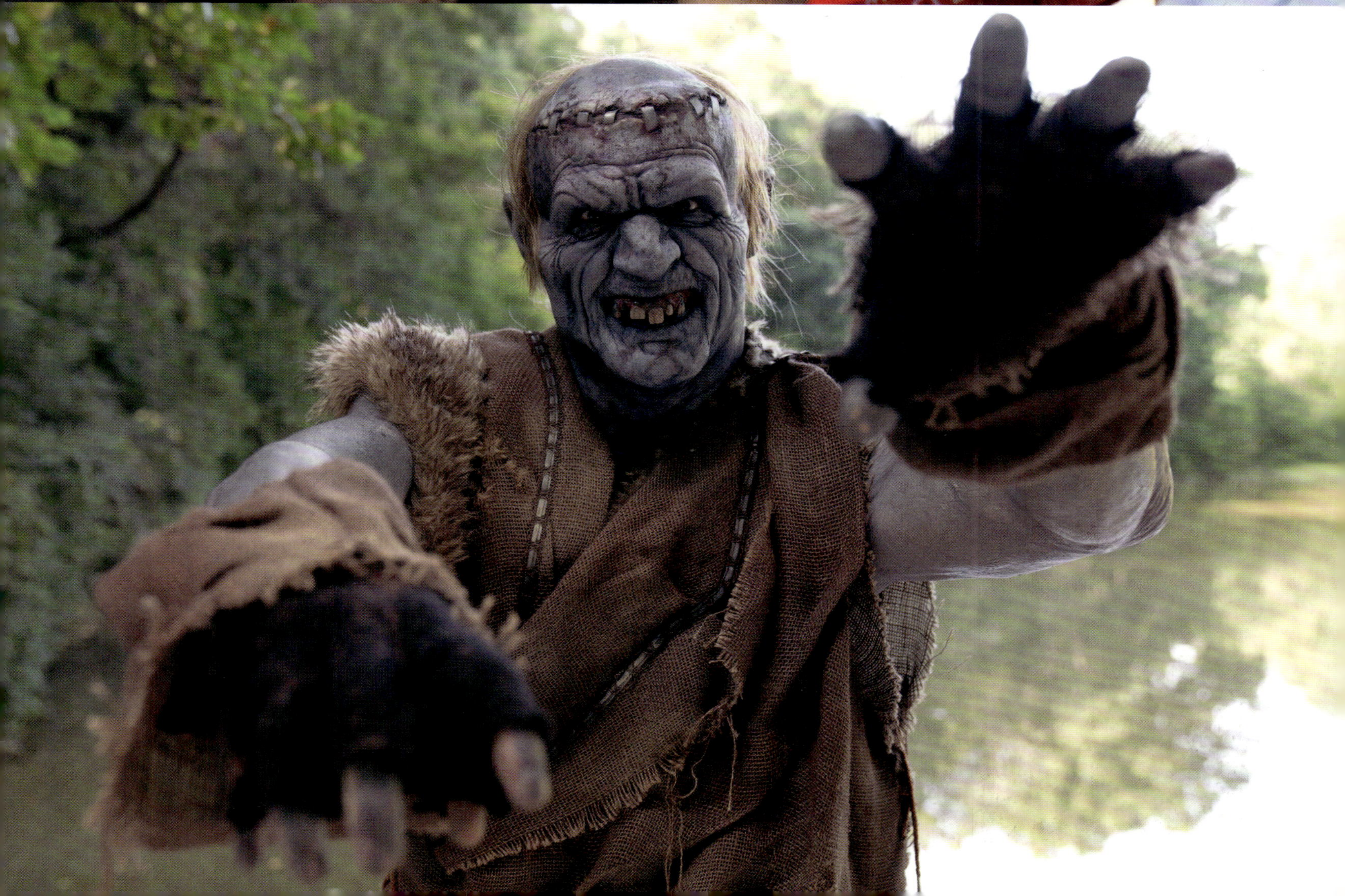

CREEPSHOW EP05
"The Man in the suitcase"
Djinn
12-12-18

KNB EFX
GROUP INC.

CREEPSHOW EP05
"The Man in the suitcase"
Djinn
12-12-18

KNB EFX
GROUP INC.

120 CHAPTER SIX

OPPOSITE: Dreaming up a demonic Djinn. It's just another example of creative conjuring by Michael Broom.

ABOVE: Andy Bergholtz's work definitely brings a smile to the face of this ethereal entity.

LEFT: Carey Jones tries on the Djinn head, then Lynn Watson gives it a supernatural 'do.

CHAPTER SIX 121

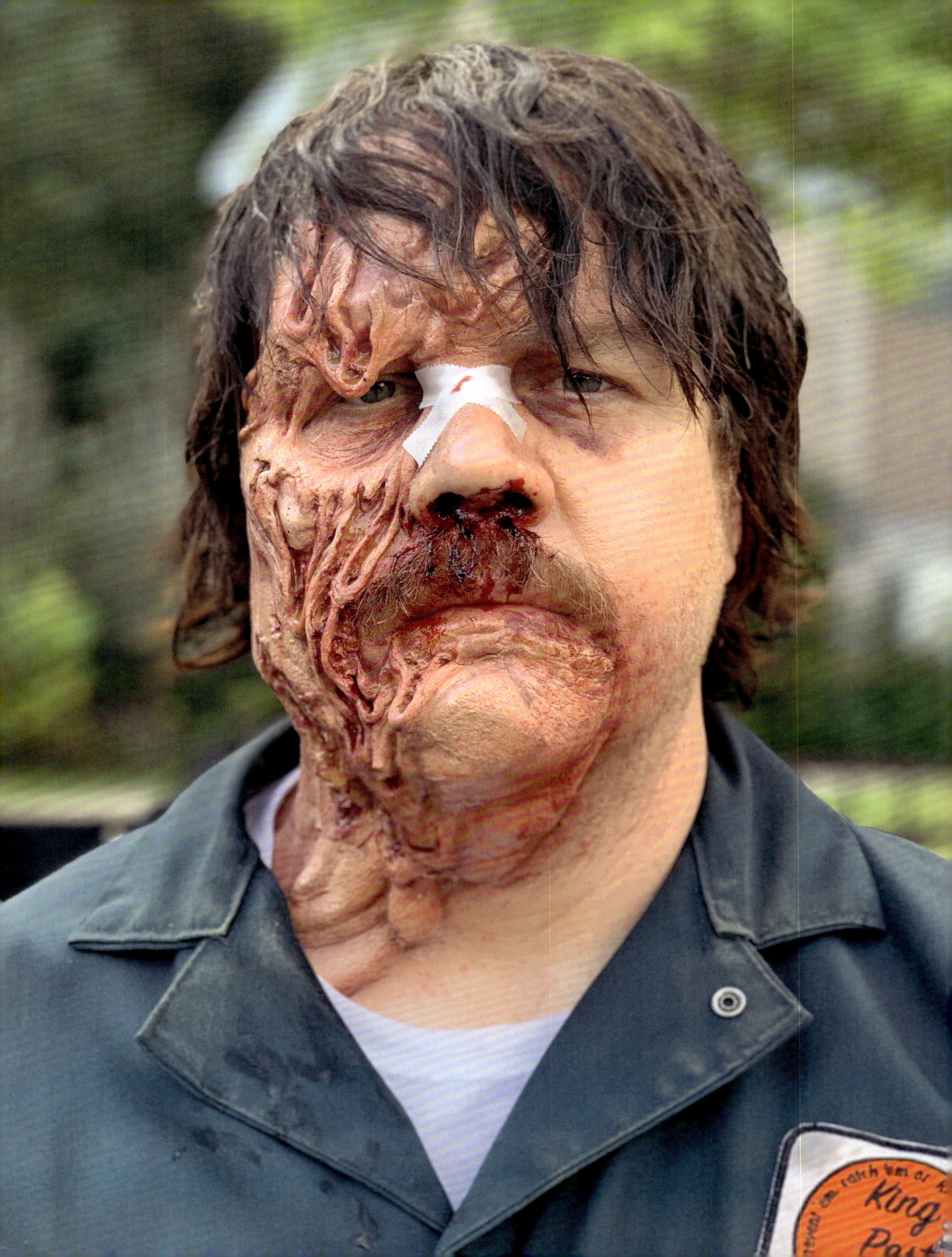

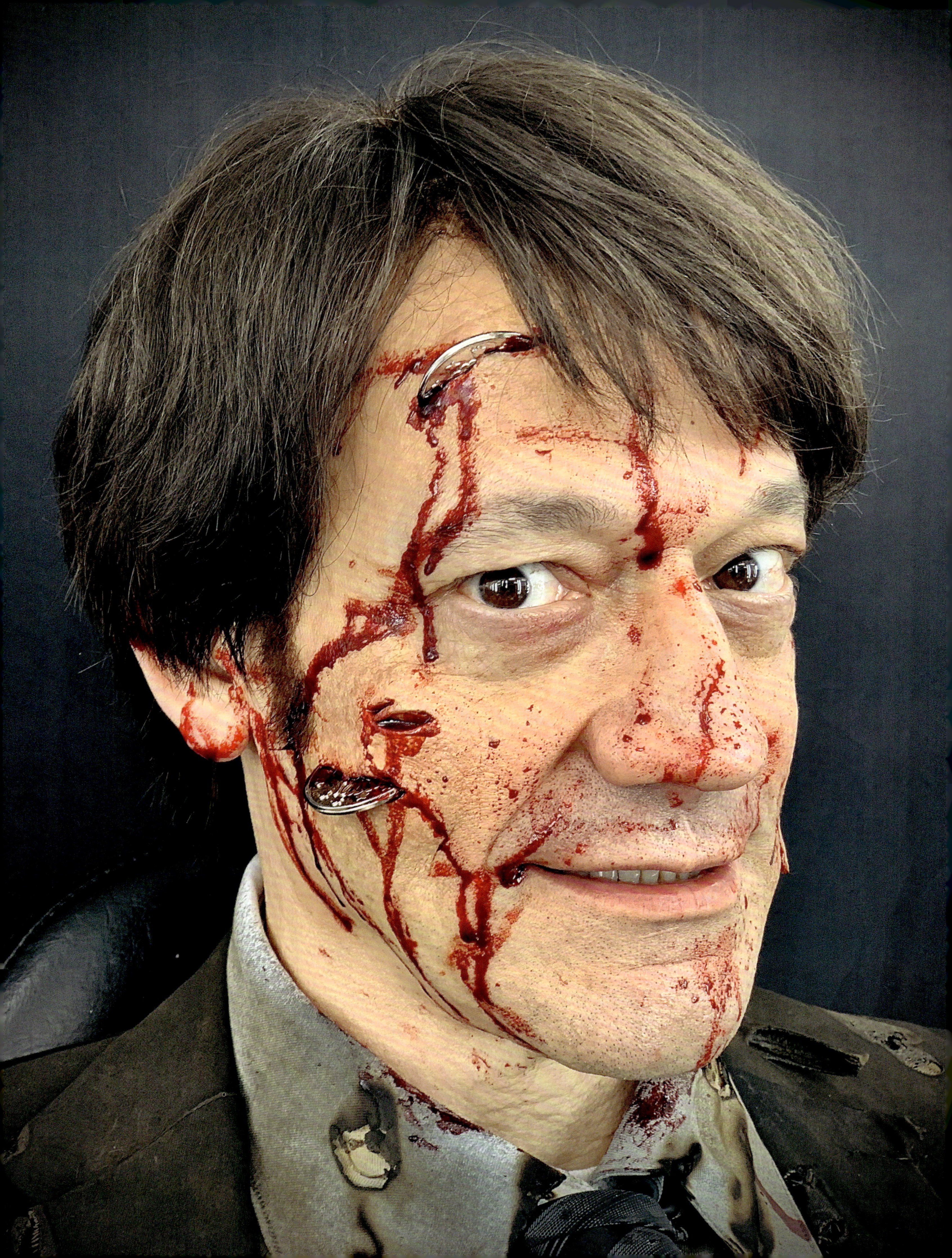

PREVIOUS SPREAD: Face the mu-sick?!

LEFT PAGE: They call poor Harlan (Josh McDermitt) ol' pizza face. Yeah, yeah—it's a cheesy joke. (From "Pesticide.")

RIGHT PAGE: Ted Raimi (as Ted Raimi) coins the phrase, "Brother, can you spare a dime?" (From "Public Television of the Dead.")

THIS SPREAD: From first look to final strike, "The Last Tsuburaya" unleashes some well-deserved comeuppance on self-obsessed Wade Cruise. Creature played by Nate Andrade.

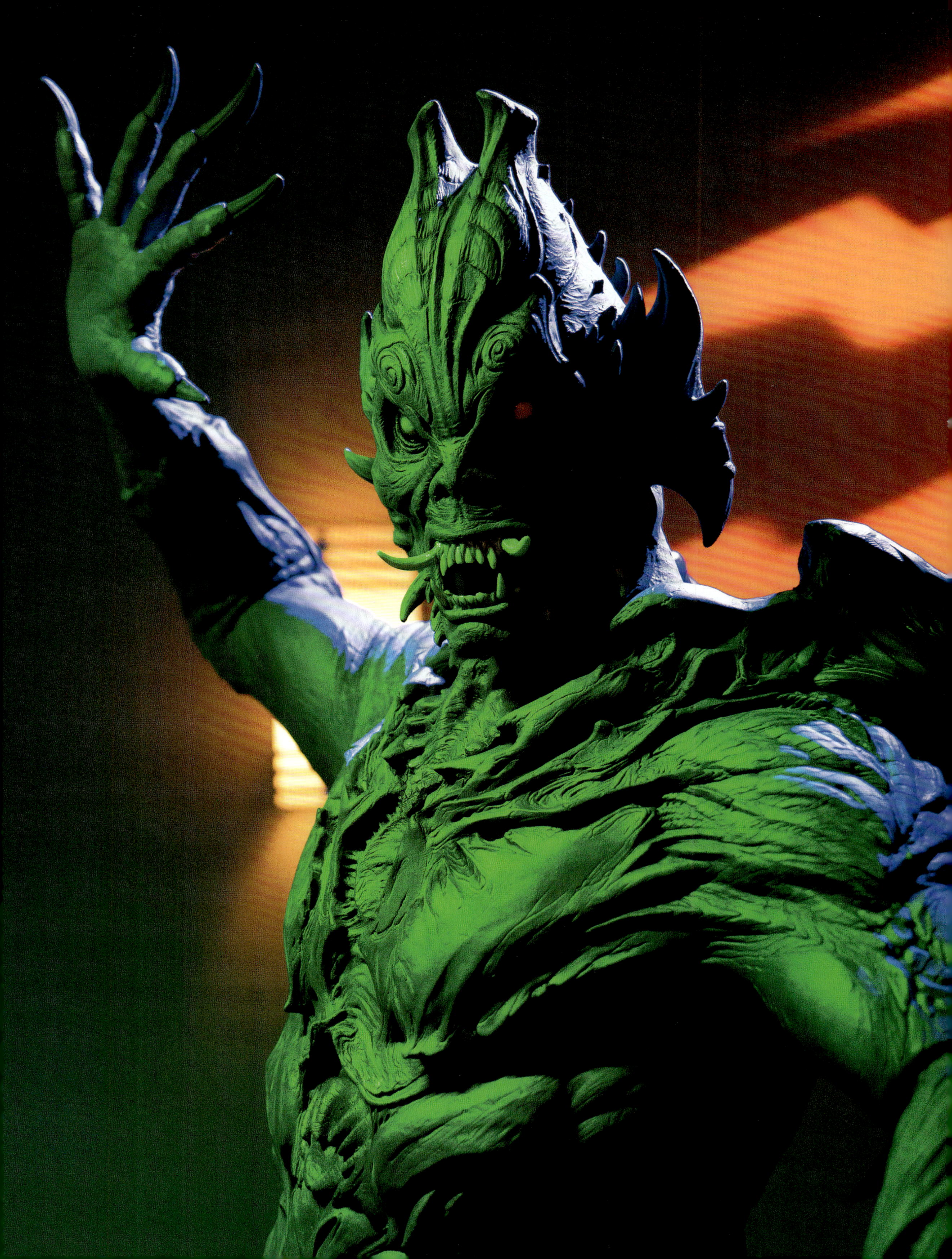

THIS SPREAD: A clever combination of puppetry and performers. You're sure to find the final face-off in "Times is Tough in Musky Holler" as truly a-peel-ing. Bottom photo is Gloria DeWeese as the zombie threatening Tony Robinson.

the *other* one that didn't fit her, I ended up putting on [Suehyla El-Attar Young] at the end, when she has the fangs and is on top of the guy…and that one fit *her* perfectly. And I also had a couple extra pieces of that prosthetic—Jonesey always sends multiples of the prosthetics so we can do multiple-day shoots or clean-up shots—so I put those aside in a drawer. Then when we did 'Drug Traffic,' and we needed makeup for the girl, I pulled out one of those extra pieces I had from 'Stranger Sings,' and it worked perfectly. And, so, I've used the same appliance designs on two different segments that are miles apart…and nobody would know it. Because of the difference in the creatures, I was able to adjust the colorings and they worked perfectly each time."

He feels good about what he pulls off in the moment, but ask him about 'Times is Tough in Musky Holler,' and he'll shake his head in disbelief. "That was *brutal*. They didn't have that set built of the elevated stage where we had to puppeteer from underneath; that was *not* built and we were literally shooting it the next day. And that night before, [construction coordinator] John Hair just sort of shrugged and said, 'We'll do our best.' And we showed up the next day to start putting things in place…and they did it; those guys pulled it off, and the baton was handed to us, so we had to get all those puppets rigged in. It was *so close* to when the cameras went up that I was literally putting my hands up through that hole and putting blood on the puppet's face right before I hear, 'OK—we're speeding…annnd…*ACTION!*' And when we finished that day, we sat back and said, 'How the fuck did we do it?'

"And it was the same thing with 'Skincrawlers' where we were there the night before rigging up the fake body from beneath the floor and feeding the monster up through the stomach and

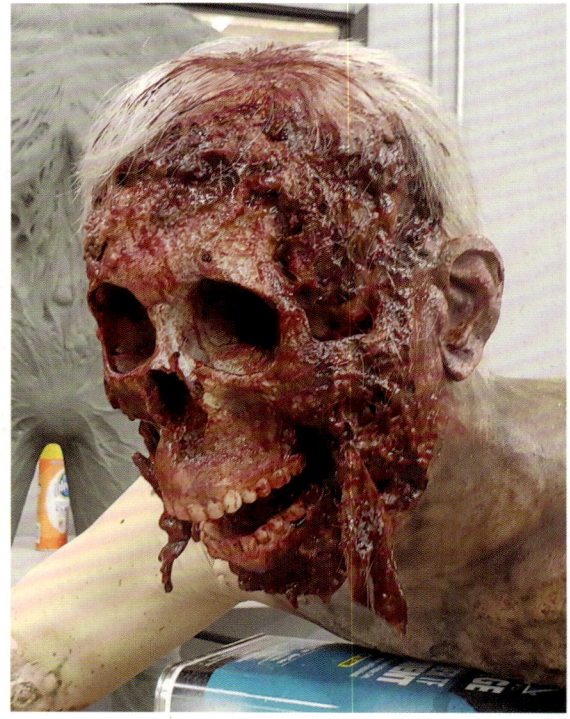

Creepshow
Brain Eating Contest
Design 006

KNB EFX
GROUP INC.

126 CHAPTER SIX

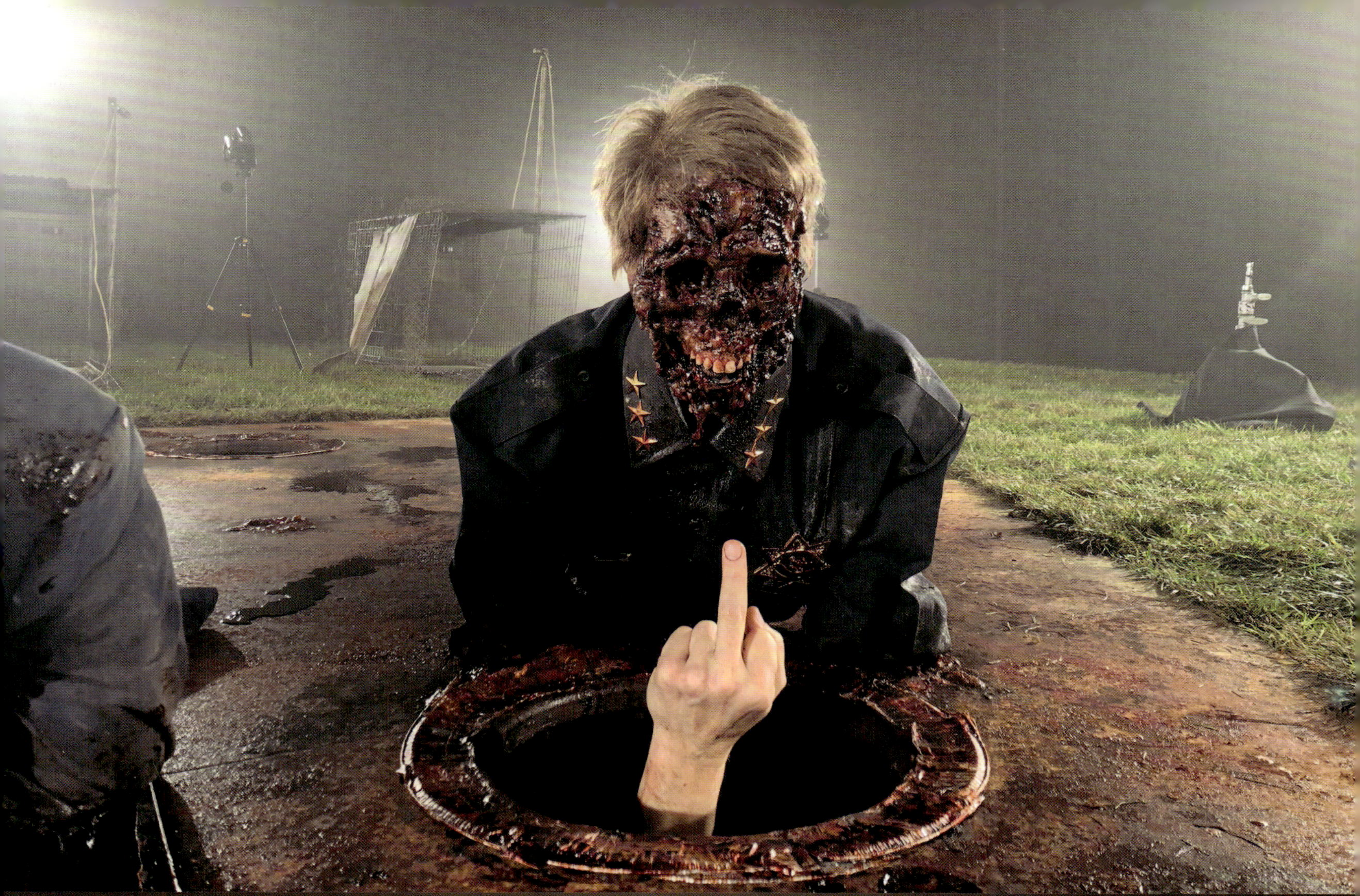

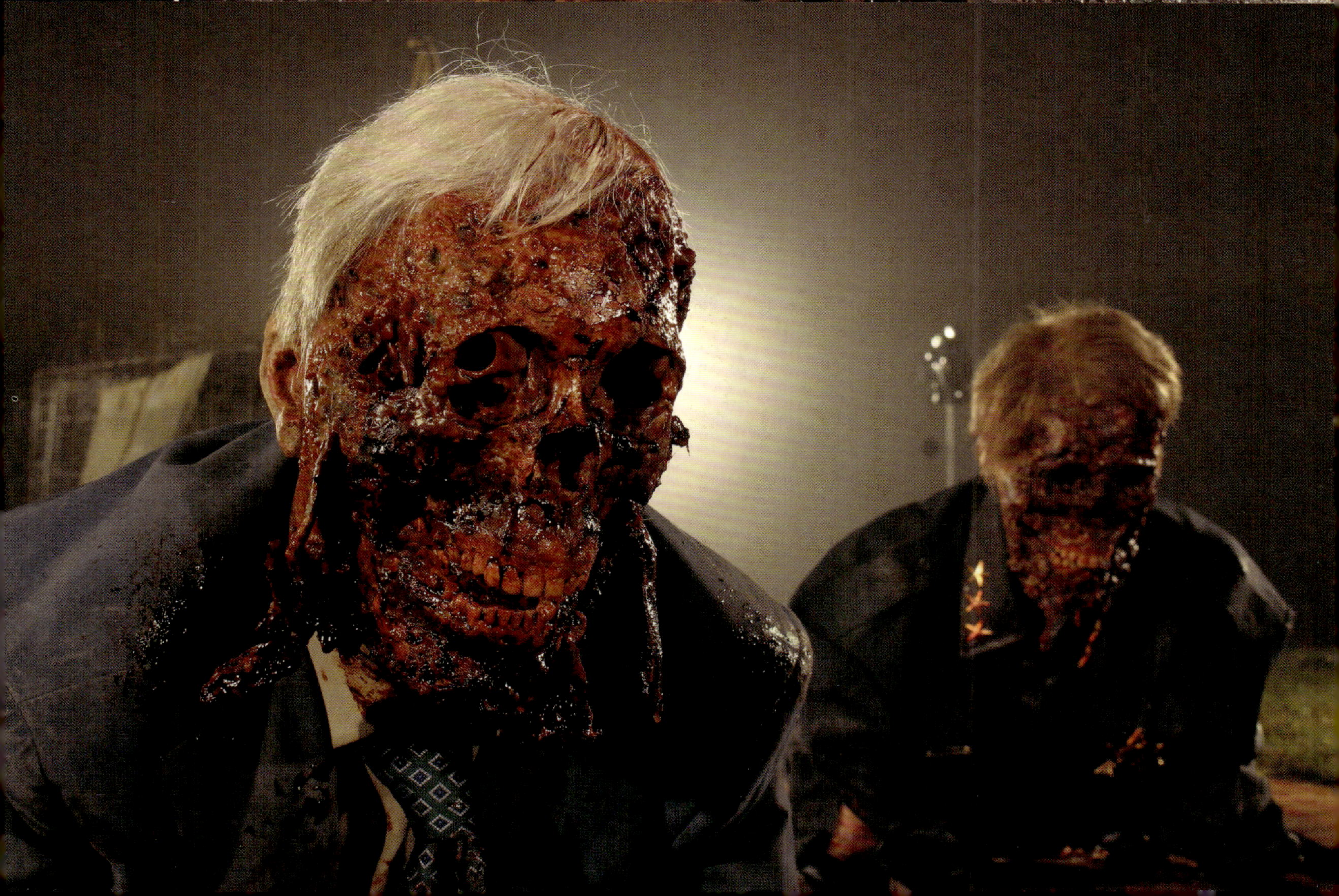

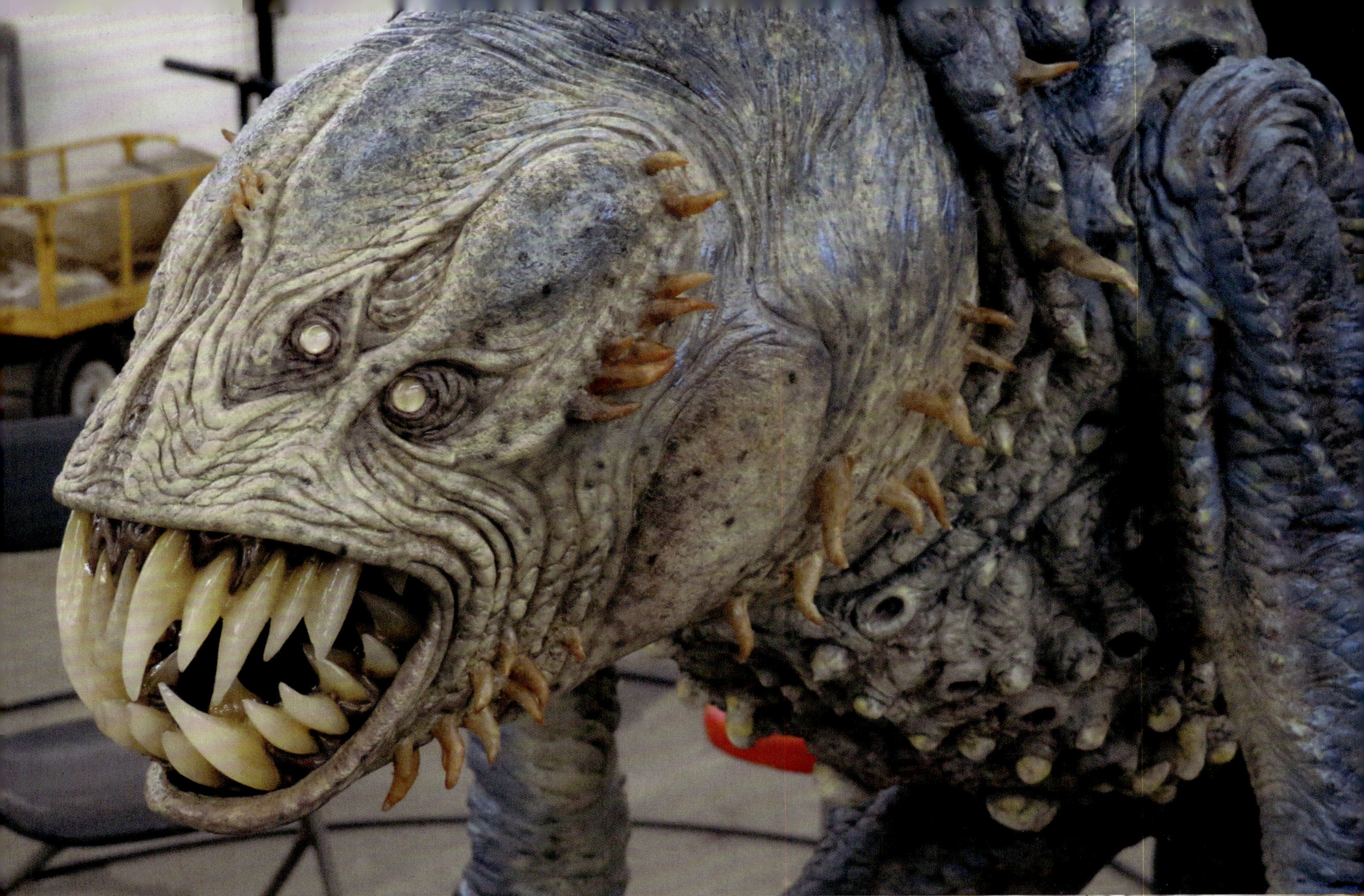

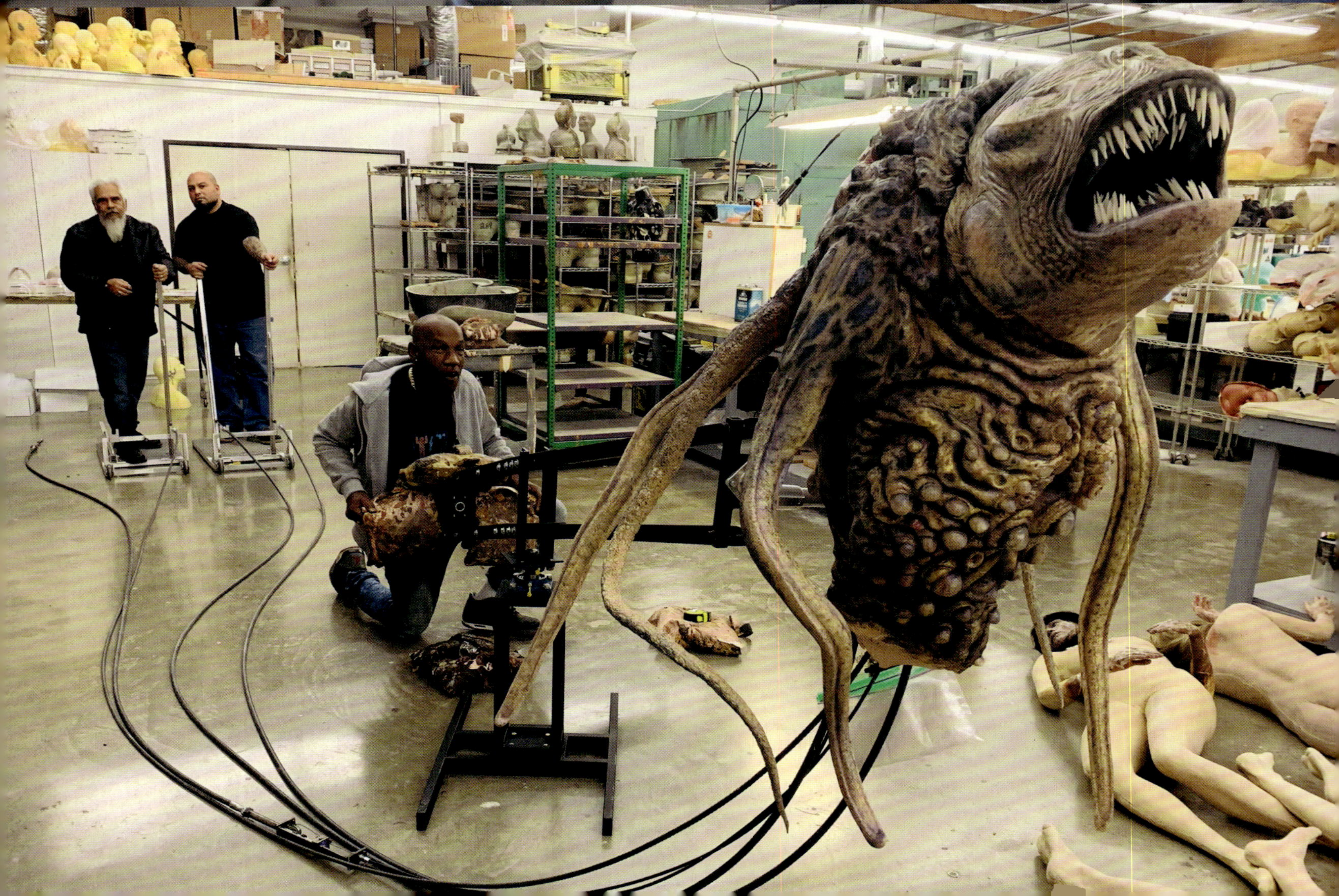

running all the cables and levers. There were five of us under that floor, with controls, getting that thing to move and rear up and stuff. And it was another close one: we were waiting for stuff from the shop, the monster shows up and it needs painting, it needs some teeth put into it, it needs cosmetic, but we gotta get in the hole tonight...and it's midnight and I'm thinking, 'Shit, I gotta get to bed 'cuz I gotta be back at 7.'"

Wrangling Creepshow's creatures is no easy task, and Gino laughingly reveals that each segment has it's "Whoa—how did we pull that off?" moments, but it's what these guys live for. They might get a bit punchy but they never punch the clock early or check out in a fit of defeat (as if). And that's all fine and good for the effects team as they usher in the show's beasties, but what about the "normies?" You know, the regular, everyday characters that carry the narrative flow? Good guys, bad guys, or otherwise, these characters are vital to every segment of Creepshow and, likewise, so is their makeup.

"Oh, yeah," Gino notes, "when you have a heavy makeup effects series, the straight makeup and hair is often overlooked, but they're like the center on a football team; no play starts without 'em, but nobody knows their names."

Well, we know their names. Meet Makeup Department Head Addison Foreman and Hair Department Head Katie Ballard. They

OPPOSITE TOP: An up-close encounter with this fat-and flesh-chewing beast will make your skin crawl.

OPPOSITE BOTTOM: Puppeteers (from left to right) Alex Diaz, Elvis Portillo, and Jeff Warren bring the beast to life.

ABOVE: Greg does a "gut check" on the creature, just it time for its gross-up... err...close-up. (From "Skincrawlers.")

BELOW LEFT: Practically a scratch-n-sniff image—you can almost smell the B.O. and bad breath on Harlan (Josh McDermitt), all thanks to the work of Katie Ballard and Addison Foreman. (From "Pesticide.")

BELOW RIGHT: Reagan Higgins as the painfully possessed Mercy, from "Meter Reader."

OPPOSITE: Oh no! Another house of the head? Nah—it's just the collection of wigs and hair pieces by Katie Ballard.

make those everyday characters look like everyday people, even when the actors portraying them don't look like this *every day*.

"I came into *Creepshow* through [Producer] Alex Orr," Katie begins, "and he gave me my first department head job back in the day, and so I've worked with him quite a bit over the years...and he's the one who brought me into the first season of *Creepshow*—and little did I know what I was getting into and how much I would come to love the project. Addison and I have known each other [for a long time], but this was the first time we've been running departments, side-by-side."

Addison adds that his first collaboration with Katie began on 2017's *Rings*, where they established an easy working relationship and a fast friendship. "When I came to *Creepshow* and learned that she was our department head for hair, I got very, very excited to be working and collaborating with her again. She's fast on her feet, has a lot of experience, and she can turn out a great wig in just three-days' time."

While Gino and his key partner in effects execution, Jake Garber, handle on-set management of everything from KNB, monster-wise or what's called "large trauma," Addison and Katie handle the day-to-day cast looks, whether facial hair grooming or beauty makeups (that is, "straight makeups"). And as Gino previously touched upon, many casting decisions are only finalized days before the actor is to show up at the studio and take a seat in the makeup chair.

"But we have to sit and wait until the deal with the actor closes," Katie sighs, "so we can't really pull the trigger on anything until that happens; and sometimes we think we've got someone but that can change at the last minute. But when we've booked an actor and we meet them, I've already done my research on them. I'll tell them, 'I know your whole Instagram history, what you've looked like through the years, and the pattern of your hairline.'"

Schedule, schedule, schedule. It's not a worry for these two, though. Once they have shooting scripts in hand, they have a collaborative review, understanding the characters and the situations, looking for how they can contribute to the storytelling in each segment through their hair and makeup work. Then come the "mood boards"—presentations of facial photos and appearance styles, and hair and makeup colors—to present to Greg and the segment director. Through discussion, the characters' visual style (that is, "mood") is determined, setting Katie and Addison off to work with the actors and implement the hair and makeup plan.

The plan typically begins with clarification of the time period. "That dictates the style of facial hair," Addison begins. "In the Eighties, most men were clean-shaven. In the Seventies, you're gonna see more moustaches and mutton chops. For modern times, it can sort of be whatever. And, at that point, it's up to the actor; does he wanna shave; does he wanna keep it? We had Josh McDermitt [for 'Pesticide']—and he's usually tanned and clean-shaven—and he really wanted to wear a moustache in his segment. 'I think my guy is gross, he has an untamed moustache, and it might be a little different from his hair color 'cuz maybe he colors one of the two and he doesn't really care.' And I said, yeah, let's do it!"

Katie laughs and adds, "Yeah, and I gave him hair extensions for that character. When he first came in, he had that really incredible mullet that we all know him for—and I was all about rocking that, but he said, 'I really wanna look different,' so we just needed to make him look more shaggy, more greasy, and grungy. So, we just made his hair look greasy every day to match the lovely look that Addison described *[laughs]*. And I wet the edges of his hair and Addison put a sheen on his face so he always looked sweaty plus had pesticide on him."

By the time this team was through with McDermitt, you could practically *smell* him from the other side of the TV screen.

"And when it comes to our female cast," Addison pivots, "it's period-based first, and then we go into what is their job or situation. Like, in 'Model Kid,' we had the mother [Tyner

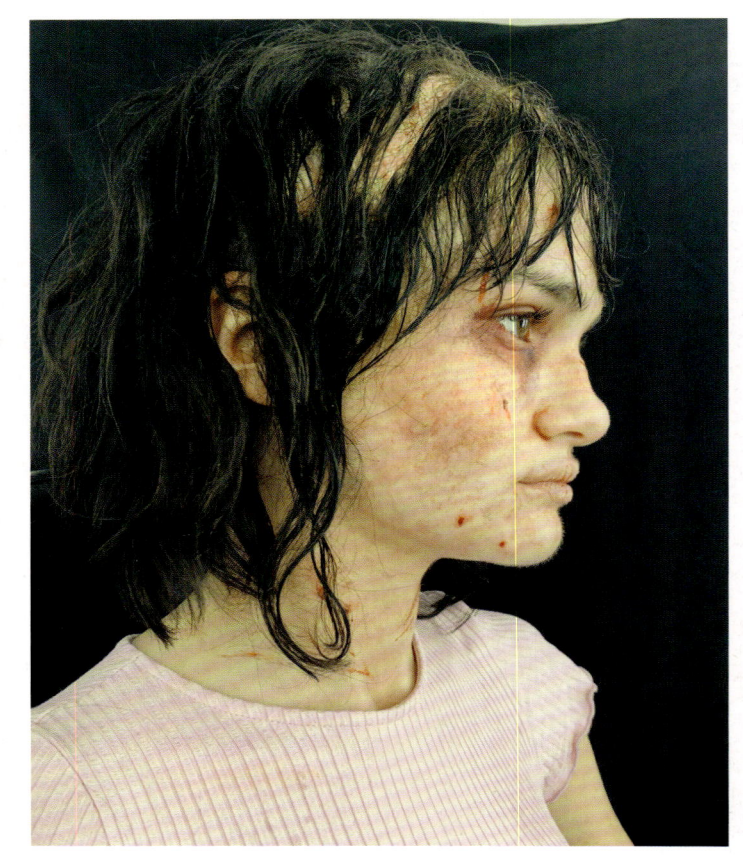

CHAPTER **SIX**

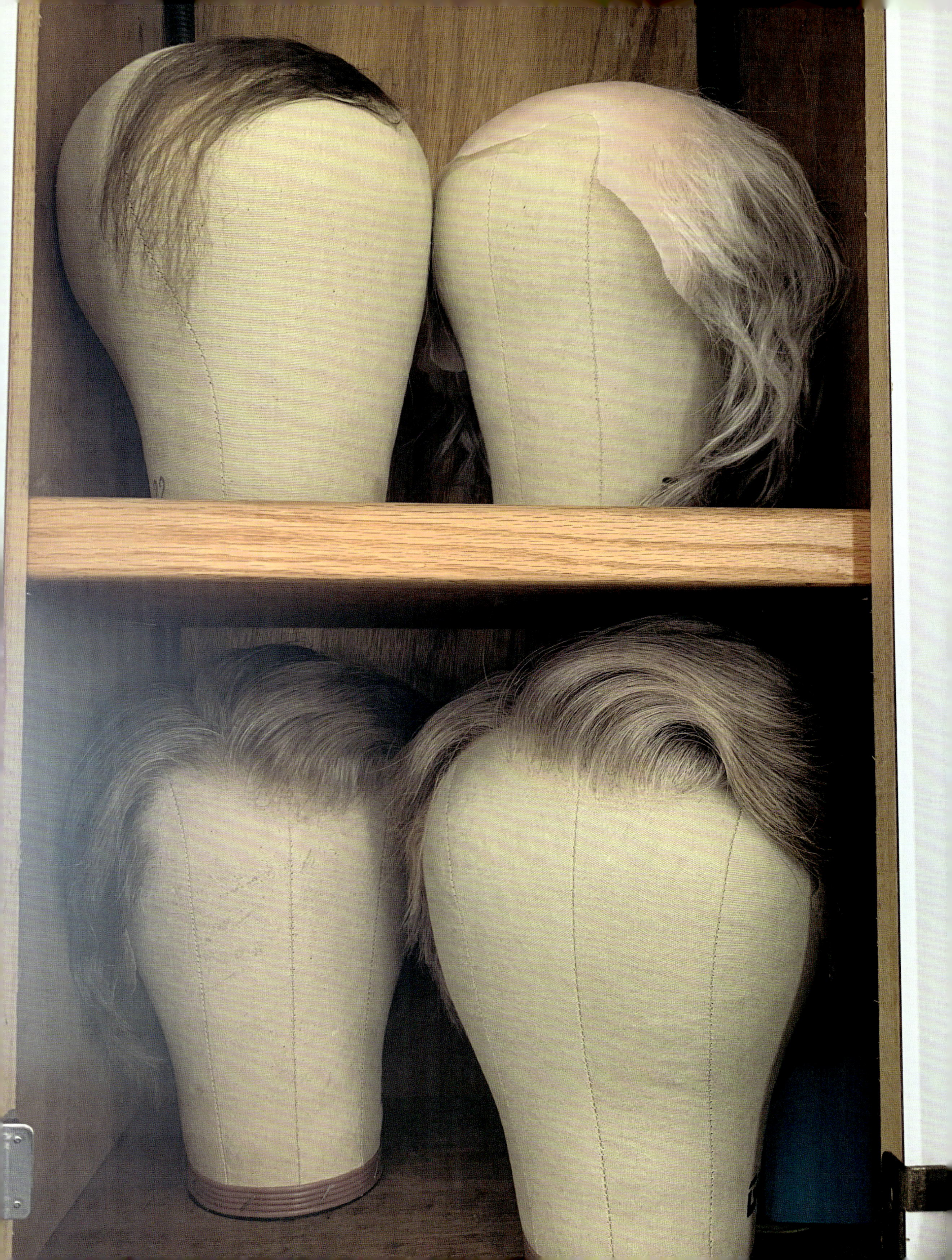

BELOW: You can place the face, but can you "square the hair?" Where are these *Creepshow* coifs headed?

OPPOSITE: Perfectly transformative treatments: a chemo-concealing bandana for "Model Kid" (top, pictured are Brock Duncan and Tyner Rushing); a well-clipped beard applied by Addison Foreman to Matthew Barnes, then transformed by Katie Ballard into a 150-year-old finale for "Time Out."

Rushing], and she had cancer, so we had to make her a little sickly...so lots of contouring shadowing there, heavy eyebags. And in 'Public Television of the Dead,' I had the most fun there because it was moustaches and mutton chops—and most of those mutton chops I hand-laid every day and the moustaches were lace pieces. My favorite aspect of my job is any time I get to play with facial hair. And Katie and I marry our crafts together typically with facial hair. Wherever the wig ends, I'll tie in the facial hair."

Katie prefers to work with wigs over an actor's real hair: "The possibilities are endless with wigs and I can make the actors' dreams come true with those...and, thanks to *Creepshow*, I've learned how to do better wigs in just a few days. But I just don't know how we'll top what we've been consistently doing as we made our way through Season Three."

But tops for both of them is, hands down, Season Three's 'Time Out.' In that twist on the time-bending trope, the character of Tim, played by actor Matthew Barnes, travels across an age spectrum of 19 to 150 years old.

"Realistic aging makeups, that's usually the sort of thing we really want to do," says Katie, "and we were so ready to do that, but we didn't close the deal with the actor until 36 hours before we started shooting *[laughs]*...and we didn't even have a hint as to who the actor might be. But we got very lucky with Matt—it couldn't have been a more ideal situation—because he has a kind of natural widow's peak, a natural recession, so I made two wigs for him that we altered to fit his head, and I made hairline lace pieces that we could bring forward for his college years, then alter them to recede as he aged. And on that first day of filming, we had to go through all five of his changes in one day!"

So much happens in one day on *Creepshow*, but for the KNB crew, what happened on Day One of their work? Lest we overlook it, amid all this excitement over strange creatures, rotting cadavers, and cleverly convincing straight makeups, what about "The Creep?"

"Oh yeah, The Creep was the first thing we did for the show," Carey says. "We weren't going to copy the original, but Greg wanted ours to be similar, like an homage to it. And I did a

CHAPTER SIX 133

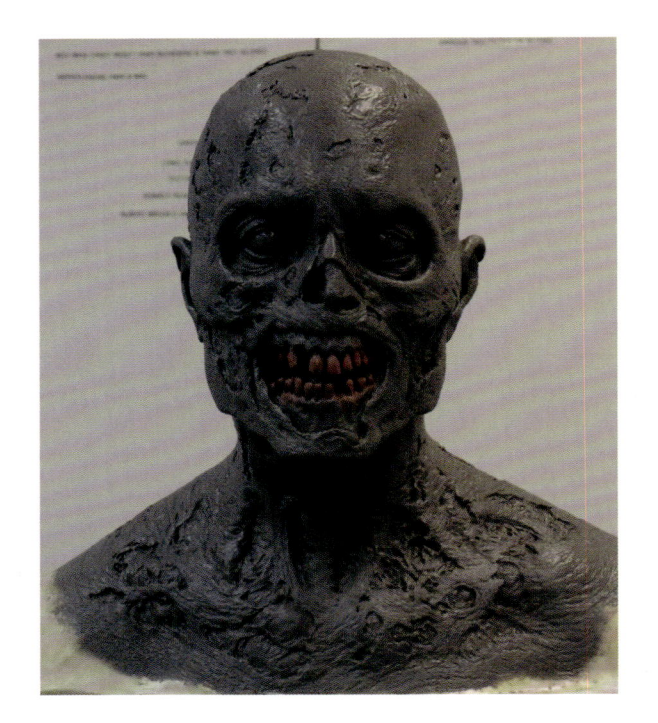

THIS SPREAD: The Creep began as an unused walker from *The Walking Dead*. With some tweaks, twists, and animated expressions, the *Creepshow* Creep takes center stage as ringleader of the wretched.

sculpture for a zombie for *The Walking Dead*, like a year previous to this, but we never used it. And Greg said, 'Hey Carey, remember that sculpture you did for *The Walking Dead*? We never shot that thing.' Yeah, yeah, and I pulled it out and photographed it and sent it to him. And he said, 'Yeah, let's use that.' Then we just tweaked it a little bit: I changed the teeth out, added a few things to the face, and an artist here, Alex Diaz, painted it. Then, I put a hood on it and took it into a room, put up a mock-moon and lit it, and photographed it again and sent it to Greg and he said, 'Oh, man, that's cool.' And now he has a lot more animation in his face—he has a four-way jaw, his neck moves, he has eye-blinks and eyebrows, and his eyes kinda look around. So, yeah, he was the first thing we did for the show."

Pushing the creative energy ever further to achieve big effects in a manageable way, there came the whole challenge of depicting the elephant-sized sea serpent in "By the Silver Water of Lake Champlain." When Rose (Sydney Wease) and Thomas (Connor Jones) stumble upon the dead Champy, washed ashore and lifeless, that's clearly a full-sized rendering of the monster. But, later, when the bigger-still Mama Champy appears and sadly pulls her dead offspring back into the lake, that's actually an

134 CHAPTER SIX

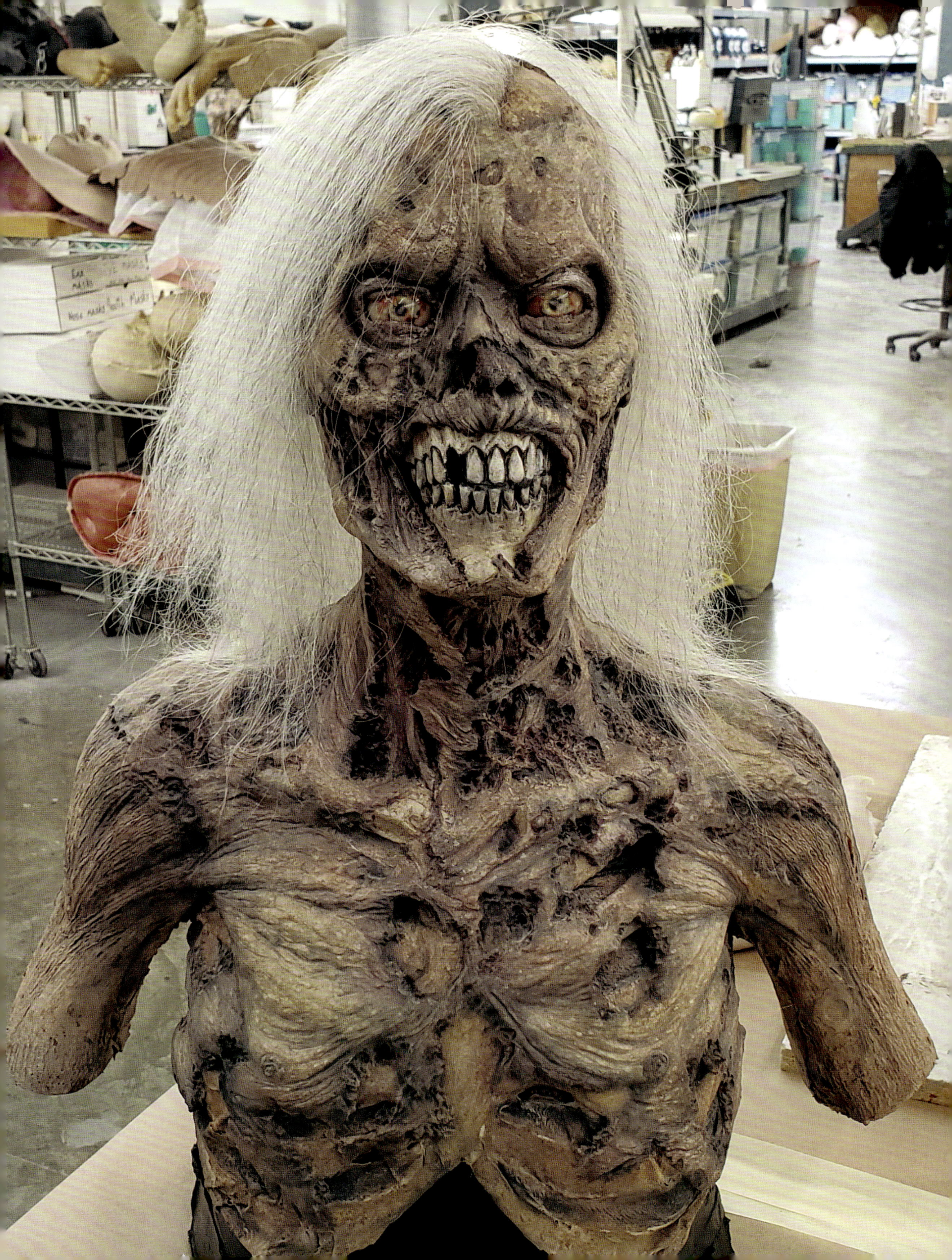

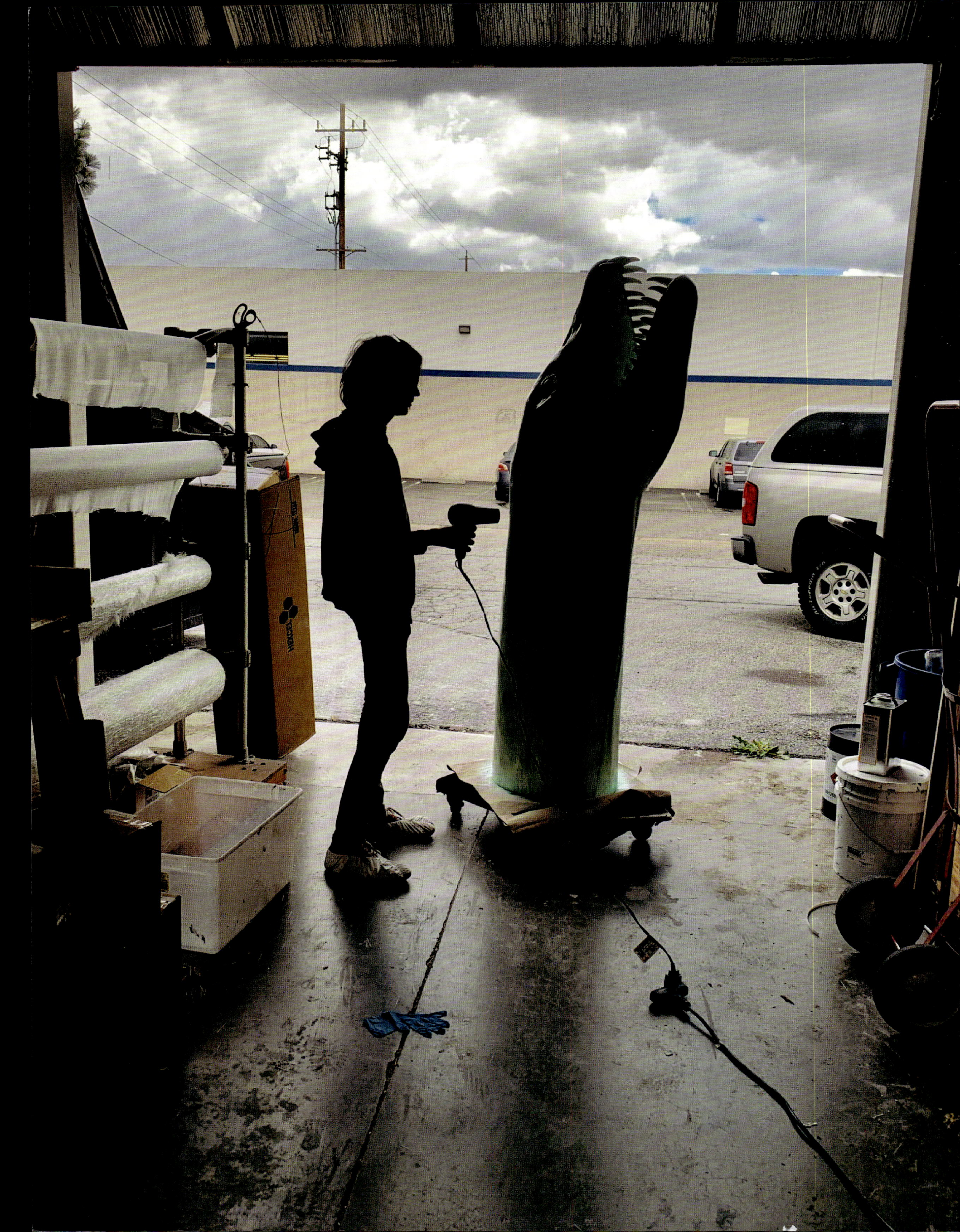

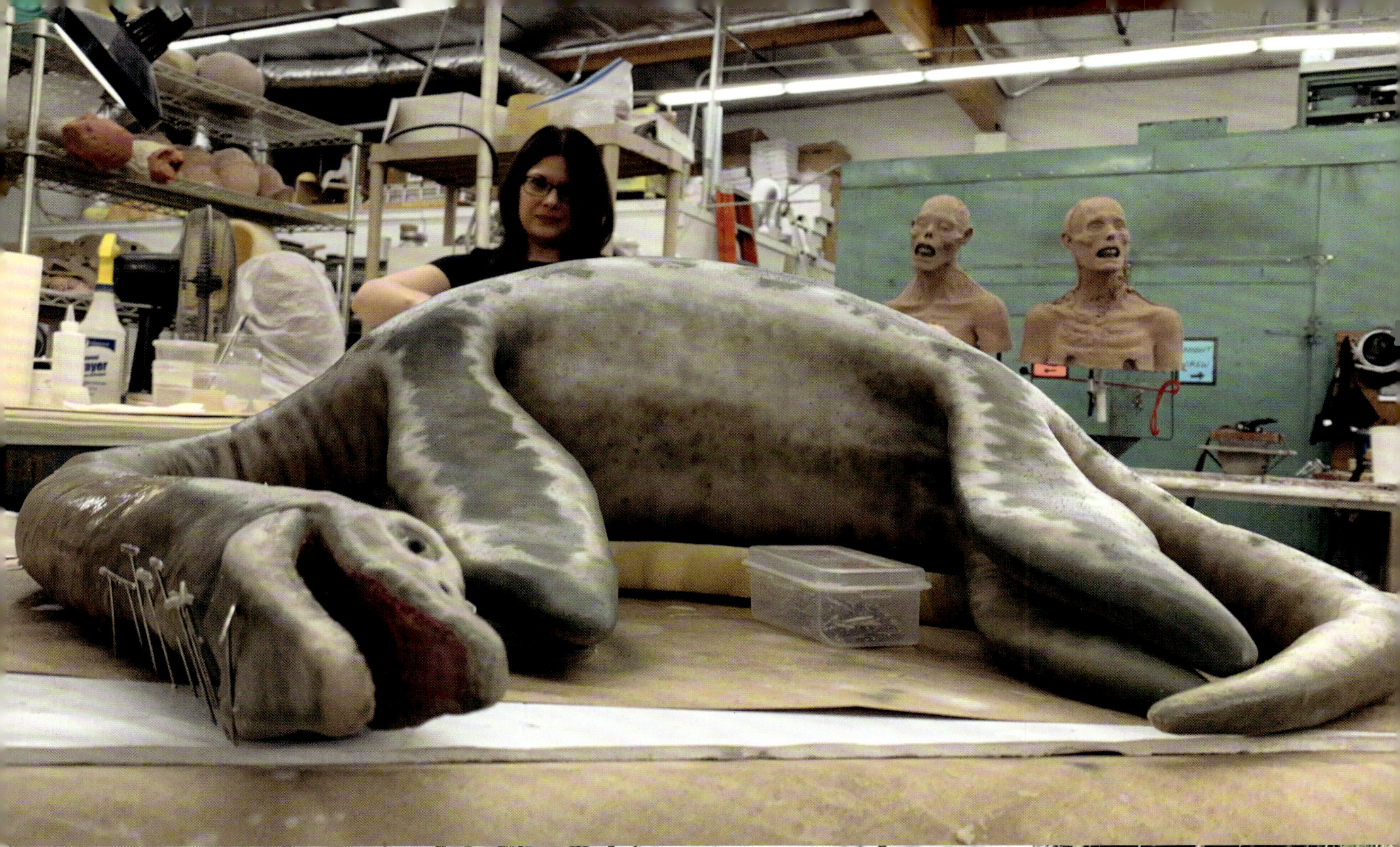

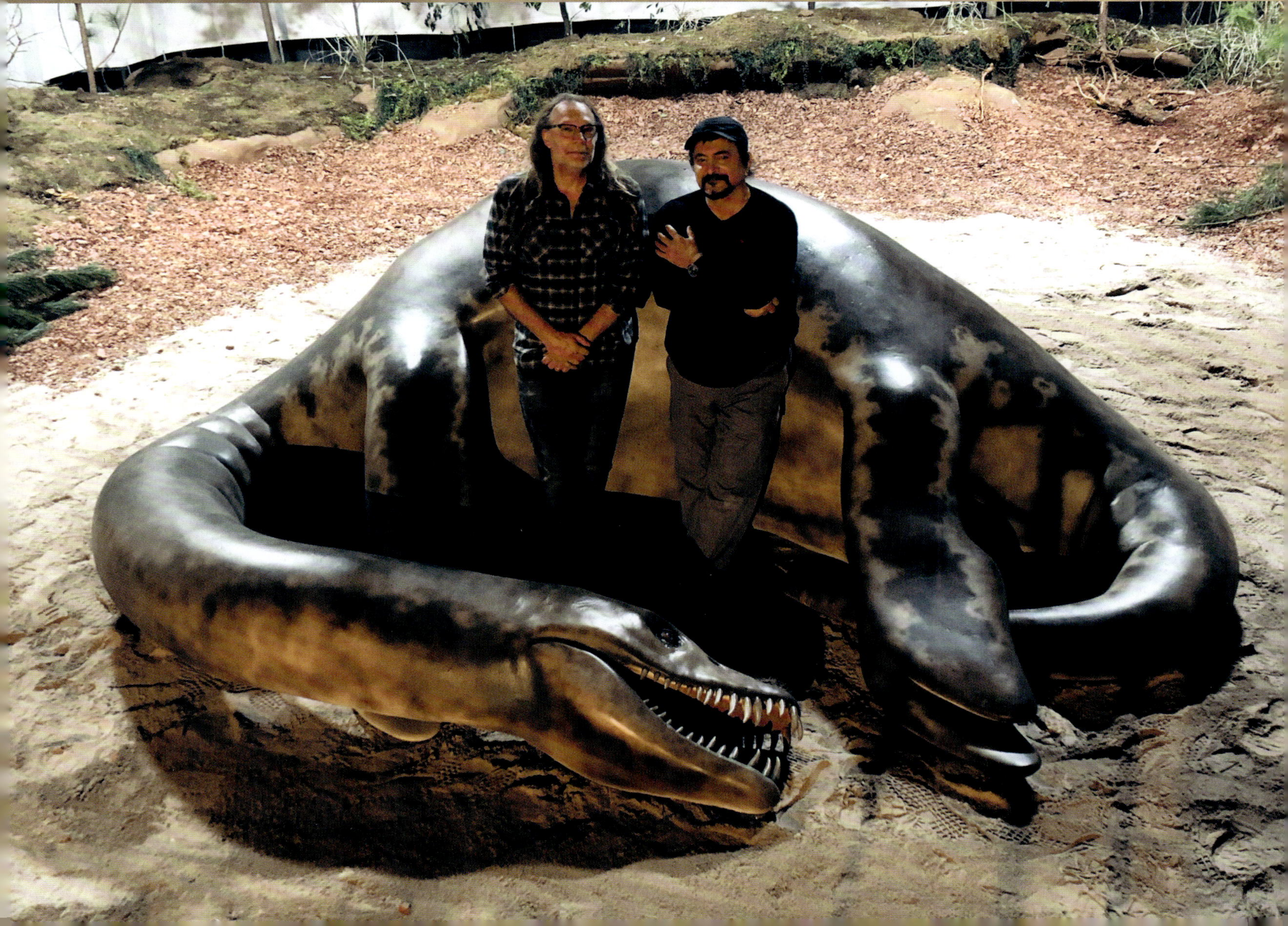

PREVIOUS SPREAD: Evolution of an evolutionary anomaly. Champy, from "By the Silver Water of Lake Champlain." Left page pictured is Chris Baer. Right pictured are Cristina Prestia (top) and Greg Nicotero and Tom Savini (bottom).

THIS PAGE: The "grue" spirit of Christmas—Big Bob from "Shapeshifters Anonymous." Lurking behind Big Bob is Aaron King.

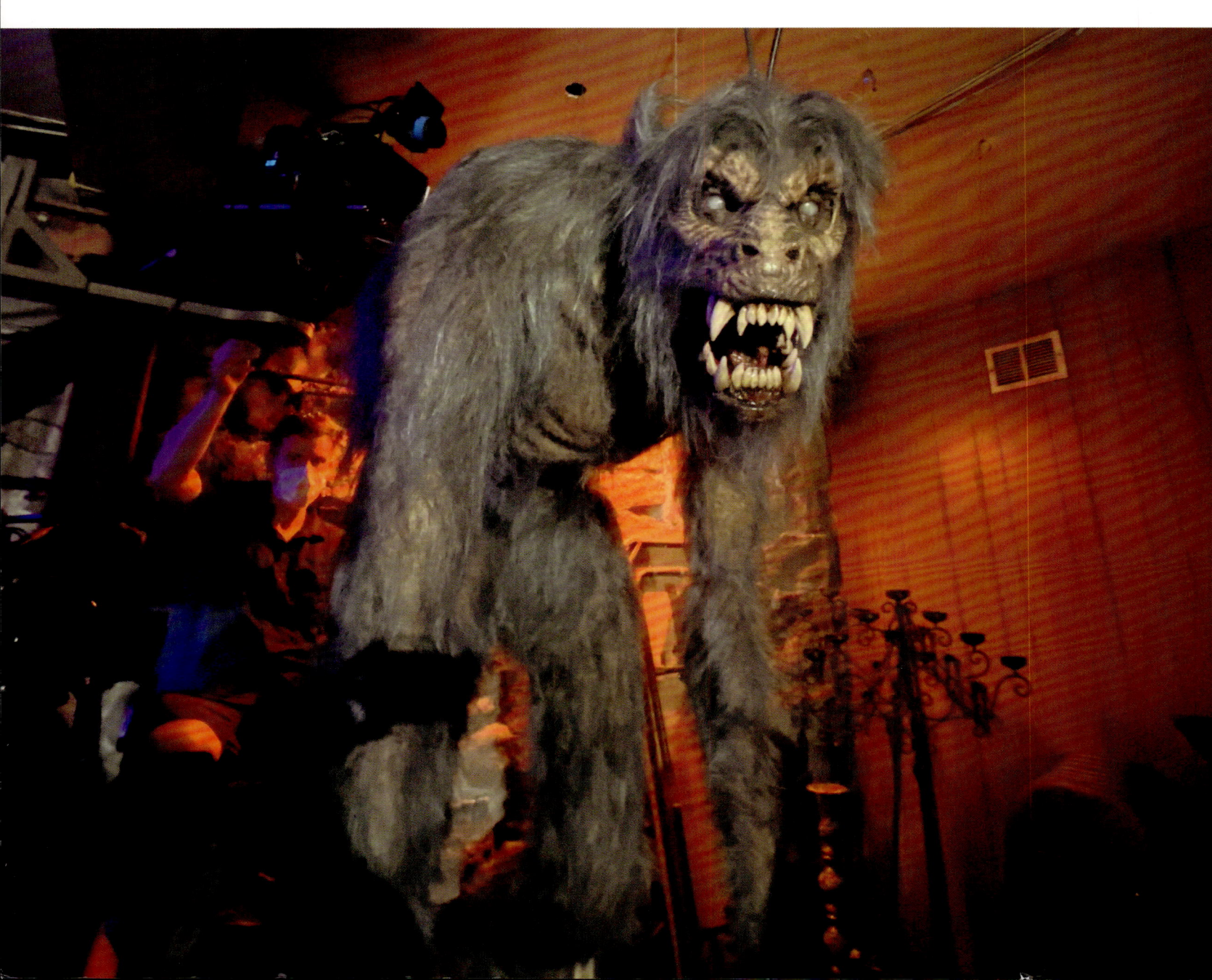

arm-length hand puppet dragging away a scale replica of Baby Champy—but you'd be challenged to realize it on first viewing. "Yeah, that's a lot from [DP] Rob Draper," Carey says, "from doing his research in terms of camera speed. And how we made it; that thing was heavy. It was solid silicone. Greg said that, when we pull this thing, it has to have the weight. And I told him the only way to do that is to actually make it heavy. And, so we did, and it worked."

Conversely, when the job called for delivering a huge creature that was truly huge—not a miniature stand-in—there came the Bob Wolf of "Shapeshifters Anonymous."

"Yeah, that thing was huge," confirms Carey. "Mike Rotella sculpted the head, and we had the idea that it's sort of an homage to Fluffy [the Crate Beast from 1982's *Creepshow*]; it has a little bit of Fluffy-look to his head, but just how big it was...it was full-practical. We had rod-puppeteering for the arms and feet, and it had a rod coming out of the top of the head and had the jaws that opened and closed. That thing was cool, just for the sheer size of it."

Leaning back to ponder the current history of this show, Greg searches for a moment, then leans forward to sort of sum it all up.

LEFT: Color concept drawing of Big Bob by John Wheaton.

BELOW: "Just hold still...this won't hurt a bit," assures KNB EFX supervisor Jake Garber.

CREEPSHOW S2
Shapeshifters Anonymous
Wereboar concept
Design 010

KNB EFX
GROUP INC.

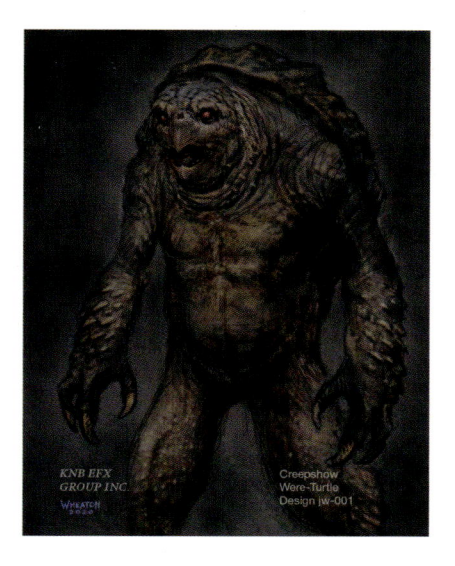

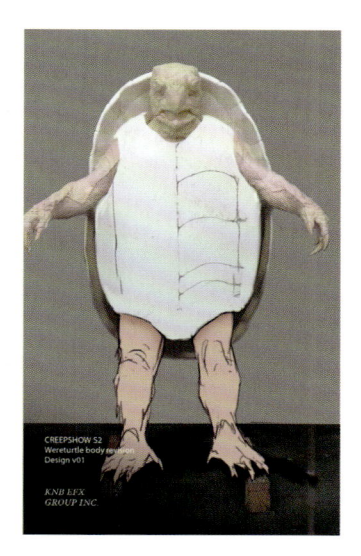

OPPOSITE: A holiday with all the intestinal trimmings (top); Were-Boar concept art by Michael Broom (bottom left); the Were-Boar is Jason Kehler, pictured with Frank Nicotero (bottom right).

THIS PAGE: It's not Yertle. It's not Tooter. And it's no ninja! It's the Were-Turtle from "Shapeshifters Anonymous," played by Scott Loeser, elbow bumping with Adam Pally.

"Look—I've been fortunate enough now to do all of the things that fascinated me as a kid. I wanted to build miniatures like what I saw in *2001*, then I wanted to do big mechanical effects like I saw in *Jaws*, and then I wanted to do makeup effects like I saw in *Dawn of the Dead*. And in Season One alone of *Creepshow*, I was able to do *all* of those things. We had makeup effects, and we had the miniatures that we used in ["Lake Champlain"], and we had these big animatronic creatures and puppets."

Gino smiles and concludes, "We like working on *Creepshow* because it feels like you're shooting movies with a bunch of your buddies in your yard where you grew up. It's got a real communal feeling—and I've been with a lot of these people for years—and that makes you wanna do good because you're with your buddies. You want to impress them: 'Dude, look what I did last night while you were sleeping, and it shoots in two hours.' And it's the stuff we love. It's *Creepshow*. It's Romero. Yeah, we're all in."

> IF YOU'VE EVER WONDERED WHO **GRINDS OUT** OUR GROTESQUERIES--WELL, NOW YOU KNOW. AND SINCE YOU SEEM TO HAVE SURVIVED THIS **ONSLAUGHT OF ODDITIES**, BRACE YOURSELF FOR WHAT'S COMING NEXT. IT'LL SURELY HAVE A **VISCERAL** EFFECT ON YOU. *HEH-HEH...*

CHAPTER SIX

ADVERTISEMENT

BOYS AND GIRLS! NOW YOU CAN GET THE OFFICIAL CREEPSHOW CREEP ROBE ...AND JOIN MY FAN CLUB TOO!

YES! TELL MOM AND DAD THAT IT'S THE GIFT YOU WANT! THE OFFICIAL

CREEPSHOW

CREEP ROBE in LONG-LASTING RAYON GABARDINE
PERFECT FOR HALLOWEEN!

ONLY **$6.95**

You get a dark, creepy threadbare cloak that looks as if it was dug right from the crypt! This OFFICIAL CREPSHOW Creep robe is a MUST for all Creepshow fans!
Don't forget to tell Mom that the suit is made to stand up under lots of hard play, or hours of midnight creeping in graveyards! It's made of fine washable rayon gabardine.
In even size from 4 to 24.

ORDER NOW!

BE THE FIRST OF YOUR FRIENDS TO GET THEM

ORDER NOW AND GET THIS **FREE** CREEP MASK!

This skeletal mask makes your CREEPSHOW Creep costume complete! Masterfully sculpted to look just like the haunting visage of your favorite undead horror host!

Please send me the following 'Creepshow' robe at $6.95 each. Check or Money order only.

Quantity					
Size					

Name _____
Address _____ Apt ____
City _____ Zone ___ State ___

CHAPTER SIX   CREEPSHOW COMIC ADVERTISEMENTS FOR AMUSEMENT ONLY.

MONSTER
S-I-Z-E MONSTERS

7 FEET TALL

In Authentic Color With **GLOW IN THE DARK EYES**

ONLY **$1.00**

Just imagine your friend's shock when they walk into your room and see the 'Monster' reaching out - bigger than life Frankenstein, the original man-made monster, that creation of an evil genius that terrorized the world! A giant 7 feet tall, his eyes glow eerily as his hand reaches out for you!
Mr. Bones the Skeleton, and then there is Mr. Bones - stark scary with nothing left but his rotten bones. A 7-foot monster straight from the grave - his empty eye sockets staring even glowing in the dark!
Money Back Guarantee
Just send $1.00 plus 35c to cover postage and handling for each monster you want.

SOLD OUT!

Rush me my 7 - foot tall glow-in-the-dark monsters. Send me ☐ Frankenstein
☐ Mr. Bones the Skeleton
I enclosed $1 plus 35c for postage
NAME _____
ADDRESS _____
CITY _____ STATE _____ ZIP _____

CREEPY FINGERS BANK
$1.95

Automatic Mechanical Pickpocket

THEY'RE CREEPING UP ON YOU!

PLACE COINS ON COFFIN & A GRUESOME GREEN HAND WITH EERIE BONY FINGERS APPEAR LIKE MAGIC FROM THE GRAVE TO SNATCH THEM.

☐ CREEPY FINGERS BANK $1.95

CREEPSHOW COMIC ADVERTISEMENTS FOR AMUSEMENT ONLY.

NOW MEET OUR *MAESTROS OF THE MACABRE*--THEY'RE THE CUNNING CRETINS WHO TAKE PLEASURE IN SCARING YOU OUT OF YOUR WITS!
THESE SEASONED FEAR-MONGERS RUN AMOK HERE AT *CREEPSHOW*, BUT WE'VE MANAGED TO SNAG A FEW TO SHARE HOW THEY MAKE YOUR NIGHTMARES COME TRUE.
STEP INTO THEIR POSH PARLOR OF *PAIN*. IT'S A SINISTER SITTING ROOM THEY CALL...
CREEP
MICHAEL BROOM 2022

THE DIRECTORS' LAIR

In a 2012 discussion, director George A. Romero expressed the importance of building strong working relationships. "I *gravitate* towards people that I feel have the same sort of [filmmaking] esthetics, and we wind up becoming friends. I mean, that's the way it was in Pittsburgh, for all those years, I worked with the same little family of technicians [...] Relationships are the most important thing, and if you've got those good relationships, you can 'shorthand' your message. You say something, and the DP knows exactly what you're talking about. You don't have to repeat yourself or over-explain."[11]

That *shorthand* communication and connection with his team were key, he says, to moving quickly, efficiently, and—most of all—enjoyably with his crew, his actors, and anyone else involved in the production at hand. Enjoying that process and sharing that shorthand language brought an infectious source of fun; it brought excitement to the team as each member would make even the most oblique of references, then see the light in the eyes of those who "got it." On Romero's sets, most did.

It's that ability to share a shorthand language that fosters the same sorts of working relationships that Greg Nicotero has also enjoyed across the span of his career. And, when it comes to Shudder's *Creepshow*, which moves at an extremely accelerated pace, that verbal shorthand is practically a requirement. Plus, it's just plain fun. He trades film and pop culture references with his team—in work and in play—and enjoys spontaneous rounds of "if you could be inside a movie, which one would it be? *Jaws*? *The Godfather*? *Horror Express*?"

Thinking back a moment, Greg recalls when he first took up the mantel of director, and he cites one of the best pieces of advice he's ever received, one that kept his naturally fun-loving style in the forefront. "When I was doing my first directing [on *The Walking Dead*], [actor/director] Michael Cudlitz said to me, 'Dude, just have fun. You gotta remember to have a good time, 'cuz if you're not having fun, don't do it.' And so, every time I'm walking on set, I remember Michael giving me those words of wisdom, and they've really served me well."[12]

Cudlitz's words carried him into and through directing episodes of *The Walking Dead*, and now they resonate for him on *Creepshow*. He took responsibility to direct the first aired segment, "Gray Matter," humbled by the opportunity to work with stars Adrienne Barbeau, Tobin Bell, and Giancarlo Esposito. Although he grappled with a self-imposed pressure to do right by the legacy of the original work, he delivered a perfectly creepy and claustrophobic segment. It set the stage for what this *Creepshow* would be...and what it could become.

With his directorial work on Season One (he directed two of the twelve flagship segments, the second being "The Finger"), Greg showed he could hit the mark dead-on, and he proved to himself that he could do right in honoring the spirit that George Romero

ABOVE: The master, George A. Romero.

[11] *In Conversation with George A. Romero*, November 2, 2012, TIFF Originals.

[12] *WonderCon@Home 2021*, AMC's *Creepshow*, March 26, 2021, Comic-Con International.

RIGHT: Greg directs on the set of "Gray Matter." Pictured from left to right are Rene Arriagada, Greg Nicotero, Hugh Braselton, Jesse C. Boyd [seated], Shawn Upthegrove, Christopher Nathan.

BELOW: Slating a shot for "Shapeshifters Anonymous."

and Stephen King had set forth—and he *did* have fun. Breathing easier, he let loose with Season Two, comfortably helming four of the regular segments, plus both segments of *The Creepshow Animated Special* and the hour-long "Shapeshifters Anonymous" extravaganza that was *A Creepshow Holiday Special*.

"Finding more humor [in the horror] is more like my personality. And, 'Shapeshifters Anonymous'—I laughed out loud when I read that story. And when I was on set with [stars] Anna [Camp] and Adam [Pally] and Frank [Nicotero]—I really loved the collaborative spirit of doing comedy, doing something that was a lot more lighthearted. We found some great, great moments that I would've probably never found if I was dealing with just a straight horror show. For us to be able to stay within the spirit of *Creepshow* and keep the tone evolving, it really made a big difference."[13]

From the outset, Greg knew he couldn't direct every segment of the series himself—and he didn't want to. With so many other directors with whom he had previously worked and whose work he deeply admired, he reached out to bring the right kind of talent to the directors' lair of Shudder's *Creepshow*. Relationships, remember? Oh, and fluency in that filmmaking shorthand? Yeah, these folks got it.

His first order of business was to tap the original bloodline; he reached out to the man who served as First Assistant Director and musical composer on the original film, and who would then go on to amass an impressive body of work in genre movies, television, and music.

John Harrison is a name well known and highly regarded in the *Creepshow* universe. He's a successful writer, producer, director, and composer. Most pertinent here, he proudly proclaims himself a graduate of the George Romero School of Filmmaking.

"Absolutely! All of us who came out of Pittsburgh [learned from Romero]. Pittsburgh was a real incubator of a lot of talent. Two partners of mine—director Dusty Nelson and editor Pat [Pasquale] Buba—put a company together called The Image Works, and we were doing commercials and industrials, and pretty much following George's pattern with what he did. Eventually, our paths were gonna cross. He was doing sports films, and we called him up, he came over to look at our stuff, and he hired us. He became one of my closest friends and my mentor. It was Richard Rubinstein, George's producing partner, who called me up to come work with George on *Creepshow* as his assistant director. I said, 'Richard, I don't know a thing about assistant directing...this is ridiculous!' But he said, 'No, no—George doesn't need a DGA-type director. He needs a friend to work with him, to keep the thing moving along, and to keep the wheels turning. Just be at his side through this thing.' And so, there I was, working at his side, throughout filming and post-production. And that led to *Day of the Dead* and on and on. And I never went to 'film school'; I went to the George Romero Film School...and, being by his side, I learned *so much*."

ABOVE: John Harrison directs a lively crew during the morgue scene in "Night of the Paw." Also pictured are Craig Owens and Hugh Braselton.

[13] *WonderCon@Home 2021*, AMC's *Creepshow*, March 26, 2021, Comic-Con International.

CHAPTER **SEVEN** 147

ABOVE: Filming an exterior shot for "Night of the Paw," John Harrison chats with Asst. Prop Master, Rene Arrigada. Also pictured is grip John Barber and camera operator Lex Rawlins.

John's learning was extended and enhanced when Romero and Rubinstein invited him to write and direct episodes of *Tales from the Darkside*. It was through those experiences (eight episodes to his directing credit) that John harnessed the skills for efficient storytelling, from both a director's and writer's perspective.

"And because those were short films, you had to be efficient in your ability to tell the story within the time and the budget—and those things were incredibly low-budget. The director, I think, was the lowest-paid guy on the crew," John laughs. "It wasn't DGA, lemme tell ya! But that wasn't the point. The point was, we—me and other directors—got an opportunity to realize our visions, as long as we stayed within the time and budget. And George and Richard trusted me to know how to tell those kinds of stories. And so, the freedom I had to do that was just unparalleled."

He says he never would have expected to have had that sort of freedom on any long-running network show, and he's carried that free and spontaneous spirit with him ever since. Plus, with an impressive amount of anthology-style work to his credit (including *Tales from the Darkside: The Movie* and television's *Tales from the Crypt*), he brought all the right stuff to Greg's *Creepshow* ensemble.

"The style of that kind of storytelling—being able to use visual vocabulary to make the projects appear bigger than they actually were—added more elegance than the budget or time could have suggested was possible. But you've gotta have great artists to collaborate with. To have a cinematographer like Rob Draper, with whom I've done a number of projects—he and I have developed a vocabulary between us that allows us to move fast and to get what we both want. We share a very similar esthetic."

The vocabulary that John references extends, artistically, to what he calls "painting with light." He applauds Rob Draper for his skill in this method, then goes on to give reverence to cinematographer Vittorio Storaro whom John has had, as he says, "the privilege and honor to have worked with." He regards Storaro as a master of the method.

"It's an ability to tell a story with the psychological use of light, whether it's black and white, light and dark, or color. So, instead of having just the two-shot or two-overs of people just talking, talking, talking, we're using the visual vocabulary of the way we move the camera and the way we create a *mise-en-scène* with the color and light in order to tell the story so we don't only need to do it with dialogue. The atmospherics we create are just as important to the story as the dialogue and the plot. It works on the audience in a psychological and subconscious way."

So, he's a visionary director—that's obvious—who uses cinematography as a tool in his director's arsenal to tell compelling stories. Even so, with the tight timing of the *Creepshow* shooting schedule, how does he prepare his approach so he can consistently deliver enticing entertainment? Actually, that prep time is another of the tools in his toolbox.

"Prep is the cheapest money you can spend on a film. A lot of people don't like it, and they just want to get on the floor and start shooting; I don't. I like to make the movie up in my mind, with my collaborators, *before* I get on the floor. I like to know and see it in my mind, because time is precious...and I would rather spend time with the actors rather than stopping to think, 'Wait a minute...how am I gonna shoot this scene?' I always have a plan—and the plan *will* change; it always does. Things come up, new ideas come up, from all kinds of sources. And this is something I definitely learned from George: I'll accept a good idea from *anybody*. But, if I've done my homework, when the difficulties arise, when we've hit the wall, when the happy accident occurs, we can dance, we can improvise."

And the dance began with John's first segment, "The House of the Head." He admits, "That one really scared me; not only for Josh Malerman's excellent story but for how I would direct it! See, when I first came out to do [Shudder's] *Creepshow*, I was slated for two segments. The first was 'Night of the Paw' by John Esposito. Fantastic! Right up my wheelhouse: haunted-house-monkey's-paw type of story. Draper and I knew we were gonna go to town on it, with all kinds of different lighting gags and in-camera time transitions. It was fantastic. And the other one was 'Times is Tough in Musky Holler,' which was just a balls-out revenge story. And I had also written 'Lydia Layne,' but Greg had asked me to let Roxanne [Benjamin] do it because he wanted the female point-of-view for it—and she did a fantastic job with it."

So, while John would go on to direct those two segments, he was also offered another two.

"[Greg] came to me while I was [on set] and said, 'Listen, I've got two other stories. Can you stick around?' I said, 'Sure, what are they?' So, he gave me 'All Hallow's Eve' and 'House of the Head.' And the reason they were put together is because they both involved kids, and we can only work with kids so many hours in a day; so, we would work with kids on the one show during one part of the day, then we'd do the other show in the other part of the day, and we'd never over-use our time allotment with the kids."

As with any *Creepshow* segment, "All Hallow's Eve" came with opportunities and obstacles.

"'All Hallow's Eve' brought its set of challenges because we basically had to do it on location because it was about a town on Halloween night; we couldn't do that on the set. 'House of the Head,' on the other hand, was a bottle episode; all in one location, which was inside the dollhouse, and in Evie's bedroom...but I had no idea how to do it."

His concerns were twofold: first, he'd have no budget to build a dollhouse, the type that he could bring a camera into and, secondly, there would be no budget to animate the family and others—the *inhabitants*—of the dollhouse. So, how was he going to do this? "And so, I said to Greg, 'This scares the shit out of me; I don't know *how* to do this.'" Greg replied to John reassuringly, "We'll figure it out...we'll figure it out."

Ultimately, John credits the crew of Shudder's *Creepshow* for the solution he so desperately needed: "[Prop Master] Lucas [Godfrey] found the dollhouse in a shop outside of Atlanta. It was big enough, it opened on both sides. It was accessible. Then I came up with a scheme to have these little dolls—they weren't animated—so, the only way to do this was to find a way to move around the dollhouse, then come back to them and we

ABOVE LEFT: Setting up the forensics scene in "Night of the Paw." As seen in foreground, Jake Garber (left), Rob Draper (center), and John Harrison (far right).

ABOVE RIGHT: Directing Connor Christie and Luke Daniels, playing several of the vengeful kids in "All Hallow's Eve."

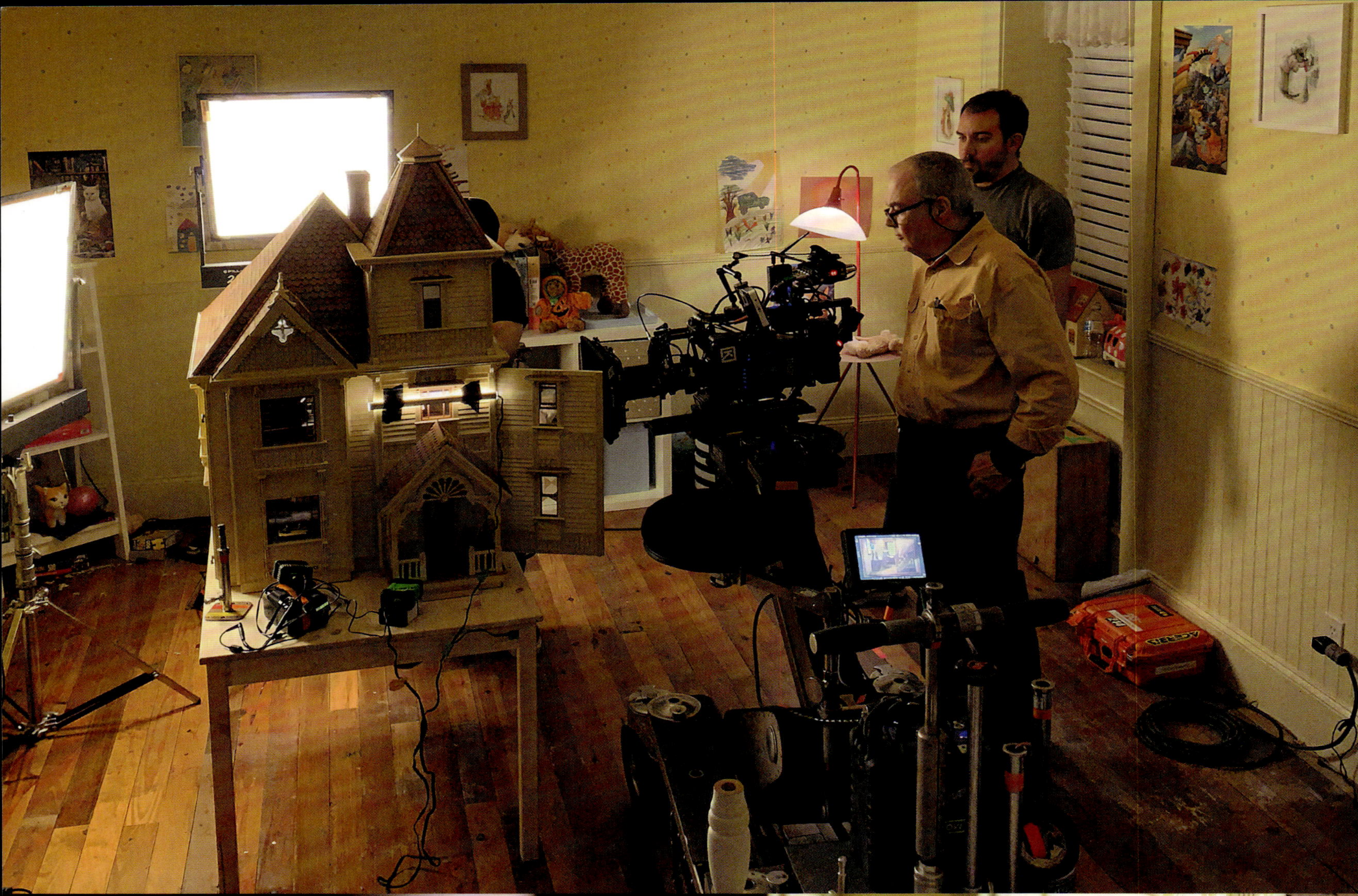

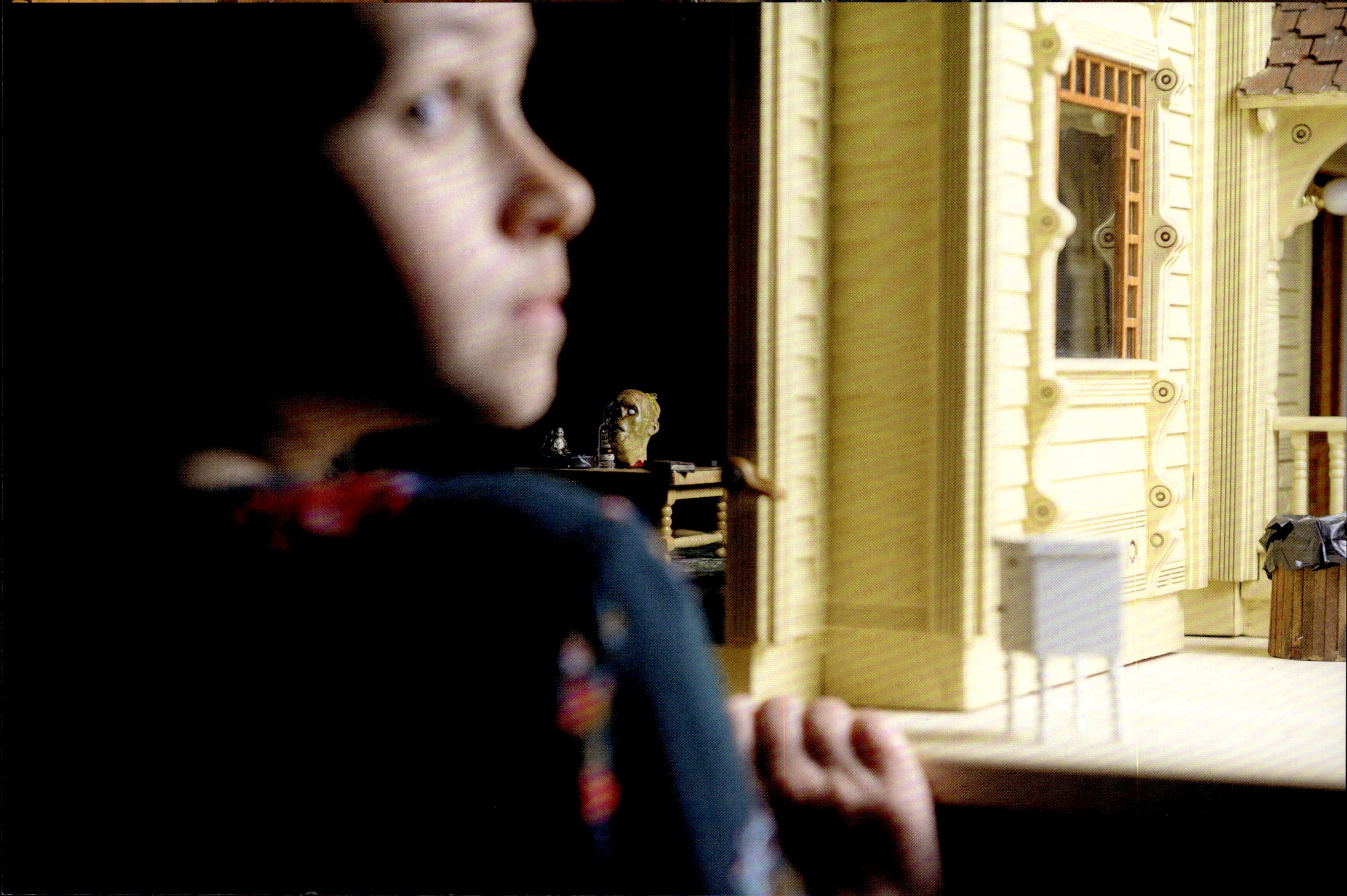

could reposition them quickly, and the way to do that was to tell the story from Evie's mind. And once I hit on that idea, I figured I'd know how to do that, then. What we're really witnessing is a horror that may or may not be in her own mind. So, I designed a lot of shots where we could come into the house, then close-up on her face...and as I moved in on her, I could transition and do shots moving around and through the house, which gave us the impression, 'Oh, it's in her head. It's in her mind.' She's actually putting herself into the house to look around for this evil head that keeps showing up and killing the little dolls.

"The story is so compelling...and it's subtle. I didn't want it to be about the dissolution of a family, and Evie's transferred that into the dollhouse...but I wanted a *little bit* of that, so there's the financial stress on the family, and the guy in the shop says how the kids often figure things out when they play in the dollhouses—and that's what Evie's doing. It just so happens that there's just this twisted thing going on in the dollhouse!"

Keeping the twists coming while continuing to tap alumni of anthology storytelling, Greg next reached out to another accomplished director whose work he enjoyed and for whom KNB had provided effects gags. His mental Rolodex runs deep and wide, and this time it landed on Rusty Cundieff for Season Two's "Sibling Rivalry" segment.

"It was quite a blast," Rusty says. "The script was fantastic. The words were just all on the page, so it was just a matter of, as it often is with a good script when you're directing, just don't fuck it up [*laughs*]. Don't make bad choices. [...] For me, it was just a matter of making sure that I got all the moments, and then enjoying all the practical mayhem of blood and guts and vampire teeth that Greg's crack team allowed us to show.

It's not that often that you get to work with practical effects nowadays, 'cause everything is so digital and so kind of processed in. So, it was kind of a blast."[14]

As mentioned, Rusty was no stranger to the director's chair nor to horror...nor to the anthology vehicle, either. His flagship horror outing was 1995's horror-comedy film *Tales from the Hood*, offering a uniquely engaging urban take on EC-style storytelling. Well-made and well-received, it would go on to spawn two sequels, the second of which immediately preceded Rusty's work on Shudder's *Creepshow*.

Greg adds, "We called [Rusty] on Season One to come down and shoot, but he wasn't available. And, for a director like Rusty, he understands the anthology world. When you hire a director on a show like this, I feel like the first thing I have to do is apologize, because you know, it's like, 'OK—you've got about three-and-a-half days[...]and it's going to be down and dirty and quick, but just have fun.'"[15]

And, for Rusty, it was fun, so much so that he returned to direct Greg's adaptation of the Joe Hill short story, "Mums."

"I've got to say," Rusty prefaces, "Greg's crew is just fantastic—his DP, Rob Draper [and everyone else], just a great group of people and just so on top of things, which you have to be when you're shooting so fast. It was never a crew problem the entire time that we shot. We had some issues, just in terms of the weather and stuff like that, but they were just so on top of it, and it was a fantastic experience[...] [The story] takes place in this little farming area and it deals with some social issues[...] and I give Greg big props for that because I love social stuff[...]but this deals with it in a very, very light way that allows the horror

OPPOSITE: John Harrison stands by while the Smith-Smiths' house is dressed for dread (top) while Cailey Fleming (bottom) asks for reasurance that the "House of the Head" isn't really haunted. It isn't, is it?

BELOW: A Shudder-ing showing—(LTR) Stephen Langford, Greg Nicotero, Paul Dini, Dana Gould.

[14] *ComicCon@Home 2021*, *Creepshow*, July 24, 2021, Comic-Con International.

[15] *ComicCon@Home 2021*, *Creepshow*, July 24, 2021, Comic-Con International.

FPS 23.976
SHUTTER 180.0
EI 800
ND -
WB 5600 K
+0.0 CC
BAT 14.9V
B014 C007
REC
CARD
0:21 h
TC 19:27:13:18
ALEXA MINI

OPPOSITE: Director Rusty Cundieff demonstrates the lethal lunge he's looking for (top) whie actress Maddie Nichols (bottom) moves in close for a hug—and a kill—from "Sibling Rivalry."

ABOVE: Rusty Cundieff directs Brayden Benson in the gruesome garden of "Mums." Also pictured is Aaron King (center).

LEFT: Rusty Cundieff readies actress Malone Thomas for a scene from "Mums."

CHAPTER SEVEN 153

BELOW: Director Roxanne Benjamin crouches off camera as Tricia Helfer struggles within the confines of her own doing, from "Lydia Layne's Better Half."

OPPOSITE TOP: "I mean, it's a blood cannon...it explodes everywhere," laughs Roxanne Benjamin (with actor Dana Gould and Jeffrey F. January) on "Skincrawlers."

OPPOSITE BOTTOM: Danielle Lyn in the "Lydia Layne's Better Half" segment.

[16] *ComicCon@Home 2021, Creepshow,* July 24, 2021, Comic-Con International.

[17] *Creepshow: The New Blood | Behind the Scenes,* September 2019, Shudder.

[18] *On the Set and Between the Pages of the New Creepshow,* October 16, 2019, AV Club.

[19] *Roxanne Benjamin Drops Creepshow Series Update at SXSW,* March 11, 2019, Movieweb.

to progress[...] And there's some great physical [effects] in a garden, and there's death and there's blood and all the good shit that Greg always brings to all of his stuff."[16]

As Rusty teases, *Creepshow* offers directors the freedom to delve into ideas in decidedly unconventional, abstract, and unusual ways. For emerging directors, it's a playground to explore and a place where they can build their shorthand fluency while learning from those who've been in the business for a while. As John Harrison previously noted, it would be director Roxanne Benjamin who would introduce viewers to "Lydia Layne's Better Half." Another in the line of multi-faceted talents, and hailing from Pennsylvania, as well, Roxanne is a familiar "newer" face in horror, yet no stranger to the anthology style of storytelling.

"Weirdly, that's where I kind of started—in anthologies," Roxanne muses, "and it really lets you play around in a shorter format that might not work in a longer format. It's a little bit of morality-tale type stuff, and I feel like that was a lot of what the original *Creepshow* was about."[17]

While she's obviously confident within the short-film framework (see her celebrated work as producer of the *V/H/S* series and director of the "Siren" segment in *Southbound*), in "Lydia Layne's Better Half," she, her cast, and crew were confined by the polished steel walls of an elevator. Actually, it was another of Production Designer Aimee Holmberg's clever sets, complete with flyaway walls yet filmed in perfectly claustrophobic angles by Cinematographer Rob Draper. As written by John Harrison and embellished with Roxanne's acuity for female character studies, it dives headlong into the world of corporate politics, personal ambitions, and human desires. Ultimately, a passed-over promotion leads to a dire confrontation between the two female leads. Roxanne pits the two against one another in agonizing assertions and accusations, with a horrific outcome. Directing her actresses to fully sink their teeth into their characters' offsetting goals, she makes it difficult for viewers to decide who's good and who's bad here. It's pitch perfect for a *Creepshow* tale.

It was in her second segment, "Skincrawlers," where all hell broke loose—and blood and gore came raining down from all directions. Written by veterans Paul Dini and Stephen Langford, this one took Roxanne out of her usual naturalistic settings and dropped her deep into a new color-saturated (and blood-saturated and laugh-infested) realm. To take the notion of "perfectly safe" fat-sucking leeches to overt and absurd lengths, Roxanne laughs as she recalls the shoot...and the blood cannon. "That was the *most* fun![...] I mean, it's a blood cannon. It explodes everywhere and then it rains for, like, thirty seconds."[18]

And, if nothing else, it's the "fun" of the material and the fun-loving nature of Greg and his crew that draws in directors of all experience levels. As a relative newcomer to directing, the capable Roxanne gives all due regard and reverence to the *Creepshow* team. "Working with Greg Nicotero is really cool, and there's a lot of history between the people who are working on [the show]...a lot of people involved in it who were involved in the original [movie], too [...] It's really cool to be a fly on the wall with these guys, and also just to benefit from their years of experience."[19]

Well, if this is going to be a "years of experience" discussion, then it has to wrap up with the guest director of Season One's

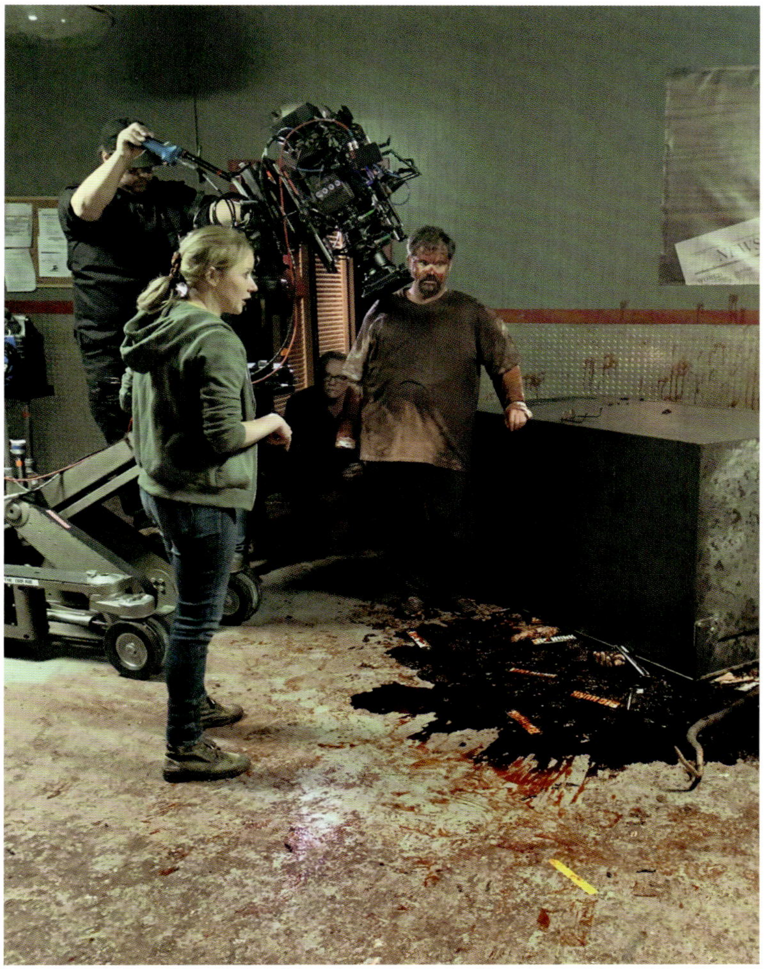

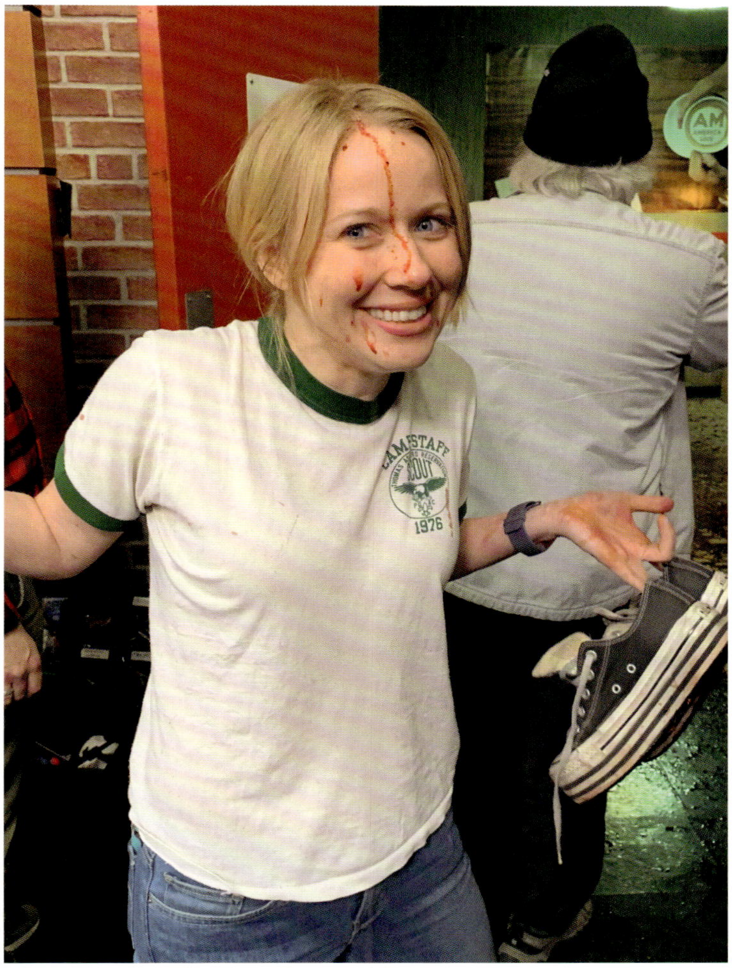

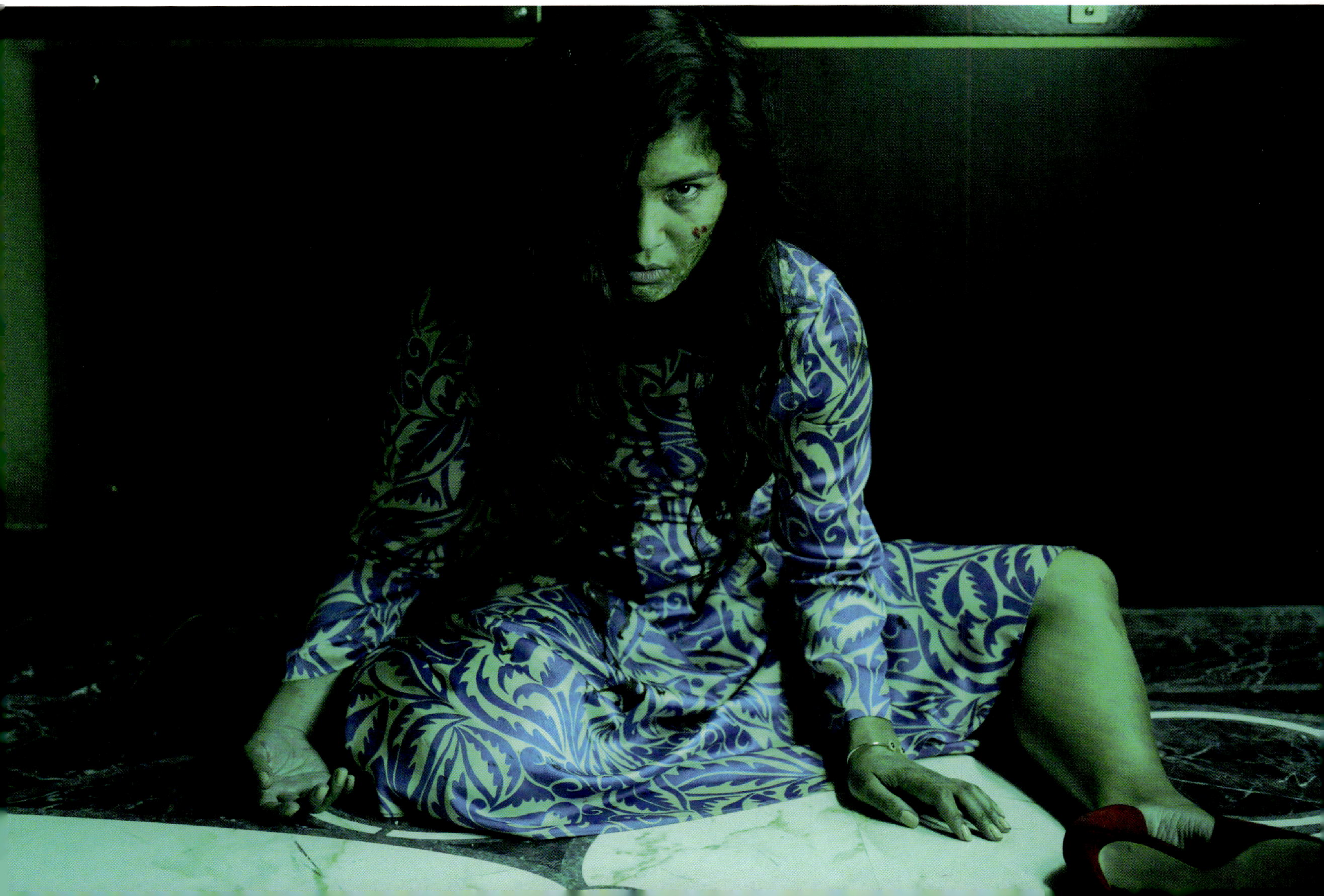

CHAPTER SEVEN

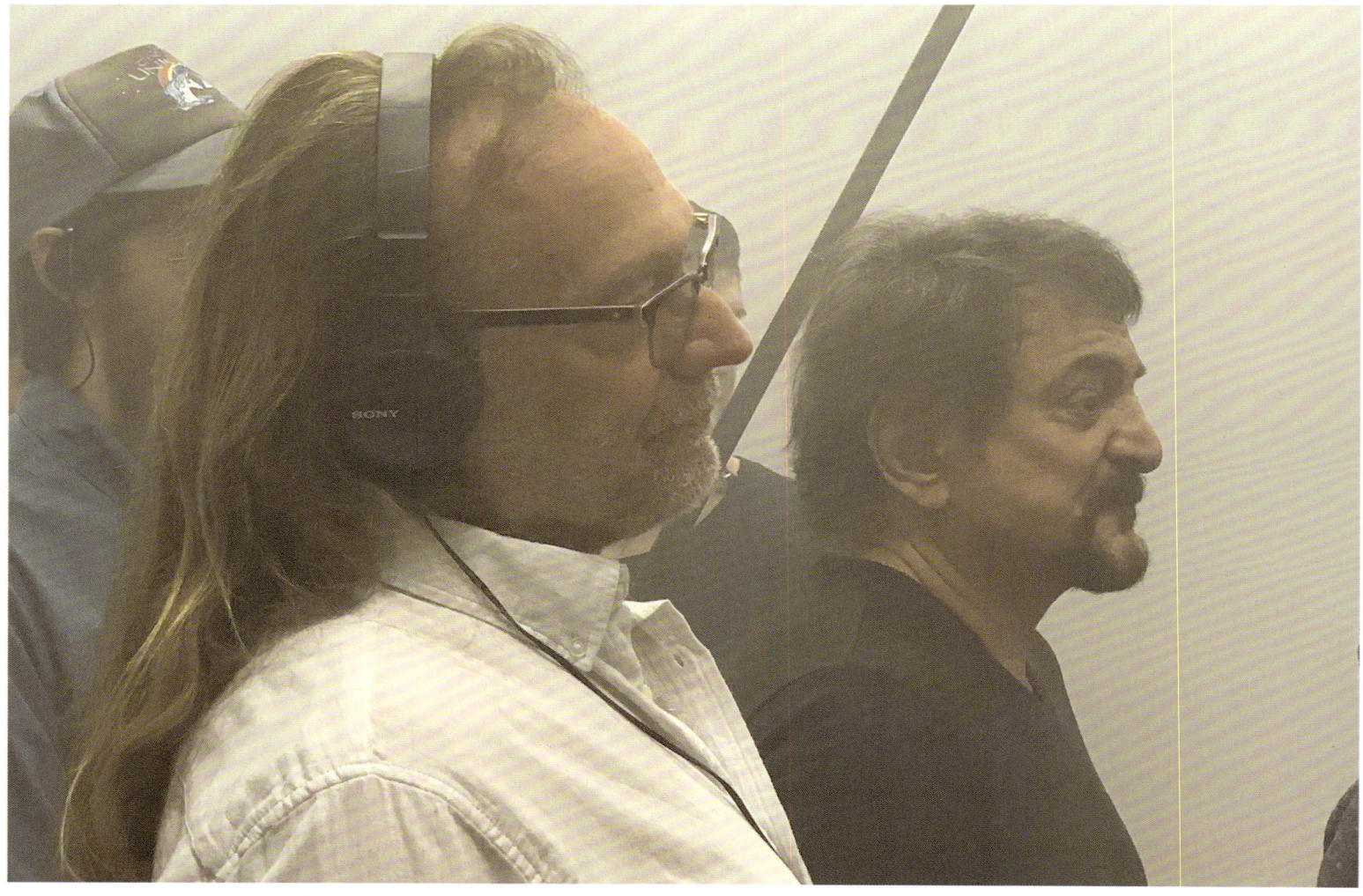

"By the Silver Water of Lake Champlain," adapted from a story by Joe Hill and directed by Greg's makeup and effects mentor, Tom Savini.

Savini's presence in the director's chair (err...*lair*) is yet another full-circle milestone for *Creepshow*. It also marks another master from the hallowed hall of makeup and effects world who firmly established himself as a director (see television's *Tales from the Darkside* and the 1990 revisitation of *Night of the Living Dead*). As Roxanne said, the *Creepshow* team all know one another, they've worked with one another, and they've shared, taught, and learned with and from one another. It's practically incestuous (cue *The Hills Have Eyes*, either version).

"The first segment [Greg] offered me was the monkey's paw segment that John Harrison ended up directing," Savini says, "but I prefer ["By the Silver Water of Lake Champlain"], no doubt about it [...] So he sent me this script, and I said, 'Greg, are all the endings to all the episodes so ambiguous?' There was no ending, no resolve to my episode. And he said, 'I'm sorry you don't like it, we could give you an episode next season if you like.' I said, 'No, no—let me try to work with this.'"[20]

Through some rewrites of the story adaptation and with some character changes, the story became what Savini regarded as truly great; it evolved into a story with real heart, all centered around the mythical sea beast that resolves the young characters' key conflict with the imposing stepfather, Chet (James Devoti)...and the resolution is satisfyingly savage. "This [segment] is sweet and sad, and then heroic," Savini says. "It's a kind of feel-good [segment]." And only in *Creepshow* can a story that features a feasting sea beast emerge as "feel-good." Gotta love that!

And, bringing it all back to Greg, Savini offers this: "I've known Greg since he was 14. He was a little kid, visited the set of [*Day*] *of the Dead*. He was my assistant on a couple of movies I did. And I said to him...'Greg, you would have all of this if you had never even met me... There's two words for why this is all happening for you: *you're good*.' [...] He was this little kid, he was 'Gut Boy' on *Day of the Dead*; he handled the pig intestines for us. Unfortunately, they had unplugged every refrigerator while we were in Florida for three weeks. The stench was—and we had to use them. You can't go buy new pig intestines at three in the morning when we did the effect. But the stench was unbelievable."[21]

Today, if ever the fridge full of intestines might spoil, Greg would likely assure his team, "We'll figure it out...we'll figure it out." And they'd have fun doing it!

OPPOSITE: Horror legend Tom Savini takes the slate (top) while Greg looks on as his mentor directs (bottom) the fog-shrouded sea serpent tale, "By the Silver Water of Lake Champlain."

ABOVE: Tom Savini directs an exterior shot for his segment, one he warmly regards for its fantastical "feel good" essence. At the right, actress Gena Shaw looks on.

WE PROMISED THIS WOULD BE THE *MOST FUN* YOU'VE EVER HAD BEING SCARED. WELL, THESE PRACTITIONERS OF PERIL HAVE SURELY DELIVERED. NOW, CONTINUE ON TO MEET THE FOLKS WHO ADD THE FINAL TOUCHES. YOU KNOW--THE FINAL *NAILS* IN YOUR *COFFIN!* HEH-HEH...

[20] *'Creepshow' Series Director and Horror Legend Tom Savini on How Cinema Saved His Life*, September 4, 2019, SlashFilm.com.

[21] *The Chattering Hour - Tom Savini*, October 14, 2021, Chris Roe Management.

HORROR HOUSE

$3.00

HORRIBLE HANDS
A frightening prop made from the same latex rubber used in Hollywood films! only $3.00 each

DO YOUR FRIENDS CALL YOU UGLY?
.....If they don't, make sure they will with this horrifying rubber werewolf mask!

$4.00

$2.00

SHRUNKEN HEAD
Looks absolutely real! This scary fleshy head will scare your friends every time!
only $2.00

$1.00

TARANTULA SPIDER
A real horrific hairy creature, sure to scare your family and friends! Listen to them scream as you drop them from above!
only $1.00

FRANKENSTEIN'S MONSTER
ALSO AVAILABLE - WITCH AND CAVEMAN
The mad doctor's creation come to life with this high-quality realistic mask! only $3.00

$3.00

$1.00

RAT IN THE BOX
Open the box and an evil-looking rat leaps from out from under the cover to attack! only $1.00

SOLD OUT!

☐ ...HEAD ☐ ZOMBIE
☐ RAT IN A BOX ☐ CAVEMAN

NAME _____ ADDRESS _____
CITY _____ STATE _____ ZIP _____

CREEPSHOW COMIC ADVERTISEMENTS FOR AMUSEMENT ONLY.

TONIGHT AT MIDNIGHT
— ONE PERFORMANCE ONLY —

You'll Meet These Monsters
FACE-TO-FACE!

Don't be afraid to screm - that cold clammy hand may belong to Dracula or the Mummy - they may even be seated beside YOU!

PLEASE TRY NOT TO FAINT

VAMPIRE! · THE CREEP! · MUMMY! · WOLF MAN!

IN PERSON - FAMOUS
MONSTERS
NEW CONCEPT IN HORROR

FRANKENSTEIN
HUNCHBACK
MR. HYDE

CAN YOU TAKE SHOCK AFTER SHOCK??!
Pure Skin-Crawling Terror!

SEE! Beautiful Girl BURNED ALIVE Before Your Terrified Eyes!

SEE! The Blood-Curdling BUZZ-SAW MURDER You MIGHT 'Lose Your Head'!

SEE! MYSTERY GIRL Without a Middle — Missing from Neck to Knee

For the Frightime of Your Lifetime
DON'T MISS THIS SHOCKER!

1,000 Free Copies Famous Monsters Magazine

ON THE SCREEN
Dawn of Frankenstein

Tickets on Sale Now!
All Seats Only 75¢

TONIGHT LATE SHOW ONLY

CREEPSHOW COMIC ADVERTISEMENTS FOR AMUSEMENT ONLY.

OK-- HERE'S ONE FOR THE NAUSEATING NERDS WITH A DIABOLICAL LOVE FOR TWISTED TECHNOLOGY.
MEET OUR DASTARDLY DEVOTEES OF POST-PRODUCTION MAYHEM AND DISCOVER THEIR TRICKS FOR TAINTING EVERY CREEPSHOW TALE WITH A FINAL DOSE OF SPINE-TINGLING TERROR...
STEP INTO THEIR STENCH-FILLED STUDIO AND BEHOLD THE WRETCHED WIZARDRY THEY FONDLY CALL...
MICHAEL BROOM 2022

UNUSUAL AFTER-EFX

As an accomplished post-producer and filmmaker in his own right, Drew Sawyer approached *Creepshow* with a practical sensibility. He knew, upon his first meeting with Greg Nicotero, that this show was not intended or expected to be a heavy visual effects ("VFX") show; rather, it was a series that would showcase the sorts of practical, on-set, in-camera effects that KNB is celebrated for; the VFX work would simply add enhancement and embellishment...and, well, a little bit more.

In the course of his duties as a co-producer on the show, Drew coordinates a team of editors, VFX artists, and sound designers. His hands are absolutely full with this extended team as he caters to the needs and demands of *Creepshow*. He calls this the hardest work he's ever done in film or television...and the most fun, too.

"I hand-picked a kind of 'Dirty Dozen' from my bullpen in the cutting room; guys and girls I knew could speak that same genre language and also listen to Greg...because when he might say, 'Uhh, let's do it like Lucio Fulci,' they had to know what that meant. And so, we all went through a boot camp, and we watched *Phantasm*, and we watched the *Evil Dead* films, and we went through all the Fulci we could stomach, and we used that to build our shorthand language so we could go really fast with Greg. So, later when we're editing and deciding to do a zoom in on a frame, I'm asking Greg, 'Are we going Fulci on this or are we going Raimi?' And he'd say, 'Yeahhh...we're going Fulci on this one.'"

Drew's hand-picked, boot-strapped editors included leads Patrick Perry and Kristina Kromer, along with Gerhardt Slawitschka, James Michael Crawford, Michael Goldberg, and Shari Coleman.

"Our challenge is to make each segment feel fresh and exciting," says Patrick Perry, "while still providing that 'core horror' experience. I was one of the first editors to start work on Season One...and a lot of that was nailing the certain look and horror anthology vibe. The difference since Season One, though, is now the show is more at ease with itself and, editorially, we're able to branch out into unexpected territory. It's become more self-referential and playful, still without betraying its original ethos."

Also a Season One veteran, Kristina Kromer echoes the sentiment that, with each successive segment, the show has found its voice and flexed its style. For her, "A Dead Girl Named Sue" was a standout segment. "It was the first black and white noir period piece that I've ever cut. It was beautifully shot and all the actors nailed that feel, and that whole look influenced the way I cut it. Instead of quick and flashy cuts—it's not slow but, rather, very deliberate. It felt like a great change of pace."

Drew had a lot of preparation to wrangle before the daily rushes landed in his lap, or else he'd be behind before he even got started. "So, on our very first meeting, when Greg asked how I thought we'd get the result in the time we'd have available, I told him that, 'I guess we're gonna go as fast as possible, we're

ABOVE: Three partners in post-production perfection: (LTR) Executive Producer Greg Nicotero, Co-Producer (Post) Drew Sawyer, Co-Producer Julia Hobgood.

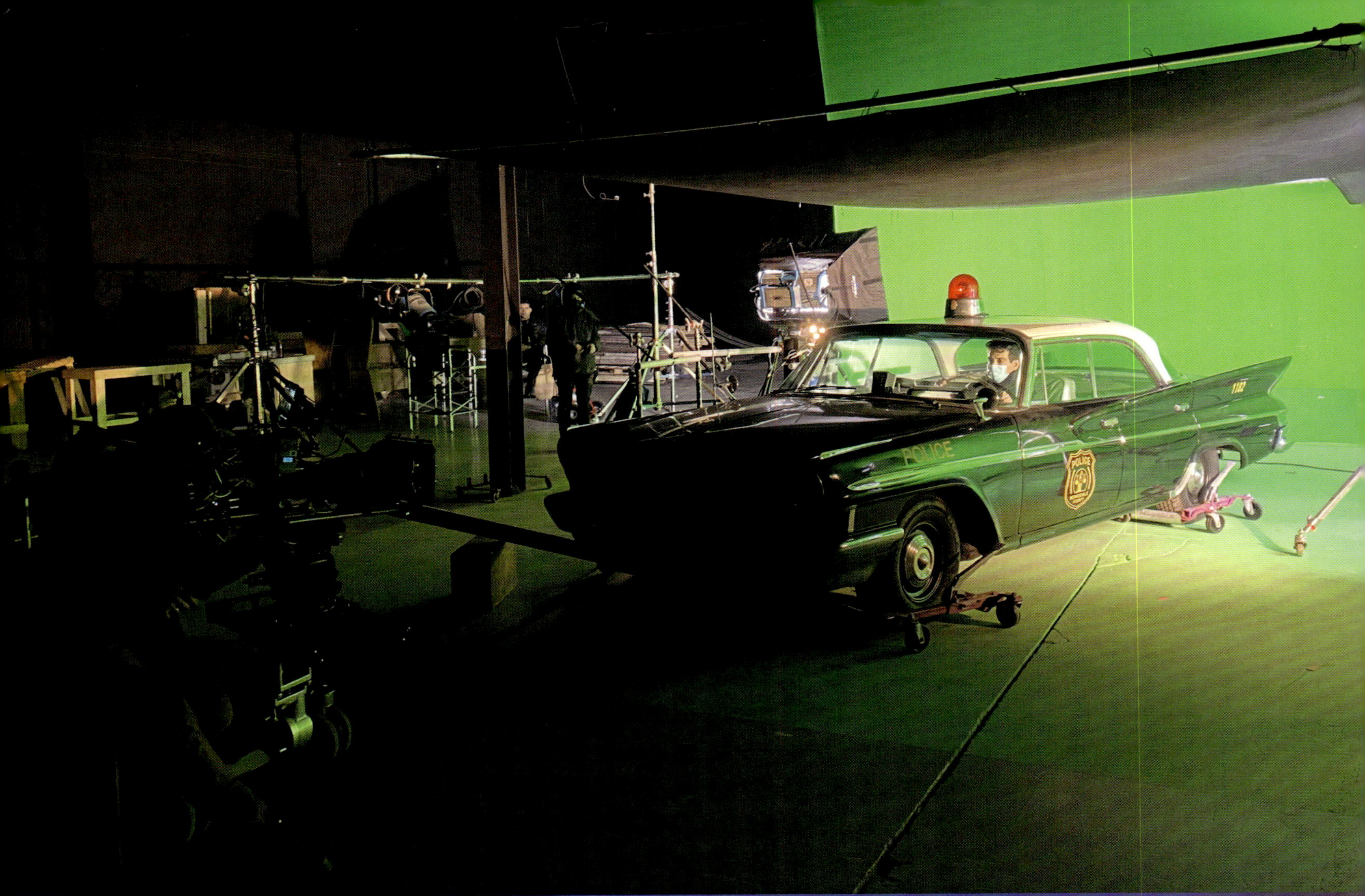
POLICE

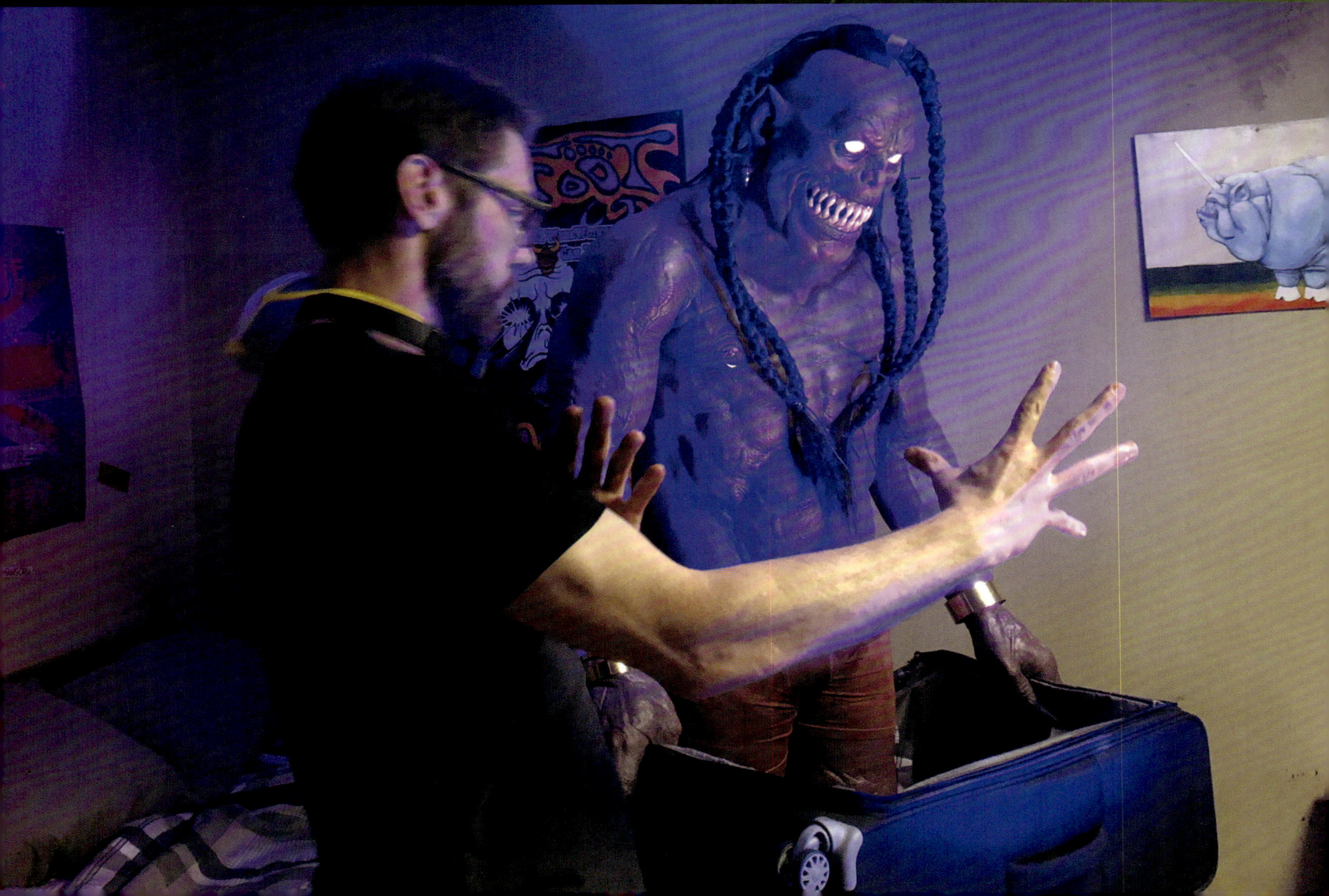

gonna do a full study of all the origin and genre material...and we're gonna make it great!' And, even with my obligations to the team in the cutting room, I was on set during most of the shooting. Literally, after a take, it was like Rob Draper would look at me, then Greg would look at me, and I'd just say, 'It's fine. That's great. We can totally work with those elements.' We were there to augment and enhance what the KNB team did, extending whatever we needed to, but never stepping in to outright replace elements."

Drew goes on to detail the collaborative discussion that unfolded during production of different segments. With the Djinn suit worn by Carey Jones in "The Man in the Suitcase," there were concerns about whether the overall effect would work onscreen. "And I said, 'Yeah, it's going to work; it's fine. You've got all the practical elements; you've given me everything I need. I'm gonna blend 'em, and then we're just gonna do a few little things that make it feel real—like the way it would affect the wall behind it… but we're not gonna replace the Djinn."

The process on "Mums" was similar, Drew reveals. "There are some beautiful on-set pieces there, and we're augmenting things so a Venus fly trap can bite, and we've got on-set dead heads and we're just adding gravel falling out of their mouths in post, but most of it's still practical."

For "Queen Bee," the editing team cut "back and forth between a miniature, an on-set piece, and a digital piece, all within shot-for-shot-for-shot. And then we go, quite literally, from a practical kill to a digital antennae brain insert."

Drew and Prop Master Lucas Godfrey go way back, hailing from the same small town, so Drew found it "hilariously full-circle" to work with Lucas when he moved in front of the camera for "Skeletons in the Closet." "That *Phantasm* ball is just stuck in him and I'm like, 'I'm going full-HAM with this and see what Greg says.' And Greg just came back with, 'More! Love it!' And that whole segment was hardcore practical; lot of stuff on strings, you know, monofilament. There's actually so much monofilament on *Creepshow* that it's hysterical. I can't believe that shit still works."

Some segments, as expected, would use more VFX than others, like the "CG extravaganza" that was "Okay, I'll Bite." "Greg hates

OPPOSITE TOP: "When we did the poor-man's process in the car, we shot that purposely so it looked like the old poor-man's process...all jerky and everything." —Rob Draper on "A Dead Girl Named Sue." Pictured in the car is Cristian Gonzalez.

OPPOSITE BOTTOM: "They shot that and then stood back and wondered if it was gonna work. And I said, 'Yeah it's gonna work; it's fine.'" — Drew Sawyer on "The Man in the Suitcase." David Bruckner directs Carey Jones as the Djinn.

BELOW: By alternating in scenes of time-lapse sprout growth, Drew Sawyer's team literally bring "Mums" to life on screen. Pictured is Aaron King at the camera with Erin Beute sprouting to life below.

CHAPTER EIGHT 163

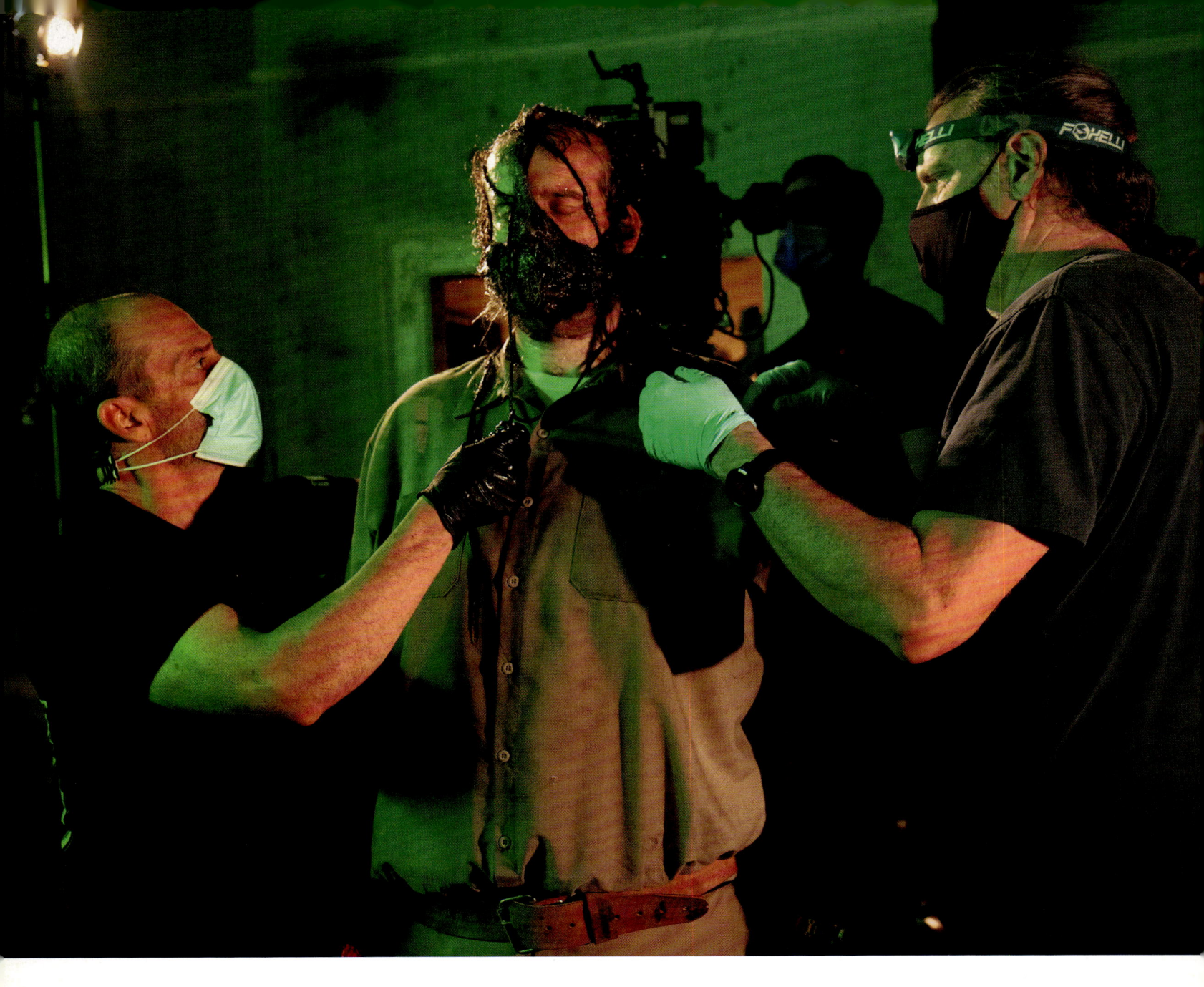

ABOVE: Gino Crognale (left) and Jake Garber (right) deploy Cloggy onto actor Eric Edelstein's face (while Aaron King visualizes the shot from behind). Post EFX will add dripping tendril effects.

OPPOSITE: "That actress [Sarah Jon] deserves some mega-trophy for what she went through. She never stopped screaming on set, making the Krasue noises, and we just rolled her around on the green screen set, changing lighting setups and getting different angles, all while she had that that intestinal beard hanging from her."—Drew Sawyer on "Drug Traffic." Carlos Mancia is the grip in greensuit.

spiders, so I don't know why he even allowed that one. The KNB guys are telling me they're going to bring a tarantula hawk spider on set, and I'm just asking, 'Have you guys talked to Greg about this? Does he know?' And during the concept meetings, Greg would just get up and leave; he wasn't gonna look at a bunch of pictures of spiders. And, yeah, there was a lot of post work in that one, but in some of the bigger shots, we were using *real* spiders, taxidermy spiders, and the CG spider, all in the same shot. And we were making them all move and wiggle at the same time."

In terms of "practical-to-digital handoffs," Season Two's "Pipe Screams" might exemplify the marrying of the methods, thanks to a slithering, sentient mass of hair named "Cloggy." Drew elaborates: "Cloggy was crazy because we wanted to see how far we could take it and have some fun...like, can we add some more poop stains to the wall back there? We wanted to make it really gross, and we wanted to give Cloggy dangly bits that try to reach out and grab at things, and that was the most fun because it wasn't to disturb the practical effect; it was just to augment it and have as much fun as possible."

Drew and the VFX team are constantly juggling new challenges to turn out convincing and carefully placed embellishments. And quickly. But he's never without a plan (well, mostly not), although often times shots needed for post do come on the fly.

"Greg always knows what he wants. He has a mind for it and is always building it all out in his head—and we'd look at a sequence and know that we're going to have to lean on some VFX, but with as much practical effects as possible. Like with 'Drug Traffic' and the *Krasue* monster, I knew what I needed for post and he knew it, too, and we were in the moment and in a hurry and we said 'fuck it'—and in his typical Greg-flannel shirt, he just grabbed the creature and perfectly placed it while the camera rolled. 'Like this?' and then 'Like this?' he'd be asking. And we were zooming through everything we absolutely had to have, shots that would usually take hours of setup. And I laughed and said, 'All right, we just got all ten elements in, like, fifteen minutes. We're good!'"

He laughs when he says that no shooting plan survives first contact on *Creepshow*. He knows the shots he needs—so does Greg—and it becomes an exercise in compromise as both men employ guerilla-style tactics to get what they want for a compelling segment. They scurry to get additional elements within the sets that remain standing for just another day. The principal actors are typically gone after a day or so, but the creatures are still available (usually) to fill the need. It often requires on-the-day gametime decisions of what they can and cannot do in their ambitious vision, squeezing every drop of blood possible out of what's available to them.

CHAPTER **EIGHT**

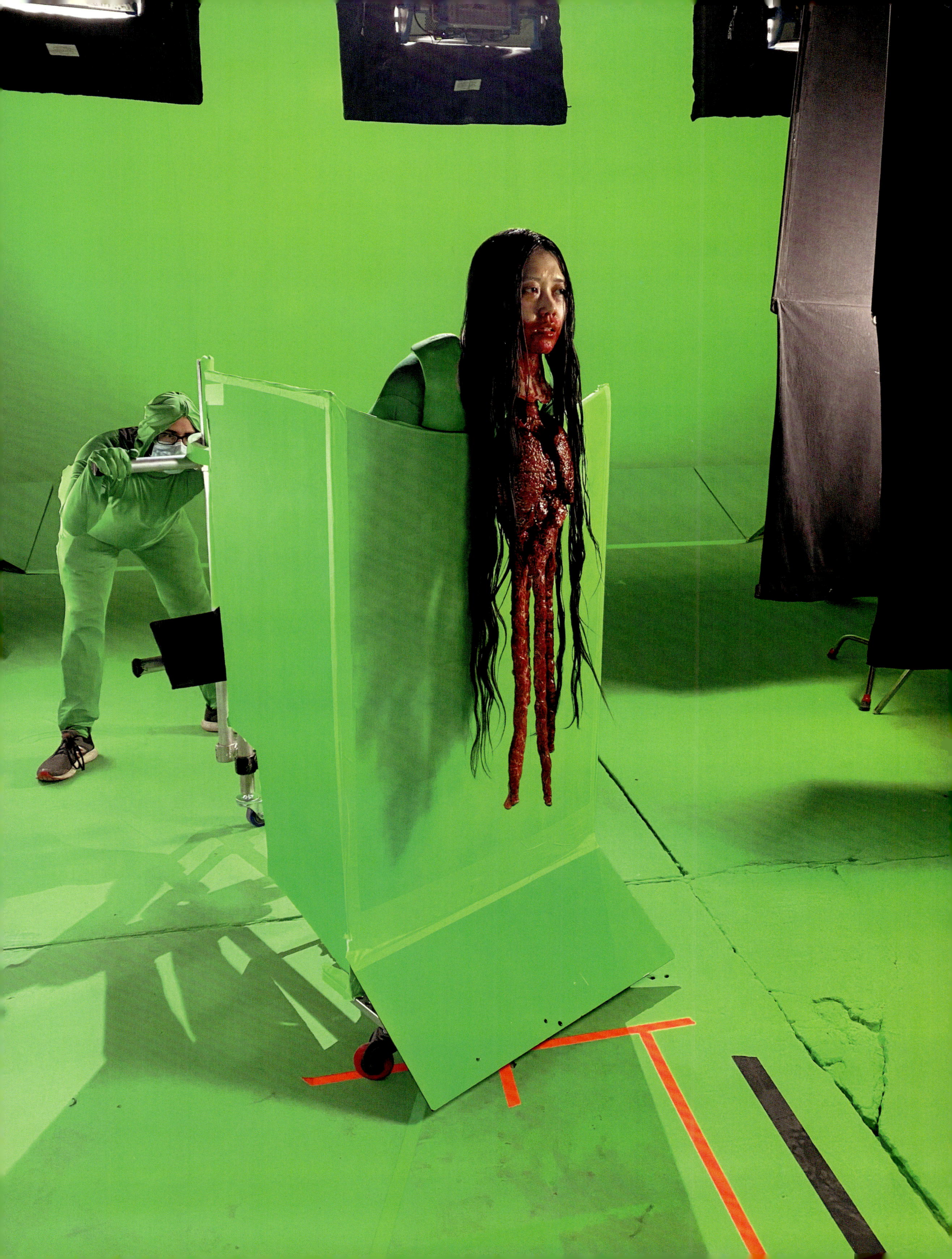

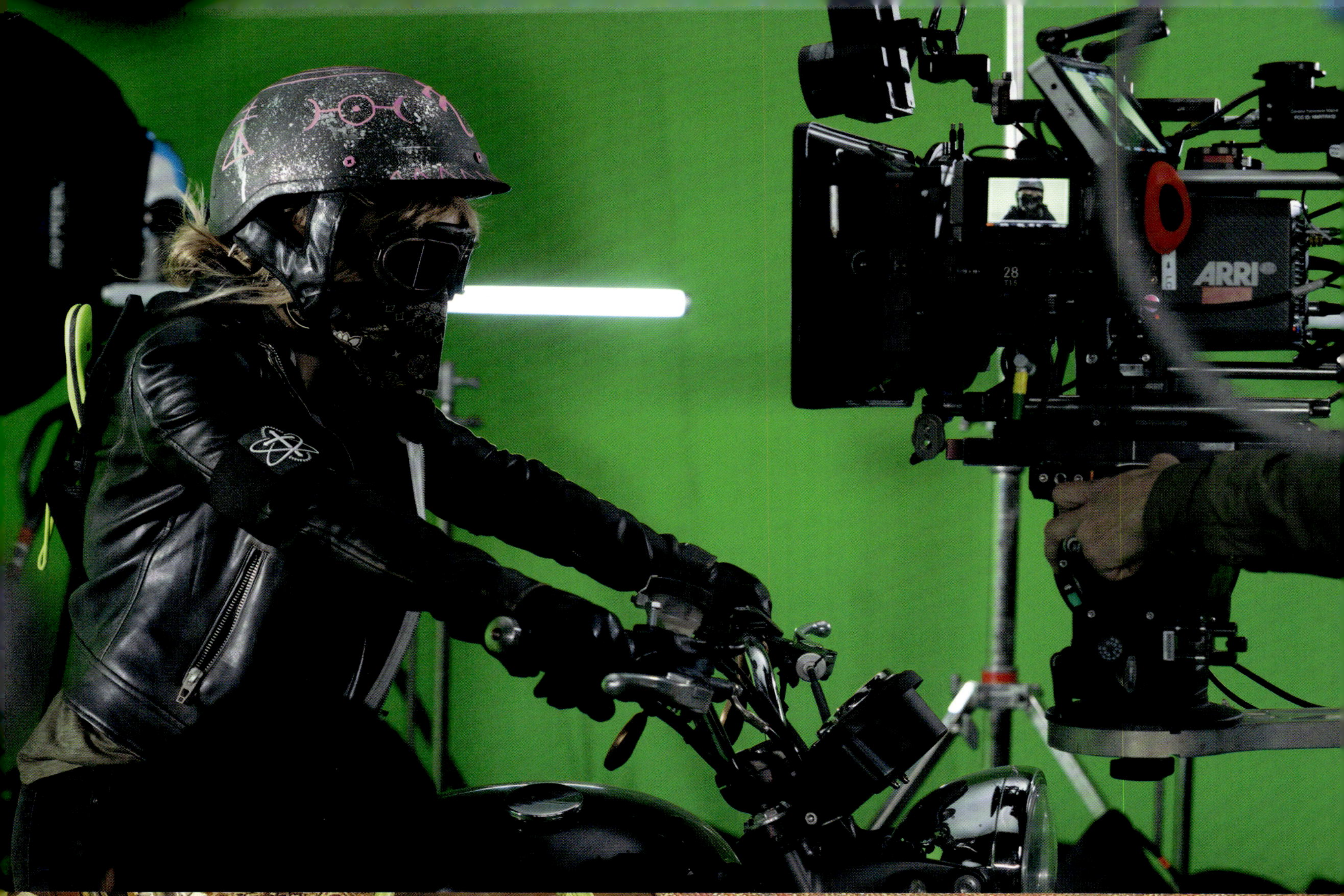
ARRI
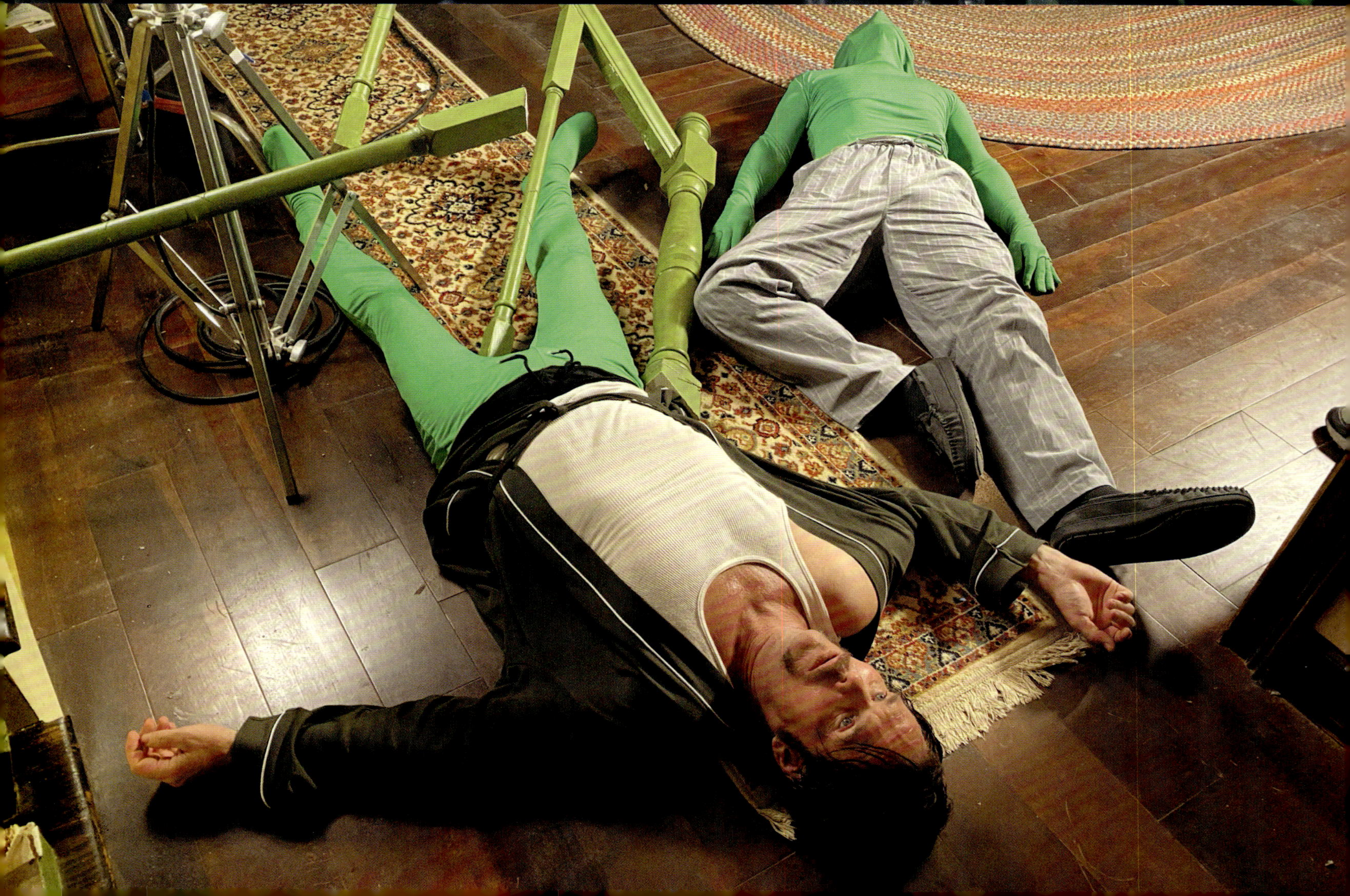

OPPOSITE TOP: No, it's not "How Green was My Valley?" Riding through what will be a bleak and barren landscape is Abigail Dolan, from "Meter Reader."

OPPOSITE BOTTOM: Little Joe Aurora decides it's time for his obnoxious Uncle Kevin (Kevin Dillon) to split. (From "Model Kid.")

LEFT: A practical blending of physical effects and post-production clean-up, as Kadianne Whyte sprouts wings (puppeteered by Jake Garber) in "Stranger Sings."

BELOW: A stuntwoman (Shellita Boxie) stands in for Brittany L. Smith as she becomes entangled in a tentacle from "Within the Walls of Madness."

CHAPTER EIGHT 167

side view

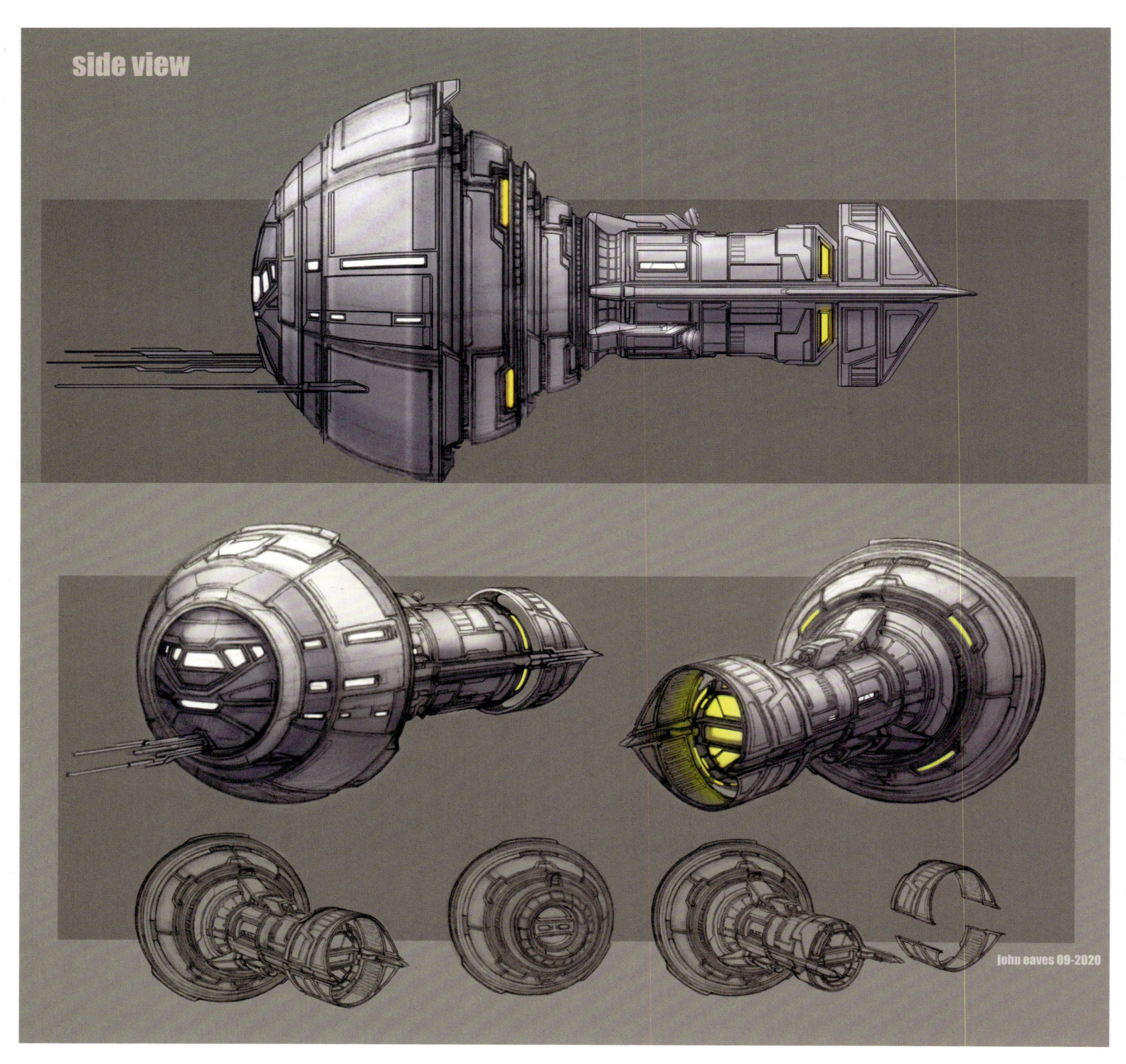

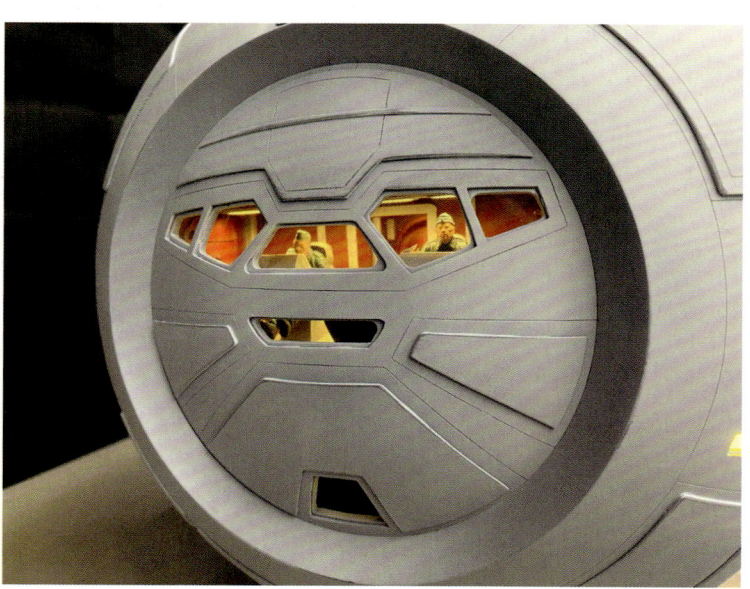

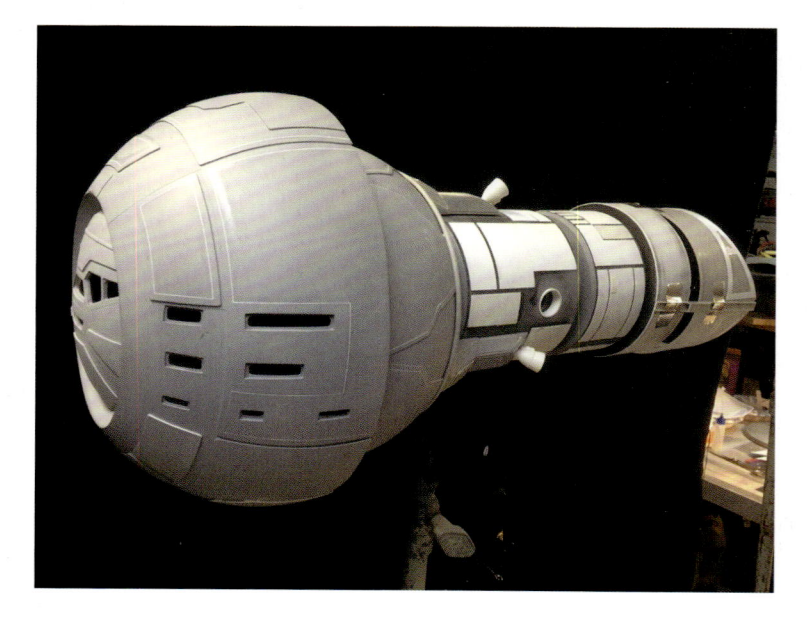

john eaves 09-2020

168 CHAPTER **EIGHT**

"And there were those miniatures! My first major TV miniature shoot was with the Champy monster [in "By the Silver Water of Lake Champlain"], and there's Tom Savini with Chet's miniature bottom half—the big Champy eats Chet—and Tom's there with these perfectly-made miniature legs of Chet, and he's playing with them and making them kick things, and I just laughed and wondered how we were gonna make this thing look legit. 'Is this gonna work?' And Rob says, 'It's all good, mate. Done this a dozen times.' Then Greg says, 'Yeah, yeah, this is gonna be fine. We do this all the time. It's normal.' So, I just said, 'OK, let's decide where we're gonna have the cutoff points where we'll blend real to normal,' and I had fun with it. These guys taught me miniatures. And when Chet got eaten, we just added some nostril flares and deep eye squints to Champy...and that was the only time in post that Greg ever said to me, 'Less blood.'"

For "The Right Snuff," Drew's challenge was how he was going to pull off a spaceship on budget and an alien on budget...and *the Void*. "And from beginning to end—from initial concept to the final conclusion, it became immensely larger in scope than we ever thought we could pull off. And Greg will say my problem is not about ever being a naysayer but, rather, always wanting to go bigger. I'd say, 'Hell yeah, we can do that...and *more!*'"

Fortunately, the production design by Aimee Holmberg made things more manageable from the get-go. "Aimee's set was gorgeous and right on target, so she established that right up front, and Rob did those amazing sweeps of the miniature and really nailed the photography with the depth of field. And once we had the model shots—and that really made it feel like a big thing—I'm just filling in the spaces [in post]. And once we were confident—me with director Joe Lynch—in those star fields, then we started sticking in nebulas. And Greg said, 'Oh, I love those gas cloud things; can we get more of that?'"

Then came the aliens in the segment, occupying the Void, and that initially posed a challenge for both director Lynch and for Drew. Would they position them within a swirling sort of mist or just empty space (a "void"), or what? But with Greg's approval of the forementioned nebulas, that language seeped into the Void. Drew went for broke and surrounded the space creatures with nebula goo. "All the guys in Greg's team always bring their 'A' game, so I had to hold up my end of the stick, so that Void got totally built in post. That was a Greg Nicotero 'how far can I take it before Drew screams *uncle*?' challenge."

Clearly, post-production work goes well beyond standard wire removal and green screen paint-outs and, due to the rapid-fire

OPPOSITE: Legendary sci-fi tech artist John Eaves renders the design for the Oculus (top) with spectular miniatures 3-D printed by KNB.

ABOVE: Filming the Oculus in deep space.

NEXT SPREAD: In space, no one can see you GREEN! From astronauts (pictured is Ryan Kwanten) to aliens in the void, VFX take us anywhere and everywhere.

CHAPTER EIGHT 169

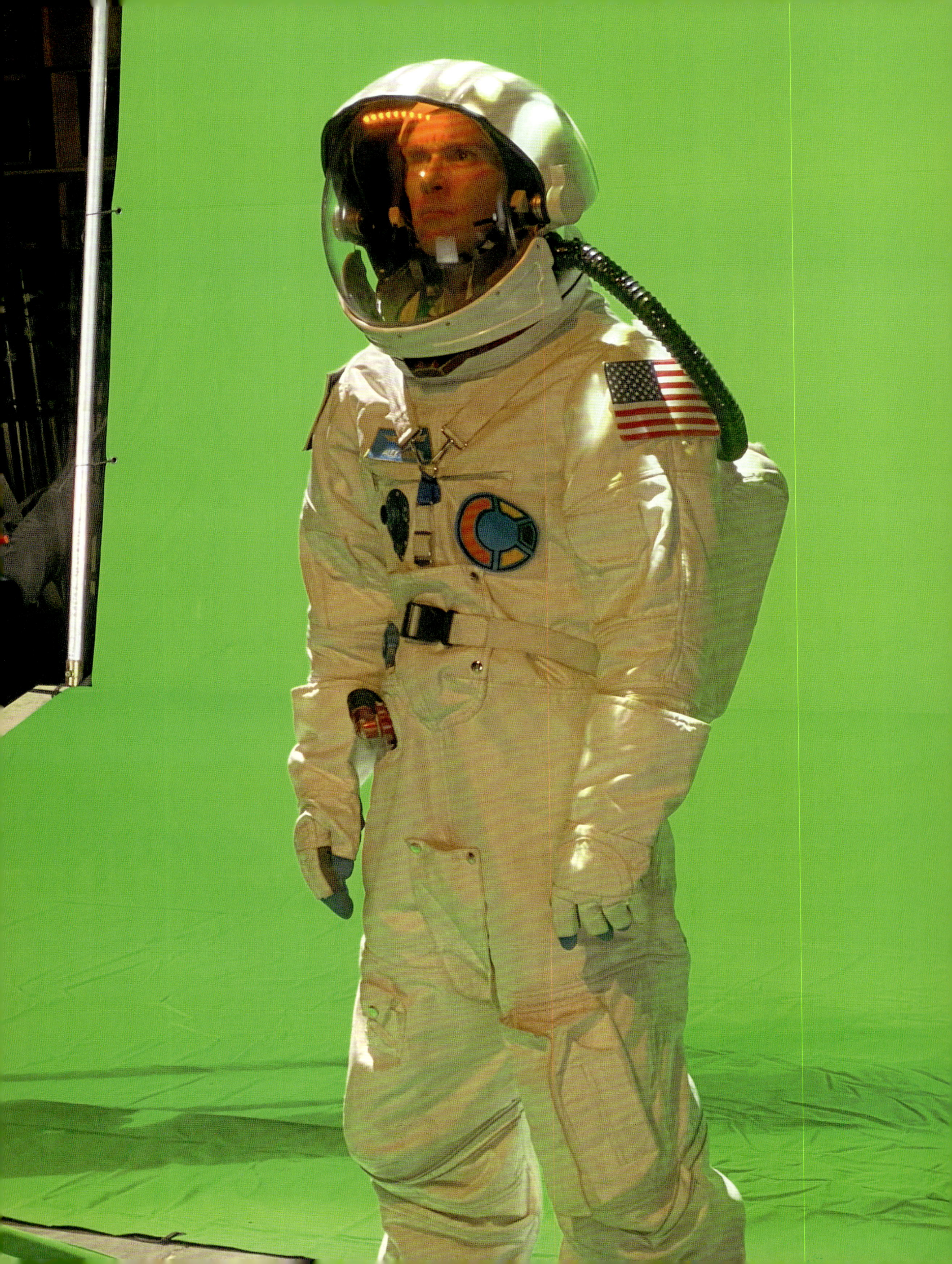

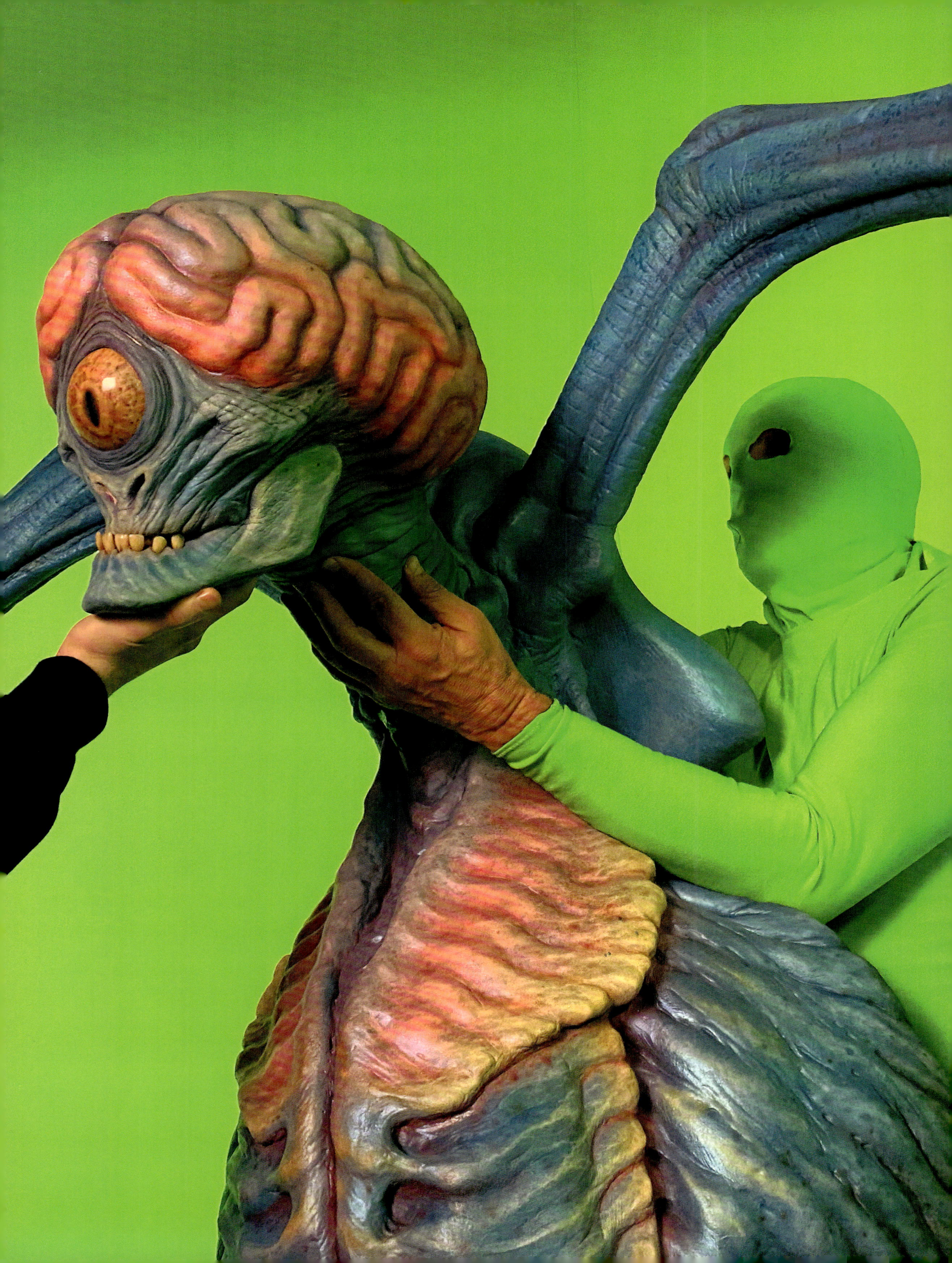

ABOVE: Renowned comic artist Kevin West illustrates the beastial Book of Bob, from "Shapeshifters Anonymous."

pace of the show and the collaborative competition to always push as far as possible, Drew is looking for every tool and technique available to him. And he benefits from what he calls a superpower: the creature concepts and detailed design work done by Mike Broom and John Wheaton.

"Yeah, those guys are really workhorses for us. They put together concept art and digital models *waaayyy* before we come into the picture, and that's a godsend for us. I'd read the scripts and try to get the details for the creatures, but then I'd have to ask what the *concept* is supposed to be. Then Greg would start flipping through photos on his phone, he'd hold it up to me and say, 'Here—this is what the creature should look like. We drew this up months ago.' So, I'd tell him to send me those digital elements and we'd prepare for that, because at least we could cut it in temporarily until the actual creature shots are done. Like, for the 'Gray Matter' [segment], those models really saved our bacon because we could prepare for the [practical to VFX] handoff. And that happened several times each season, and those guys were generating so much concept work that it really took a lot of the guesswork out of it for us and it gave our team more time to expand their minds, editorially, to do better storytelling up to the big conclusion at the end."

But the other superpower—well, more of a secret weapon—for the VFX team comes by way of the essence of *Creepshow* itself:

the in-world comic book! As Greg once explained, "My original intention for *Creepshow* was that I needed to preserve the idea that you were reading a comic book."

It's exactly what Drew and the VFX crew did. The presence of the comic art not only preserves the tone and style of the original material, it also enables the storytelling to go far beyond what any budget of time or money—in a television series—could ever dare to attempt. The comic content, like the actors and the creatures, is an undeniable character throughout each episode, grounded by The Creep himself.

"We don't want anyone's performance undercut," adds Drew, "and we certainly don't want the creatures' performances undercut. We have to make sure both sides—both equally important—are well established, but we still need to have maximum flexibility in the cut. So, in Season One, we were still trying to build the tone together, us and Greg. We wanted to discover how far we could push things, and how far we could build out graphical elements and the comic book elements— and that's when it *really* got interesting, when we started having those comic book conversations to augment the story and to also get from place to place or to jump time or to even make the creatures more terrifying or comical through those elements. And we'd really get into that."

ABOVE: In "Shapeshifters Anonymous," Kevin West's illustrations cleverly tell the intense backstory as animated page turns (along with narration).

CHAPTER EIGHT 173

THIS PAGE: Kelley Jones illustrates some of the most dramatic moments in Shudder's Creepshow, including the segments "The Finger" and "Gray Matter."

Kelley Jones brings the scares to *Creepshow*'s development. Kelley is a world renowned comic book illustrator, best known for *Batman and Dracula: Red Rain* and *Swamp Thing* at DC Comics, and *Aliens: Hive* at Dark Horse Comics.

CHAPTER **EIGHT** 175

For the "Bad Wolf Down" segment, Drew recounts the excitement at a comic book approach to the werewolf transformations: "We should do those werewolves—you know, the 'wolfing out'— we should do that as a comic flipbook real quick. That would be great!"

"And coming up with that in the moment, in those production meetings," Drew continues, "then seeing it through that we *can* do that...it's like...it's the most fun I've had. And for segues and transitions, those comic elements are the ultimate tool for us to use. They're awesome, and we wanted to maximize them and have the absolute most fun and put the viewers places where we couldn't normally get to."

In "Night of the Paw," the comic art opening allows efficient establishing of the dark killer character and the ultimate car crash that puts her in Mr. Whitlock's care, quickly and effectively. In "Bad Wolf Down," a massive theater of war is revealed and the viewer is thrust literally into the horror of a firefight, from above and on the ground, all through efficient use of the comic art. And, of course, we become quickly acquainted with the tragically comedic anti-hero, Clark Wilson, of "The Finger."

"Yeah, I drew the opening comic page for that," says veteran comic artist and *Creepshow* contributor Kevin West; you might be familiar with his work for DC Comics, including *A Nightmare on Elm Street*, *Modern Warfare*, and *Blue Beetle*. "The *Creepshow* work was right up my alley because, as [Shudder's *Creepshow* Executive Producer] Brian Witten explained when I met him at San Diego Comic-Con, they really needed that comic style—the EC comic style—and I was comfortable with that, so it wasn't a reach for me at all. But the funny thing is that I came into *Creepshow* quite by accident. I met Brian earlier in the day, and later I was at the *Heavy Metal* booth promoting some of my work for them. And Greg was there at the table where I was signing—he was signing the limited *Creepshow* comic—and, in the meanwhile, I had been doodling The Creep, just for fun. Then, someone passes my drawing down the table to Greg—he was far down the table from me so I couldn't see him. And the next thing I hear is, 'I want it! How much?' That was Greg."

THIS SPREAD: Comic page renderings by Kevin West ("The Finger"), Ron Frenz ("Night of the Paw"), Michael Broom and Ron Frenz ("Times is Tough in Musky Holler"), and Kelley Jones ("Bad Wolf Down").

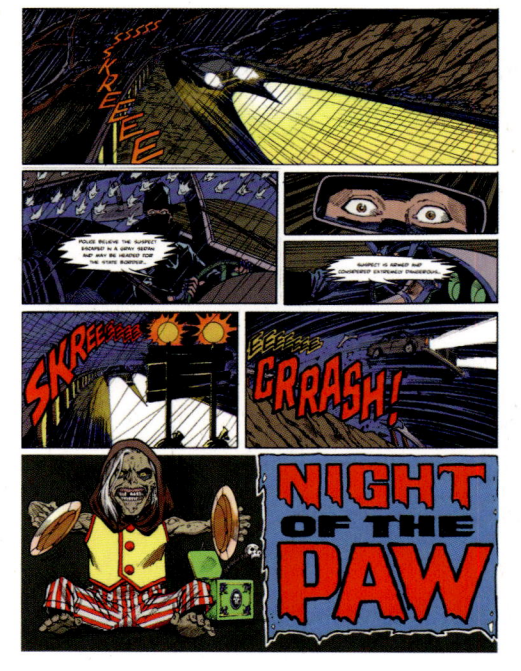

STEP RIGHT UP MY FEAR FANCIERS AS OUR RED BLOODED AMERICAN BOYS ARE DOING THEIR BEST FIGHTING OFF THE NAZI'S IN FRANCE, 1944. BOMBERS CIRCLE OVERHEAD AS A BATALLION OF GERMAN SOLDIERS MOVES IN ON CAPTAIN TALBY AND HIS MEN. LITTLE DO THEY KNOW, A FIENDISHLY FURRY FRIEND IS ABOUT TO TURN THE TIDES ON THEIR LUCK IN SICKENING SAGA I CALL

BAD WOLF DOWN

THE BATTLEFIELD IS LITTERED WITH FRESH CORPSES AS AMERICAN SOLDIERS RETREAT TOWARD A DEAD FOREST. A YOUNG NAZI SPOTS THEM AND, WITH AN EVIL GRIN, FIRES HIS MAUSER. TWO AMERICANS ARE STRUCK, AN UNNATURAL AMOUNT OF BLOOD EXPLODES FROM THEM AS THEY FALL DEAD.

DER AMERIKANISCHE ABSCHAUM!!!!!!

FALL BACK! NOW, LET'S MOVE!

CHAPTER EIGHT   177

178 CHAPTER EIGHT

Kevin's additional work in Season One (he came on board late in the season) includes fade panels that occur later in "The Finger" plus the opening splash art seen in the first episode's "Gray Matter." For Seasons Two and Three, Kevin has been a continual contributor, his comic work seen throughout the segments, including "Dead and Breakfast," "Skeletons in the Closet," and his personal favorite, "Shapeshifters Anonymous."

"I consider that 'Shapeshifters' segment as my stellar achievement, because I was a primary artist on that one—along with Mike Broom's work—and the story was fantastic. I drew the shapeshifters, that decked-out Santa with the claws, and all the scenes for the Book of Bob. Plus, that page with The Creep with the Santa hat on!"

Kevin, of course, is very much in awe of the other great artists that have been enlisted into the show, including lead artist Mike Broom as well as well-known talents like Kelley Jones, Ron Frenz, Hilary Barta, Jim Terry, and Phineas X. Jones, among others. "Thanks to these artists' work," Drew interjects, "we get to build these massive worlds that we wouldn't get to do otherwise. We came up with a lot of that on the fly, Greg and I. And Greg would

OPPOSITE: Kevin West sets the merry scene for the strangest holiday gathering on record, from "Shapeshifters Anonymous."

BELOW: A jolly old elf and eight tiny reindeer? Not exactly. More art from The Book of Bob, illustrated by Kevin West.

CHAPTER EIGHT 179

180   CHAPTER **EIGHT**

OPPOSITE: The Book of Bob reveals the true mission of the man in red, from "Shapeshifters Anonymous."

THIS PAGE: The Creep does his thing! A selfie with Raul from "Skeletons in the Closet" (top); Season 2 announcement (bottom left); a Harrowing indulgence from "Gray Matter" (top right); checking in for "Dead and Breakfast" (bottom right).

CHAPTER EIGHT 181

throw things at us and, in the cutting room, we'd decide that, actually, we could totally segue at a point [in the story] and build the rest out later in comic art. It's kind of funny because we're limited by how much time we had, but because of the style and tone set forth in the original film, creatively we were limitless in the ideas we could pursue."

Then comes the sound, and the team at Bare Knuckles Creative. Specifically, Chris Basta, whose job it is to look at every working cut of a segment, and take notes of the sounds required to flesh out the action, especially the monsters. Chris, by the way, enjoys the distinction of having provided the voice of The Creep. *Heh-heh-heh.*

"Sound is always my favorite part," Drew says, "especially on a show like this; it makes everything *real* and it gives everything *weight*. The guys and girls [at Bare Knuckles Creative] who work on this...they're killers. Effects and Foley alone are in a world

RIGHT: Chris Basta gives a sinister voice to The Creep.

BELOW: An animation still from "Twittering from the Circus of the Dead."

182 CHAPTER EIGHT

all their own here, so we have to turn to some pretty unusual sources for our sound design. Usually, it's the local junkyard... and our pets. There were a lot of pets that were barking and yipping in there, and Chris decided, 'Yeah, I'm gonna record those today.'"

Drew continues, "And Foley is always its own can of crazy, and we've got a scarecrow monster that weighs about two tons walking around—we can't just throw our regular hammers and hay at it. With that one, it was the messiest Foley room we've ever had. And our Foley artist [Leah Marie Puffenberger] would daily bring in a Red Flyer wagon with super random stuff from Home Depot and garden centers and whatever...and it was fun."

And the sound for "Twittering from the Circus of the Dead" broke a special sort of series record. "Oh, and that animated segment. The sound design for that alone—that's the most amount of people we ever killed for *Creepshow*, period. Tops 'em all. Most carnage, ever. But I guess that was just a bunch of squishy-squish."

As for the series scoring, Drew applauds composer Christopher "Chris" Drake for "hitting it on the head." Without the benefit of established musical themes running throughout the show, save for the main title (alternately scored by Tyler Bates and Tim Williams for a handful of Season One episodes), Chris is tasked with creating unique musical soundscapes, themes, cues, and "stings" within each segment, all different and all needed to maintain the tone and accentuate the dread, punctuate the scares, and lend some occasional levity to the goings-on—and there's always so much going on in the *Creepshow* universe. And, yes, he has to turn out his scores in a matter of just days.

"I met Greg through my acquaintanceship with Bob Burns, the longtime horror and sci-fi prop collector and friend to just about everyone in the business. Bob invited me to his home in Southern California in 2001 to prep for his big Halloween display—I offered to write a musical score to accompany it—and Greg was there to help out as Bob opened up his garage full of incredible movie memorabilia and everything else. And he and I immediately got along great. When I heard about [Shudder's] *Creepshow*, I messaged Greg. Then he messaged me back and said, 'Hey, I'd really like you to do this.' And I said I'd be there. And that was my *welcome aboard* moment."

So, how would he approach, first, an extension of John Harrison's original theme? In a word, *carefully*. Due to the tangled lines of rights and ownership and so forth, repurposing the original theme was a no-go, but that was all right because this is that forementioned extension; it had to *exist* in the *Creepshow* universe, but it also needed to travel beyond the origin material.

"And so, John came over and was a super collaborator with me, and my intention was to always respect John's legacy in this music...and that sound palette—that analog style—and he had only a four-track Steinway piano and a Prophet-5 synthesizer—

LEFT: The 1982 Creepshow soundtrack re-release from Waxwork Records. Cover art by Gary Pullin.

CHAPTER EIGHT 183

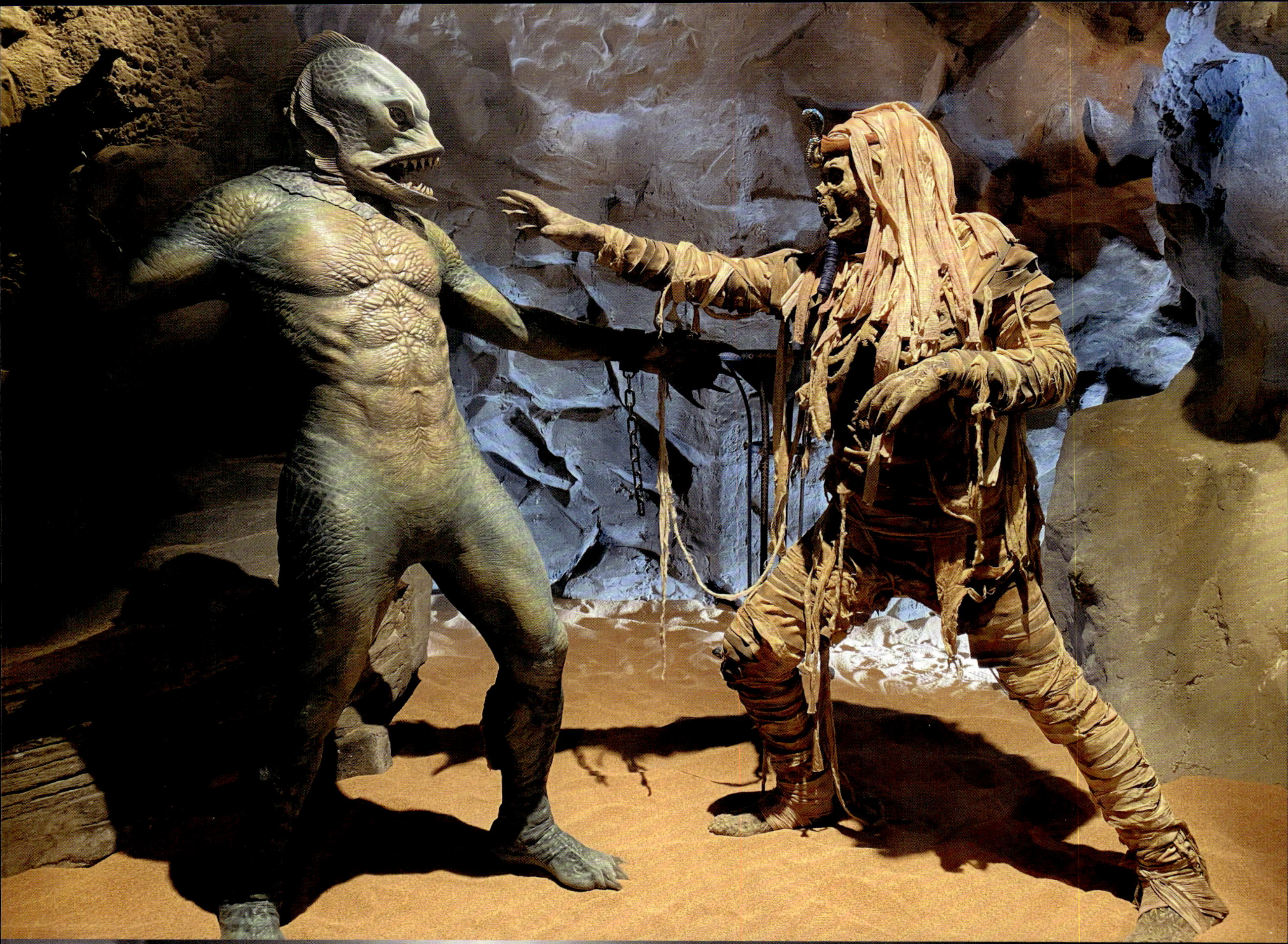

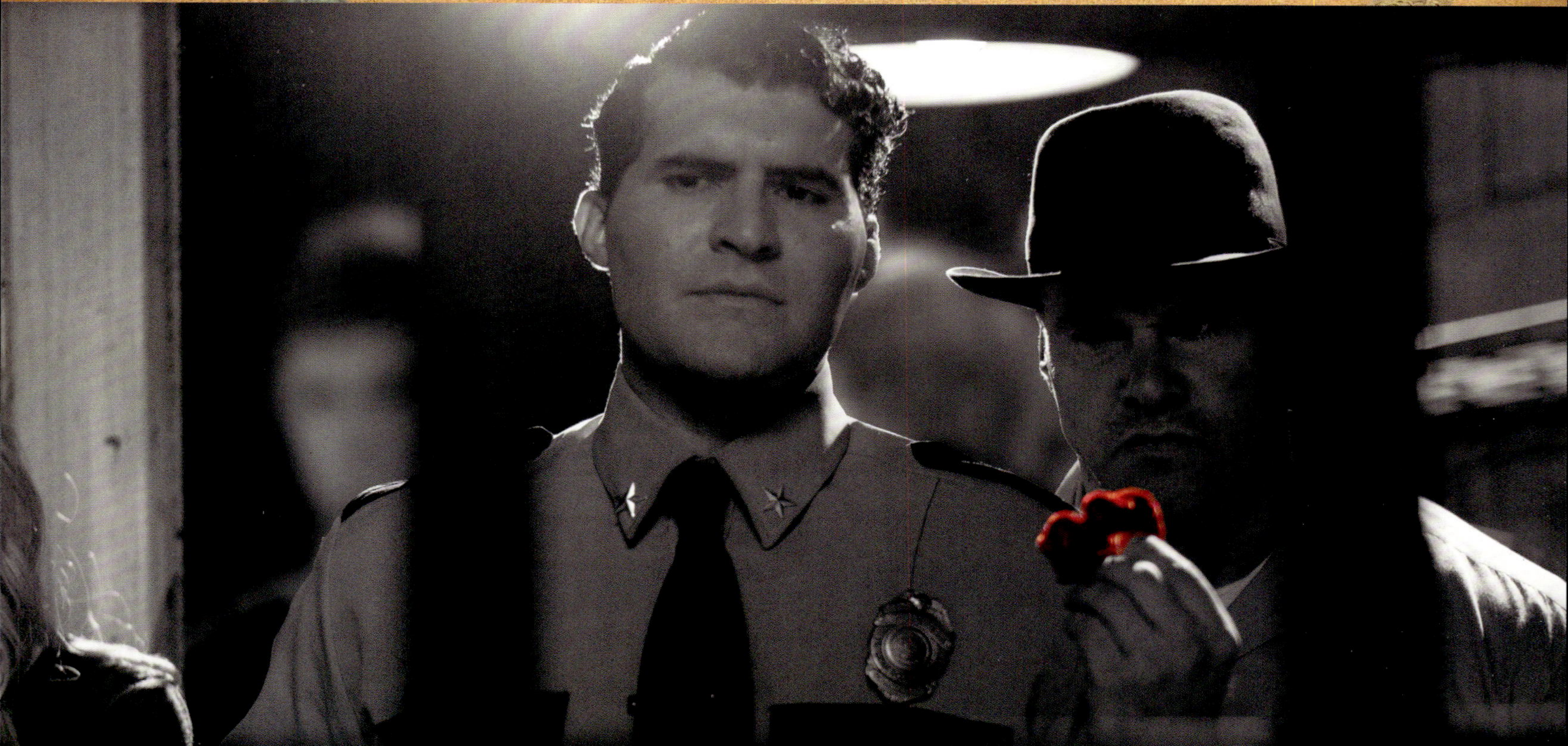

and that's it! And it's always been amazing to me that he created that original iconic music this way; it was like he caught lightning in a bottle."

To move forward as composer, Chris had to clarify a few things first with Greg. "I mean, are we rebooting Creepshow? And Greg emphasized that it isn't a reboot; it's a continuation. So, I took that very seriously, honoring the work of John Harrison. I got a Prophet-5, then John came over and asked if he remembered what patches he used in his score, and he said, 'Yeah, they're just pre-sets.' And so, I have them all here—the sounds from Fluffy's appearance and the bass beats from 'Something to Tide You Over,' and all that. And I used all those instruments—all those *patches*—in my score. And it makes it sound and feel familiar but sort of subliminal."

So, for "Night of the Paw," the Season One segment that just so happens to be directed by John himself, Chris says, "That bass patch in the score is the exact same one as in the original film's 'Something to Tide You Over.' And I've been able to do that same thing throughout the series score, using the same instrument patches, just in a different orchestral arrangement. And when Greg originally said to me about the new title theme, that it has to sound like Creepshow, I knew exactly what that meant. It meant piano, it meant it has to be playful, and it has to have the Prophet-5 to get that sound, and while mine isn't exactly Harrison's theme, it's in the same spirit and celebrates it. It uses the same sonic language and textures as Harrison did. So, the main title and the comic elements are all Harrison-esque, but once we go into different stories, there are no rules; I can use an orchestra; I can go retro; I can make it sound like an Eighties synth-horror movie; I can make it sound like The Andromeda Strain. During our spotting sessions, Greg would say, 'I want this to sound like Frankenstein Meets the Wolf Man,' and I know what that is; he doesn't have to explain it. He and I, musically, can speak to each other in a kind of shorthand when it comes to film scores."

Sound familiar?

"So, specifically about that intro for 'Model Kid,' with the Gillman versus the Mummy, that was 'Swan Lake' inspired; the piece Universal used for *Dracula* and *The Mummy*. So, I had to program and perform it, then I put it in mono, I distressed it to make it sound like an old music library cue. And I took great pains to do the same thing in Harrison's segment 'A Dead Girl Named Sue.' That whole score is in mono and I wrote it in a style that would make you wonder if it was actually an old Capitol Records Library cue. In the original 'Night of the Living Dead,' they were taking those library tracks and putting them through a tape delay to get that weird throbbing, almost like a synthesizer sound, when the zombies are eating the people; and I did the same thing with my music—I put it on an Echoplex to get some of that same reverb. It's that attention to detail that I wanted to bring to the show and, besides, where else am I going get this opportunity to completely geek out? And I know that's what drives Greg, too. This is a celebration of the stuff we love."

Drew then leans in to succinctly sum it all up, "Pound for pound, this show has managed to punch way above its weight class—and it all goes back to the team. We're having the most fun of our lives."

OPPOSITE: A monstrous clash between the Gill Man (Carey Jones) and the Mummy (Jake Garber) from "Model Kid" (top photo). A clever color spot featured in "A Dead Girl Named Sue," featuring Cristian Gonzalez, with Rey Hernandez to the right.

ABOVE: Chris Basta adds finesse to the frightful sounds of Creepshow at his malevolent mixing board.

> WELL, THAT TIES IT ALL TOGETHER QUITE NICELY--LIKE A 13-LOOP *NOOSE!*
>
> THESE GUYS HAVE REALLY STUCK THEIR *NECKS* OUT TO DELIVER THE GRUESOME GOODS FOR YOU. HOPEFULLY, THEIR WORK WILL BRING YOU NON-STOP *NIGHTMARES* FOR EVERMORE...
>
> SEE YOU IN YOUR *SCREAMS!*

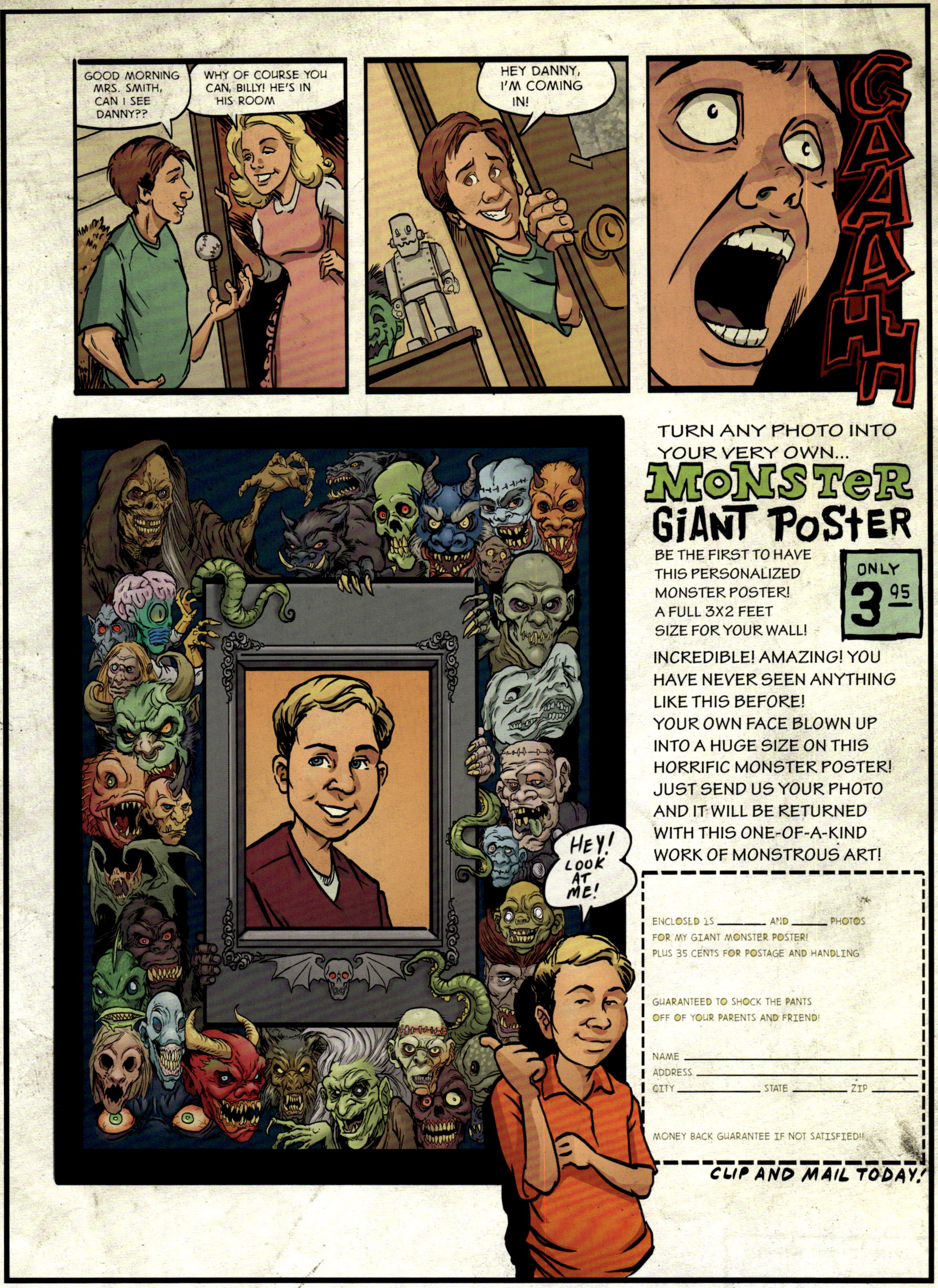

CREEPSHOW COMIC ADVERTISEMENTS FOR AMUSEMENT ONLY.

Genuine Soil from FRANKENSTEIN'S CASTLE

Authentic Soil from Frankenstein's Castle in Germany

DUST from FRANKENSTEIN'S DOMAIN, Actual Earth (Guaranteed Authentic) from the crumbling ruins of Castle Frankenstein, the location that inspired Mary Shelly to write the famous literary masterpiece FRANKENSTEIN. Only 5000 of these unusual iron pendants will be produced of this fabulous work of art

One Gram of Soil in Each Amulet

From the silver-plated chain (guaranteed to deter werewolves as well!) is suspended a transparent miniature coffin containing one gram of genuine earth from the exact place where the mad scientist Baron Von Frankenstein once made macabre history and brought forth a monster, stitched from the remains of sewn-together corpses, from beyond the grave!
No mystic powers are claimed for this amulet, and yet - who could fail to feel a tingle up and down their spine when viewing onself in a mirror, observing this rare soil lying close to one's still-beating heart? Who wouldn't feel fear at the touch of the same ground that the bodies from which the monster was created?

Certificate of Authenticity

Each Pendant is $9.95 and comes with a Certificate of Authenticity. This is not a gag, not a spoof, not a gimmick, not a put-on. The soil in this unique piece of jewelry actually CAME FROM FRANKENTEIN'S CASTLE, high in the mountains of Germany - where the Baron discovered the horrifying secrets and mysterys of life and death!
Encased in clear plastic, artistically secured on a silver chain, this dust of Frankenstein can now be preserved through lifetimes to come, Starting with YOU!
Sorry, orders are limited; no more than 2 (two) per customer.

SOLD OUT!

NAME
ADDRESS
CITY
STATE   ZIP

CREEPSHOW COMIC ADVERTISEMENTS FOR AMUSEMENT ONLY.

BY NOW, YOU MIGHT HAVE NOTICED SOME CURIOUS LITTLE RELICS SCATTERED ABOUT DURING THIS TERRIFYING TREK THROUGH SHUDDER'S CREEPSHOW. GREG AND HIS TEAM ARE THE CURATORS OF THESE CRYPTIC CLUES AND CLOISTERED CALLBACKS THAT YOU'LL DISCOVER IN EVERY SEGMENT.
YOU DID FIND THEM, DIDN'T YOU? IF NOT, MAYBE A LITTLE HELP FROM YOUR FIENDS IS IN ORDER. ALLOW US TO ASSIST YOU IN YOUR HUNT FOR THESE DELIGHTFULLY DECREPIT...
MICHAEL BROOM 2022

DEVILED EGGS

It all started with a green marble ashtray.

Lore has it that it began as a fun little on-set joke suggested by George Romero's key grip, Nick Mastandrea, during filming of the original *Creepshow* film. The marble ashtray Aunt Bedelia uses to crack Nathan Grantham's skull in the "Father's Day" segment would become the film crew's own Easter egg, appearing in all of the five segments. Now, with the new series underway, Greg Nicotero playfully—and respectfully—believed the ashtray deserved placement in every episode of his *Creepshow*, too.

And Prop Master Lucas Godfrey says the ashtray was only the beginning.

"The amount of Easter eggs we were sliding into the sets was absolutely ridiculous. And [Set Decorator] Nick [Morgan] was doing so many that were so deep, just hidden in the sets, and we knew we'd never shoot 'em all because it's a TV show and, half the time, you never even see what's on the walls. But, if you look closely, you'll see there's so many fun little things in there."

And perhaps one of the best Easter eggs of all to appear—and it's *not* little—appears immediately in the Season One, Episode 1 intro teaser—that is, the full-sized Crate.

"I got [the Crate] from Savini when he was remodeling his attic, years ago," Greg says, "and I realized that we had to open it for the teaser and fill it with comic books, so we had to take the nails out and take the chains off…and it hadn't been opened since the movie was made, so I was really curious to find out what might be inside. Of course, there was nothing in there; I was kinda bummed. So, anyway, we shot the teaser then took the Crate back to the [KNB] shop and I told the guys they had to reattach the chains as they were originally, so they did that and then they put it in my office. And I asked if they took all the comic books out of it first. 'Oh, shit…we forgot to do that,' they said, so all the *Creepshow* comic books are still in there!"

The egg hunt is for fun, obviously, because it adds a bit of "gaming" to each segment and gives incentive for repeated viewings. And, as Nick Morgan sees it, it's another layer of his set decoration duty and artistry.

"With the Easter egg thing, I do that on *everything* I've done. And this is a testament to the crew; on the second or third day, they started to notice them…and I've gotten through whole seasons—and multiple seasons—of other shows where no one had picked up on my Easter eggs. But on [the] *Creepshow* [series] they started to see it right away, and once Greg saw what I was doing he gave his full endorsement and said, 'Go for it—that's what this is all about.'"

So, on with the hunt. We'll point out where to find the ashtray in a handful of episodes to get you started, and give you a short list of a few other objects and references you'll find througout the series. Of course, we won't give away all the eggs within all the episodes; that would spoil the fun.

ABOVE: The "traveling ashtray," iconized from the original *Creepshow* film. Can you spot it in the next few pages?

BELOW: It's "All Hallow's Eve," and a distraught Mrs. Hathaway (Erica Frene) appears that she's been trick-or-treated to near-death. The ashtray is at her left elbow.

OPPOSITE TOP: In "Night of the Paw," undertaker Avery Whitlock busies himself with a current "customer." See the ashtray on the far worktable?

OPPOSITE BOTTOM: From "Dead and Breakfast," a creepy couple (C. Thomas Howell, Ali Larter) are determined to get the Sinister House trending…for terror. The table lamp illuminates the ashtray.

GRAY MATTER
- Missing pets on bulletin board—"Church" and "Cujo" from *Pet Sematary* and *Cujo*
- Timmy's yellow raincoat from *It*
- Marsh Wheeling cigar box from *Jaws*
- Dead mouse Mr. Jingles from *The Green Mile*
- Grady Twins in newspaper from *The Shining*
- Bucket of Blood on counter from *Carrie*
- Jack's typewriter (deep background) from *The Shining*
- Chief's "King County" shoulder patch
- Car model on Timmy's desk from *Christine*

HOUSE OF THE HEAD
- Tape recorder from *Evil Dead*
- Freddy's hat from *A Nightmare on Elm Street*
- ET's purse from *ET*
- Chop Top's camera from *The Texas Chainsaw Massacre 2*
- Bub's headphones from *Day of the Dead*
- Patrick Bateman's axe from *American Psycho*
- Pumpkin from *Halloween*
- Necronomicon from *Evil Dead*
- Lemmy's bass guitar from Motörhead
- Leatherface's chainsaw from *The Texas Chain Saw Massacre*
- Old Chief Wood'nhead from *Creepshow 2*
- Rug from Kubrick's *The Shining*
- Freddy Krueger's tongue phone from *A Nightmare on Elm Street*
- Ash's shotgun from *Evil Dead*
- The Crate from *Creepshow* (1982)

BAD WOLF DOWN
- Character names—"Talby," a take on *The Wolf Man*'s Larry Talbot, "Quist," a reference to *The Howling*'s Marsha and Eddie Quist
- Jeffrey Combs' gloves from *The Frighteners*
- Werewolf styles from *The Howling*, *An American Werewolf in London*, *Silver Bullet*

THE FINGER
- Pint of the Stuff in the freezer from *The Stuff*
- Full-sized rug from *The Shining*
- Harrow's Lite beer from "Gray Matter"

ALL HALLOW'S EVE
- Mockingbird Lane road sign from *The Munsters*
- Silhouette of neighbor with George Romero's square-frame glasses

THE MAN IN THE SUITCASE
- *A Touch of Genie* is an actual porn film
- *Fangoria* magazine and stickers
- *Ghastly Gals* comic

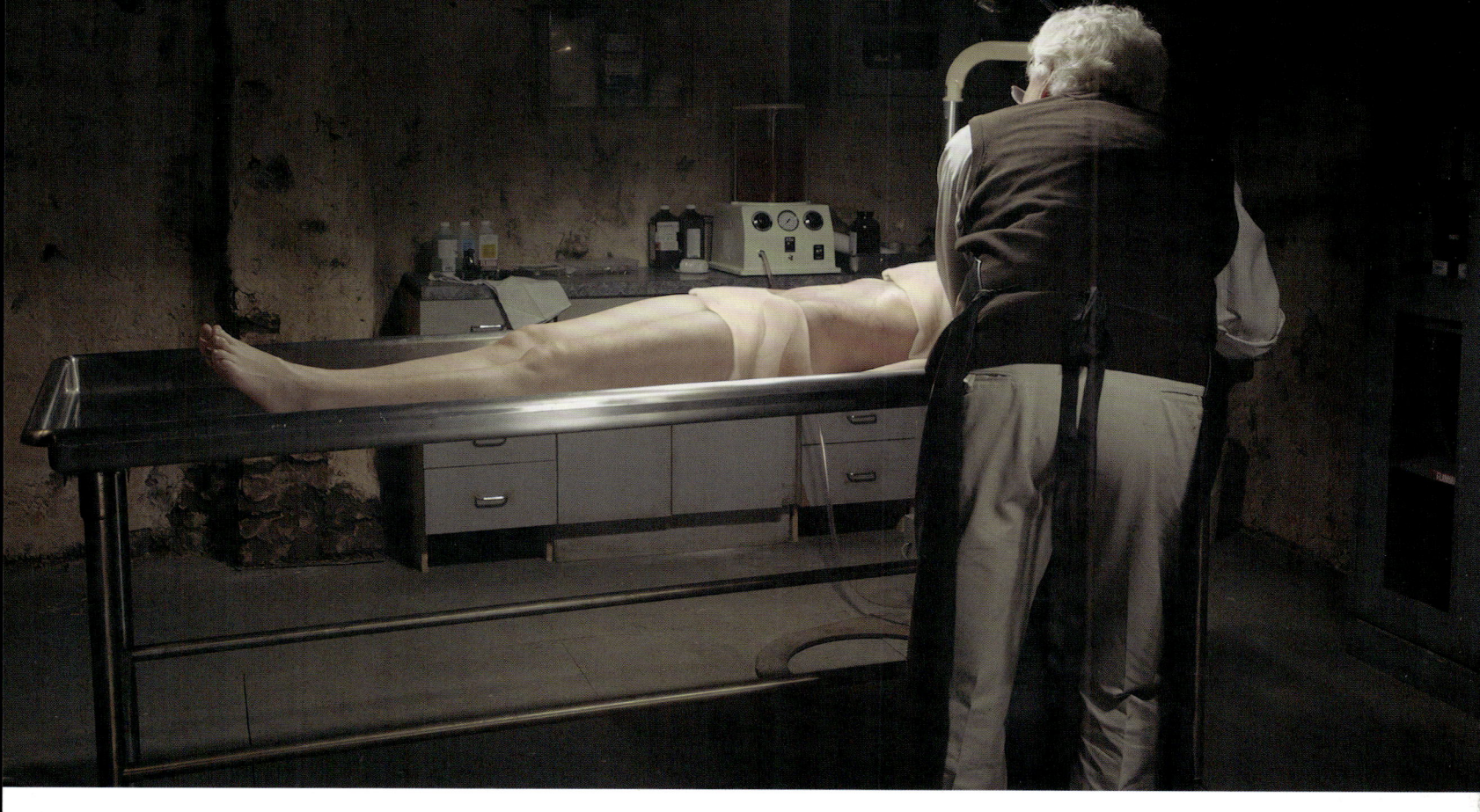

THE COMPANION
- Andrew Romero's artwork on Billy's door
- Harold's *Creepshow* comics
- Raincoat from "Gray Matter"

NIGHT OF THE PAW
- Names in guestbook
- Homewood Cemetery, Pittsburgh PA

SKINCRAWLERS
- Statuette of Pazuzu from *The Exorcist*
- "Horlicks" observatory, a nod to *Creepshow* (1982)
- Paragon Tribune, also seen in "Gray Matter"

BY THE SILVER WATER OF LAKE CHAMPLAIN
- S.S. Champy paper boat, a nod to *It*
- Harrow's Supreme beer from "Gray Matter"

ABOVE: Don't worry—this mix of "Pesticide" is all OSHA approved and perfectly safe for ridding your home of whatever bugs you. The ashtray is to the right of the chemical concoctions.

OPPOSITE TOP: Smile—you're on Can-dead Camera (a big egg as seen in 1978's *Dawn of the Dead*), from "Public Television of the Dead."

OPPOSITE BOTTOM: Would you sell your soul to possess this accursed coffee table book? The ashtray is in the display drawer just below. Recognize anything else?

MODEL KID
- Photo of makeup artist Jack Pierce on Joe's makeup mirror
- Model kits of The Creep, "Pesticide" tarantula, and "Companion" scarecrow
- "All Hallow's Eve" devil mask
- "Gray Matter" *Creepshow* comic
- Milk carton from *The Lost Boys*
- Zuni fetish doll from *Trilogy of Terror*
- Imagineering kits for Vampire Blood, Scar Stuff, and Vampire Teeth
- Monster Scenes' Pain Parlor model kit

PUBLIC TELEVISION OF THE DEAD
- TV cameras same as used on *Dawn of the Dead*
- Full-sized Zuni fetish doll from *Trilogy of Terror*
- Michael Myers mask from *Halloween*
- Cane from *The Wolf Man*
- Statuette of Pazuzu from *The Exorcist*
- Fertility idol from *Raiders of the Lost Ark*
- Bubo the mechanical owl from *Clash of the Titans*
- Painting of cabin from *Evil Dead*
- Chet's Zippo lighter from "By the Silver Waters of Lake Champlain"

DEAD AND BREAKFAST
- *Last Podcast on the Left* stickers on phone/computer
- Livestream followers/commenters names

PESTICIDE
- Puzzle box drink coaster, a reference to *Hellraiser*
- Box of sunglasses, a reference to *They Live*
- Raincoat from *The Hitchhiker*
- Dover sign from *Creepshow 2*

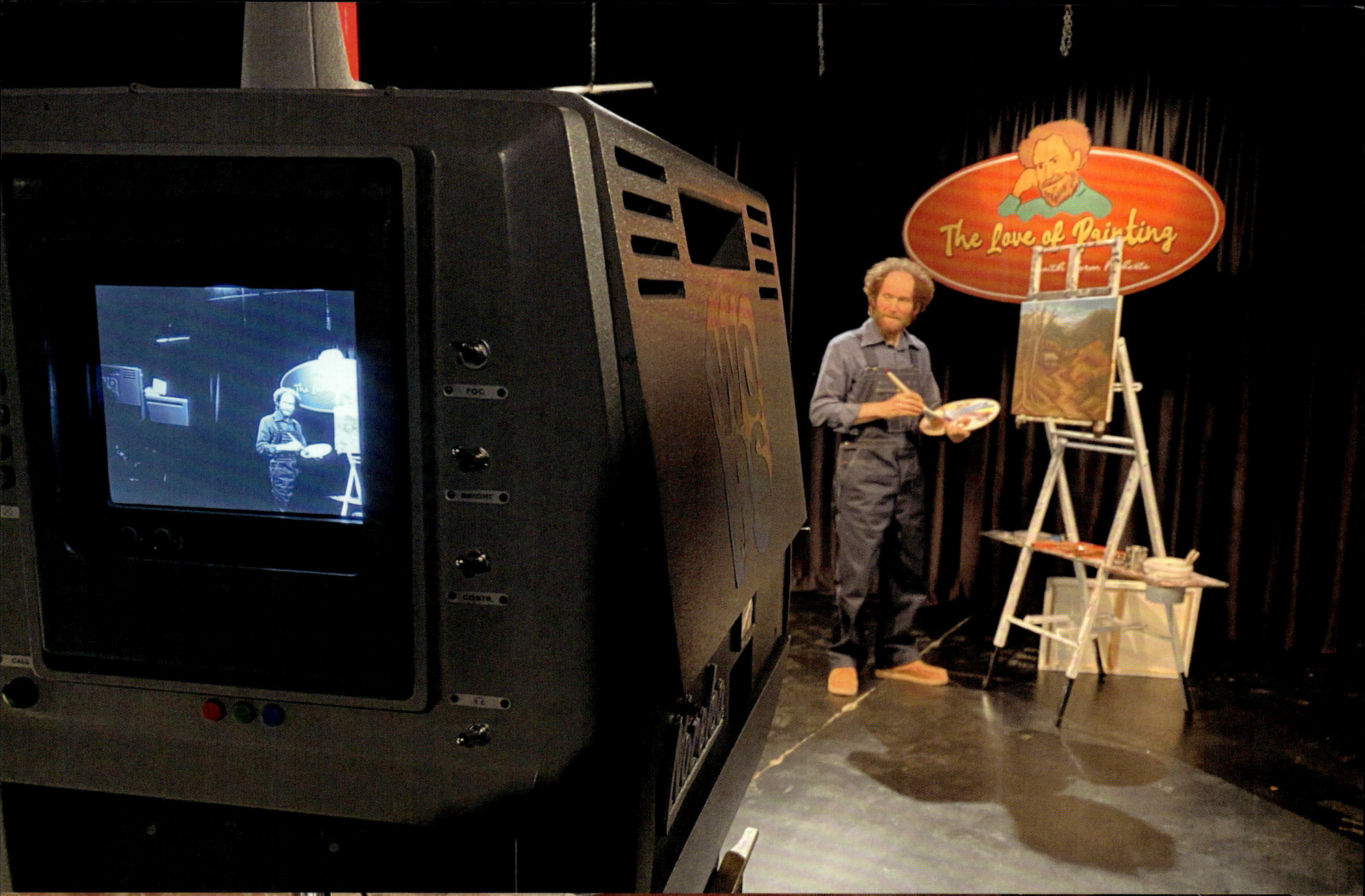
The Love of Painting

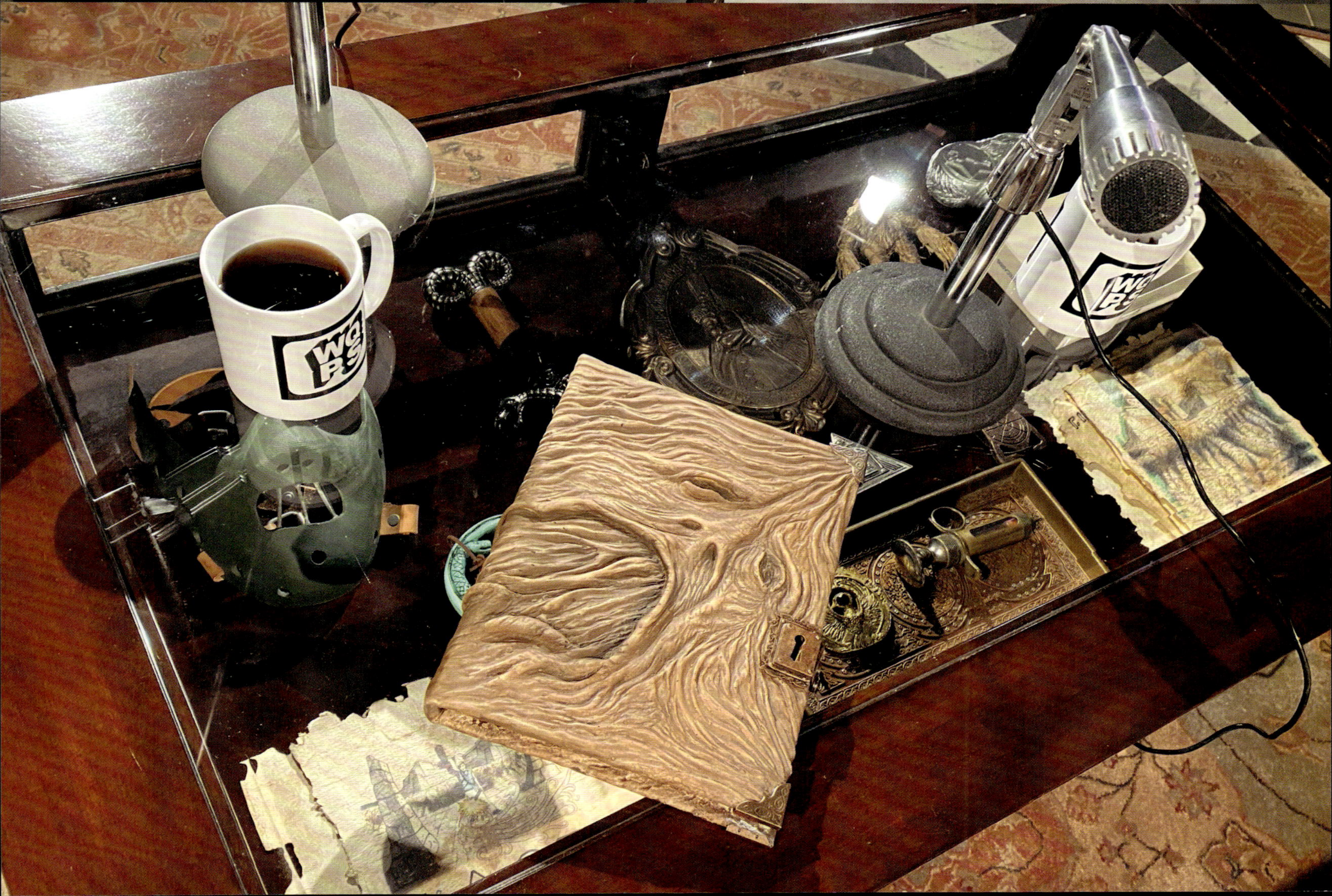

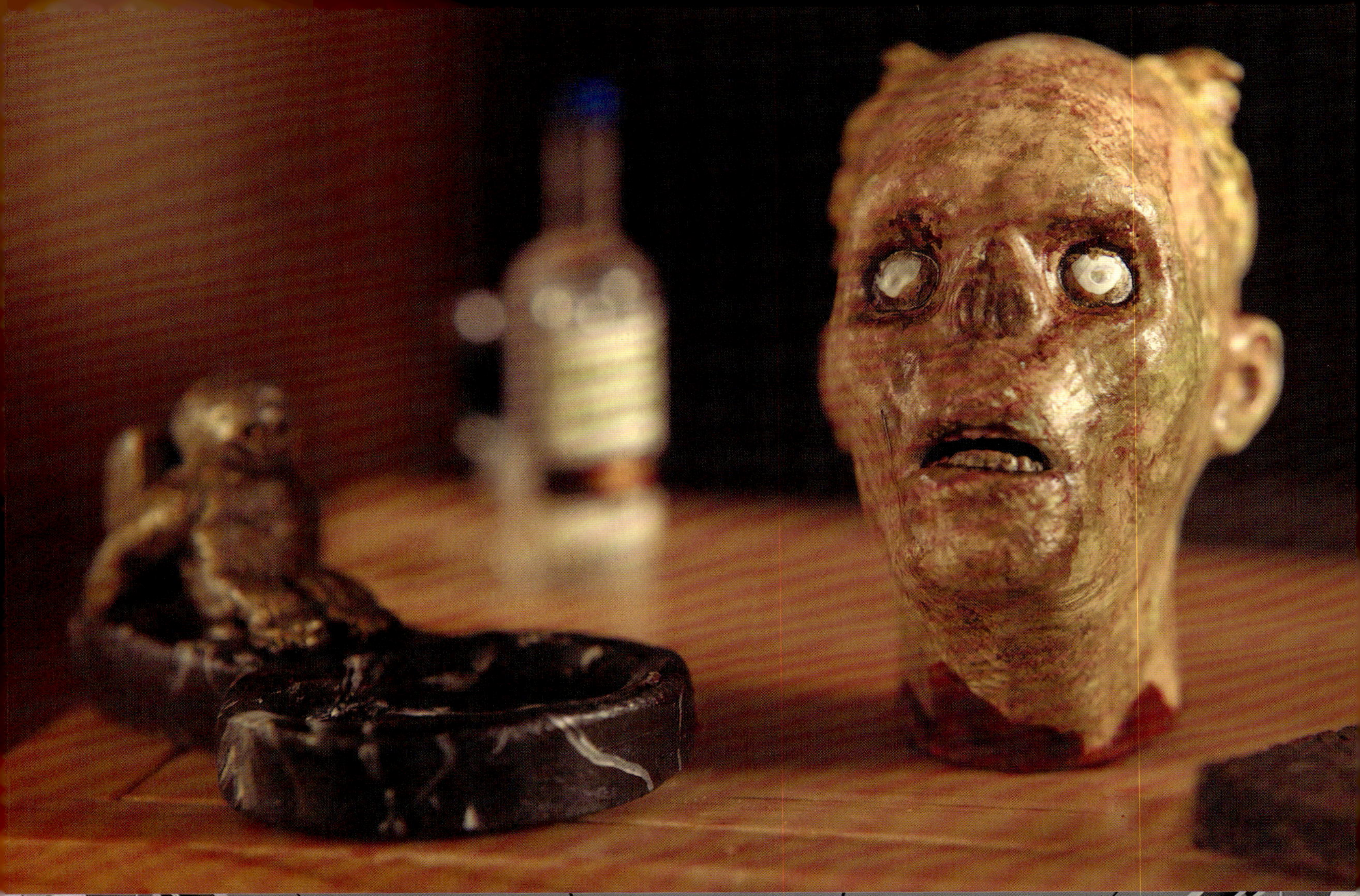

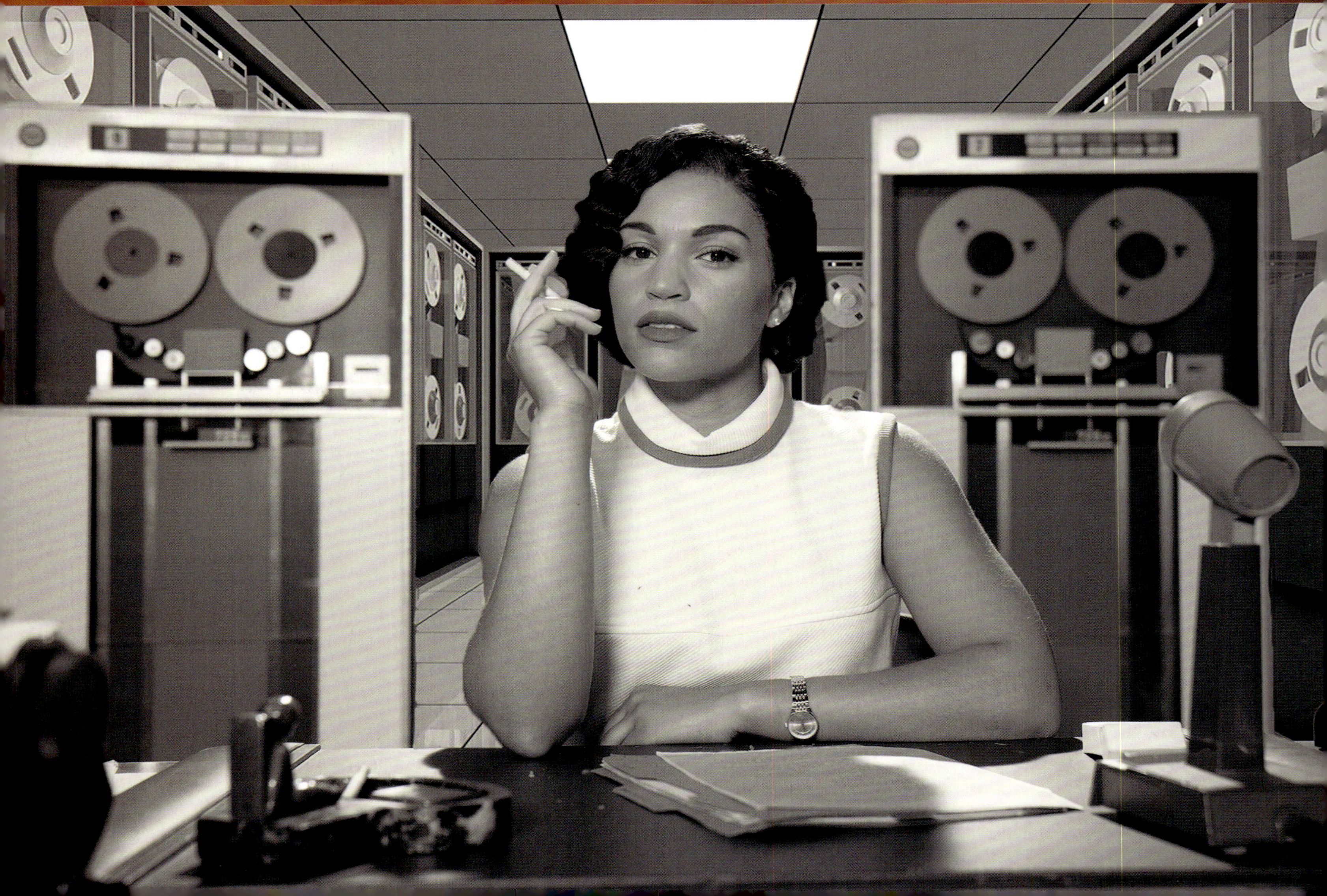

THE RIGHT SNUFF
- Flight Director "Barlow" reference to *'Salem's Lot*
- "KNB" on control panel monitor
- "HAL" on control panel monitor, a reference to *2001: A space Odyssey*
- Lockwood name a reference to *2001: A Space Odyssey*
- Toomey name a reference to Stephen King's "The Langoliers"
- Key necklace from *Andromeda Strain*

SIBLING RIVALRY
- *Dolores Claiborne* pet name reference
- Boy carrying *Creepshow* comic

PIPE SCREAMS
- "Fluffy" cat collar
- Fluffy's crate

WITHIN THE WALLS OF MADNESS
- Trollenberg reference to *The Crawling Eye*
- Cartwright reference to *Alien*

TWITTERING FROM THE CIRCUS OF THE DEAD
- Animated cameos by Greg Nicotero and author Joe Hill
- 1982 *Creepshow* comic

So, there's your start for your own hunt. Think we missed some eggs from those first two seasons? Of course we did! Go back and find the rest, then move along to fill your own basket from what you'll find in Season Three. Oh—one more hint for you: be on the lookout for "in-world" eggs; that is, Seasons Two and Three contain elements from previous *Creepshow* segments, as you've likely noticed in the previous list. Remember, these crew members live for this stuff, with everything and anything potentially being an Easter egg (even what's written on scraps of paper). Pay attention. Look sharp. Don't blink. You might miss an egg...or two...or more!

OPPOSITE TOP: "The House of the Head" features the tiniest ashtray cameo, front and center in the dollhouse.

OPPOSITE BOTTOM: At last! Sandra (Gabrielle Byndloss) puts the ashtray to good use in "The Right Snuff." Be sure to crush those butts out-
-dead out!

ABOVE: Dr. Trollenberg (Denise Crosby) dares to troll an ethereal being in "From Within the Walls of Madness." The ashtray is silhouetted to the right.

WHAT A GAG-WORTHY GAME, RIGHT? WHO DOESN'T ENJOY A DEVILISH EGG HUNT? WELL, MAYBE IT WASN'T TO THE TASTE OF THAT USUAL BASKET CARRIER, BUT I'M SURE THAT I'LL FIND HIM TO BE DELICIOUS!! HEH-HEH...

GIANT
LIFE SIZE
CREEP
PIN-UP

OVER 6 FEET TALL!

DRAWN BY MICHAEL BROOM

Never anything like it before! A gigantic, unbelievable drawing of the FRANKENSTEIN MONSTER, over 6 feet tall—by America's greatest cartoonist-artist JACK DAVIS. This is the most striking thing you ever saw! A masterpiece of reproduction that will startle anyone who sees it. The FRANKENSTEIN PIN-UP will supply 100 hours of laughs and thrills: have your picture taken alongside your favorite ghoul; scotch-tape it to the inside of your bedroom or den door; put it between someone's bed sheets, or just pin it on the wall. A million dollars worth of value for a low, low price! Order your's now—supply limited.

only $2.00

MONEY-BACK GUARANTEE—MAIL COUPON TODAY

SOLD OUT!

NAME
ADDRESS
CITY .... ZONE
STATE

CREEPSHOW COMIC ADVERTISEMENTS FOR AMUSEMENT ONLY.

MONSTER GLOW PUZZLES

Assemble your own Monster! It's easy! It's fun! It's....what? Against the Law? Remember what happened to Dr. Frankenstein? Don't worry! these are PUZZLES ans the only one who will be out to get yu is your brother, if you assemble one of these "glow in the dark" msterpieces on his pillow and leave it waiting for him in his dark room. These full-color 14-1/4"x17-1/4" puzzles, containing over 300 pieces, are reproduced from CREEPSHOW cover art: Creepshow #301's Frankendead Monster, the 1965 Yearbook's "House of the Head" and the CREEP from the 1969 Yearbook. They're neat! They're scary! They glow in the dark! Perfect for a rainy day in the castle!

BUY ALL THREE!

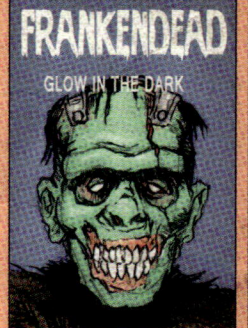

FRANKENDEAD MONSTER #2685/$3.00

HOUSE OF THE HEAD #2684/$3.00

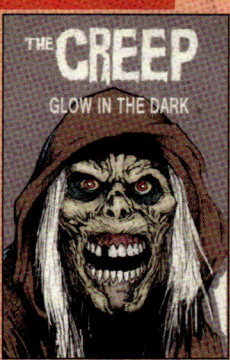

GLOW IN THE DARK CREEP #2683/$3.00

PAINT-A-MONSTER STATUES

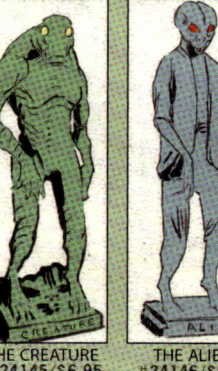

THE DEMON #24144/$6.95

THE CREATURE #24145/$6.95

THE ALIEN #24146/$6.95

CREATE A FULL-COLOR MONSTER!

Test your artistic skill! Create full-color statues of three of your favorite monsters! Wolfman! Frankenstein! The Creature From the Black Lagoon! Each kit comes complete with a 12" white bisque-clay statue, two paint brushes and five exciting acrylic colors. Paint each statue according to the enclosed directions or create your own full-color design. Fun to paint! Fun to display! Get all three. Own a trip of monster miniatures! Irresistible monsterrific fun!

ZOMBIE NOSE!

TURN YOURSELF INTO A ZOMBIE!

Now you can own the same unique, high quality latex appliance that was used to turn Gavin Walters into his monstrous characterization, the Zombie. Apply to your face with spirit gum (avaiable at most drug stores) or with Creepy Skin paste, advertised below. and, when the hand-painted nose is fixed to your face, apply the gruesome Rotten Flesh, available below. You will be a complete Zombie. There are two large airholes in the appliance, for easy breathing. so life-like, you'll scre your friends to death!

Become a makeup artist, and, while you're at it, order our Zombie TeethDead eyes, and other make-up items. You may be the next Jack Pirce! #2666/$1.39

LADY FRANKENSTEIN & CREEPSHOW T-SHIRTS!

LADY FRANKENSTEIN T-SHIRTS....Now in DAY-GLOW colors! Sure to make you the talk of the town! Shirts are washable and won't fade. The cost of each is only $3.98. Specify size: #2704, Adult small, size 34-36; #2105, Adult Medium size 38-40; #2706, Adult Large size 42-44; #2707, Boy's Medium size 10

THE CREEP PLASTER CASTING COIN BANK

SAVE YOUR MONSTER MONEY IN THIS AUTHENTIC 'CREEPSHOW' COIN BANK!

Fun! Excitement! Creativity for you and the whole family! Get this exciting Frankenstein Plaster Casting Hobby Kit and see for yourself! Kit comes complete with flexible plastic mold, two 13 oz bags of special grade casting plaster, plastic mixing bags, a roll of masking tape, sandpaper, paint brushes and 4 bottles of acrylic paints. Simply mix the plaster according to the easy instructions and pour it into the mold provided. Wait 45 to 90 minutes while the plaster heats and hardens by a chemical process. Then very carefully remove the mold. Trim the edges, file down the rough spots, fill in the holes. Allow the mold to dry out, from 24 to 48 hours. When it is completely dry, it's time to paint your masterpiece. The kit provides red, yellow, blue and white acrylic paint and includes instructions on mixing any color you might want from grays to flesh-tones Now paint Frankenstein statue in realistic hues You will have a work of art you can be proud of. And you will have enough equipment left to mold another! #24147 $5.95

CREEPSHOW COMIC ADVERTISEMENTS FOR AMUSEMENT ONLY.

THEY SAY BEAUTY IS IN THE EYE OF THE BEHOLDER. WE AGREE. THAT'S WHY WE'VE ADORNED EVERY COVER OF SHUDDER'S CREEPSHOW WITH THE MOST UNFORGETTABLY GARISH MONSTROSITIES AND MISHAPS.
TAKE A LOOK AT OUR ABOMINABLE ART, EACH FEATURING THE FINEST IN BESTIAL BEAUTY EVER TO SLITHER ALONG THE DECREPIT CATWALK. HERE COMES OUR PETRIFYING PARADE NOW. IT'S OUR FINEST COLLECTION OF...
MISS CRYPT
MISS CEMETERY
MISS CREEP
MICHAEL BROOM 2022

COVER GHOULS

In the EC days, the terrifying comic cover art for *Tales from the Crypt*, *The Haunt of Fear*, and the other horror and crime titles was pivotal in grabbing readers' attention, compelling them by shock, surprise, and a morbid curiosity to peek inside—and to purchase the comic! With the *Creepshow* film from 1982, the referential comic cover art of young Billy's book drew moviegoers into the comic sensibility of the film, all the while paying proper homage to its inspirational source material from some thirty years prior. And now, with Shudder's *Creepshow*, the in-world comic cover art not only pays double homage—to EC and to the original film—but it also serves to draw the reader into the fright-filled free-for-all horror comic experience; it's a method still as effective as it was back in the 1950s.

As we said at the beginning of this book, the EC style and the in-world *Creepshow* comic method is timeless, and it resonates with audiences today.

Michael Broom, the creature concept artist you've previously met, is also one of the artists responsible for the frighteningly fun comic covers that splash across the screen in every episode of the show. While Michael is an artist of many styles and disciplines—he especially enjoys his very "painterly" work using classic artists' oils—he has an obvious knack for the *Creepshow* look and is able to let his imagination run wild with every cover he designs.

"I took a lot of influence from [Jack] Davis and the original EC covers; I wanted to mimic that style. And I would typically do thumbnails for Greg to consider for the different covers, then he'd cherry-pick through those and choose the one he liked best. But sometimes he'd give a thumbnail sketch to me of what he wanted, so I'd use that as my direction for the art."

When time allows, Michael takes a classic approach to the work, creating pencil sketches for thumbnails, then proceeding to create hand-inked detailed line art. For coloring, he'd scan his inked art and digitally add color using Photoshop. "That makes it easy for me to change colors, if I'm asked to, without having to start again from scratch." Of course, if there is a time crunch, he'll work directly in the digital process, using CorelDRAW for his early thumbnails and the detailed ink renderings.

And while Broom has been a long-time team member at KNB EFX Group, he recalls his first meeting with Greg Nicotero, years prior, all thanks to a comic book.

"I met Greg because he bought a comic book from me at a convention years ago. I was selling zombie comics back in the '90s and he came by and bought one. And so, when I visited the KNB offices, he walked to his shelf and pulled out my comic book and said, 'Remember this?'"

Nothing about Shudder's *Creepshow* appears to be accidental, right?

So, enjoy this look at the in-world comic cover art from Michael (plus the guest-artist work of John Wheaton for the "Skincrawlers" issue). It's a ghoulish gallery, a petrifying parade, of horror comic art in the most nerve-jangling, jugular vein.

HEH-HEH-HEH...

BELOW: Artist Michael Broom, the man behind the *Creepshow* in-world comic covers that love to lure you in.

GN
STRANGE, EERIE, TERRIFYING
10¢
CREEPSHOW
TALES OF SUSPENSE AND HORROR!!!
WHO WILL SURVIVE?
HARROW'S SUPREME BEER
HEEELP!
NO! PLEASE...
OH MY GOD...

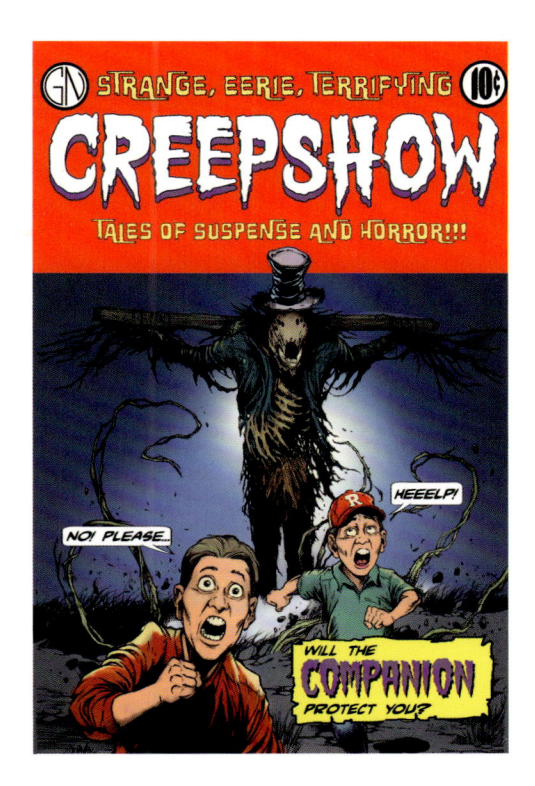

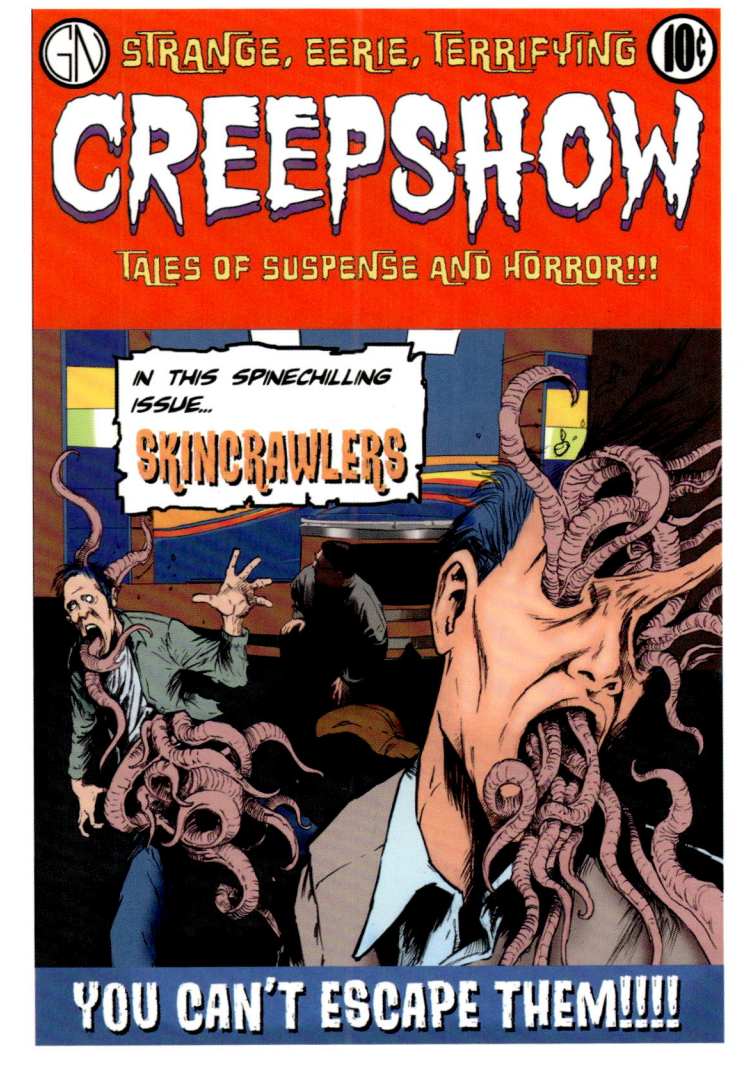

SEASON ONE: When it comes to the stories for *Creepshow*, executive producer and Monster Agency Productions partner Brian Witten weighs in: "The stories had to have a certain feel [of classic EC] but still they could be very different as long as we stayed in that [classic] tone." These Season One covers show a pitch-perfect approach to delivering that classic horror.

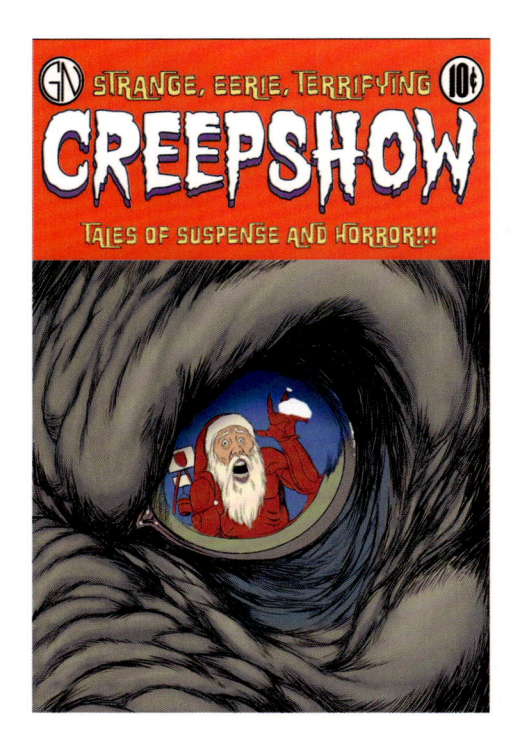

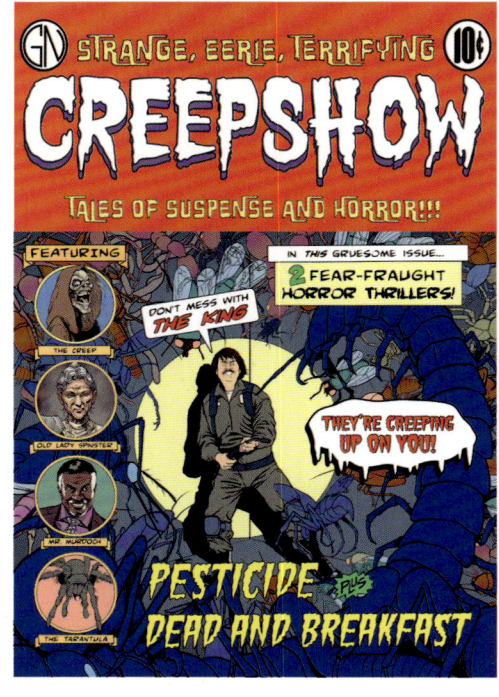

SEASON TWO: Brian Witten reveals the angst (and irony) of his youth: "When I was a kid, I was picked on and bullied for bringing comic books to school for show-and-tell, and for doing reports about comic books. [And now], all of that shit that people made fun of me for is an asset. My first interview [at a production company] was literally about comic books!"

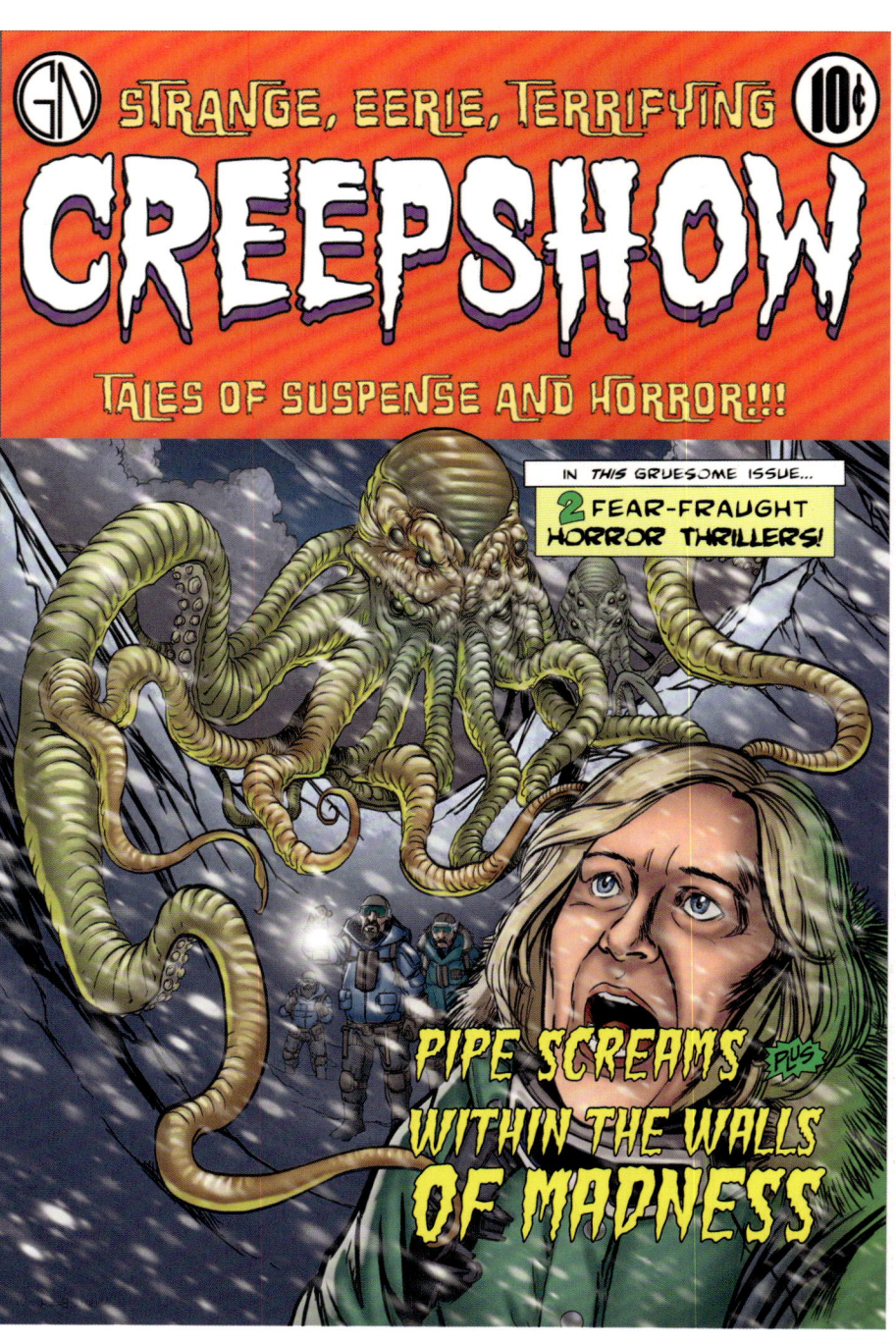

GN
STRANGE, EERIE, TERRIFYING
10¢
CREEPSHOW
TALES OF SUSPENSE AND HORROR!!!
FEATURING
THE CREEP
SIMON
THE COUNTESS
RENEE
IN THIS OTHERWORLDLY ISSUE...
A FEAR-FRAUGHT HORROR THRILLER!
NIGHT OF THE LIVING LATE SHOW

GN
STRANGE, EERIE, TERRIFYING
10¢
CREEPSHOW
TALES OF SUSPENSE AND HORROR!!!
FEATURING...
IN THIS BLOODCURDLING ISSUE...
2 FEAR-FRAUGHT HORROR THRILLERS!
THE CREEP
TRENICE
THE NURSE
MUMS
PLUS
QUEEN BEE

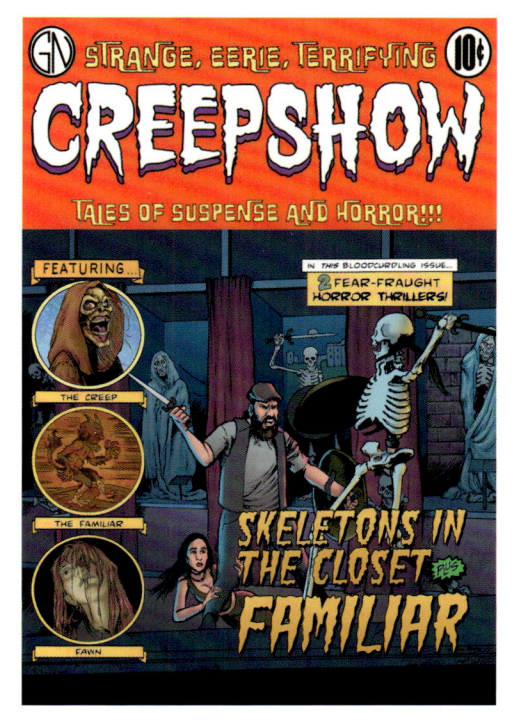

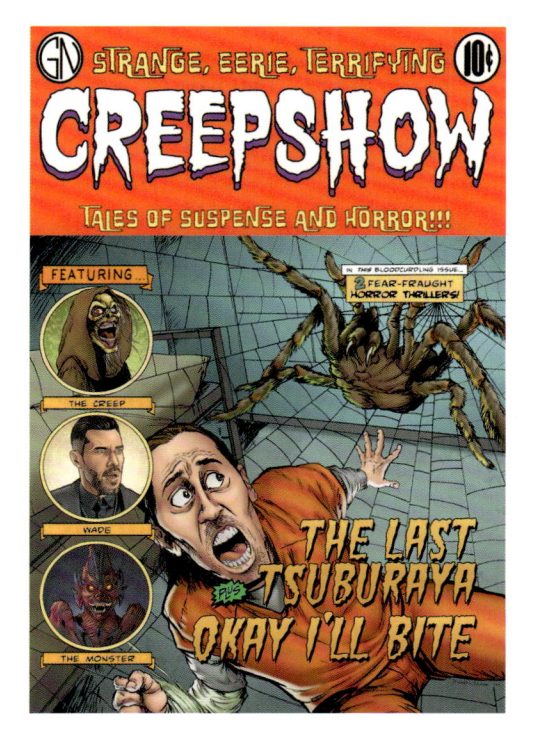

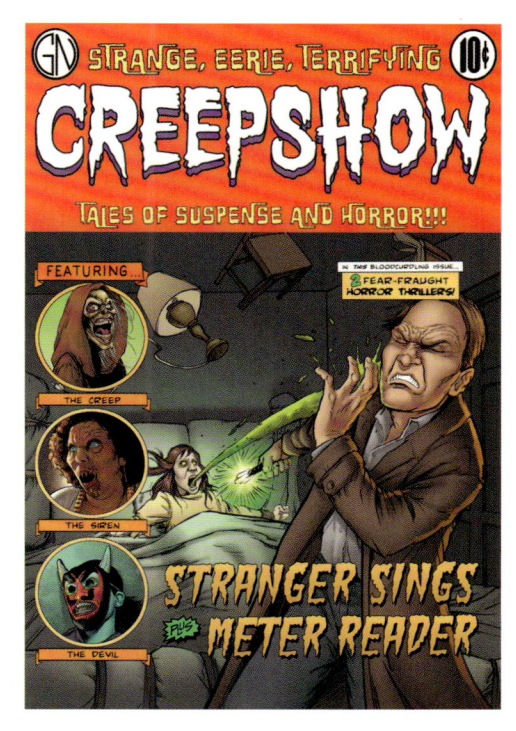

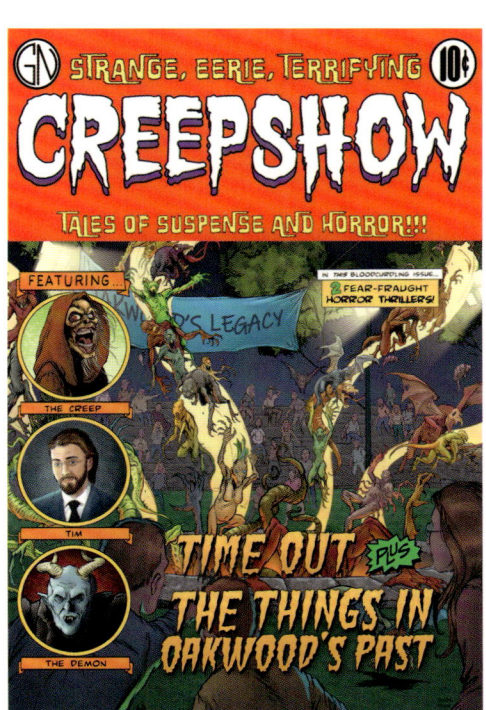

SEASON THREE: By this season's end, the proof was apparent: from top to bottom, front to back, cover to cover, the entire *Creepshow* team lived and breathed the passion for their work. It's the most fun you'll have being scared!

THERE YOU HAVE IT--*SHUDDER'S CREEPSHOW!* WE TRUST YOU'LL ENJOY YOUR *EXTENDED* STAY WITH US... BECAUSE ONCE YOU CHECK IN...WELL... *WE'LL* DECIDE *IF* YOU EVER CHECK OUT.

AHH-HA-HA-HAAA...

CHAPTER TEN 205

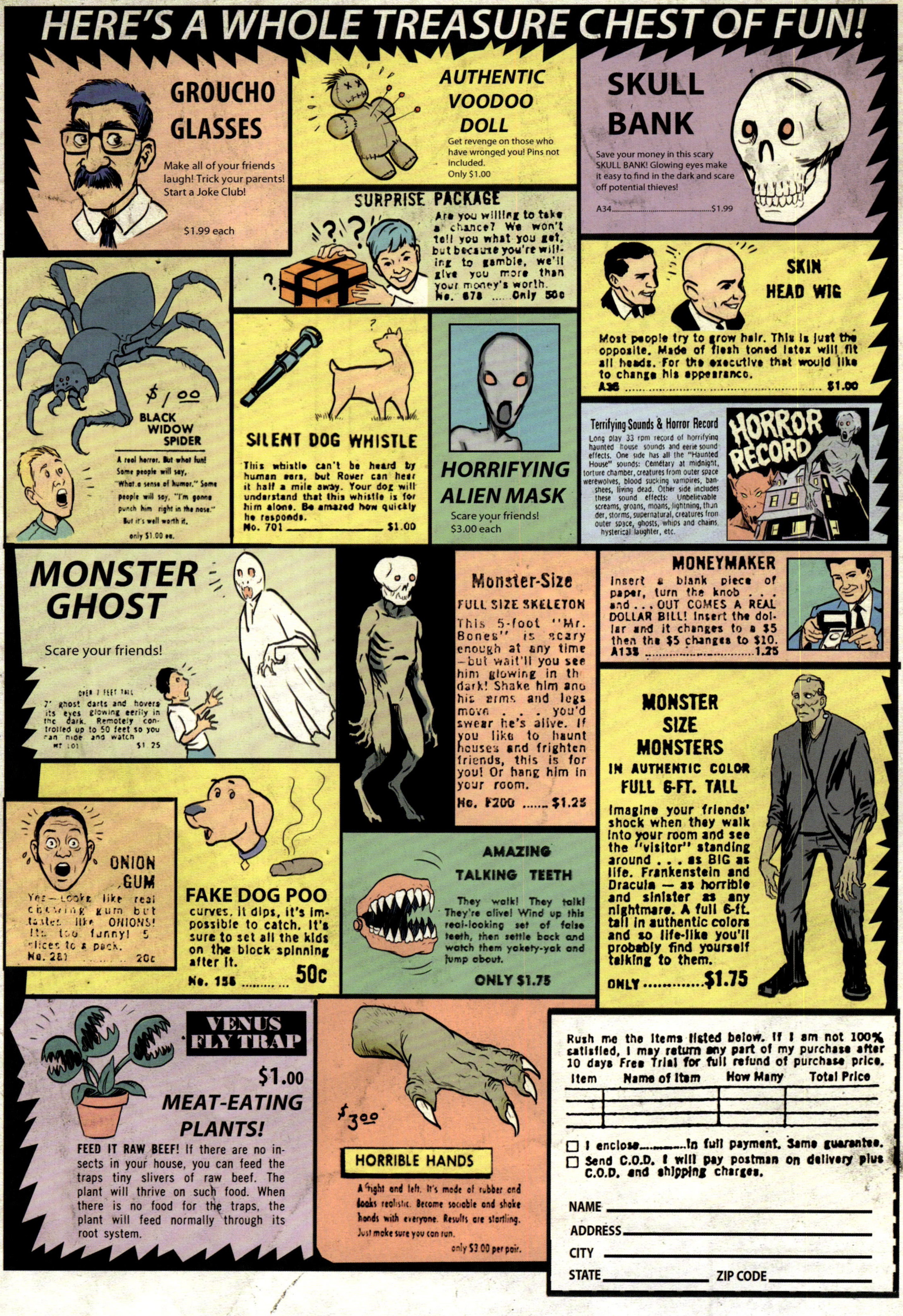

HERE'S A WHOLE TREASURE CHEST OF FUN!

GROUCHO GLASSES
Make all of your friends laugh! Trick your parents! Start a Joke Club!

$1.99 each

AUTHENTIC VOODOO DOLL
Get revenge on those who have wronged you! Pins not included.
Only $1.00

SURPRISE PACKAGE
Are you willing to take a chance? We won't tell you what you get, but because you're willing to gamble, we'll give you more than your money's worth.
No. 678 ...... Only 50¢

SKULL BANK
Save your money in this scary SKULL BANK! Glowing eyes make it easy to find in the dark and scare off potential thieves!
A34 .... $1.99

BLACK WIDOW SPIDER
$1.00
A real horror. But what fun! Some people will say, "What a sense of humor." Some people will say, "I'm gonna punch him right in the nose." But it's well worth it.
only $1.00 ea.

SILENT DOG WHISTLE
This whistle can't be heard by human ears, but Rover can hear it half a mile away. Your dog will understand that this whistle is for him alone. Be amazed how quickly he responds.
No. 701 _____ $1.00

HORRIFYING ALIEN MASK
Scare your friends!
$3.00 each

SKIN HEAD WIG
Most people try to grow hair. This is just the opposite. Made of flesh toned latex will fit all heads. For the executive that would like to change his appearance.
A36 .... $1.00

Terrifying Sounds & Horror Record
Long play 33 rpm record of horrifying haunted house sounds and eerie sound effects. One side has all the "Haunted House" sounds: Cemetary at midnight, torture chamber, creatures from outer space, werewolves, blood sucking vampires, banshees, living dead. Other side includes these sound effects: Unbelievable screams, groans, moans, lightning, thunder, storms, supernatural, creatures from outer space, ghosts, whips and chains, hysterical laughter, etc.

HORROR RECORD

MONSTER GHOST
Scare your friends!
OVER 7 FEET TALL
7' ghost darts and hovers, its eyes glowing eerily in the dark. Remotely controlled up to 50 feet so you can hide and watch.
MT 101 .... $1.25

Monster-Size FULL SIZE SKELETON
This 5-foot "Mr. Bones" is scary enough at any time — but wait'll you see him glowing in th dark! Shake him and his arms and legs move . . . you'd swear he's alive. If you like to haunt houses and frighten friends, this is for you! Or hang him in your room.
No. F200 .... $1.25

MONEYMAKER
Insert a blank piece of paper, turn the knob and . . . OUT COMES A REAL DOLLAR BILL! Insert the dollar and it changes to a $5 then the $5 changes to $10.
A138 .... 1.25

MONSTER SIZE MONSTERS
IN AUTHENTIC COLOR
FULL 6-FT. TALL
Imagine your friends' shock when they walk into your room and see the "visitor" standing around . . . as BIG as life. Frankenstein and Dracula — as horrible and sinister as any nightmare. A full 6-ft. tall in authentic colors and so life-like you'll probably find yourself talking to them.
ONLY $1.75

ONION GUM
Yes—looks like real chewing gum but tastes like ONIONS! It's too funny! 5 slices to a pack.
No. 281 .... 20¢

FAKE DOG POO
curves, it dips, it's impossible to catch. It's sure to set all the kids on the block spinning after it.
No. 156 .... 50¢

AMAZING TALKING TEETH
They walk! They talk! They're alive! Wind up this real-looking set of false teeth, then settle back and watch them yakety-yak and jump about.
ONLY $1.75

VENUS FLY TRAP
$1.00
MEAT-EATING PLANTS!
FEED IT RAW BEEF! If there are no insects in your house, you can feed the traps tiny slivers of raw beef. The plant will thrive on such food. When there is no food for the traps, the plant will feed normally through its root system.

HORRIBLE HANDS
$3.00
A right and left. It's made of rubber and looks realistic. Become sociable and shake hands with everyone. Results are startling. Just make sure you can run.
only $3.00 per pair.

Rush me the items listed below. If I am not 100% satisfied, I may return any part of my purchase after 10 days Free Trial for full refund of purchase price.

Item	Name of Item	How Many	Total Price

☐ I enclose _____ in full payment. Same guarantee.
☐ Send C.O.D. I will pay postman on delivery plus C.O.D. and shipping charges.

NAME _____
ADDRESS _____
CITY _____
STATE _____ ZIP CODE _____

CREEPSHOW COMIC ADVERTISEMENTS FOR AMUSEMENT ONLY.

MONSTER S·I·Z·E MONSTERS

7 FEET TALL

In Authentic Colors With GLOW in the DARK EYES

ONLY $1.00

TEN DAY FREE TRIAL

Just imagine your friends shock when they walk into your room and see the "Monster" reaching out—bigger than life-Frankenstein, the original man-made monster, that creation of evil genius that terrorized the world. A giant 7 feet tall, his eyes glow eerily as his hand reaches out—as aweful and sinister as the wildest nightmare. Yes—Frankenstein is 7 feet tall, in authentic colors on durable polyethelene, and so lifelike you'll probably find yourself talking to him. Won't you be surprised if he answers? Comes complete with eyes that glow even in the pitch dark for a special thrilling chill.

Boney the Skeleton. And then there is Boney—stark scary with nothing left but his bare bones. A 7 foot monster out of the grave—his bones white, his eyes staring—even glowing in the dark.

Money Back Guarantee.

Just send $1.00 plus 25c to cover postage and handling for each monster you want. Your money back if not satisfactorily horrified.

SOLD OUT!

...oney the Skeleton
...for postage and handling for each...
...get shivers of delight. I can return my purchase within 10 days and you will refund the full purchase price.

NAME
ADDRESS
CITY ___ STATE ___ ZIP
New York State Residents please add ___ sales tax.

AUTHENTIC MONKEY'S PAW

100% REAL

ONLY $4.98

You've never seen anything like this before! A genuine mummified MONKEY'S PAW, WHICH WILL GUARANTEE YOU THREE WISHES! This authentic Simian appendage will be your gateway to happiness, life-long riches and more! Just hold it in your hand, stroke it twice and make your wish. It's as easy as that! A million dollars worth of value for the low, low price of only $4.98 (plus shipping and handling). Order yours now! Supply is extremely limited!

MONEY BACK GUARANTEE!

Please rush me my Authentic Lucky Monkey's Paw for which I have enclosed $4.98. My money back if I'm not completely satisfied.

☐ I enclose $4.98 plus 62¢ shipping charge.
☐ Send C.O.D. I will pay postman on delivery plus C.O.D. and shipping charge.

Name _____
Address _____
City _____ State _____ Zip _____

CREEPSHOW COMIC ADVERTISEMENTS FOR AMUSEMENT ONLY.

SO, NOW YOU'VE CRAWLED THROUGH THE GUTS OF WHAT MAKES SHUDDER'S CREEPSHOW SO AGONIZINGLY IRRESISTIBLE.
IF EVER YOU NEED A TERRIBLE TALLY OF WHAT HAS PUT YOU IN YOUR WRETCHED CONDITION, HERE'S THE LIST OF EVERY EVIL BIT YOU'VE INGESTED ALONG THE WAY. I CALL IT...
CREEPSHOW SEASON 2 EPISODE 1&2
CREEPSHOW
SWAMP MUMMIES FROM MARS
DRACULA'S SWAMP
THE DEAD CIRCUS
HELL OF THE MUMMIES
REVENGE of the ALIENS
ZOMBIES of JUPITER
CASTLE OF THE APES
TOMBS of the WEREWOLF
VAMPIRE HOLOCAUST
VAMPIRES ALWAYS WEAR BLACK
EVIL CRYPT
THE SALEM DONESAW MASSACRE
MIDNIGHT DEATHSHOW
MOON OF THE MUMMY
CASTLE OF THE WEREWOLF
HYENA PEOPLE
THE UNHOLY BLOODSUCKERS
DAWN OF THE WEREWOLF
EVIL NIGHTMARE
BLOOD TOADS
THE EVIL ZOMBIES
CREATURE FROM THE VOLCANO
THE SATANIC RITES OF FRANKENSTEIN
ZOMBIE BLENDER MASSACRE
13 VAMPIRES
13 DOORS of BLOOD!
THE EVIL OF THE CLOWNS
THE DAWN OF THE HAUNTED
THE FOREVER
MICHAEL BROOM 2022

THE CREEPSHOW COMPENDIUM

ABOVE: The Creep grins and scares it for the first three seasons of Shudder's *Creepshow*.

SEASON ONE | EPISODE ONE
GRAY MATTER

Written by: **BYRON WILLINGER / PHILIP DE BLASI**

Based on the short story by **STEPHEN KING**

Directed by: **GREG NICOTERO**

Starring: **ADRIENNE BARBEAU, GIANCARLO ESPOSITO, TOBIN BELL, CHRISTOPHER NATHAN, JESSE C. BOYD**

Air Date: **September 26, 2019**

Run Time: **22 mins.**

Hurricane Charlie threatens to be the most devastating storm to hit this coastal town in nearly 70 years, but it's not the Category 4 assault that has young Timmy Grenadine so stricken with fear. His daddy's sick—and he's getting worse—all since Mom died. And the nightly case of Harrow's beer that Timmy faithfully takes to his beloved father doesn't seem to be helping matters any. In fact, it might have been a bad can of the swill that has caused a truly awful change in Timmy's dad. He promised he'd quit drinking...but now it seems it's much too late for that.

SEASON ONE | EPISODE ONE
THE HOUSE OF THE HEAD

Written by: **JOSH MALERMANI**

Directed by: **JOHN HARRISON**

Starring: **CAILEY FLEMING, RACHEL HENDRIX, DAVID SHAE, GUY MESSENGER, DIANE D CARTER**

Air Date: **September 26, 2019**

Run Time: **20 mins.**

Evie happily tends to the needs of the Smith-Smiths, the toy family that lives in the elaborate doll house in her bedroom. She imagines a calm bliss for Mother, Father, son Ethan, and pet dog Dane, until an uninvited guest appears—a ghastly disembodied head. Now, Evie witnesses the terrified reactions of the Smith-Smiths as the ghostly head pursues each of them, with murderous intent...and then it sets its sights on Evie herself.

SEASON ONE | EPISODE TWO
BAD WOLF DOWN

Written by: ROB SCHRAB
Directed by: ROB SCHRAB
Starring: DAVID A. MACDONALD, CALLAN WILSON, SCOTT MESCUDI, NELSON BONILLA, JEFFREY COMBS, KATE FREUND
Air Date: October 3, 2019
Run Time: 18 mins.

It's 1944 on a war-torn French battlefield, where a small group of American soldiers find themselves hopelessly out-flanked by a battalion of Nazi soldiers. The vengeful Commandant Reinhard vows death to these Americans who took down his own son in a volley of bullets. Now, trapped in an abandoned jail house, American Captain Talby turns to an unthinkable solution to save his remaining men...while sacrificing their very humanity.

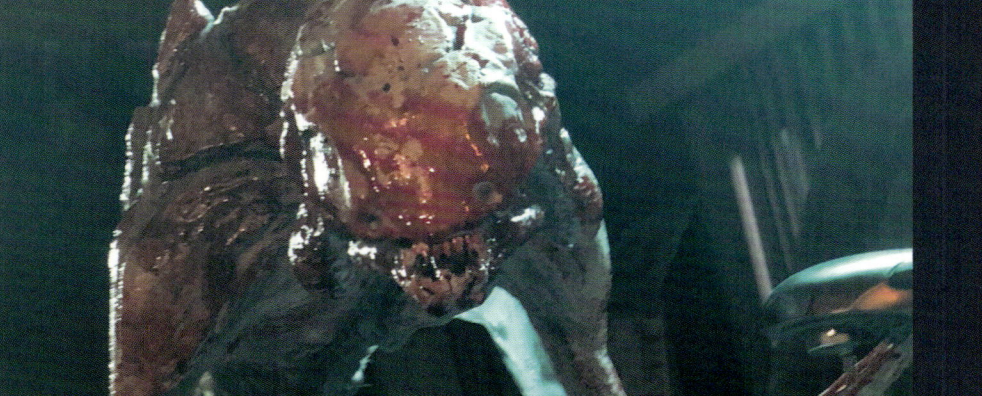

SEASON ONE | EPISODE TWO
THE FINGER

Written by: DAVID J. SCHOW
Directed by: GREG NICOTERO
Starring: DJ QUALLS, ANTWAN MILLS, JAKE GARBER
Air Date: October 3, 2019
Run Time: 22 mins.

Oh, the shit we collect in life. Random bits of this-and-that. Castoffs that others have left strewn in our path. Things we pick up and put in our pocket. Miserable divorcée and hopeless hoarder Clark Wilson has just stumbled across a...well...it's a *finger*. But a finger from what? Don't know, but he takes it home to investigate it anyway. And just as it seems it might just become another useless artifact in his growing collection of his life's disappointments, the finger begins growing. What it becomes—and what it does—turns out to be of no disappointment to Clark.

SEASON ONE | EPISODE THREE
ALL HALLOW'S EVE

Written by: **BRUCE JONES**

Directed by: **JOHN HARRISON**

Starring: **CONNOR CHRISTIE, MADISON THOMPSON, JASUN JABBAR, ANDREW EAKLE, MICHAEL MAY, JULIA DENTON, SCOTT DANIEL JOHNSON, TOM OLSON, ERICA FRENE**

Air Date: **October 10, 2019**

Run Time: **18 mins.**

Every Halloween, kids gather to collect their just desserts. But in this suburban town of Smithville, the five youths who make up the Golden Dragon club have more than Milk Duds and mini-Mounds bars on their minds. The horror of that one Halloween, five years ago when Eddie Hathaway and his crew pulled their fiery prank, has kept them coming back. All have atoned for that night of terror...all except Eddie. One more time around the block, Golden Dragons?

SEASON ONE | EPISODE THREE
THE MAN IN THE SUITCASE

Written by: **CHRISTOPHER BUEHLMAN**

Directed by: **DAVID BRUCKNER**

Starring: **WILL KINDRACHUK, RAVI NAIDU, MADISON BAILEY, IAN GREGG, ANTWAN "BIG BOI" PATTON, NASIM BOWLUS, CAREY JONES**

Air Date: **October 10, 2019**

Run Time: **23 mins.**

Dammit! They've lost Justin's luggage. That's all he needs, what with Carla having broken up with him and now Dad's pissed about the bad grades. Frickin' airports, always losing...wait—there's his bag. Only, it turns out it's not his bag. In fact, the man inside the bag (yes, inside the bag) promises Justin that his luck is about to change, if he'll just help the man safely extract himself from his carry-on confinement. But, can Alex make good choices after he learns that there's profit in this man's pain?

212 CHAPTER ELEVEN

SEASON **ONE** | EPISODE **FOUR**
THE COMPANION

Written by: **MATT VENNE**

Based on a short story by **JOE LANSDALE, KASEY LANSDALE, & KEITH LANSDALE**

Directed by: **DAVID BRUCKNER**

Starring: **LOGAN ALLEN, AFEMO OMILAMI, CAREY JONES, VOLTAIRE COUNCIL, DYLAN GAGE, ADDISON HERSHEY**

Air Date: **October 17, 2019**

Run Time: **19 mins.**

Since when does a kid's own brother become his most-feared bully? For Harold, that's been a way of life, day after miserable day. But when bastard brother Billy tracks Harold down at his favorite fishing stream, the terrified boy tears into the deep woods where he encounters an unlikely ally. Now it's Billy's turn to be stalked, and Harold's new companion is just the one to root out the big brother's bad temperament.

SEASON **ONE** | EPISODE **FOUR**
LYDIA LAYNE'S BETTER HALF

Written by: **JOHN HARRISON**

Story by: **GREG NICOTERO & JOHN HARRISON**

Directed by: **ROXANNE BENJAMIN**

Starring: **TRICIA HELFER, DANIELLE LYN, MICHAEL SCIALABBA, JORDAN PATRICK**

Air Date: **October 17, 2019**

Run Time: **21 mins.**

Lydia Layne has done well for herself. She's grown her Medtech equity group to be one of the richest in the country, and she lifts up those loyal employees who have helped her reach such enviable heights. But when she passes over right-hand partner—in every sense of the word—Celia for a deserved promotion as company CFO, it becomes apparent that "loyalty" is a one-way street. In a tragic turn of events, Lydia finds she has more to mend than Celia's shattered trust. How about a shattered skull, for instance?

CHAPTER **ELEVEN**

SEASON ONE | EPISODE FIVE
NIGHT OF THE PAW

Written by: **JOHN ESPOSITO**

Directed by: **JOHN HARRISON**

Starring: **BRUCE DAVISON, HANNAH BAREFOOT, SUSANNAH DEVEREUX, GRACE TOSO, RYAN CLAY GWALTNEY**

Air Date: **October 24, 2019**

Run Time: **27 mins.**

Ah, the monkey's paw. It's known to have the astounding power to return our dearly departed to us, back to soothe our grieving hearts...but then come the guilt-ridden results and terrifying consequences of ill-considered wishes made. For mortician Avery Whitlock...well, he's thought through the loss of his beloved Marjorie, carefully and completely, and has a plan to undo her previous unwise wish for money and his heart-broken wish for her resurrection. And what about pretty Angela? Well, her nearby car wreck seemed to be an unfortunate and unplanned event that has put her under widower Whitlock's care. Was her crash an accident, or was it the result of Whitlock monkeying around with the hand of fate?

SEASON ONE | EPISODE FIVE
TIMES IS TOUGH IN MUSKY HOLLER

Written by: **JOHN SKIPP & DORI MILLER**

Directed by: **JOHN HARRISON**

Starring: **DANE RHODES, KAREN STRASSMAN, DAVID ARQUETTE, TOMMY KANE, TRACEY BONNER, KERMIT ROLISON, CONNOR HAMMOND**

Air Date: **October 24, 2019**

Run Time: **14 mins.**

A tight community is a strong community...until the corruption takes hold. From the town mayor, the trusted pastor, and even local media and law enforcement, the *good* people of Musky Holler are staging their day of reckoning. They're breaking the chains that have been holding them down, shackled by those community leaders who treated it all like a game—taking from and trampling the good townspeople, all while enriching themselves. Well, the real game is now underway. Welcome to the people's court!

SEASON **ONE** | EPISODE **SIX**
SKINCRAWLERS

Written by: **PAUL DINI & STEPHEN LANGFORD**

Directed by: **ROXANNE BENJAMIN**

Starring: **DANA GOULD, CHAD MICHAEL COLLINS, HINA KHAN, MELISSA SAINT-AMAND, BETH KEENER, JASON GRAHAM, DARIN TOONDER**

Air Date: **October 31, 2019**

Run Time: **19 mins.**

Imagine—the body of your dreams. The look you deserve. Lean. Luscious. Sexy beyond your wildest dreams. It's all yours. No exercise. No diet. No kidding. You're not dreaming—Skin Deep by Sloan makes the dream a reality. Come, experience for yourself the amazing new method that literally melts fat away in mere days. It's all natural, made possible by the rare *anguiloforms* of South America—they literally feed on your fat with no pain, no discomfort, and no after-effects. The results speak for themselves. Your satisfaction is guaranteed. What could possibly go wrong?

SEASON **ONE** | EPISODE **SIX**
BY THE SILVER WATER OF LAKE CHAMPLAIN

Teleplay by: **JASON CIARAMELLA**

Based on the short story by **JOE HILL**

Directed by: **TOM SAVINI**

Starring: **SYDNEY WEASE, CONNOR JONES, DAVID ALEXANDER KAPLAN, JAMES DEVOTI, GENA SHAW**

Air Date: **October 31, 2019**

Run Time: **22 mins.**

The local legend of Lake Champlain's sea serpent is regarded as a silly myth by most, but young Rose believes, just as her father did. She's never seen "Champy" with her own eyes but, rather, through her father's belief and his stack of documentation. He died searching for the beast, and now Rose's irascible and unpredictable stepfather, Chet, promises to put an end to Rose's nonsense. If only Rose, aided by boyfriend Thomas, could actually find proof that there's nothing mythical about the lake's mysterious monster.

CHAPTER **ELEVEN**

SEASON TWO | EPISODE ONE
MODEL KID

Written by: JOHN ESPOSITO
Directed by: GREG NICOTERO
Starring: BROCK DUNCAN, TYNER RUSHING, JANA ALLEN, KEVIN DILLON, CHRIST SCHMIDT, NICK MORGAN

Air Date: **April 1, 2021**
Run Time: **26 mins.**

Joe likes monsters—so what? He'll probably grow out of it, someday. Mom doesn't mind, and she bonds lovingly with her imaginative son in his world of gill men and musty mummies. But when Mom loses her long battle with cancer, Joe is left to fend off his obnoxious Uncle Kevin, a mock-worthy man who believes boys should play with footballs, not plastic freaks. Joe will make his unhinged uncle believe in monsters....

SEASON TWO | EPISODE ONE
PUBLIC TELEVISION OF THE DEAD

Written by: ROB SCHRAB
Directed by: GREG NICOTERO
Starring: MARK ASHWORTH, MARISSA HAMPTON, COLEY CAMPANY, PETER LEAKE, TODD ALLEN DURKIN, TED RAIMI AS TED RAIMI, JASON KEHLER

Air Date: **April 1, 2021**
Run Time: **22 mins.**

Public television goodness, made possible by government funding and your generous membership pledges. There's delightful story time with sweet Mrs. Bookberry. There's the escape into natural beauty brought to canvas with Norm Roberts and *The Love of Painting*. And, what hidden fortunes lie among our own belongings? *The Appraiser's Road Trip* is ready to unlock the secrets of life's odds and ends, this week featuring visitor Ted Raimi and his unusual leather-bound "Necronomicon" book. What might be lurking within its oddly illustrated pages...and what riches might it have in store for Mr. Raimi?

SEASON **TWO** | EPISODE **TWO**
DEAD AND BREAKFAST

Written by: **MICHAEL ROUSSELET & ERIK SANDOVAL**
Directed by: **AXELLE CAROLYN**
Starring: **ALI LARTER, C. THOMAS HOWELL, IMAN BENSON, PAMELA RICARDO, STARR LAJOIE, DOMINIQUE HARRIS**
Air Date: **April 8, 2021**
Run Time: **22 mins.**

What sick people seek out the crime scenes of history's most infamous serial killers—for a night of chills followed by continental breakfast in the morning?! Plenty of people, that's who. But despite the legend of the Spinster Murder House, where Grandma Spinster ran amok with an axe on her hotel guests, there's little traction in that tale. Now, it's up to desperate grandkids and current Spinster House hotel owners, Sam and Pam, to entice a social media influencer to stay a night and help infuse some life into this dying "dead and breakfast" destination.

SEASON **TWO**| EPISODE **TWO**
PESTICIDE

Written by: **FRANK DIETZ**
Directed by: **GREG NICOTERO**
Starring: **JOSH MCDERMITT, KEITH DAVID, ASHLEY LAURENCE**
Air Date: **April 8, 2021**
Run Time: **24 mins.**

Harlan King is a name to be feared...if you have eight tiny legs and a fat thorax. He's been ridding the community of roaches, spiders, and any sort of stinkbug that has infested your slice of Paradise. No pest is too wily for Harlan, that is until he's pointed toward a most unique—and lucrative—pest for elimination. Will he take the task? Will he do the unthinkable? And will there be a price to pay for his disregard for the humane? Careful—some pests will demand a payback!

CHAPTER **ELEVEN** 217

SEASON **TWO** | EPISODE **THREE**
THE RIGHT SNUFF

Written by: **PAUL DINI, STEPHEN LANGFORD, GREG NICOTERO**

Directed by: **JOE LYNCH**

Starring: **RYAN KWANTEN, BRECKIN MEYER, GABRIELLE BYNDLOSS, KARA KIMMER**

Air Date: **April 15, 2021**

Run Time: **24 mins.**

Captain Alex Toomey and Major Ted Lockwood are international heroes. Aboard the Ocula space station, the two astronauts have tested and are perfecting the Major's gravity wave device, allowing for the actual control and directional use of gravity itself. And while Lockwood is the acknowledged genius of the mission, Toomey is living in the shadow of his celebrated astronaut father, the first man on Mars, and his accusations that his son will never measure up to the same level of greatness. Toomey's pain is enough to cause him to lose his bearings and descend into a space-induced—and guilt-fueled—madness...even murder?

SEASON **TWO** | EPISODE **THREE**
SIBLING RIVALRY

Written by: **MELANIE DALE**

Directed by: **RUSTY CUNDIEFF**

Starring: **MADDIE NICHOLS, ANDREW BRODEUR, JA'NESS TATE, JERRI TUBBS, MOLLY RINGWALD**

Air Date: **April 15, 2021**

Run Time: **20 mins.**

Of course Lola Pierce knows how crazy it sounds—that her brother is trying to kill her—especially in the face of Counselor Porter's dismissive stare. Despite the young girl's pleading, the perplexed Miss Porter is struggling to determine if Lola's is a cry for help or a cry for attention (they're so often one and the same in the world of teen angst). But, as Miss Porter will soon find out, Lola's brother had sound instincts and justifiable cause to fear his sister, and no level of scholastic snark will help Miss Porter now.

SEASON TWO | EPISODE FOUR
PIPE SCREAMS

Written by: **DANIEL KRAUS**
Directed by: **JOE LYNCH**
Starring: **ERIC EDELSTEIN, BARBARA CRAMPTON, SELENA ADUZE**
Air Date: **April 22, 2021**
Run Time: **19 mins.**

Victoria Smoot, the landlord, lords over the shittiest tenement in this area as she wields her intolerant attitude towards her tenants. She doesn't discriminate; she despises 'em all equally! But now she is making it Linus Carruthers' problem, the plumber who thinks he's traced the source of the black whatever-it-is that's taken up residence in the tenement's pipe system. Is that black gunk really from the tenants, or is it an embodiment of vitriolic Victoria's dark soul?

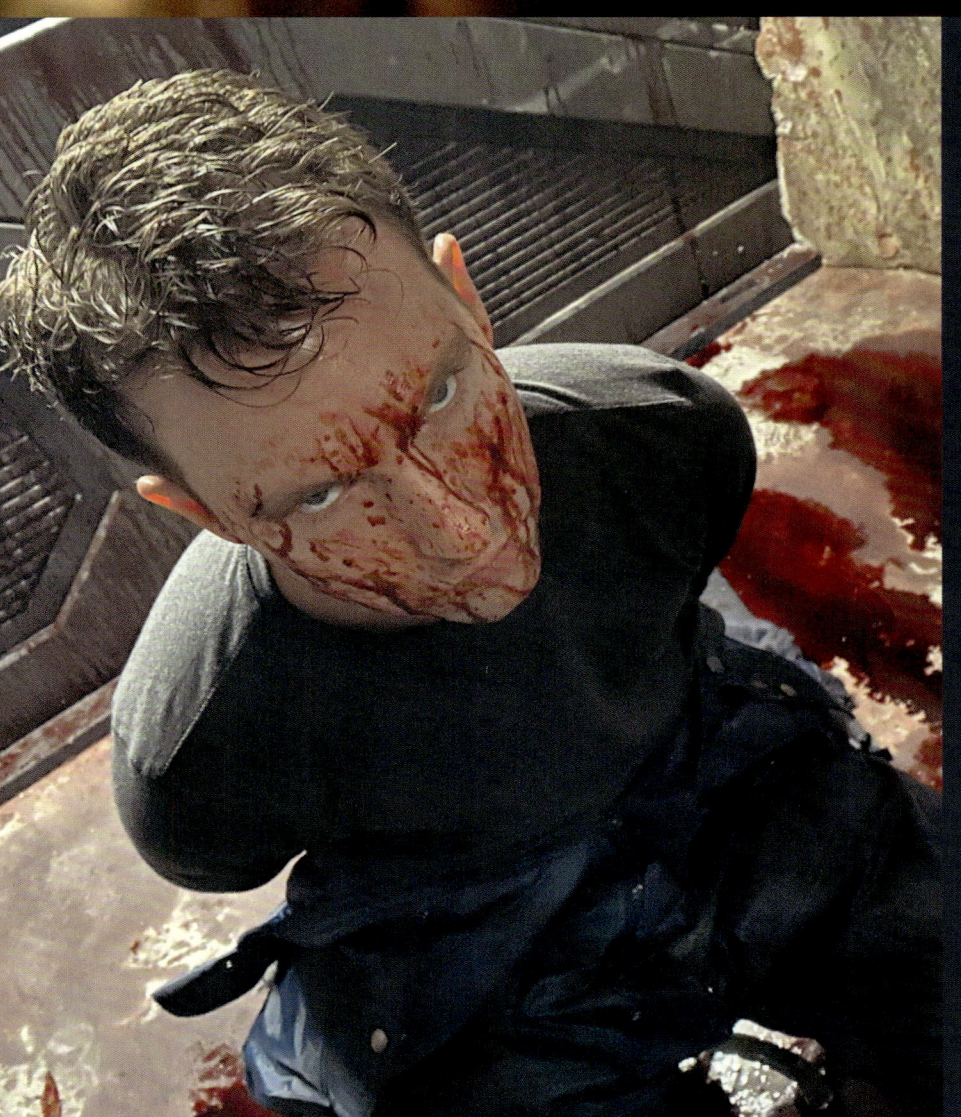

SEASON TWO | EPISODE FOUR
WITHIN THE WALLS OF MADNESS

Teleplay by: **JOHN ESPOSITO**
Story by: **GREG NICOTERO & JOHN ESPOSITO**
Directed by: **JOHN HARRISON**
Starring: **DREW MATTHEWS, DENISE CROSBY, BRITTANY SMITH, NICHOLAS LOGAN, BROOKE BUTLER, LEONARD BUTLER**
Air Date: **April 22, 2021**
Run Time: **20 mins.**

Things aren't what they seem at Install-511, a professed biotech research facility that has undergone a recent containment breach... with horrific consequences. Station intern Zeller was the only one to understand what happened, the only one who actually saw whatever it was that breached the other-dimensional wormhole and now emanates from the very walls of the sub-Arctic installation. Now, Zeller is being held in maximum security, charged with the gruesome deaths of his colleagues, but he knows the true origin of the entity that punched a hole into our world...and he knows how to summon it again.

SEASON **TWO** | EPISODE **FIVE**
NIGHT OF THE LIVING LATE SHOW

Written by: **DANA GOULD**
Directed by: **GREG NICOTERO**
Starring: **JUSTIN LONG, D'ARCY CARDEN, HANNAH FIERMAN**

Air Date: **April 29, 2021**
Run Time: **37 mins.**

Inventor Simon Sherman's affinity for technology is only matched by his love for classic horror movies. Now, he's brought both worlds together with his Immersopod, the first virtual reality media bridge that actually puts him inside his all-time favorite film, *Horror Express*. But his wealthy new bride, Renee, soon suspects her husband's obsession with his invention goes far beyond a fanboy's standing shoulder-to-shoulder with the likes of film legends Christopher Lee and Peter Cushing. Is Simon actually attempting to step out on his young bride while he steps into the movie?

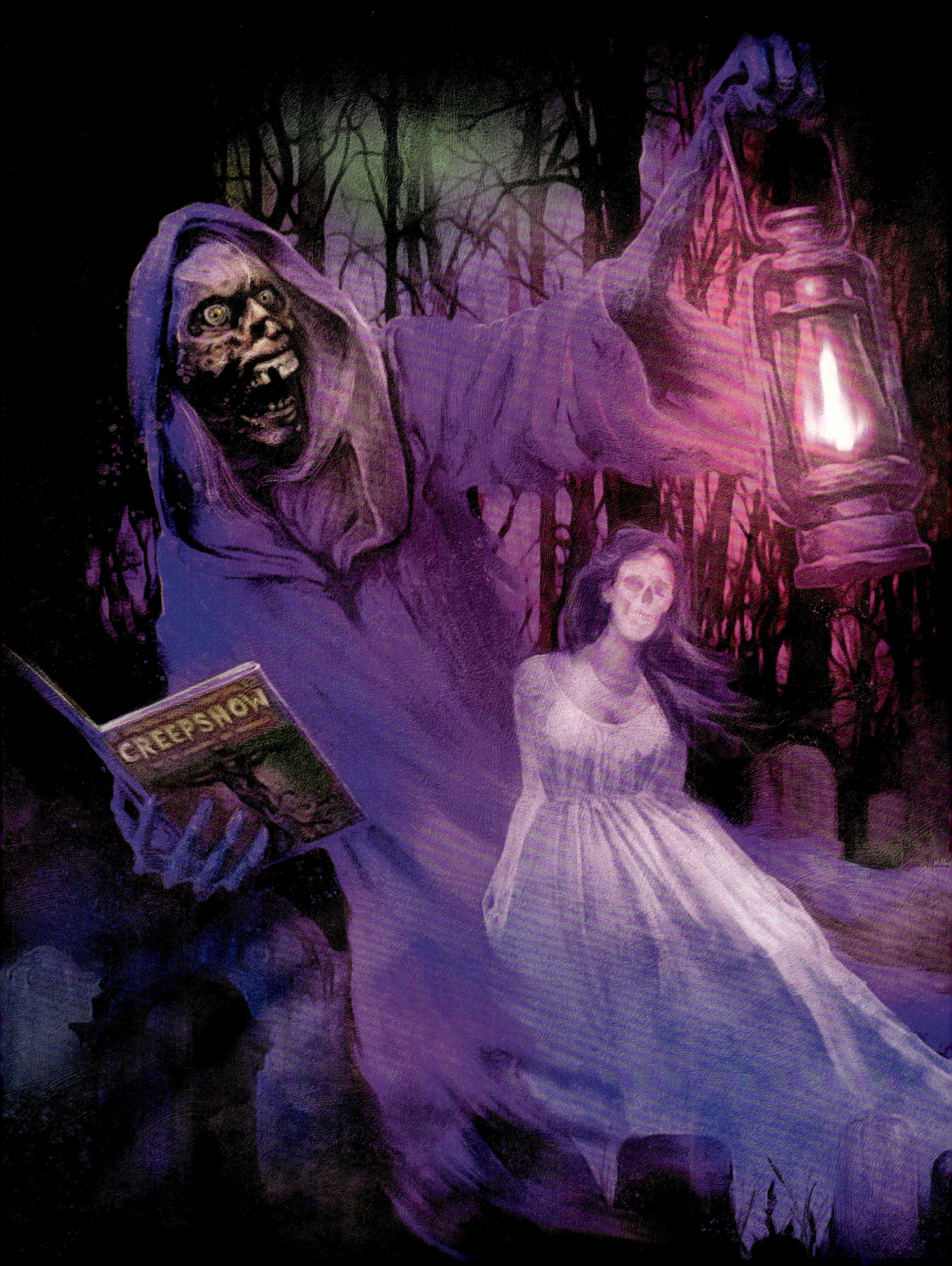
CREEPSHOW

SEASON THREE | EPISODE ONE
MUMS

Written by: GREG NICOTERO & DAVID J. SCHOW
Based on a short story by JOE HILL
Directed by: RUSTY CUNDIEFF
Starring: ETHAN EMBRY, BRAYDEN BENSON, ERIN BEUTE, MALONE THOMAS, LOWREY BROWN
Air Date: September 23, 2021
Run Time: 23 mins.

The only thing Bloom loves more than her flower garden is her young son Jack. But when she attempts to take the boy and flee from her abusive husband Hank, her survivalist spouse thwarts her escape. After the unthinkable happens, Jack takes up tending to his departed mother's garden, and there he discovers that blood is thicker than water and that nature always finds a way to right that which has gone wrong.

SEASON THREE | EPISODE ONE
QUEEN BEE

Written by: ERIK SANDOVAL & MICHAEL ROUSSELET
Directed by: GREG NICOTERO
Starring: KAELYNN GOBERT-HARRIS, MONICA LOUWERENS, HANNAH KEPPLE, OLIVIA HAWTHORNE, NICO GOMEZ, BRUCE ANTHONY SHEPPERSON
Air Date: September 23, 2021
Run Time: 21 mins.

Oh my god! Can you believe it—the amazing Regina is here in our town and rumor has it she's delivering her baby at the local hospital? Professed superfans Trenice and Debra, with tag-along pal Carlos, can hardly contain themselves. Wouldn't it be the bomb if we snuck into the hospital to be there when she welcomes her beautiful baby into this world? As her superfans, it only makes sense that the trio take flight to be by their pop queen's side when it happens. If only they had been calmer and cooler in their exuberance. They're about to feel the sting that comes from the ugly underbelly of show business.

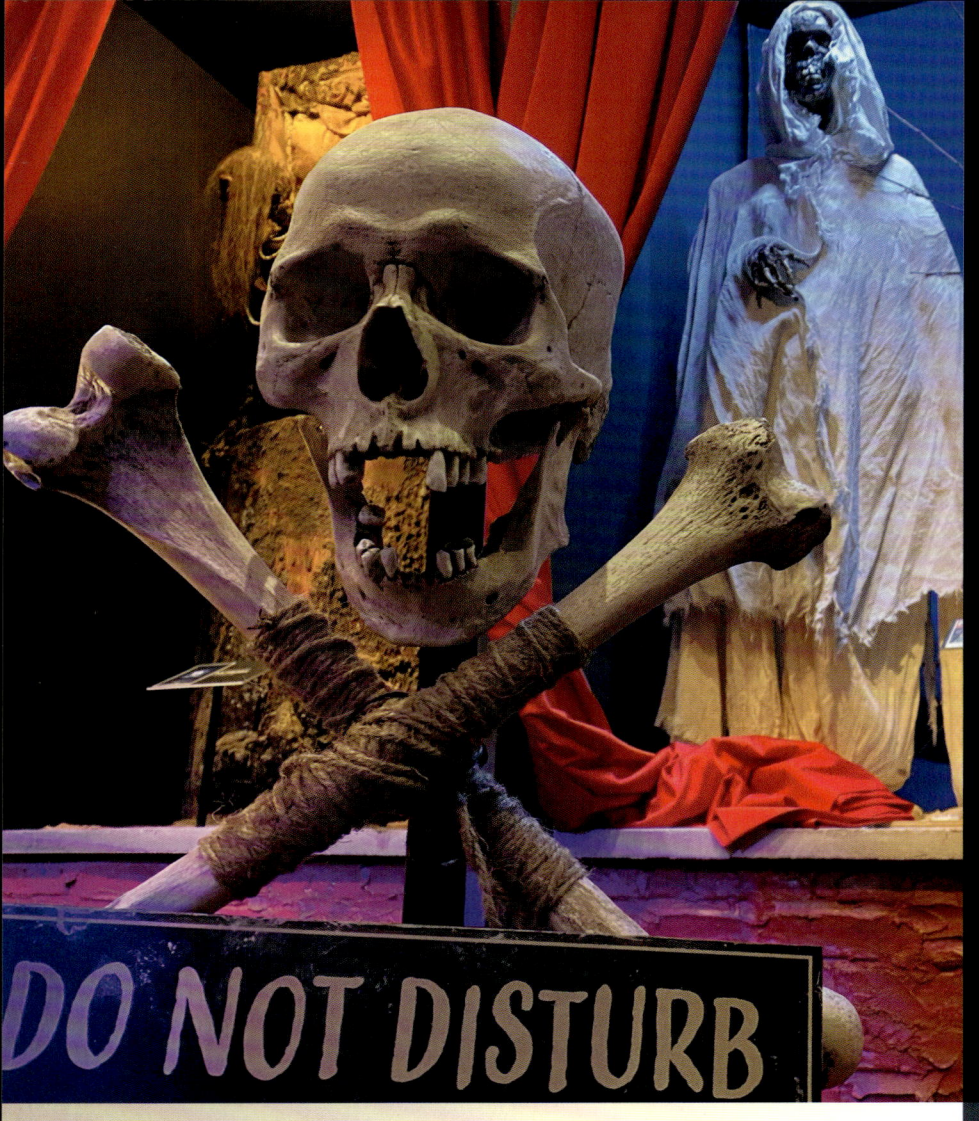

SEASON **THREE** | EPISODE **TWO**
SKELETONS IN THE CLOSET

Teleplay by: JOHN ESPOSITO
Story by: GREG NICOTERO & JOHN ESPOSITO
Directed by: GREG NICOTERO
Starring: JAMES REMAR, VICTOR RIVERA, VALERIE LEBLANC, LUCAS GODFREY
Air Date: September 30, 2021
Run Time: 24 mins.

With literally millions of dollars' worth of rare and original movie props, Lampini's Skeletons in the Closet museum is a treasure trove of filmdom's most-coveted relics. Lampini will go to any extent to collect and curate the finest in screen-used artifacts...*any extent.* But when rival collector Bateman threatens blackmail to wrest away one of Lampini's most cherished exhibits, the gauntlet has been thrown down. Either Lampini surrenders a prized piece or Bateman spills the beans on the true provenance of one of the museum's most ghoulish attractions.

SEASON **THREE** | EPISODE **TWO**
FAMILIAR

Written by: JOSH MALERMAN
Directed by: JOE LYNCH
Starring: ANDREW BACHELOR, HANNAH FIERMAN, KEITH ARTHUR BOLDEN
Air Date: September 30, 2021
Run Time: 22 mins.

Jackson doesn't go in for any of that fortune teller stuff, but he'll humor girlfriend Fawn when she leads him into Boone's Third Eye parlor. Fawn's amusement quickly turns to amazement as the all-seeing Boone reveals details of her past and present. For Jackson, however, he delivers an unspoken warning of something that lurks in his future. He passes no judgment; only a scribbled note: *Something bad followed you in here.*

CHAPTER ELEVEN

SEASON **THREE** | EPISODE **THREE**
THE LAST TSUBURAYA

Written by: **PAUL DINI & STEPHEN LANGFORD**

Directed by: **JEFFREY F. JANUARY**

Starring: **BRANDON QUINN, JADE FERNANDEZ, GIA HIRAIZUMI, KENNY ALFONSO, JOE ANDO-HIRSH, JOSEPH STEVEN YANG**

Air Date: **October 7, 2021**

Run Time: **26 mins.**

It seems Bobby Tanaka's fortune is changing. As the only living descendant of Ishido Tsuburaya, a contemporary artist whose chilling renderings of Japanese ghosts and monsters have earned him legendary status, a final and never-before-seen illustration is now Bobby's. Curator at Tokyo's Ota Museum of Art, Dr. Mai Sato, is eager to gain Bobby's agreement to add Tsuburaya's final work to the collection. Rival art collector and obnoxious billionaire Wade Cruise purchases the piece out from under Sato, then hosts a private party where he'll be the first—and only—to see the art. In a flash of flames, Cruise destroys the piece, making himself the only individual ever to have laid eyes upon it. But something other-worldly was released in those flames, and it intends to lay its wrath on Cruise.

SEASON **THREE** | EPISODE **THREE**
OKAY, I'LL BITE

Written by: **JOHN HARRISON**

Directed by: **JOHN HARRISON**

Starring: **NICK MASSOUH, NIC STARR, DEBORAH BOWMAN, JACKSON BEALS, TONY DEMIL, GLENN MAGEE**

Air Date: **October 7, 2021**

Run Time: **24 mins.**

All these years, locked in this coat closet of a prison cell...a guy's gotta make whatever friendships he can. That's exactly what former pharmacist Elmer Strick does, turning to his collection of eight-legged cell mates to help him pass the days, weeks, years. Today, though, he'll have his parole hearing and they'll be sure to see that he's paid his due. Corrupt prison guard Dill, however, sabotages Strick's parole hearing in order to keep the inmate's coerced production of opiates flowing. It's a lucrative operation for the guard and his goons, but it leads Strick to make a most unusual bid for freedom, all while unleashing his eight-legged wrath.

SEASON THREE | EPISODE FOUR
STRANGER SINGS

Written by: **JORDANA ARKIN**

Directed by: **AXELLE CAROLYN**

Starring: **SUEHYLA EL-ATTAR YOUNG, KADIANNE WHYTE, CHRIS MAYERS**

Air Date: **October 14, 2021**

Run Time: **19 mins.**

We all hear sirens, every day, but Barry has been lured by the unique tones of Sara, a woman he's just met at a local bookstore. Although he falters in his attempt to ask Sara for a date, it's she who puts out the compelling call for Barry's attention—or was it Sara's mysterious friend, Miranda. No matter, because Barry's a practicing OB-GYN, and Sara and Miranda have entrapped him into performing an odd procedure. Barry complies as if his life depends on it... because it does!

SEASON THREE | EPISODE FOUR
METER READER

Written by: **JOHN ESPOSITO**

Directed by: **JOE LYNCH**

Starring: **JOHNATHON SCHAECH, ABIGAIL DOLAN, CYNTHIA EVANS, BOSTON PIERCE, SAMANTHA WORTHEN, REAGAN HIGGINS**

Air Date: **October 14, 2021**

Run Time: **23 mins.**

What's the point in going on? Ever since the plague descended upon our planet, each day is just the delaying of an inevitable, inescapably horrifying end. The demons roam the Earth now, feeding upon the weak and the strong-willed equally. Our last hope for humanity: the Meter Readers, sacred vigilantes who do battle with the dark forces, all in a final attempt to save whatever might be left of mankind. But if the Meter Readers fail, then who can possibly save us?

SEASON **THREE** | EPISODE **FIVE**
TIME OUT

Written by: BARRINGTON SMITH & PAUL SEETACHITT
Directed by: JEFFREY F. JANUARY
Starring: MATTHEW BARNES, DEVON HALES, JIBRE HORDGES, LAUREN RICHARDS, SHANNON EUBANKS, KAMRAN SHAIKH

Air Date: October 21, 2021
Run Time: 26 mins.

There are only so many hours in a day, but Tim Denbrough just found a way to squeeze as much time out of each day as he chooses. Upon inheriting a mysterious armoire, he discovers it to be a refuge from the nagging tick-tocking of the clock's incessant reminder that the hour is running late. Inside the clothes locker, time passes normally for its occupant, but outside, time stands still. It becomes Tim's secret ally in ascending to heights he never believed he'd have time enough to reach. It all seems so easy, but will there be a price to pay for stealing away the hours?

SEASON **THREE** | EPISODE **FIVE**
THE THINGS IN OAKWOOD'S PAST

Written by: DANIEL KRAUS & GREG NICOTERO
Directed by: DAVE NEWBERG & GREG NICOTERO
Animation directed by: ENOL JUNQUERA & LUIS JUNQUERA
Starring: MARK HAMILL, DANIELLE HARRIS, RON LIVINGSTON, FAYNA SANCHEZ, KATE THULIN, ANDY DALY

Air Date: October 21, 2021
Run Time: 17 mins.

Oakwood, Maine. Quaint. Routine. Well, all except that time in 1821, where the entire town population just up and vanished. Poof! All gone. It's been the mystery of the ages—literally—but all the years of contemplating and theorizing will be put to rest this Friday. That's when local librarian Marnie Wrightson will open a recently-found time capsule. Long lost town journals dating back to the 1800s led her to it, but she's since discovered even darker details that indicate the townspeople didn't abandon Oakwood—they were...they were.... The time capsule—? Does it offer protection to the town, or offer it up for Friday's next round of the 200-year curse?

SEASON **THREE** | EPISODE **SIX**
DRUG TRAFFIC

Teleplay by: **CHRISTOPHER LARSEN**
Story by: **MATTIE DO & CHRISTOPHER LARSEN**
Directed by: **GREG NICOTERO**
Starring: **MICHAEL ROOKER, SARAH JON, REID SCOTT**
Air Date: **October 28, 2021**
Run Time: **28 mins.**

U.S. Congressman Evan Miller has lofty political aspirations, and he's getting plenty of mileage out of a recent bus trip into Canada where citizens have gone to get their much-needed medications. While stumping on the deplorable U.S. healthcare system that neither provides nor allows low-cost medications to its citizens, a U.S. border guard detains a woman, her obviously-ill daughter, and the curious unmarked medications they're attempting to smuggle into the country. Forget the politics and the social grandstanding because there's something seriously wrong with this woman's daughter, and all hell is about to break loose on the U.S.-Canadian border.

SEASON **THREE** | EPISODE **SIX**
A DEAD GIRL NAMED SUE

Teleplay by: **HEATHER ANNE CAMPBELL**
Based on the short story by **CRAIG ENGLER**
Directed by: **JOHN HARRISON**
Starring: **CRISTIAN GONZALEZ, JOSH MIKEL, J.R. RODRIGUEZ, BRYAN BRENDLE, REY HERNANDEZ, KARLTON DAVIS**
Air Date: **October 28, 2021**
Run Time: **24 mins.**

Pittsburgh, 1968: the dead have risen and are feeding on the flesh of living humans. The unbelievable news sweeps the region as small communities struggle to cope with the unprecedented onslaught. The dead are walking! Amid the chaos, one group of vigilantes are dealing with another matter, their way. With what Mayor Ridgeway's degenerate son has now gone and done—and to that sweet, innocent little Sue—well, this has gone too far. Can the police chief contain the mob's thirst for revenge and retribution, and will the mayor get his despicable son off yet again? There just might be something more horrible than the walking dead.

CHAPTER **ELEVEN** 227

A CREEPSHOW ANIMATED SPECIAL
SURVIVOR TYPE

Teleplay by: **GREG NICOTERO**
Based on a short story by **STEPHEN KING**
Directed by: **GREG NICOTERO**
Starring: **KIEFER SUTHERLAND, FAYNA SANCHEZ**
Air Date: **October 26, 2020**
Run Time: **20 mins.**

Just how far would a man go to stay alive while stranded on a tiny uncharted island? Without a speck of food in sight, and with a badly injured foot that…well, as a skilled surgeon, he knows it *has* to come off if he's to stop the spread of infection. And he has to have *something* to eat, right? But after that, then what? What more can he humanly forsake of himself to stave off starvation until a rescue party arrives? Sometimes, the survival instinct can go a bit too far.

A CREEPSHOW ANIMATED SPECIAL
TWITTERING FROM THE CIRCUS OF THE DEAD

Teleplay by: **MELANIE DALE**
Based on a short story by **JOE HILL**
Directed by: **GREG NICOTERO**
Starring: **JOEY KING, FAYNA SANCHEZ**
Air Date: **October 26, 2020**
Run Time: **22 mins.**

Blake is so bored…to death, she swears it. Her only connection with reality—and her tween-age sanity—is her tweet stream, TYME2WASTE. Seriously, these family road trips are absolutely the worst, and she's screaming about it, 280 characters at a time. But when Dad spots a roadside curiosity—really, *Circus of the Dead?*—Blake and her family get more than stretch break. And the obviously-fake zombie clowns inside this sickening sideshow give Blake plenty to tweet about. Ugh—these family vacations. #KillMeNow

A CREEPSHOW HOLIDAY SPECIAL
SHAPESHIFTERS ANONYMOUS

Teleplay by: GREG NICOTERO

Story by: J.A. KONRATH

Directed by: GREG NICOTERO

Starring: ANNA CAMP, ADAM PALLY, FRANK NICOTERO, PETE BURRIS, CANDY MCLELLAN, DEREK RUSSO, TOM GLYNN, DONNIE EVANS, KEITH FLIPPEN, HOLLY STEVENSON, KARA KIMMER, LIL YACHTY

Air Date: December 18, 2020

Run Time: **41 mins.**

It's not the annual festival of tinsel and twinkling lights that has Robert Weston anxious. He's at his wits' end over his troubling condition, and his last hope is a clandestine support group called "Shapeshifters Anonymous." While he finds the acceptance and encouragement he's so desperately needed for his unusual affliction, he also learns about the shapeshifters' obscure lore and that history's mightiest red-armored warrior is coming to town—with his legion of helpers—to sort out who's naughty and nice. You better watch out!

SO, SETTLE IN, KIDDIES. I **WARNED** YOU AT THE BEGINNING THAT ONCE YOU STARTED THE **DESCENT** INTO THE WORLD OF **CREEPSHOW**, THERE'D BE NO TURNING BACK. REST ASSURED, THESE CREEPY TALES WILL KEEP YOU ON THE EDGE OF YOUR SEAT--AND ON THE **EDGE OF MADNESS**--AS YOU WATCH THEM AGAIN AND AGAIN--FOR EVER...AND EVER...**AND EVER**...

AHH-HA-HA-HA-HA!

THE DEAD LETTER OFFICE

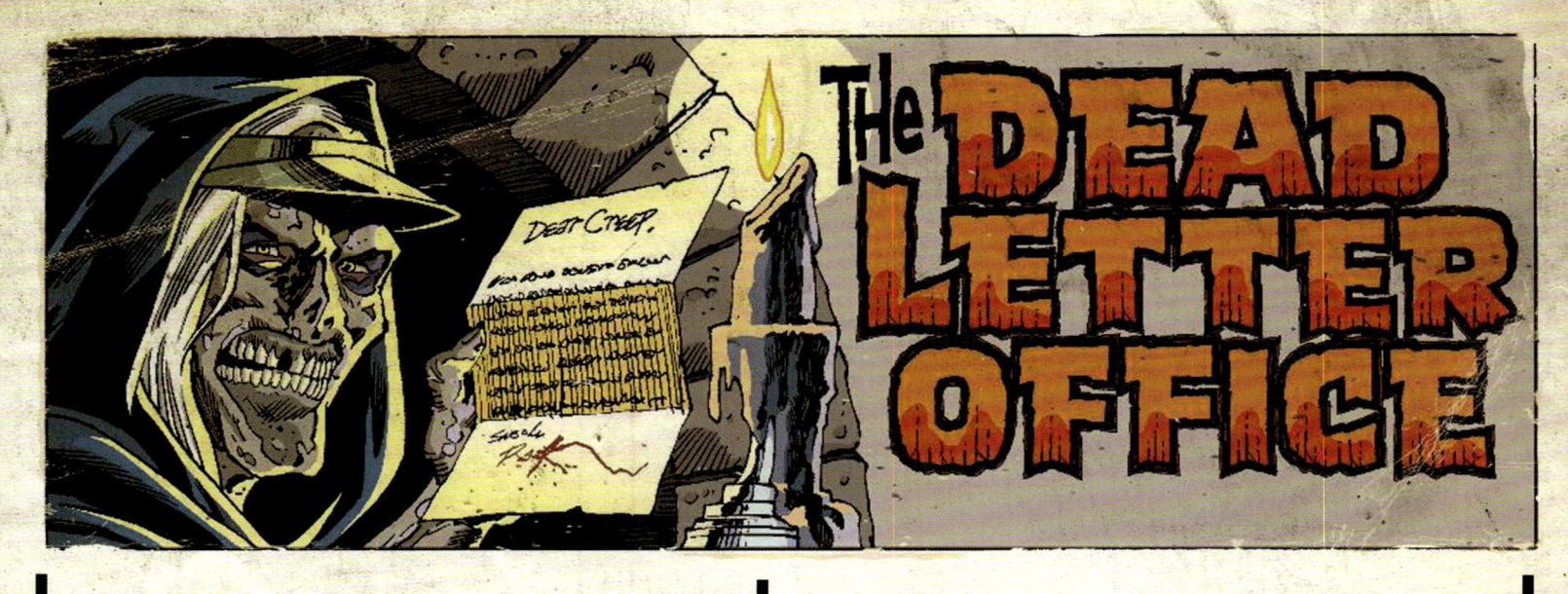

DEAR CREEP,

MY NAME IS STEPHEN AND I'M 14 YEARS OLD AND I JUST WANTED TO ASK IF THERE WAS ANY CHANCE I COULD BUY THE MONKEY'S PAW FEATURED IN YOUR STORY **NIGHT OF THE PAW**. I COULD REALLY USE IT AND I PROMISE I WON'T WISH ANYTHING BAD ON ANYONE.

STEPHEN
BANGOR, MAINE

DEAR CREEP,

CREEPSHOW ISSUE #3 WAS ABSOLUTELY FANTASTIC. I'D LIKE TO CONGRATULATE EVERYONE INVOLVED. THE "ALL MOSTER" ISSUE IS BY FAR MY FAVORITE AND THE COVER WAS INCREDIBLE.

LARRY
BLOOMFIELD, N.J.

DEAR CREEP,

I WANTED TO SAY HOW MUCH I LOVED **THE FINGER**. IT WAS VERY FINNY AND SCARY AND "BOB" MAY BE THE COOLEST PET I'VE EVER SEEN. WHERE CAN I GET ONE?!

ALYSSA
LOS ANGELES, CA

I HAVE TO SAY THAT I AGREE WITH SOME OF OUR READERS THAT I WOULD LOVE TO SEE A SEQUEL TO **"THE CRATE"** THAT YOU PUBLISHED SO MANY YEARS AGO. A SUPER COOL STORY WITH A SUPER COOL MOSTER!

GREG
PITTSBURGH, PA

DEAR CREEP,

I JUST READ ISSUE #6 AND THINK IT WAS MY FAVORITE. LET'S HAVE MORE STORIES ABOUT DRAGONS AND WEREWOLVES. I JUST LOVE THE WAY YOUR ARTISTS CREATE THESE CREATURES FROM THEIR IMAGINATION.

WELL DONE!

TOM
BLOOMFIELD, PA

DEAR CREEP,

EVER SINCE I WAS A LITTLE KID I'VE ALWAYS LOVED ZOMBIE. SOMETHING SO CREEPY AND SCARY ABOUT HOW THEY CRAWL OUT OF THE GROUND AND WANT NOTHING MORE THAN TO EAT YOU ALIVE. UGGGGGGGH! SO COOL. I'D LOVE TO SEE MORE STORIES ABOUT ZOMBIES AND HOW THEY COME BACK TO LIFE.

JOHN
LEVITTOWN, NY

CREEPSHOW COMIC ADVERTISEMENTS FOR AMUSEMENT ONLY.

MAKE A MONSTER!

LABORATORY-TESED HOBBY KITS FOR THE BOY WHO HAS EVERYTHING!

frightfully easy to assemble! CREATE YOUR VERY OWN CHAMBER OF HORRORS!

america's newest, most spine-tingling hobby! Build 'em with your bare hands!
SUPERNATURAL REALISM

PERFECTLY DETAILED DOWN TO THE SMALLEST FANG!
DECORATE YOUR ROOM! SURPRISE YOUR MOTHER! *they're a scream!*

98¢ each

GET THEM BEFORE THEY GET YOU!

AORTA

CREEPSHOW COMIC ADVERTISEMENTS FOR AMUSEMENT ONLY.

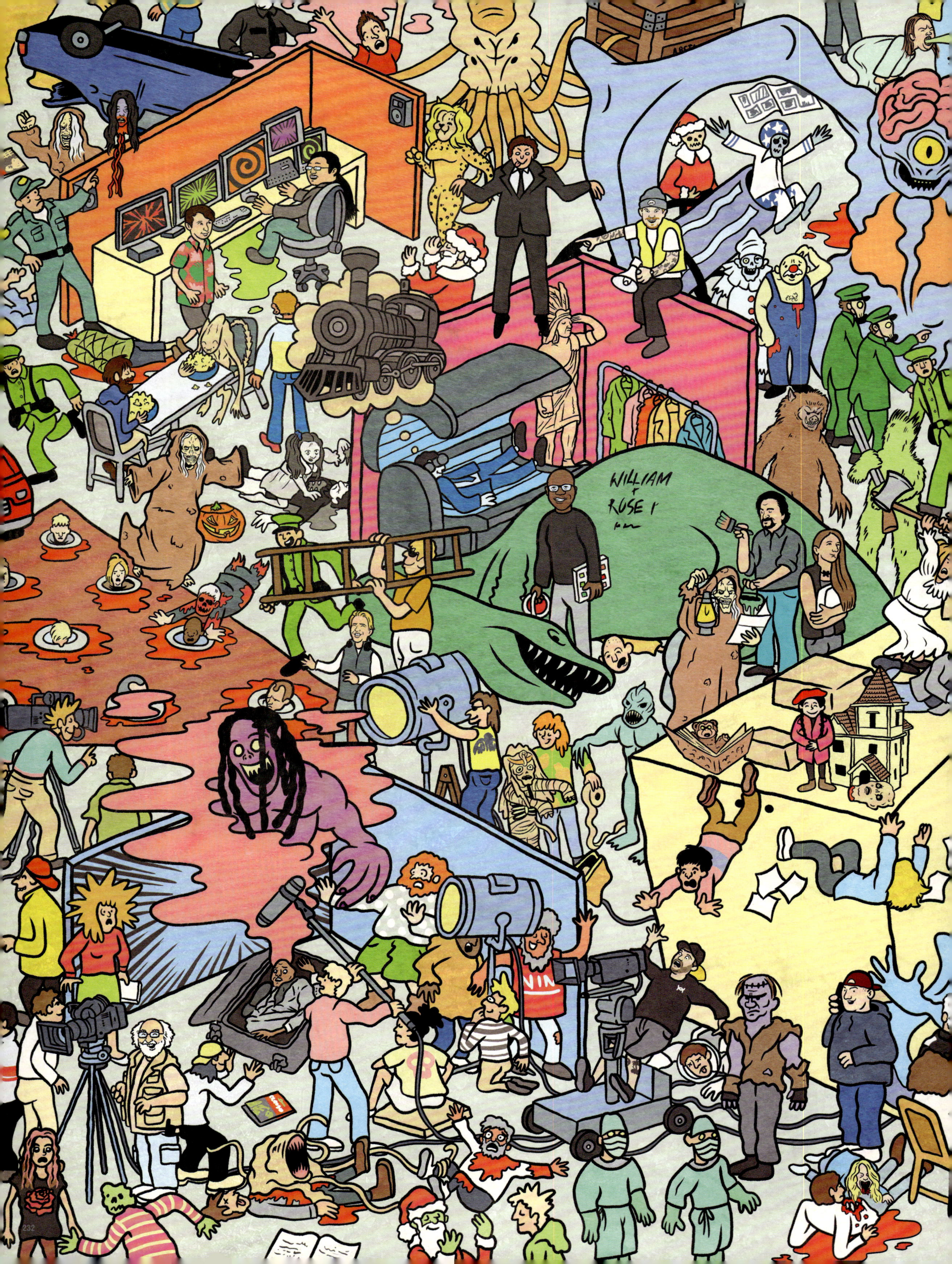
WILLIAM + ROSE !

CREEPSHOW

M. LINEHAN

STRANGE, EERIE, TERRIFYIN
CREEPSHOW
TALES OF SUSPENSE AND HORROR!!!

AFTERWORD
by KIRK HAMMETT

Here it is, a book I hope you enjoyed sinking your teeth into!

First off, I am so excited because I really love *Creepshow*. Second, because I dig this series. It's everything a big *Creepshow* fan like me could want—more *Creepshow*! More stories, more monsters, and more great special effects. I'm ecstatic that they are keeping it pretty old-school with their effects, and that it's all executive produced by Greg Nicotero.

Greg and I actually go all the way back to before Metallica's *...And Justice For All* (1988) album. That's how long we've known each other. It's great to see him involved in this now, coming full circle, because I know those original *Creepshow* movies were really close to his and Tom Savini's hearts. They were close to the hearts of millions of fans all over the world, too, including mine.

I started watching the Shudder series in 2020, so I might be a little late to the game, but I've gone back and binge-watched every episode, a few more than once. I don't have the space to list all of the fantastic contributors and collaborators, but there are some brilliant stories written by Joe Hill, John Esposito, and Greg Nicotero, as well as some great appearances by actors like Dana Gould, Kiefer Sutherland, Adrienne Barbeau, Michael Rooker and so many other outstanding names. I feel it's a true successor to the original. The characters, the props, the horror references are all spot on, and I love the way it can reach across all the worlds of horror.

I was hooked immediately. I mean, all three seasons have such strong episodes, but the very first episode is one I've gone back to a few times. The second story was superb, as well. It's called "The House of the Head" and it's about a dollhouse. I'm not going to throw any spoilers your way; let's just say that episode has stuck with me.

BIOGRAPHIES

GREG NICOTERO
EXECUTIVE PRODUCER / DIRECTOR / SPECIAL FX MAKE-UP SUPERVISOR

Entering his 36th year in the industry, Greg Nicotero has never forgotten his roots. Growing up in Pittsburgh in the '70s, it never occurred to this young movie and special effects buff that Hollywood was literally in his backyard. Auteur director George Romero would be the first of many to recognize something in Nicotero and forge a relationship of collaboration as a special effects make-up artist.

Within two years he was in Los Angeles working with Sam Raimi, James Cameron, and Wes Craven on landmark films such as *Evil Dead 2*, *Aliens*, and the *A Nightmare On Elm Street* series. The climate that embraced practical make-up effects allowed Nicotero to partner with Howard Berger. Together they created the longest running effects house in Hollywood, The KNB EFX Group, Inc. Founded in 1988 and still as vital as ever, Nicotero and his team have worked on nearly 700 film and television programs that stretch through cinema as a who's who of horror, science fiction, and thrillers. With titles such as *Reservoir Dogs*, *Spawn*, *The Mist*, *Scream*, and *Sin City*, this unique troupe of artists have brought life to stories and characters of all kinds, while innovating and perfecting their craft.

Partnering with directors such as Frank Darabont, Steven Spielberg, Quentin Tarantino, and Robert Rodriguez, Nicotero fine-tuned his craft as an effects artist and gradually moved into providing 2nd unit direction on several feature films. After a stint on a number of movies across the globe, including *Inglourious Basterds*, *The Book Of Eli*, *Predators*, and *Transformers*, Nicotero found himself in 2010 designing zombies for the AMC series, *The Walking Dead*. Within months he'd become the producing director on the hit show and to this date has directed more than 30 episodes of the series.

His work on *The Pacific*, *The Walking Dead*, and *Breaking Bad* have garnered him nearly a dozen Emmy nominations and four wins. As the zombie epic entered its tenth season, Nicotero debuted his new series *Creepshow*, an anthology comprised of terrifying tales inspired by the original 1982 film of the same name. He is the Executive Producer/Showrunner and also directed multiple segments for the show.

Nicotero also had a hand in producing *Fear The Walking Dead* and *The Walking Dead: World Beyond*, while supervising make-up effects for HBO's *The Watchmen* and Quentin Tarantino's *Once Upon a Time in Hollywood*.

STAN SPRY
CEO, CARTEL ENTERTAINMENT

Stan Spry is a Founding Partner of the Cartel and is a Literary Manager and Producer. Stan represents top tier writers, directors, producers, show runners, and production companies for feature films, television, new-media. Stan has nearly fifteen years of experience in the entertainment industry, most recently as a Partner at Artist International, a production and management subsidiary of Hollywood Studios International.

Prior to joining Artist International, Stan was a Literary Agent for Dytman & Associates Talent and Literary Agency. For two years prior to becoming an agent, Stan was a Literary Manager and Vice-President of Production and Development for ASE, and began his career in Development and physical production.

Some of Stan's producing credits include recent feature films such as, *Guns Girls & Gambling*, *Jeepers Creepers 3*, *Love at the Shore*, *Sun Sand & Romance*, *Love at First Glance*, *The Fixer Upper Mysteries*, *The Wrong Mother*, *Give Me My Baby*, *911 Nightmare*, *Online Abduction*, *Wrong Swipe*, *The Wedding Pact*, *Out of Reach*, *Avalanche Sharks*, *Defending Santa*, *Merry ExMas*, *Crimes of the Mind*, *Dracano*, *Anatomy of Deception*, *Fire Twister*, *The Town Came A-Courtin'*, *Sink Hole*, *Stepdaughter*, *Dragon Wasps*, *Terror Experiment*, *Dangerous Company*, *Deadly Pursuit*, *Demo Girl*, to name a few.

In the television arena, Stan Executive Produced the US version of the long-running UK reality show *A Place in the Sun* for Discovery Networks and Executive Produced the series, *Ties That Bind*, for Up Network. Stan has been involved in setting up, packaging and selling movies and television shows to Netflix, Amazon, WGN, ABC, ABC Family, Starz, The Hub, CBS Paramount, SyFy, Universal, HBO, Sony, Cartoon Network, Lifetime, Vh1, Twentieth Century Fox, FX, Showtime, USA, MTV, Syfy, Up, Ion, Warner Brothers and Disney just to name a few.

RUSSELL BINDER
PRESIDENT, STRIKER ENTERTAINMENT

Russell Binder is a founding partner of Striker Entertainment, an independent boutique entertainment licensing, merchandising, and production company. Russell is graduate of The University of California Santa Barbara class of 1990 with a Bachelor of Arts degree and a 24-year veteran of the entertainment and brand licensing business.

In 2007 Russell started his own full-service global agency calling it Striker Entertainment. With the innovative management of intellectual property as the central focus of Striker's business, Russell has successfully built a business in the Pop Culture Licensing/Consumer Products and entertainment space.

Binder has overseen the licensing of several billion dollar retail brands including *The Walking Dead*, *Five Nights at Freddys*, *Angry Birds*, and *The Twilight Saga*, while working with some of the biggest film makers and content creators along the way.

On the production side of the business, in 2017 Russell served as an Executive Producer on the *Candy Crush* game show on CBS with Lionsgate Television, and in 2018, Striker concluded a first look deal with Blumhouse Television to build a television production business designed as a foundation to a larger branded content business for franchises. Binder is attached to Executive Produce the *Five Nights at Freddy's* motion picture at Blumhouse, *Creepshow* at Shudder, *Trivia Quest* and *Peanut Bear* both at Netflix, *Weight of the Stars* at Westbrook, and more.

Striker has been nominated for over 15, and was the recipient of eight, of LIMA's most prestigious awards including the 2008 Best Film, Television, and Entertainment Brand of the Year. Russell has also credited as one of the "Top 40 under 40" in License Magazine, as a "Maverick in the Marketplace" by Royalties Magazine, and a member of licensing's Elite from Daily Variety. Russell is a regular speaker at UCLA, Game Developers Conference, Digital Entertainment World and other forums. Russell also serves on the Board of Advisor for REALM, a scripted audio podcast producer and distributor, and To the Stars Academy of Arts and Sciences founded by Blink 182's front man Tom Delonge.

Russell is happily married with two amazing children and two lucky dogs.

JULIA HOBGOOD
PRODUCER

Julia Hobgood is currently a Co- Executive Producer on *Creepshow*, Shudder's anthology series comprised of three seasons inspired by the original 1982 film of the same name with a fourth season on the way. She was also an Associate Producer on AMC's hit series *The Walking Dead*, which is currently airing its eleventh and final season. Julia has a passion for creative storytelling, especially in the genre world of horror, fantasy, and suspense.

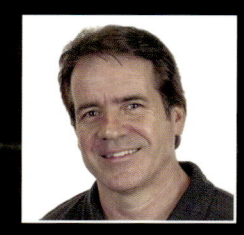

DENNIS L. PRINCE
WRITER

Dennis L. Prince is an author, biographer, film & television analyst, and pop culture enthusiast. He fell in love with *Creepshow* in 1982 while working as a Northern California theater usher where the film debuted. He cherishes the wax-coated *Creepshow* soda cups that he collected from the snack bar, a couple of them shared with special friends in the forty years since then.

Prince's body of work now includes nearly thirty books plus scores of articles published over the past three decades, delivering in-depth analysis in a range of topics: entertainment, technology, consumer trends, and pop culture history.

His most recent books include the widely praised *Joe Alves: Designing JAWS* and the model kit fan favorite, *Aurora Monster Scenes: The Most Controversial Toys of a Generation.*

MEREDITH BORDERS
EDITOR

Meredith Borders is the Senior Contributing Editor at *Fangoria*. Her essays have been published in genre study books including *Science Fiction Theatre*, *Creepy Bitches*, and *My Favorite Horror Movie,* and she has contributed as a programmer, jury member, or panelist at Fantastic Fest, Telluride Horror Show, SXSW and more. She's the former editorial director of Birth.Movies.Death. and the editor of several books covering topics from film theory to American history to werewolves. Meredith is currently living in Germany and working on her first novel.

JOHN J. HILL
CREATIVE DIRECTOR & DESIGNER

John J. Hill is a Portland, OR based creative director / producer / designer working in comics, technology, publishing and entertainment. An alumnus of the University of Michigan, he has been the creative lead for 52mm, Eruptor Entertainment, Big Stage Entertainment, Crayon Pixel, and Printed in Blood.

John is best known for working in the comic book industry on logos, branding, trade paperback design, and lettering for *Harley Quinn*, *Batman*, *Superman*, *Robin*, *Batgirl*, *Swamp Thing*, *StarCraft*, *Overwatch*, *Nailbiter*, *Painkiller Jane*, *God Country*, and *Crossover* to name just a few. He is also currently working with AMC Networks on multiple projects and was the creative director for their publishing division's debut book *The Art of AMC's The Walking Dead Universe*.

John has worked with Adobe, AfterShock, Atlantic Records, DC Comics, Disney, The Hollywood Theatre, GM, Image Comics, Legendary, NHL, Paperfilms. Random House, and many others. His work has been shown at the Art Directors Club, Cooper-Hewitt National Design Museum, Ward-Nasse Gallery, and the Low Res Film Festival.

MIKE ZAGARI
HEAD OF AMC NETWORKS PUBLISHING

After over 15 years of experience at Marvel, Disney, Lucasfilm, Pixar and DC Comics, Mike Zagari joined AMC Networks in 2018. A native New Yorker, Mike received his BFA from the School of Visual Arts. He has extensive experience developing digital (VR, AR, interactive apps, eBooks), print (books, comics, storybooks), media (TV, film, animation), and consumer product (toys, apparel, collectibles) cooperative ecosystems. In addition to being Head of AMC Networks Publishing, Mike leads strategy, creative, and story-telling for critical initiatives on the Franchise team, covering new and existing intellectual properties.

INDEX

001 *Artwork:* Rich Hilliard
002-003 *Artwork:* Nick Charge
006 *Artwork:* Sanjulian
007 *Photography of Stephen King:* Shane Leonard
008 *Artwork:* Michael Broom
009 Photography by Charles 'Teenie' Harris/Carnegie Museum of Art/Getty Images.
010 *The Haunt of Fear* Issue #19 Artwork is copyrighted material owned by William M. Gaines, Agent, Inc. All Rights Reserved.
011 *Artwork:* Comic book mock-ups by KNB Art Department
013 *Night of the Living Dead* Art is copyright Image Ten, Inc. All Rights Reserved.
014 *Creepshow* Theatrical One-Sheet is copyright Taurus Entertainment Company. All Rights Reserved.
015 *Artwork:* TOP: Creepshow Art Department / BOTTOM: *Artwork:* Michael Broom
016-017 *Artwork:* Parody ads by Creepshow Art Department
018 *Artwork:* Michael Broom
019 *Pictured:* Brock Duncan
020 Photograph of George A. Romero is copyright Geraint Lewis / ArenaPAL. All Rights Reserved.
021 *Fangoria* Issue #1 Artwork is copyright Fangoria Publishing, LLC. Godzilla is copyright Toho Co., Ltd. All Rights Reserved.
022 *Pictured:* Tom Savini, Debbie Pinthus, Antone DiLeo, Bruce Miller, Robert Harper. Photography: Tom Savini & Greg Nicotero. Creepshow film is copyright Taurus Entertainment Company. All Rights Reserved.
024 *Photography:* Greg Nicotero. Day of the Dead film is copyright Taurus Entertainment Company. All Rights Reserved.
025 *Day of the Dead* Theatrical One-Sheet is copyright Taurus Entertainment Company. All Rights Reserved.
026 *Pictured:* TOP: Greg Nicotero / BOTTOM: Greg Nicotero, Garrett Zehner (Walker)
027 *Pictured:* Greg Nicotero, Brock Duncan
028 *Pictured:* Greg Nicotero
029 *Pictured:* Greg Nicotero / *Artwork:* Michael Broom
030-031 *Artwork:* Parody ads by Creepshow Art Department
032 *Artwork:* Michael Broom
037 *Artwork:* BOTTOM: Michael Broom
038-039 *Artwork:* Parody ads by Creepshow Art Department
040 *Artwork:* Michael Broom
041 *Pictured:* Greg Nicotero
042 *Pictured:* TOP: Giancarlo Esposito, Tobin Bell / BOTTOM: Adrienne Barbeau, Christopher Nathan
043 *Pictured:* TOP: Puppet / BOTTOM: Cailey Fleming
044 *Pictured:* Andrew Bachelor, Brandon Jones (The Familiar demon)
045 *Pictured:* TOP: Brock Duncan, Austin Blythe, Aaron King / BOTTOM: Alex Hill (Frankenstein), Chris Schmidt, Jr
046 *Pictured:* TOP: Puppet / BOTTOM: James Remar, Valerie LeBlanc, Victor Rivera
047 *Pictured:* Puppet
048 *Artwork:* Robin Raaphorst
049 *Pictured:* Sarah Jon, Katie Ballard
050 *Pictured:* TOP: Jeffrey Combs, Daniel Stone, Ryan Dempsey / BOTTOM: Andy Rusk
051-053 *Artwork:* Rob Schrab
054 *Pictured:* Peter Leake
055 *Pictured:* Maddie Nichols / *Artwork:* Animation still by Octopie animation studio
056 *Pictured:* TOP: Cristian Gonzalez, Josh Mikel / BOTTOM: Olivia Hawthorne, Nico Gomez, Puppet
057 *Pictured:* Ali Larter
058 *Pictured:* Justin Long
059 *Pictured:* D'Arcy Carden, Justin Long / *Artwork:* Michael Broom
060-061 *Artwork:* Parody ads by Creepshow Art Department
062 *Artwork:* Michael Broom
063-067 *Artwork:* Creepshow Art Department
068 *Artwork:* Chet Zar
069 *Pictured:* Greg Nicotero / *Artwork:* Painting by Bethany Arriagada
070 *Artwork:* KNB Art Department / *Pictured:* Joe Giles
071 *Pictured:* Shawn Upthegrove, Lucas Godfrey, Gino Crognale, [Dead Uncle], Tom Savini, Jake Garber, Greg Nicotero, Rene Arriagada
072-076 *Artwork:* Creepshow Art Department
078 *Pictured:* TOP: Puppet / BOTTOM: Greg Nicotero
081 *Artwork:* Michael Broom
082-083 *Artwork:* Parody ads by Creepshow Art Department
084 *Artwork:* Michael Broom

085 *Pictured:* Rob Draper
086 *Pictured:* TOP: Carey Jones (Werewolf) / BOTTOM: Maddie Rose Chandler, Kevin Marshall, Jeffrey Hawkins Jr.
087 *Pictured:* TOP: Suehyla El-Attar Young / BOTTOM: Rob Draper, Jake Garber (The Mummy)
088 *Pictured:* Jeffrey F. January, Rob Draper, Nate Andrade
089 *Pictured:* Rob Draper, John Harrison, David Waters
090 *Pictured:* BOTTOM: Drew Matthews
092 *Pictured:* TOP: Giancarlo Esposito, Tobin Bell / BOTTOM: Andy Rusk, Giancarlo Esposito, Tobin Bell
093 *Pictured:* Giancarlo Esposito
094 *Pictured:* Puppet, Rob Draper
096 *Pictured:* TOP: Josh Mikel, Cristian Gonzalez / BOTTOM: Chloe Williamson
097 *Pictured:* Cristian Gonzalez, Rob Draper / *Artwork:* Michael Broom
098-099 *Artwork:* Parody ads by Creepshow Art Department
100 *Artwork:* Michael Broom
101 *Pictured:* TOP: Greg Nicotero / BOTTOM: Josh McDermitt
102 *Artwork:* John Wheaton, Michael Broom
103 *Artwork:* John Wheaton, Michael Broom
104 *Artwork:* Michael Broom
105 *Artwork:* Michael Broom, Dave Grasso
106 *Artwork:* John Wheaton
108-109 *Artwork:* KNB Art Department
110-111 *Artwork:* Michael Broom, John Wheaton
112 *Pictured:* TOP: Carey Jones
113 *Pictured:* Dave Wogh / *Design & Construction:* Dave Wogh
114 *Artwork:* John Wheaton
115 *Pictured:* Dave Grasso
116 *Artwork:* Michael Broom / *Pictured:* Andy Rusk
117 *Pictured:* TOP: Jeffrey Combs, Carey Jones / BOTTOM LEFT: Jonathan Thomas
118 *Pictured:* Gino Crognale, Alex Hill (Frankenstein) / *Artwork:* Michael Broom
119 *Pictured:* Alex Hill (Frankenstein), Gino Crognale
120 *Artwork:* Michael Broom
121 *Pictured:* TOP: Andy Bergholtz / BOTTOM LEFT: Carey Jones / BOTTOM RIGHT: Lynn Watson
122 *Pictured:* Josh McDermitt
123 *Pictured:* Ted Raimi
124 *Artwork:* KNB Art Department
125 *Pictured:* Nate Andrade
126 *Artwork:* KNB Art Department / *Pictured:* Gloria DeWeese, Tony Robinson
128 *Pictured:* Alex Diaz, Elvis Portillo, Jeff Warren
129 *Pictured:* Greg Nicotero
130 *Pictured:* BOTTOM LEFT: Josh McDermitt / BOTTOM RIGHT: Regan Higgins / *Design & Construction:* Katie Ballard, Addison Foreman
133 *Pictured:* TOP: Brock Duncan, Tyner Rushing / BOTTOM LEFT: Addison Foreman, Matthew Barnes / BOTTOM RIGHT: Katie Ballard, Matthew Barnes
136 *Pictured:* Chris Baer
137 *Pictured:* TOP: Cristina Prestia / BOTTOM: Greg Nicotero, Tom Savini
138 *Artwork:* KNB Art Department / *Pictured:* Aaron King
139 *Pictured:* Jake Garber / *Artwork:* John Wheaton
140 *Pictured:* TOP: Jason Kehler / BOTTOM RIGHT: Jason Kehler, Frank Nicotero / *Artwork:* Michael Broom
141 *Pictured:* BOTTOM: Scott Loeser, Adam Pally / *Artwork:* Michael Broom
142-143 *Artwork:* Parody ads by Creepshow Art Department
144 *Artwork:* Michael Broom
145 *Pictured:* George Romero
146 *Pictured:* TOP: Rene Arriagada, Greg Nicotero, Hugh Braselton, Jesse C. Boyd, Shawn Upthegrove, Christopher Nathan / BOTTOM: Frank Nicotero, Derek Russo
147 *Pictured:* John Harrison, Craig Owens, Hugh Braselton
148 *Pictured:* John Harrison, Rene Arrigada, John Barber, Lex Rawlins
149 *Pictured:* TOP LEFT: Jake Garber, Rob Draper, John Harrison / *Pictured:* TOP RIGHT: Connor Christie, Luke Daniels
150 *Pictured:* TOP: John Harrison, Hugh Braselton / BOTTOM: Cailey Fleming
151 *Pictured:* Stephen Langford, Greg Nicotero, Paul Dini, Dana Gould
152 *Pictured:* TOP: Rusty Cundieff, Maddie Nichols, Tim Blanchard, Gino Crognale / BOTTOM: Maddie Nichols
153 *Pictured:* TOP: Brayden Benson, Aaron King, Rusty Cundieff / BOTTOM: Rusty Cundieff, Malone Thomas
154 *Pictured:* Roxanne Benjamin, Tricia Helfer, Dana Gould, Jeffrey F. January

155 *Pictured:* TOP LEFT: Dana Gould, Jeffrey F. January, Roxanne Benjamin / TOP RIGHT: Roxanne Benjamin, Rob Draper / BOTTOM: Danielle Lyn
156 *Pictured:* BOTTOM: Greg Nicotero, Tom Savini
157 *Pictured:* TOP: Tom Savini, Hugh Braselton, Mike Brune, Aaron Byrnes, Gena Shaw / *Artwork:* Michael Broom
158-159 *Artwork:* Parody ads by Creepshow Art Department
160 *Artwork:* Michael Broom
161 *Pictured:* Greg Nicotero, Drew Sawyer, Julia Hobgood
162 *Pictured:* TOP: Cristian Gonzalez / BOTTOM: David Bruckner, Carey Jones
163 *Pictured:* Drew Sawyer, Aaron King, Erin Beute
164 *Pictured:* Gino Crognale, Jake Garber, Eric Edelstein, Aaron King
165 *Pictured:* Sarah Jon, Carlos Mancia (greensuit)
166 *Pictured:* TOP: Abigail Dolan / BOTTOM: Kevin Dillon
167 *Pictured:* Shellita Boxie, Jake Garber / BOTTOM: Brittany L. Smith
168-169 *Artwork:* KNB Art Department
170 *Pictured:* Ryan Kwanten
172-173 *Artwork:* Kevin West
174-175 *Artwork:* Kelley Jones
176 *Artwork:* Kevin West, Ron Frenz, Michael Broom
177 *Artwork:* Kelley Jones
178-181 *Artwork:* Kevin West
182 *Pictured:* Chris Basta / *Artwork:* Animation still by Octopie animation studio
183 *Artwork:* Gary Pullin. Image is copyright Waxwork Records. All Rights Reserved.
184 *Pictured:* TOP: Carey Jones, Jake Garber / BOTTOM: Cristian Gonzalez, Rey Hernandez
185 *Pictured:* Chris Basta / *Artwork:* Michael Broom
186-187 *Artwork:* Parody ads by Creepshow Art Department
188 *Artwork:* Michael Broom
190 *Pictured:* Erica Frene
191 *Pictured:* BOTTOM: C. Thomas Howell, Ali Larter
193 *Pictured:* TOP: Mark Ashworth
194 *Pictured:* BOTTOM: Gabrielle Byndloss
195 *Pictured:* Denise Crosby / *Artwork:* Michael Broom
196-197 *Artwork:* Parody ads by Creepshow Art Department
198 *Artwork:* Michael Broom
199 *Pictured:* Michael Broom
200-205 *Artwork:* Michael Broom, Creepshow Art Department
206-207 *Artwork:* Parody ads by Creepshow Art Department
208 *Artwork:* Michael Broom
210 *Pictured:* TOP: Andy Rusk, Christopher Nathan / BOTTOM: Cailey Fleming
211 *Pictured:* TOP: Carey Jones / BOTTOM: Puppet
212 *Pictured:* TOP: Madison Thompson, Connor Christie, Luke Daniels / BOTTOM: Ravi Naidu
213 *Pictured:* TOP: Puppet / BOTTOM: Tricia Helfer
214 *Pictured:* BOTTOM: Puppet
215 *Pictured:* TOP: Puppet / BOTTOM: David Alexander Kaplan
216 *Pictured:* TOP: Brock Duncan / BOTTOM: Peter Leake
217 *Pictured:* TOP: Ali Larter / BOTTOM: Josh McDermitt
218 *Pictured:* TOP: Ryan Kwanten / BOTTOM: Maddie Nichols, Jerri Tubbs
219 *Pictured:* TOP: Eric Edelstein / BOTTOM: Drew Matthews
220 *Pictured:* TOP: Justin Long, D'Arcy Carden / BOTTOM: Justin Long
221 *Artwork:* Rich Hilliard
222 *Pictured:* TOP: Brayden Benson / BOTTOM: Olivia Hawthorne
223 *Pictured:* TOP: Puppets / BOTTOM: Brandon Jones
224 *Pictured:* TOP: Nate Andrade / BOTTOM: Nick Massouh, Glenn Magee
225 *Pictured:* TOP: Kadianne Whyte, Chris Mayers / BOTTOM: Johnathon Schaech
226 *Pictured:* TOP: Matthew Barnes / BOTTOM: *Artwork:* Animation still by Octopie animation studio
227 *Pictured:* TOP: Sarah Jon / BOTTOM: Cristian Gonzalez, Josh Mikel
228 *Artwork:* Animation stills by Octopie animation studio
229 *Pictured:* Tom Glynn / *Artwork:* Michael Broom
230-231 *Artwork:* Creepshow Art Department
232 *Artwork:* Matthew Lineham
234 *Artwork:* Graham Humphreys
235 *Photography of Kirk Hammett:* Ross Halfin
240 *Artwork:* Devon Whitehead

ACKNOWLEDGEMENTS

SEASON 1

PRODUCERS / DIRECTORS
Greg Nicotero
Brian Witten
Stan Spry
Anthony Fankhauser
Laurel Murphy
Alex Orr
Julia Hobgood
David Bruckne
John Harrison
Roxanne Benjamin
Rob Schrab
Tom Savini

PRODUCTION
Cameron Boling
Won Chung
Tiffany D. Moore
C.J. DeCant
Sara Sometti Michaels
Ryan Dempsey

ACCOUNTING
Tim Honiball
Jamie Davenport
Christine Sines
Alex Huebner

ART DEPARTMENT
Aimee Holmberg
Jason Vigdor
Diem Ngo

ASSISTANT DIRECTORS
Jeffrey F. January
Mike Brune
Laura O'Keefe
Britt Dvorak
Wen Ramon
Briana Johnson
Caitlin Wolfe
Dennis Shanaberg
Joe Crognale

CAMERA
Rob Draper, ACS
Bill McClelland, SOC
Lex Rawlins
Christy Fiers
Hugh Braselton
Matt McGinn
Austin Blythe
Daniel Irons

CASTING
Tara Feldstein Bennett, CSA
Chase Paris, CSA
Patrick Ingram

CATERING
Silver Screen Catering
Jeff Gardner
Larry Johnson
Melody Garrison

CONSTRUCTION
John Hair
Michael Solano
Greg Moncrief
Jay Murphy
Jay Carter
Adam Rogers
Michael Jeremy Watts
Andre Spencer
Zach Meyers
Daniel Robinson
Michael Wingo
Jarrod Womack
Peter Anderson
James West
Robert Peoples
Jeremiah Shari
Ryan Edward Davis
John Matthew Rogers
Sean Millerick
Keron Cutkelvin
William Palmer
Micah Myers
David Murphy
Kristin Fox
Matthew Cisneros
Michael Robert Zieper
Brent Addison
Rob Yeary

COSTUMES
Jaclyn Akeju
Jose L. Ramos Jr.
Kendall "Ken" Rodgers
Jonathan Thomas

CRAFT SERVICE
John Mekhail
Tony Mekhail
Dalton Greenwalt
Keitel Small

ELECTRIC
Mitchell McDannald
Patrick Strunk
Chris Cox
Joshua McCready
Javier Pesquera
Jeremy Bradley

GRIP
Craig R. Owens
Garrett Miller
John C. Barber
Justin Dunn
Albert Omstead
Jeffrey Hawkins Jr.

HAIR
Katie Ballard
Heather M. Morris

LOCATIONS
Tony Holley
Luke Welden
Haley Billue
Unda Romero
Jay Elgin
Michael Slack
Anthony Lowery II
April Easterwood Thornton

MAKEUP
Addison Foreman
Ashley Pleger

MAKEUP FX
Jake Garber
Gino Crognale

MEDIC
Tasha M. Wdowin
Jaimee Partain

POST PRODUCTION
Drew Sawyer
Patrick Perry
Michael Goldberg
Gerhardt Slawitschka
Kristina Kromer
James Crawford
Jenny Lindamood
Kristina Kromer
John Petersen
Hannah Rockette
Gabi Camirano
Grant Reynolds

PROPS
Lucas Godfrey
Rene Arriagada
Shawn Upthegrove

SCRIPT
Aimee Bell

SET DECORATION
Nick Morgan
Calvin Myers
Blake Myers
Clarke Williams
Eric E.R. Brown
Andres Miller
Josh Gould
Jason Altreche
William Egan

SOUND
Paul Reed
Aaron Byrnes

SPECIAL EFFECTS
Caius Man
Andi Sowers
Richie Bearden

STUNTS
Andy Rusk
Jason Kehler

SEASON 2

PRODUCERS / DIRECTORS
Greg Nicotero
Kady Dewees
Brian Witten
Stan Spry
Anthony Fankhauser
Laurel Murphy
Mitchell Galin
Julia Hobgood
Rusty Cundieff
Joe Lynch
John Harrison
Axelle Carolyn

PRODUCTION
Cameron Boling
Won Chung
Kelsey Muir Beattie
Clarke Douglas
Christina Fuentes
Barbara Llewellyn
Haley Stevens
Lindsey Ewing
P.J. Desutter

ACCOUNTING
Laveda Lewis
Brandon Calhoun
Avery Beekman
Hasan Texeira

ART DEPARTMENT
Aimee Holmberg
Jason Vigdor
John Jozef Veres
Diem Ngo
Jessie Dubyoski

ASSISTANT DIRECTORS
Spencer Jarvis
David Muddy Waters
Laura O'Keefe
Chris Wright Jr.
Nate Galesic
Michael Brownlee
Megan Molloy
Victoria Rupert
Parker Womble

CAMERA
Rob Draper, ACS
Aaron King
Chris Larsen
Amanda E. Ray
Hugh Braselton
Matt McGinn
Austin Blythe
Laura Knox
Joe Crognale

CASTING
Chase Paris, CSA
Tara Feldstein Bennett, CSA
Paul Ruddy, CSA
Patrick Ingram

CATERING
Elizabeth's Catering

CONSTRUCTION
John Hair
Jarrod Womack
Michael Solano
Marshall Downey
Steven M. Adams
Haley Coker
Brooke Beall
Ashley Santos Washinski
Tyler Whisnant

COSTUMES
Jaclyn Banner
Jose L. Ramos
Tomoko Goddard
Brooks May

CRAFT SERVICE
Christopher Gary Wood
Daniel Arriagada

ELECTRIC
Bobb Lovett
Douglas Brannon
Daniel McDowell
Rob Russell
Aaron Sickman
Will Dameron
Josh Warren

GRIP
Craig R. Owens
Albert Omstead
Dusty Mitchell
Jeffrey Hawkins Jr.
David Lee
Carlos Mancilla
Garrett Miller

HAIR
Katie Ballard
Jeremiah Newcombe

HEALTH AND SAFETY
Paul Bednarz
Thaddaeus Tad Mercer

LOCATIONS
Jason Underwood
June Shin
Matt Bender
Joseph Gagliardi

MAKEUP
Addison Foreman
Ashley Pleger

MAKEUP FX
Jake Garber
Gino Crognale

MEDIC
Thaddaeus Tad Mercer
Jaimee Partain

POST PRODUCTION
Drew Sawyer
Jacob Velcoff
Patrick Perry
Gerhardt Slawitschka
Kristina Kromer
J. Michael Cheeves
Marquis Mosley
James Crawford
Travis Preston
Anna Holley

PROPS
Lucas Godfrey
Rene Arriagada
Nicholas Ragazzo

SCRIPT
Jana Davis
Karlyn Taylor

SET DECORATION
Nick Morgan
Nicholas Gjoka
Blake Myers
Eric E.R. Brown
Luke Myers
Will Davis
Mitchell Baxter
Clarke Williams

SOUND
Serena Simpson
Aaron Byrnes
Julian Cabrera

SPECIAL EFFECTS
Andi Sowers
A.J. Dzenowagis
Richie Bearden

STUNTS
Andy Rusk
Jason Kehler

SEASON 3

PRODUCERS / DIRECTORS
Greg Nicotero
Kady Dewees
Brian Witten
Stan Spry
Anthony Fankhauser
Laurel Murphy
Mitchell Galin
Julia Hobgood
Rusty Cundieff
Jeffrey F. January
Axelle Carolyn
Joe Lynch
Dave Newberg
Enol Junquera
Luis Junquera
John Harrison

PRODUCTION
Cameron Boling
Won Chung
Kelsey Muir Beattie
Brett J Bagwell
Clarke Douglas
Mariana Lacuesta
Christina Fuentes
Barbara Llewellyn
Haley Stevens
Lindsey Ewing
P.J. Desutter

ACCOUNTING
Laveda Lewis
Brandon Calhoun
Avery Beekman
Hasan Texeira

ART DEPARTMENT
Aimee Holmberg
Jason Vigdor
John Jozef Veres
Jessica Sanchez
Diem Ngo
Jessie Dubyoski

ASSISTANT DIRECTORS
Spencer Jarvis
David Muddy Waters
Matthew Goodwin
Hayley Luhrs
Jamie MacDonald
Chris Wright Jr.
Austin Franco
Victoria Rupert
Katherine Schooler
Megan Molloy
Parker Womble
Deven Nicotero

CAMERA
Rob Draper, ACS
Richard Chapelle, ACS
Aaron King
Danny Eckler
Chris Larsen
Chase Schultz
Hugh Braselton
Matt McGinn
Austin Blythe
Laura Knox
Joe Crognale

CASTING
Chase Paris, CSA
Tara Feldstein Bennett, CSA
Paul Ruddy, CSA
Patrick Ingram

CONSTRUCTION
John Hair
Jarrod Womack
Michael Solano
Steven M. Adams
Haley Coker
Brooke Beall
Ashley Santos Washinski
Marshall Downey Jr.
Tyler Whisnant
Andre Spencer
Dennis Ford
Ryan Davis

COSTUMES
Jaclyn Banner
Jose L. Ramos
Tomoko Goddard
Brooks May

CRAFT SERVICE
Christopher Gary Wood
Daniel Arriagada

ELECTRIC
Mitchell McDannald
Hollywood Heard
Bob Lovett
Chris L. Cox
Ben Bowling
Dan Wittenburg
Vince Jordan
Matt Mercier
Noah Hammer
Kevin Brenner
Nick Gaston

GRIP
Craig R. Owens
Albert Omstead
Sherwin Kannukkaden
Dusty Mitchell
Darwin Conort
Jeffrey Hawkins Jr.
Eddie Sarkisov
David Lee
Carlos Mancilla
Dakota Curtis
Michael Cape
Warren Jenkins
Adam Patterson
Brad Mcgaughey
Vlad Narcisse
Garrett Miller
Petar Angelov

HAIR
Katie Ballard
Jeremiah Newcombe
Sonya Riviere
Steve Battaglia

HEALTH AND SAFETY
Paul Bednarz
Thaddaeus Tad Mercer
Chris Shotwell

LOCATIONS
Jason Underwood
June Shin
Bob Wagstaff
Ben Beeler
Joseph Gagliardi
Johnny Nguyen
Alisha Smith

MAKEUP
Addison Foreman
Melanie DeForrest
Nataleigh Verrengia
Aida Scuffle
Katelyn Barton Howard
Brittanie Cruz

MAKEUP FX
Jake Garber
Gino Crognale

MEDIC
Thaddaeus "Tad" Mercer
Jaimee Partain

POST PRODUCTION
Drew Sawyer
Jacob Velcoff
Patrick Perry
Kristina Kromer
James Crawford
J. Michael Cheeves
Anna Holley
Travis Preston

PROPS
Lucas Godfrey
Rene Arriagada
Nicholas Ragazzo

SCRIPT
Jana Davis
Karlyn Taylor
Yvonne Chan

SET DECORATION
Nick Morgan
Nicholas Gjoka
Blake Myers
Eric E.R. Brown
Luke Myers
Will Davis
Mitchell Baxter
Clarke Williams

SOUND
Serena Simpson
Marcus Petruska
Julian Cabrera
Philip Scheidt
Aaron Byrnes
Stokes Turner

SPECIAL EFFECTS
Andi Sowers
Richie Bearden
Jesse Trevino

STUNTS
Andy Rusk
Jason Kehler

GEORGE A ROMERO FOUNDATION

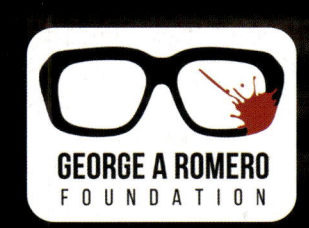

Suzanne Romero
Founder and President

Jeff Whitehead
Chief Operations Officer

Christian Stavrakis
Artistic Director

GEORGEAROMEROFOUNDATION.ORG

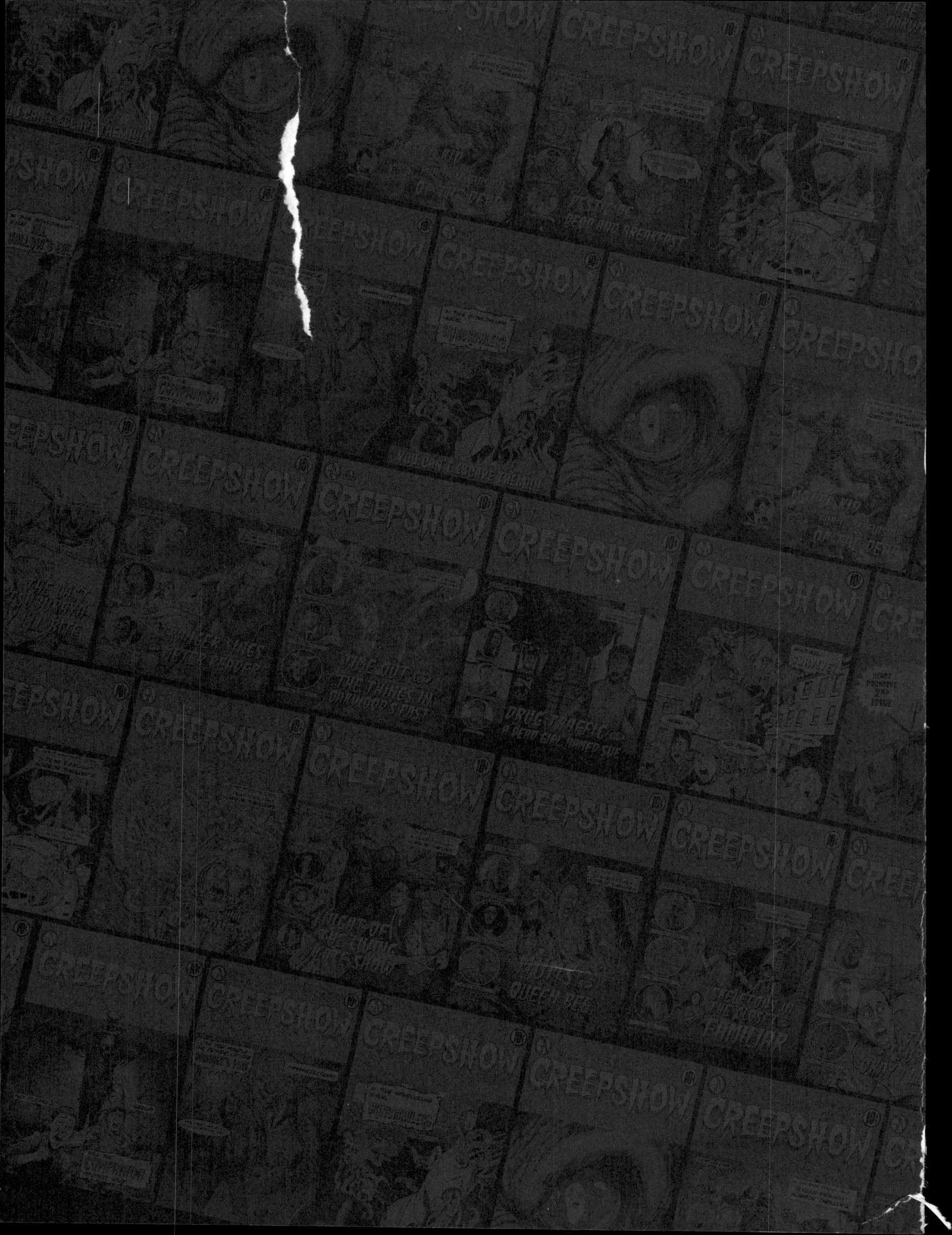